MW00777528

Exploring

THE MINOR
PROPHETS

THE JOHN PHILLIPS COMMENTARY SERIES

Exploring

THE MINOR
PROPHETS

An Expository Commentary

JOHN PHILLIPS

kregel
PUBLICATIONS

Grand Rapids, MI 49501

Exploring the Minor Prophets: An Expository Commentary

© 1998 by John Phillips

Published in 2002 by Kregel Publications, a division of Kregel, Inc., P.O. Box 2607, Grand Rapids, MI 49501.

ISBN 0-8254-3475-0

Printed in the United States of America

3 4 5 6 / 08 07 06

CONTENTS

Preface   7

Introduction   9

The Twelve and Their Times   15

1. Hosea: Prophet of the Broken Heart   37

2. Joel: Prophet of the Plague   67

3. Amos: The Country Cousin   85

4. Obadiah: Prophet of Edom's Doom   117

5. Jonah: The Rebellious Prophet   135

6. Micah: A Tale of Two Cities   157

7. Nahum: Goodbye, Nineveh   183

8. Habakkuk: Prophet with a Problem   201

9. Zephaniah: The Royal Prophet   221

10. Haggai: First Things First   243

11. Zechariah: Looking Ahead   263

12. Malachi: The Gathering Gloom   313

Notes   339

PREFACE

The prophecies of the twelve minor prophets are found in the second division of the Hebrew Bible (the first being "Law," the second "Prophets," and the third "Writings"). There they are treated as one book and given the common title, "Book of the Twelve."

In all Hebrew manuscripts and printed Hebrew Bibles these prophecies appear in unbroken sequence. The Hebrew text of the "Book of the Twelve" is divided into twenty-one segments (called *sedarim*) for convenience in public reading, but the divisions were made without regard to where one prophecy ends and another begins. For instance the fourth reading begins with Hosea 14:7 and continues to Joel 2:26. The next reading begins with Joel 2:27 and ends with Amos 2:9.

From earliest times, then, the twelve prophecies were regarded as one book and ultimately they were bound together in a single volume because they were so small. As separate scrolls some of them might otherwise have been lost.

The internal arrangement of the twelve prophecies in our Bible is the same as that of the Hebrew Bible: the order corresponds roughly to the dates of the prophets. The "Book of the Twelve" spans the entire prophetic era from the early Assyrian period to the early Persian period.

As we study the "Book of the Twelve" we will be stirred by the clarion sound of trumpets of war and by the measured tramp of marching feet. We will see great empires rise and fall. We will find ourselves in towns, villages, and world capitals, on mountaintops, and out in the raging deep. We will stand in busy markets and wilderness wastes; we will pause alongside temples and tombs. We will hear the shrill cry of the huckster, the siren voice of the harlot, the song of the drunkard, the wrathful voice of the king, the wail of the widow, the desolate sobs of the orphan, the despairing cry of the captive, the oily voice of the venal magistrate, and the unctuous tones of the apostate priest. We will stand where Eden's garden bloomed and in cities stricken by siege, famine, and plague. We will listen to the music of a babbling brook and hear the din of war.

Above the rest we will hear the voice of the living God and the urgent voice of the prophet. We will hear that "more sure word of prophecy" (2 Peter 1:19)—warning, wooing, weeping, welcoming the unborn ages, and saying farewell to the ages being swiftly filed away as history.

In the "Book of the Twelve" we will find pageantry, prophecy, eternal principles, and enduring promises. So *Exploring the Minor Prophets* ought not to be dull!

John Phillips

INTRODUCTION

The voice of the prophet was heard in Israel only in times of national apostasy. God normally communicated with His people through kings and priests, but when these channels failed, He spoke through prophets. When a prophet was chosen and anointed, he took precedence over both king and priest. There was no prophetic succession like that of Israel's kings and priests, but in time a prophetic order did emerge.

The prophets were God's "ministers without portfolio." Drawn from all ranks and from all regions of the country, they owed allegiance to no one but God. They spoke with a divine authority and occasionally their words were reinforced by miracles. Speaking for God, the prophets addressed the moral depravities, social injustices, and spiritual apostasies of their times. Many of them were political statesmen of the highest order who understood the world of their day and had a wide view of the future.

Sometimes they were *foretellers,* inspired by God to lift the impenetrable veil of the future and give glimpses of things to come. Always they were *forth-tellers,* inspired by God to denounce prevalent sins, demand repentance and reform, and declare His purposes for mankind.

To understand the prophets we must understand the calling and election of Israel. This specially favored nation is the only one with which God has made a treaty. God created Israel to be His nation and chose the Israelites to be His representatives to the other nations, His ambassadors to the world. The "chosen people," as they are sometimes called, were ordained to be "kings and priests unto God" (Revelation 1:6). All other nations were to be blessed by their contacts with Israel, for through her they were to be brought into "the light of the knowledge of the glory of God" (2 Corinthians 4:6).

To this end, God placed Israel at the world's geographic center. He gave the chosen people the most strategic location on earth. They were to dominate the Middle East; their territory was to stretch from the Nile to the Euphrates. Had the Israelites remained true to their calling and had they properly administered their vast land, it would have become the heart of a world empire and the center of spiritual blessing for all mankind. Now the goal will not be reached until the millennium. Israel's repeated failure even to approximate this divine ideal gave rise to the prophetic ministry in that country.

The era of prophecy began with Elijah and ended with John the Baptist, who came in the spirit of Elijah (Luke 1:17). The ministries of Elijah, John, and all the other prophets cannot be divorced from the times in which they lived. For example Baal worship during the reign of Ahab and Jezebel called for the spectacular, miracle-filled ministries of Elijah and Elisha. To understand the times of the prophets we need to review the history of the prophetic era. There were four major turning points:

1. After the accessions of Jeroboam II in the North and Uzziah in the South, the fighting farmers of the sister kingdoms of Israel and Judah changed into a race of sophisticated city-dwellers. The transition was fraught with perils. As the Hebrews became mercantile, they had heady contacts with other nations and acquired many of the vices that often accompany wealth and power. At the same time, the emergence of the writing prophets brought a new sophistication to Biblical prophecy.

2. Hard on the heels of urbanization, a new and sinister factor entered the equation: Assyria. Assyria changed the world. There was nothing benign about Assyrian aggression; it was imperialism in its most savage and malignant form. The need for writing prophets became more urgent than ever. God's Word needed to be confirmed in writing so that the godly remnant could take something tangible with them into their captivities, dispersions, and exiles. The Hebrews needed a Book.

3. The dissolution of the northern kingdom of Israel and the mass deportation of her people by the Assyrians left the little country of Judah isolated and alone. Then what Assyria had done to Israel, Babylon did to Judah. But the Babylonian captivity was benign. Many Jews learned to like Babylon. They settled down, prospered, developed the commercial instincts for which they have become famous, and rose to positions of power. However, success brought with it the lure of the world. So there was a need for exilic prophets and apocalyptic teaching.

4. The final turning point came when Judah regathered and returned from exile. This momentous development also called for prophets because the repatriated Jews soon grew discouraged, then neglectful. Finally they became bogged down in formalism and hypocrisy, and God could not leave them in that state without having one last word.

If we are to understand the prophets, it is essential that we understand their times. The chart of kings and prophets on pages 12-13 will help the reader place each prophet in his historical context. The analysis beginning on page 15, "The Twelve and Their Times," should also prove helpful, for it gives a more detailed history of the prophetic era and includes visual aids. The books of the minor prophets are not in *strict* chronological sequence in our Old Testament, but for the purposes of our study it seems best to follow the Biblical order.

CHART OF KINGS AND PROPHETS

Dates	Hebrew History		Prophets	Other Events
B C	Judah	Israel		
931	Rehoboam	Jeroboam		
913	Abijah (Abijam)			
911	Asa			
910		Nadab		
909		Baasha		
886		Elah		
885		Zimri		
		Tibni		
		Omri		(The commencement of
874		Ahab	Elijah (?–852)	Elijah's ministry is uncertain.
873	Jehoshaphat			He prophesied until about 852.)
853	Jehoram (Joram)	Ahaziah		
852		Jehoram (Joram)	Elisha (852–795)	
841	Ahaziah (Jehoahaz)	Jehu		
841	Athaliah			(Daughter of Ahab)
835	Jehoash (Joash)			
830			Joel ? (830–820)	
814		Jehoahaz		
798		Jehoash (Joash)		
796	Amaziah			
793		(Jeroboam II, regent)		
790	(Uzziah, regent)			
785			Jonah ? (785–770)	
783				Shalmaneser IV (783–773)
782		Jeroboam II		
767	Uzziah (Azariah)			
765			Amos (765–755)	
755			Hosea (755–715)	
753		Zachariah		
752		Shallum		
		Menahem		
750	(Jotham, regent)			
745				Tiglath-pileser III (745–727)
742		Pekahiah		
740		Pekah		
739	Jotham		Isaiah (739–690)	
736			Micah (736–700)	
735	(Ahaz, regent)			
732		Hoshea		
731	Ahaz			
727				Shalmaneser V (727-722)

Dates	Hebrew History		Prophets	Other Events
B C	**Judah**	**Israel**		
722		**Fall of Samaria**		Sargon II (722–705)
715	Hezekiah			
705				Sennacherib (705–681)
695	(Manasseh, regent)			
669				Ashurbanipal (669-633)
645			Nahum (645–620?)	
642	Amon			
640	Josiah			
635			Zephaniah (635–625?)	
627			Jeremiah (627–575)	
620			Habakkuk (620–610)	
612				Fall of Nineveh
609	Jehoahaz (Shallum)			
	Jehoiakim (Eliakim)			
605			Daniel (605–536)	Nebuchadnezzar (605–562)
				Battle of Carchemish
597	Jehoiachin (Jeconiah)			
	Zedekiah (Mattaniah)			
593			Ezekiel (593–558?)	
592			Obadiah (592–572)	
586	**Fall of Jerusalem**			
550				Cyrus (550–530)
539				Fall of Babylon
538	Zerubbabel			
536				Decree of Cyrus
535	Temple Begun			
530				Cambyses (530–521)
521				Smerdis
				Darius Hystaspes (521–486)
520	Temple Resumed		Zechariah (520–490)	
			Haggai (520–505)	
516	Temple Finished			
486				Xerxes (486–464)
478	Esther Becomes Queen			
473	Feast of Purim			
464				Artaxerxes (464–424)
458	Ezra			
445	Nehemiah			
435			Malachi (435–395?)	
423				Darius II (423–404)
336				Alexander the Great (336–323)
63	Pompey Captures Jerusalem			
30				Augustus Caesar

Note: Most dates are based on the chart of Old Testament kings and prophets by John Whitcomb, Jr. Some of the regencies and dates, especially those of the prophets, are uncertain.[1]

13

BACKGROUND READING

Bible students will find it helpful to read the historical narrative related to each prophet. The following chart is a general guide to background reading.

The Prophets	Their Times	Their Dates (B.C.)
Joel	2 Kings 11–12	830–820 ?
Jonah	2 Kings 13–14	785–770 ?
Amos	2 Kings 14:23–15:7	765–755
Hosea	2 Kings 15:1–18:1	755–715
Isaiah	2 Kings 15–20	739–690 ?
	2 Chronicles 26–32	
Micah	2 Kings 15:8–20:21	736–700
	2 Chronicles 27–32	
	Isaiah 7–8	
	Jeremiah 26:17-19	
Nahum	Jonah	645–620 ?
	Isaiah 10	
	Zephaniah 2:13-15	
Zephaniah	2 Kings 22–25	635–625 ?
	2 Chronicles 34:1–36:4	
Jeremiah	2 Kings 22–25	627–575
	2 Chronicles 34:1–36:21	
Habakkuk	2 Kings 23:31–24:20	620–610
	2 Chronicles 36:1-10	
Daniel	2 Kings 23:35–25:30	605–536
	2 Chronicles 36:5-23	
Ezekiel	2 Kings 24:17–25:30	593–558
	2 Chronicles 36:11-21	
Obadiah	2 Kings 25	592–572 ?
	2 Chronicles 36:11-21	
Haggai	Ezra 1–6	520–505
Zechariah	Ezra 1–6	520–490
Malachi	Nehemiah 8–13	435–395

Note: Dates are approximate. Each prophet ministered within the margins given, but the dates do not represent the duration of his ministry.

THE TWELVE AND THEIR TIMES

From the beginning, the ten-tribe nation of Israel, separated from the Davidic kingdom, was idolatrous. The founder of the northern kingdom, Jeroboam I, introduced calf worship as the state religion and he was not deterred by the visit of a prophet, a series of miracles, or a scathing denunciation. Invariably he is called "Jeroboam the son of Nebat, who made Israel to sin."

The people sacrificed to golden calves at Dan and Beth-el instead of going up to Jerusalem. New priests, new feasts, and new rituals were established to replace the old. But however objectionable and false the new religion was, it still claimed to be the worship of the true God. Then conditions degenerated during the reign of Ahab and Jezebel, who made a new era of prophecy necessary in Israel.

First Kings 16:30-31 says, "Ahab the son of Omri did evil in the sight of the Lord above all that were before him.... He took to wife Jezebel the daughter of Ethbaal king of the Zidonians, and went and served Baal." Incidentally Jezebel was the great-aunt of Dido, the founder of Carthage, but Ahab's wife needed no such claim to fame, for she was able to make history herself—with high-handed disregard for the consequences.

Jezebel imported the filthy worship of Baal (the sun god of the Phoenicians) and the licentious worship of Astarte (the moon goddess) into Ahab's kingdom. Ahab erected (in the promised land!) the vile and suggestive pillars associated with the porno-graphic worship of Baal. Soon every form of moral wickedness was practiced in the name of religion. God's prophets were ruthlessly persecuted. Murder and mayhem went hand in hand with such apostasy.

The situation called for a new breed of prophet. So God sent miracle-working prophets who could not only speak, but also take action: Elijah and then Elisha. However, in spite of repeated prophetic warnings, Ahab, spurred on by Jezebel, committed one wicked act after another, thus sealing the ultimate fate of the northern kingdom.

Meanwhile in the southern kingdom of Judah, King Jehoshaphat, whose character was far different from Ahab's, ascended the throne of David. He did his best to reform the religious life of his little land and he could have become a truly great king, had he not become infatuated with the more sophisticated Ahab and his attractive, forceful, and determined wife. To his own sorrow and the eventual undoing of Judah, Jehoshaphat compromised his convictions and sought alliances with Ahab. Dreaming of an end to the divided kingdom, Jehoshaphat married his son to Ahab's daughter Athaliah. It seems that Jehoshaphat hoped for healing of the seventy-year breach between the North and the South, but the ill-fated marriage had disastrous results for Judah, for Athaliah was a true daughter of Jezebel. Jehoshaphat also allowed himself to be drawn into a military alliance with Ahab against Syria, and again the consequences were lamentable.

Against this background Elijah ministered, towering like a veritable Sinai against the stormy Old Testament sky. He is best known for the episode on mount Carmel, where he single-handedly confronted hundreds of Ahab's Baal-cult priests. After exposing them as frauds, he supervised their subsequent execution and brought down on his head the wrath of Jezebel. He also denounced Ahab and his formidable consort for the murder of Naboth and the theft of his vineyard and told the guilty pair how and where they would die.

Jehoshaphat lived to see two of Ahab's sons ascend the throne of Israel: Ahaziah and Jehoram. It is difficult to untangle the histories of Israel and Judah during this time frame, partly because both kingdoms had a Jehoram and an Ahaziah. The chart on page 20 will help you sort out the kings of the period.

Ahaziah of Israel continued the vile religious practices of his parents. Jehoshaphat continued his policy of compromising with Israel and joined with Ahaziah in a trading venture, but the expedition came to nothing. After falling through a window and sustaining serious injuries, wicked Ahaziah sent messengers to ask Baal-zebub, the god of Ekron, for succor and advice. The messengers were intercepted by Elijah, who sent them back to the apostate king with the warning that he should prepare for death. Ahaziah died shortly afterward, having reigned a scant two years.

Ahaziah was succeeded on the throne of Israel by his brother Jehoram. About the same time Elijah was translated and he was succeeded by the less fiery but equally powerful prophet Elisha. Jehoram slightly moderated the evil practices of his parents and brother. Perhaps he had been intimidated by Elijah when he demonstrated his power and prescience to Ahaziah. Doubtless Jehoram had been impressed by Elijah's pronouncement of doom on his brother and the prophet's invulnerability to arrest. In any case Jehoram "wrought evil in the sight of the Lord; but not like his father, and like his mother: for he put away the image of Baal that his father had made" (2 Kings 3:2).

The miraculous ministry of Elisha fills up many chapters of the Bible. In his day Israel seems to have been halting between two opinions, her ultimate doom not yet having been decreed. Active hostility toward God's prophet ceased and there were tokens, albeit unsubstantial and insincere, of some kind of return to the Lord. But it was only the calm before the storm, for by the time of the prophet Amos, Israel had passed the point of no return and judgment had become inevitable.

Jehoram, like his brother and father, cultivated friendly relations with Judah. He sought Jehoshaphat's help in quelling Moab and they went to battle together, but their expedition would have ended in disaster had not Elisha intervened. Jehoram should have been more concerned about Syria, for the Syrians invaded his realm several times. After one of these invasions the terrible famine of Samaria ensued. It was miraculously relieved as foretold by Elisha.

In the meantime Jehoshaphat died. His son, Jehoram of Judah, came to the throne brooding over the fact that his father had installed other sons in strong cities and had amply funded them from the royal treasury. Had Jehoram been married to anyone other than Athaliah, he might have acted differently. One suspects it was at her instigation that Jehoram solved the problem of possible rivals to the throne by having his brothers massacred. The sacred text says that Jehoram "walked in the way of the kings of Israel . . . for he had the daughter of Ahab to wife: and he wrought that which was evil in the eyes of the Lord" (2 Chronicles 21:6).

Jehoram introduced into Judah the same terrible idolatries that Jezebel had imported into Israel. And like a voice from another world, a posthumous letter from Elijah came predicting calamity. Evil King Jehoram and his vile wife Athaliah must have been shocked to receive the letter, but it did little good and calamity did come. The Philistines and Arabians rebelled, stormed Jehoram's palace, and killed all his wives and children—except Athaliah and his youngest son Ahaziah. Later Jehoram died of a horrible disease.

Jehoram was succeeded on the throne of Judah by Ahaziah, who continued his father's idolatrous practices. We should not be surprised, for his mother was Athaliah and 2 Chronicles 22:3 says that she "was his counsellor to do wickedly." About this time Ahaziah's uncle, Jehoram of Israel, decided to try to free Ramoth-gilead from Syrian control and he invited his nephew to join him in the enterprise. The Judean king would have been wise to decline the invitation, for his death was in it. Elijah had prophesied against the house of Ahab and the time had come for the prophecies to be fulfilled (1 Kings 21:21).

Uncle and nephew met at Jezreel, where divine vengeance overtook them. God's instrument was Jehu, a general in the army of Jehoram of Israel. A young prophet sent by Elisha had secretly anointed Jehu as king, and Jehu wasted no time in making his calling and election sure. He waded to the throne of Israel through seas of blood. Jehu killed Jehoram of Israel and Ahaziah of Judah as well.

Tidings of Jehu's uprising reached Jezebel. She knew that her doom was sealed and fatalistically she attired herself like a queen and waited at a window. Jehu thundered up to the palace and ordered her attendants to throw her out the window. They did as they were told, Jehu spurred his horses, and his chariot wheels crushed the fallen woman's mangled body, which was left for the dogs to devour. After he had eaten, in a moment of compunction he gave orders for her remains to be buried, but all that could be found was her skull, the palms of her hands, and her feet. Elijah had predicted, "The dogs shall eat Jezebel by the wall of Jezreel" (1 Kings 21:23) and his prophecy was literally fulfilled.

Having dealt summarily with the principal representatives of Ahab's detestable dynasty, Jehu moved swiftly to consolidate his power. The capital city, Samaria, which was fortified and defended by the bulk of the army, sheltered seventy sons of Ahab. Jehu demanded immediate submission by the city fathers, who proved their loyalty by executing all the royal princes. He also intercepted forty-two princes of the house of Ahaziah of Judah who were on a friendly visit to Samaria and had them executed. One way or another, Jehu make a clean sweep of all Ahab's kin and his followers in Jezreel and Samaria.

It was also in Jehu's interests to put an end to Baal worship and all its adherents. This Jehu accomplished in short order by trickery. With his customary thoroughness he even turned the demolished temple of Baal into a public latrine.

Although Jehu reigned for twenty-eight years, he was as contemptuous of God as the other kings of the northern kingdom had been. Before long Syrian power encroached on his domain and the decline of Israel began.

Meanwhile one vigorous shoot of the Ahab stock remained strong and outside Jehu's reach: Athaliah. She became the curse of the southern kingdom just as her mother Jezebel had been the curse of Israel. The marriage of Jehoram of Judah to Athaliah brought calamity to the house of David.

When Athaliah learned that her son Ahaziah was dead, she seized the reins of government and inaugurated a massacre of his descendants. On what a slender thread hung the Messianic hope and the royal line to Christ! From this fearful purge, one son of Ahaziah escaped. He was rescued by Ahaziah's sister Jehosheba, who was married to the high priest Jehoiada. With commendable presence of mind and courage, the princess smuggled the infant Jehoash (Joash) out of the palace and hid him in the temple for six years. It is a pungent comment on the apostasy of the times that God's deserted temple in Jerusalem was the safest place to conceal the little refugee. The house of God had been broken up and plundered; everything of value had been removed to the temple of Baal (2 Chronicles 24:7).

During the seventh year of Athaliah's oppression, Jehoiada led a successful counter-revolution, using Joash as the rallying point. The priesthood seems to have been solidly behind Jehoiada's determination to seat his nephew on the throne as the legitimate heir of David, so the high priest crowned Joash in the temple amid the acclamation of the people. Hearing the noise, the wicked queen mother rushed into the temple, in rage tore her clothes, and cried out, "Treason, Treason" (2 Chronicles 23:13). According to Josephus, she then called for the immediate execution of the young king. Instead she was seized, hurried from the temple, and executed on Jehoiada's orders while he completed the inauguration of Joash by solemnly binding the new king and the people to the divine covenant.

God rewarded Jehoiada with long life. Second Chronicles 24:15 tells us he was "full of days when he died." The expression "full of days" is used to describe only four other people in Scripture: Abraham, Isaac, David, and Job.

Jehoiada kept King Joash steady, but after the high priest died, Joash (who had just finished restoring the temple) yielded to the pressure of the nobility and restored the abominable worship of Baal. The death of Elisha removed another restraining influence from the life of this weak king. About this time the voice of Joel was raised in prophetic warning. Thus we enter the era of the writing prophets.

How did King Joash reward his deceased benefactor, Jehoiada? By murdering Jehoiada's son Zechariah, who in the power of the Holy Spirit had dared to preach to the people against their renewed apostasy. And what was Joash's reward for this unprincipled

ROYAL FAMILY TIES

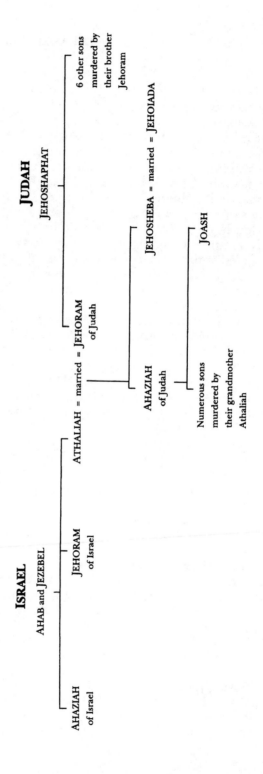

ISRAEL
AHAB and JEZEBEL

AHAZIAH
of Israel

JEHORAM
of Israel

ATHALIAH = married = JEHORAM
                              of Judah

JUDAH
JEHOSHAPHAT

6 other sons
murdered by
their brother
Jehoram

AHAZIAH
of Judah

JEHOSHEBA = married = JEHOIADA

Numerous sons
murdered by
their grandmother
Athaliah

JOASH

murder? God smote him with vile diseases and while he lay on his sickbed, his servants conspired against him and slew him.

In the meantime Jehoahaz of Israel succeeded the ruthless, careless Jehu, and the Syrians once again proved troublesome. The Bible attributes Israel's defeats to the continued royal policy of maintaining the false worship instituted by Jeroboam.

Jehoahaz was succeeded on the throne of Israel by his son Jehoash. Jehoash continued the policy of his father Jehoahaz and grandfather Jehu. The Jehu dynasty supported a religious return, not to the Lord, Jerusalem, and the temple, but to the false religion of Jeroboam. Indeed Jehu had found that religion to be a comfortable alternative to the true worship of Jehovah, a convenient tool for consolidating his grip on the throne of Israel, and a useful counterpoise to the worship of Baal. The intent to continue this settled policy was expressed in the name Jehoash gave to his son: Jeroboam.

In spite of this compromise with the calf worship instituted by Jeroboam, the Lord did not leave the weak Jehoash of Israel without a witness. The dying Elisha gave him his last prophecy (2 Kings 13:14-20). The Lord answered one of Jehoash's prayers and also delayed the judgment that had been impending for so long.

Meanwhile in Judah, Amaziah became king. He began fairly well, doing "that which was right in the sight of the Lord." Scripture, however, qualifies the statement twice by adding "but not with a perfect heart" in 2 Chronicles 25:2 and by adding "yet not like David his father" in 2 Kings 14:3. Just as the kings of Israel were measured by the yardstick of "Jeroboam the son of Nebat, who made Israel to sin," so the kings of Judah were measured by the yardstick of David.

Inspired by the successes of the northern kingdom in its campaigns against Syria, Amaziah of Judah set out to reconquer Edom. To ensure success he recruited one hundred thousand mercenaries from Israel and hired them at an enormous cost. Warned by a prophet that such an expedient would prove disastrous, Amaziah reluctantly dismissed his hired help and they returned home in a rage. His own army was victorious—even against the formidable stronghold of Petra (Selah)—but among the plunder that Amaziah brought back to Jerusalem were Edom's idols. He worshiped the idols and then sneered at the prophet God sent to him.

Next war broke out between Israel and Judah. The conflict was probably fomented by the mercenaries that Amaziah of Judah had dismissed and the results were disastrous for Judah. Amaziah's army fled and he was taken prisoner. The Israelites marched to Jerusalem unopposed, breached the wall, plundered the temple and palace, and carried away a number of hostages. Never had the fortunes of Judah sunk lower.

Amaziah returned to Judah, but he turned away from the Lord. A palace revolution followed and the wretched king fled to the strongly fortified town of Lachish on the road to Egypt. But walls, no matter how strong, could not protect the king from his doom. He was caught and killed, and his corpse was brought back to Jerusalem for burial.

In the next period of the history of Israel and Judah, the number of writing prophets increased. They sealed the doom of both kingdoms. Both Israel and Judah entered the era on a rising tide of outward success. Both saw the greatest expansion of their national territories since the days of David and Solomon. Inwardly, however, Israel and Judah were riddled with complacency, injustice, and growing religious disorder.

On the throne of Israel sat the vigorous Jeroboam II, who reigned for more than forty years. His reign was by far the longest of all the kings of Israel. His father Jehoash, whose military arms the dying Elisha blessed, won back in eighteen years all the cities the Syrians had seized during the reign of Jehoahaz. Then Jeroboam II, fulfilling the prophecy of Jonah, restored the border of Israel from the pass of Hamath to the Dead Sea and occupied at least part of Damascus (see 2 Kings 14:25). The disastrous war of Syria with Assyria and the alliance of Israel with Assyria account for the conquests of Jeroboam II.

By the time Amos appeared, a generation of Israelites had grown up not knowing defeat. The country of Israel, however, was marked by moral corruption and religious apostasy, for the worship of the golden calves was supplemented with the worship of Baal. The prophets Hosea and Amos raised their voices in warning, but Jeroboam II and his priest at Beth-el actively persecuted the Lord's prophets.

God's prophets had always reproved, warned, guided, and encouraged His people, but now a new phase of witness began. The prophetic horizon expanded and other nations were brought into view. In a time when the world was hardened beyond the hope of recovery, the prophets proclaimed the hope of a Messianic kingdom yet to come.

Little is said in the Biblical historical narrative about Jeroboam II, but he was the last king of Israel to rule with any semblance of divine authority. Nearly all his successors ascended the throne by murdering their predecessors.

Meanwhile in Judah, Uzziah (Azariah) became king when the

country was at its lowest ebb. A vigorous leader, he swiftly took steps
to recover the fallen fortunes of his kingdom. Uzziah reorganized
the army; invented new instruments of war; and pushing southward
to the Red Sea and eastward to the coast, crushed the Philistines.
He also built towers on the frontiers facing the desert in order to
cow the nomads into subjection. All his efforts were combined with
a determination to do "that which was right in the sight of the Lord"
(2 Chronicles 26:4).

However, Uzziah's continuing success went to his head and he
became intolerant of any other power in the land. He even wanted
to unite the functions of the priest with those of the king. Accordingly he went into the temple, seized a censer, pushed his way into
the holy place, and attempted to offer incense on the golden altar.
Then and there he was smitten with leprosy and he remained
leprous until his death.

The leprosy perhaps explains his double name. Originally it
seems he was called *Azariah*, the name which identifies him on
Assyrian monuments. After he became a leper he was called *Uzziah*,
which means "my strength is Jehovah." The new name was a sign of
his repentance and a confession that the help he had received had
come from God.

Toward the end of Uzziah's long reign the youthful Isaiah began
to feel the first stirrings of the Holy Spirit in his soul.

Meanwhile the northern kingdom of Israel was preparing for its
final plunge into oblivion. Jeroboam II was succeeded by his son
Zachariah, the fourth and last king of the Jehu dynasty. Shallum,
who publicly murdered Zachariah and seized the throne, reigned
for one month. Shallum in turn was assassinated by Menahem, who
managed to hang onto the throne for ten years.

But the dreaded Assyrians were moving toward center stage.
After a period of decadence a military adventurer seized the throne
of Assyria and established himself as Tiglath-pileser III. (See the
chart on page 24.) He campaigned first in Babylon. Because his
armies were bogged down there for several years, Syria and Israel
were deluded into believing that the Assyrians would not hammer
at their doors.

In the meantime Menahem was succeeded on the throne of
Israel by Pekahiah, who two years later fell victim to a military
conspiracy led by Pekah. Pekah joined Syria in the Syro-Ephraimitic
alliance against Judah. Neither Israel nor Syria wanted a potentially
hostile neighbor on their southern flank.

After a long reign the leper-king of Judah died and was succeeded by his son Jotham, who had been coregent with Uzziah for

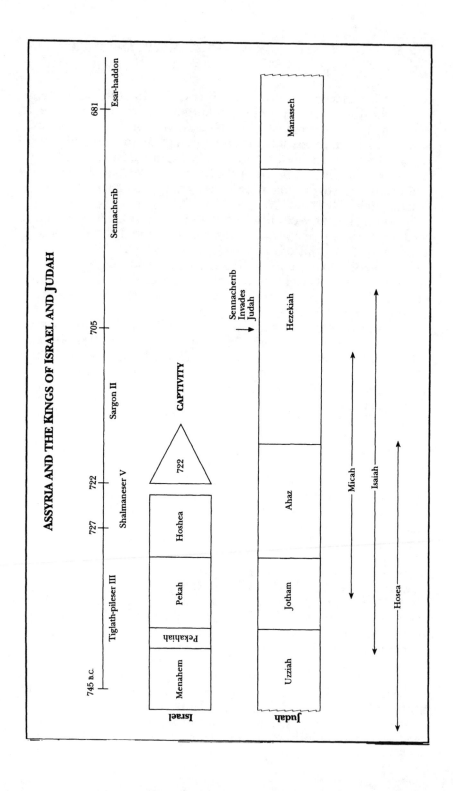

ASSYRIA AND THE KINGS OF ISRAEL AND JUDAH

some years. Jotham continued his father's sound religious and political policies. He strengthened the fortifications of Jerusalem and was victorious over the Ammonites. However, success proved to be heady wine for the people of Judah, who were guilty of all the sins we read about in Isaiah 1–6.

During Jotham's reign the Syro-Ephraimitic alliance commenced its great struggle against Judah. It seems that eventually the league embraced the Ammonites, Edomites, Philistines, and various other southern powers, so Judah was surrounded by foes. Jotham, however, saw only the beginning of this formidable alignment and he was strong enough to keep it in check.

Jotham's son Ahaz was weak and wicked, and his reign was disastrous for Judah. An unbeliever who was ready to swallow the grossest religious superstitions, Ahaz restored Baal worship and served the cruel god Moloch, whose devotees included child sacrifice in their rituals. Ahaz also restored the vile worship of the goddess Ashtoreth. He ordered a new altar (patterned after one dedicated to an Assyrian idol in Damascus) for the temple and gave it precedence over God's brazen altar; all sacrifices had to be placed on the new heathen altar.

The Syro-Ephraimitic league began to exert its influence. Its principal partners, Syria and Israel, hoped to shake off the Assyrian menace and perhaps even depose the hated Tiglath-pileser, but first they had to make themselves invulnerable to any threats from Judah. They directed their efforts against Ahaz himself (2 Kings 16:5); the conspirators hoped to dethrone him and install a commoner in his place (Isaiah 7:6). The alliance, then, was really directed against the house of David and against the Messianic hope, which Satan was determined to destroy. This explains why God took up the cause of wicked Ahaz.

At this time Isaiah told Ahaz, "Fear not," and gave his famous prophecy of the virgin birth of Christ (Isaiah 7:4,14), but the king refused to listen to the voice of the great prophet. Instead of repenting and trusting the Lord, Ahaz appealed to Assyria for help. No more foolish or fatal policy could be imagined.

Ahaz bought Assyrian help at an enormous cost. He had to acknowledge Assyrian sovereignty and pay a large cash fee for the Assyrians to do something their foreign policy would have required them to do anyway—that is, to crush Israel and Syria (2 Kings 16:7-8). It was as if Ahaz were inviting the cat into the birdcage to keep peace between the canaries. The Syro-Ephraimitic threat to Judah was simply replaced by the Assyrian threat. Pekah of Israel's triumphs over Judah were short-lived, whereas for a time Judah was nothing more than a vassal state of Assyria and was forced to pay tribute.

The Assyrians moved against Israel, Philistia, Phoenicia, Edom, Moab, and Ammon. Many cities in Israel were captured and Pekah was murdered by Hoshea, who seated himself on the throne. He was the last king of Israel. Tiglath-pileser advanced in a straight line from north to south. He made Galilee and the territory of the trans-Jordanian tribes an Assyrian province that served as a base for further aggression and he reduced Hoshea to a mere puppet.

The Assyrians turned their attention to Damascus, which after a stubborn resistance fell to the conqueror (2 Kings 16:9). Tiglath-pileser then summoned the princes of conquered and allied domains to Damascus to take an oath of allegiance. Ahaz was among them and it was during that time in Damascus that he saw the altar that he coveted for Jerusalem.

Ahaz sank into his grave unsung and unlamented. He left behind a Judah in which a formal, lifeless worship of Jehovah was coupled with the worship of Baal, Moloch, and Ashtoreth; necromancy and witchcraft were practiced openly; and wealth and luxury walked hand in hand with social injustice and immorality.

In vain did Joel, Hosea, Isaiah, and Micah raise their prophetic voices. Darkness was already descending on the promised land, especially on the kingdom of Israel, which was now on the brink of its final doom.

Hoshea reigned in Israel for nine years. Tiglath-pileser, who died about five years after Ahaz met him in Damascus, was succeeded by Shalmaneser V. The new Assyrian monarch was not nearly so successful a leader as his predecessor, but Hoshea submitted to him, as did most of the Phoenician cities—except Tyre.

Encouraged by the stubborn resistance of Tyre, Hoshea sought to enlist Egypt in an alliance against Assyria, but the pharaoh was too wise to swallow the bait. Shalmaneser V was already disillusioned with his vassal because Hoshea had stopped paying tribute, so when news of the discussions with Egypt reached the Assyrian king, he seized Hoshea and cast him into prison (2 Kings 17:4).

A full-scale invasion of Israel followed. During Assyria's siege of Samaria, which lasted about three years, Shalmaneser V died and was succeeded by Sargon II. Samaria finally fell in 722 B.C. and approximately 27,300 of its people were led into exile. Many more were rounded up from the various tribes and deported.

Sargon II then transported captives from other conquered lands into the territory of the northern tribes. These newcomers adopted a spurious form of Jehovah-worship in which Hebrew truths, traditions, and corruptions were liberally mixed with the pagan rites and beliefs that the captives brought from their homelands. These people and their descendants became known as Samaritans. A bitter hatred and rivalry developed between the Samaritans and the Jews of the South.

So the kingdom of Israel came to an end and the empires of Assyria and Egypt glowered at one another. These rivals were separated only by strategic little Judah.

At that time Judah was ruled by one of its greatest and godliest kings, Hezekiah. Guided by his friend Isaiah, Hezekiah led his country "back to the place where its tent and its altar had been at the beginning"—back to God. Hezekiah's first governmental decree abolished all idolatry. Then he restored the temple to its pristine purity and called for a celebration of the sabbath. He invited all the tribes (or what remained of them), not just Judah, to the celebration; being a man of God, he turned the other cheek to Israel, who had so bitterly warred against his own land. Another of Hezekiah's projects was to make a formal collection of the Psalms, to which he added numerous hymns that he had written.

While he was dealing with internal matters, Hezekiah did not forget the ominous, brooding power of Assyria. For a while he threw off the yoke that his father had fastened on Judah's neck, but in the face of Sargon's victories, Hezekiah had to submit to Assyria. Sargon died and was replaced by the terrible Sennacherib. About this time the Philistine, Phoenician, and Egypto-Ethiopian powers seem to have formed another anti-Assyrian league. Taking advantage of this new widespread rebellion, Hezekiah rebelled again. He put his country, and particularly Jerusalem, in as strong a position as possible to repel the expected siege.

It was not long in coming. The Assyrians laid waste a large part of Judah and captured Lachish. They sent an ambassador to Jerusalem to demand its immediate surrender, and although the ambassador's clever propaganda speech failed to accomplish his purpose, the population inside the city were wavering and the arrogant Assyrian host outside the city were seemingly invincible. Hezekiah had only one recourse: God. How thankful he must have been for the prayers and prophecies of Isaiah. God struck the terrible foe and the power of Assyria was broken as one angel in one night killed 185,000 troops. Sennacherib departed for Assyria, where he was later assassinated while worshiping one of his pagan gods.

Hezekiah's health problems seem to have begun just before the Assyrian invasion. Isaiah told his royal friend to prepare for death, but in answer to Hezekiah's desperate prayer, God sent Isaiah back with a promise and a sign. The king would recover and the shadow on the sundial would go back ten degrees as proof.

News of Hezekiah's healing spread far and wide. From far-off Babylon, Merodach-baladan sent ambassadors to Hezekiah, ostensibly to congratulate him on his recovery. Really their purpose was to ask for a treaty against Assyria, with whom Babylon had long been at war. Greatly flattered, Hezekiah was sorely tempted to sign a mutual assistance pact. He did not go that far, but in order to impress his foreign visitors, he foolishly showed them all his treasures. We can be sure that the ambassadors made notes for the authorities in Babylon—for future reference. Isaiah rebuked Hezekiah for his folly. The prophet could see that Judah's ultimate peril lay not with nearby Assyria, but with distant Babylon.

When Hezekiah died, he was succeeded on the throne by his twelve-year-old son Manasseh, who was born during the fifteen-year extension of Hezekiah's life. Manasseh, the child that should never have been born, reigned longer than any other Judean king.

Self-willed, reckless, weak, and cruel, Manasseh led the country back into religious apostasy, moral depravity, social injustice, and political folly. He restored the worship of Baal and Ashtoreth, introduced the Assyro-Chaldean worship of the stars, built altars to the hosts of heaven in the inner courts of the temple, and even set up the sex symbol Ashtaroth in the temple itself. Manasseh's reign was a time of such depravity that homosexuality was encouraged and Sodomites' houses lined the road to God's temple. It was also a time of martyrdom for God's saints. According to tradition, the king actually had the aged prophet Isaiah placed in the hollow trunk of a tree and sawn asunder.

Babylon was now under the Assyrian yoke, and the Assyrian emperor Ashurbanipal apparently resided in Babylon. Assyria maintained its supremacy over Judah, and Manasseh was taken as a prisoner to appear before Ashurbanipal in Babylon. Manasseh's experience there was a foretaste of Judah's coming exile. While in Babylon, Manasseh repented of his sins (2 Chronicles 33:12-13) and thereafter, in the providence of God, he was restored to his kingdom and throne. Once back home, he seems to have made some attempt at reform, but at best it was superficial. The damage had already been done.

After Manasseh died, his son Amon took the throne. He did his best to restore idolatry—in a form that was even worse than his father's. Amon only lasted two years; a palace coup put an end to his brief and inglorious reign.

When Amon's son Josiah ascended the throne, a new age began

for Judah. Josiah was only eight years old at the time, but he loved the Lord and his way was lighted by the prophet Jeremiah, and by Zephaniah and Habakkuk as well. Josiah introduced sweeping religious reform. It was he who took the initiative; the reform was not a movement of the people. He assigned men to restore the temple and while the extensive repairs were being made, a copy of the Mosaic Law was found; when a scribe read the book to Josiah, the king rent his clothes to express his grief over how far the nation had departed from God.

The discovery of God's Word served to intensify Josiah's efforts to reform his nation. He eradicated Baal worship and defiled the valley of Topheth, which was associated with Moloch worship and child sacrifice. He destroyed pagan shrines and high places, the houses of ill repute near the temple, the horses and chariots used in sun worship, and the altars that Ahaz and Manasseh had installed in the temple courts. Josiah carried his reforms north to the territory formerly occupied by the ten tribes. Above all, he reinstituted the Passover.

When the cruel reign of Ashurbanipal ended, decay set in and Assyria was no longer able to interfere in Palestine. In Babylon, Nabopolassar pushed for independence and allied himself with the Medes against the detested Assyrians. Egypt marched to the aid of Assyria, but for some unknown reason Josiah opposed Pharaoh Necho's passage through Judah and fought a decisive battle at Megiddo. Josiah was killed and the death knell sounded for Judah, which became a pawn of rival world superpowers.

Josiah had four sons. The eldest, Johanan, seems to have been killed at Megiddo. The three surviving were Eliakim (later called Jehoiakim), Shallum (later called Jehoahaz), and Mattaniah (later called Zedekiah). These sons became three of the last four kings of Judah.

After Josiah died, Shallum became king and he took the name Jehoahaz. He seems to have been the choice of the people because of his anti-Egyptian sentiments. Jehoahaz reigned a scant three months and "did that which was evil in the sight of the Lord" (2 Kings 23:32). Presumably he restored the lascivious rites that his grandfather had encouraged. Pharaoh Necho deposed Jehoahaz and carried him off to Egypt, where he died in captivity.

In the place of Jehoahaz, Necho installed Eliakim on the Judean throne and changed his name to Jehoiakim. Egypt demanded tribute from Jehoiakim, but the amount was astonishingly small— an incidental testimony to the impoverishment of the land. The reign of Jehoiakim was disastrous. He reinstated all the former

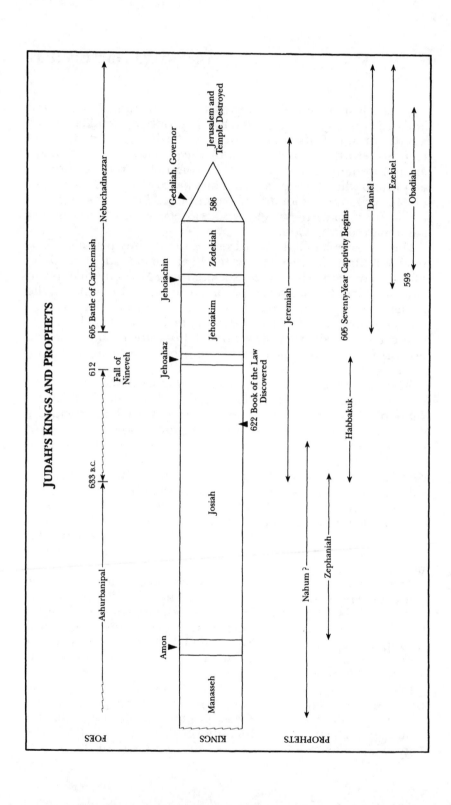

JUDAH'S KINGS AND PROPHETS

FOES

Ashurbanipal

633 B.C.

Fall of Nineveh

612

605 Battle of Carchemish

Nebuchadnezzar

KINGS

Manasseh

Amon

Josiah

622 Book of the Law Discovered

Jehoahaz

Jehoiakim

Jehoiachin

Zedekiah

586

Gedaliah, Governor

Jerusalem and Temple Destroyed

PROPHETS

Nahum ?

Zephaniah

Jeremiah

Habbakuk

605 Seventy-Year Captivity Begins

Daniel

Ezekiel

593

Obadiah

idolatries, which resulted in the demoralization of the people. The king lived in luxury while the people lived in poverty. Violence, oppression, immorality, social injustice, and covetousness were the order of the day. Habakkuk and Jeremiah raised their voices in vain.

Meanwhile Nineveh had fallen (612 B.C.) to a combined Medo-Babylonian army, and Egypt was vying with Babylon for an empire. Three years after the battle of Megiddo, Pharaoh Necho again sallied forth to war. His army met the Babylonians at Carchemish in 605 B.C. The Egyptians were no match for the brilliant young Nebuchadnezzar, and world dominion passed decisively into the hands of Babylon.

Wasting no time, Nebuchadnezzar marched westward. Jehoiakim, enraged by Jeremiah's prophecies of coming Babylonian victories, contemptuously cut up Jeremiah's prophecies and threw them into the fire. The king's tantrums, however, changed nothing and Nebuchadnezzar captured Jerusalem. He allowed Jehoiakim to remain on the throne as a vassal king, but took the vessels and treasure of the temple and deported Daniel and the cream of the Judean nobility to Babylon.

Jehoiakim, rebellious as ever against the preaching of Jeremiah, decided—probably with the encouragement of Egypt—to throw off his pledged allegiance to Babylon. Immediately Jehoiakim found himself embroiled in hostilities. "The Lord sent against him bands of the Chaldees, and bands of the Syrians, and bands of the Moabites, and bands of the children of Ammon" (2 Kings 24:2), for it was now the settled purpose of Heaven to put an end to the Judean monarchy. Having found Egypt to be a broken reed that he could not rely on, Jehoiakim died unmourned and dishonored.

His eighteen-year-old son Jehoiachin became king but lasted only three months. About this time (597 B.C.) Nebuchadnezzar again appeared in Jerusalem. Infuriated by the treachery of Jehoiakim and the queen mother's continuing intrigues with Egypt, Nebuchadnezzar acted decisively. He despoiled the temple and palace and carried off Jehoiachin, his mother, and his wives. Jehoiachin languished for thirty-seven years in a Babylonian prison. Then Evil-merodach, son and successor of Nebuchadnezzar, freed Jehoiachin and allowed him to eat at the royal table until he died.

Also deported to Babylon in 597 B.C. were the prophet Ezekiel, all the important Judean officials, and any able-bodied men who might later have formed the nucleus of an armed rebellion.

Before Nebuchadnezzar departed for Babylon, with astonishing generosity he seated another son of Josiah on the vassal throne of Judah: Mattaniah, whose name was changed to Zedekiah. Evil

THE YEARS OF EXILE AND RETURN

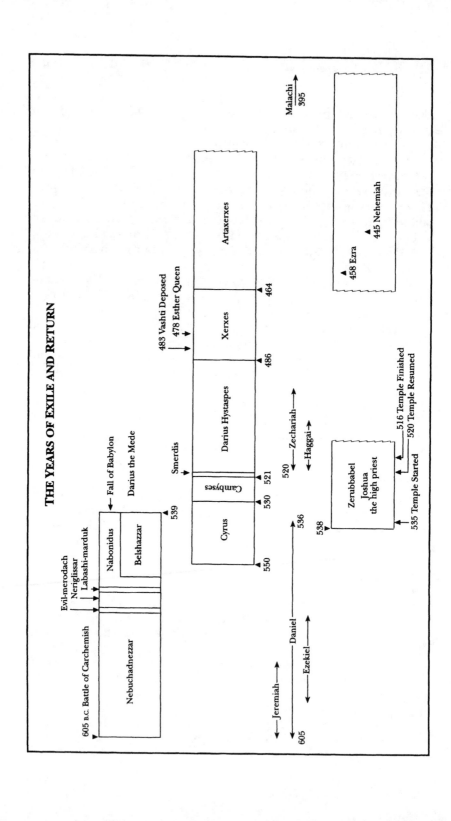

through and through, Zedekiah allowed the capital and temple once again to become scenes of idolatry.

Surrounding kingdoms were rife with schemes for overthrowing the Babylonian yoke, and false prophets fostered Zedekiah's hopes for political freedom. Jeremiah, who prophesied doom, was accused of high treason and flung into a miry pit. At last Zedekiah, in spite of his solemn oath of fidelity, openly rebelled against Nebuchadnezzar. The Babylonians swiftly countered the Judeans and overran their country. The conquerors frightened off the Egyptians and began the final siege of Jerusalem.

Jerusalem fell in 586 B.C. and Nebuchadnezzar exacted a fearful vengeance on the false and foolish Zedekiah. Jerusalem was put to the torch, Zedekiah's sons were slain before his eyes, and then he was blinded and carried off to Babylon.

Jeremiah, on the other hand, was honored by the Babylonians and given a choice of going with them or staying behind. He elected to remain with the small community of Jews who were left in the desolate city of Jerusalem under the rule of a Babylonian governor. He continued to prophesy, but as always his words went unheeded. When the Jews fled to Egypt, they forced Jeremiah to go with them.

Thus ended the Judean kingdom. Savage neighbors exulted in its destruction—especially the Edomites, who saw profit for themselves in the fall of Jerusalem. They even helped the conquerors from Chaldea (a name referring to all of Babylonia) capture fleeing refugees and took possession of a portion of the deserted land. The prophet Obadiah had words of certain judgment to come for the Edomites.

God did not leave Himself without a witness to His exiled people. Ezekiel and Daniel ministered to them with extraordinary power.

Although the throne of David was destroyed, the line of David remained. When the seventy-year captivity ended, a prince of the tribe of Judah—a descendant of David named Zerubbabel—led a remnant of Jews back to the promised land.

Nebuchadnezzar died and four kings followed him in rapid succession. The last of these, Nabonidus, had little taste for the onerous work of government. As soon as possible he handed the running of the kingdom over to his son Belshazzar.

By 550 B.C. a new and prophetically significant name was being headlined in the media of the day: Cyrus the Persian. His coming had been foretold by Isaiah more than a hundred years earlier (Isaiah 44:28). In 539 B.C. Babylon fell to a combined Medo-Persian army, and Cyrus appointed Darius the Mede to take charge of the imperial city.

The foreign policy of Cyrus was the exact opposite of the policy of the Assyrians. They used terror and deportation to hold captive peoples in line; Cyrus used humane means. In 538 B.C. he issued his famous decree whereby the Jewish exiles in Babylon could return to their ancestral home. A comparatively small number of Jews took advantage of the opportunity. The majority had settled down to a comfortable life in Babylon and the prospect of hard pioneering in Palestine had little or no appeal. Zerubbabel and his colleague Joshua, the high priest, led the first small contingent back.

The repatriates faced formidable obstacles and opposition when they arrived in their homeland. Nevertheless they set up God's altar in Jerusalem, cleared the temple site, and laid the foundation for the second temple. Neighboring peoples, especially the Samaritans, first derided the Jews, then demanded a share in the work, and finally petitioned the Persian royal court to stop the work. These adversaries asked in effect, "Do you really want these troublesome Jews to rebuild Jerusalem and her formidable walls? Have you forgotten the fanaticism with which they fought for their independence?"

The charges, innuendoes, and misrepresentations in the petition had their intended effect: the Jews were forced to cease building the temple. They refrained from that work during the reigns of Cyrus, Cambyses, and Smerdis—a period of some sixteen years—but they busied themselves constructing and embellishing their homes.

The Jews were in peril, for without a temple they were likely to become irreligious or lapse into the gross idolatry that the Babylonian exile had so effectively burned out of their souls. So two new voices sounded above the din of business and pleasure. Haggai and Zechariah spoke for God and cut through the complacency of the repatriates. Under the goading and guidance of these prophets, the Jews resumed work on the temple in 520 B.C.

Tatnai, the Persian territorial governor, wrote to Darius Hystaspes (who had succeeded Smerdis) and challenged the rebuilding of the temple. A search of the archives confirmed the right of the Jews to rebuild and for once the inflexible "law of the Medes and Persians, which altereth not" (Daniel 6:12) worked in favor of God's people. The temple was completed in 516 B.C.

Time passed and the despotic Xerxes came to power in Persia. Suddenly the Jews learned how tenuous was their position in Gentile lands. With the king's backing, a powerful and vindictive Persian official named Haman launched a crusade to exterminate all Jews in Persian territory. The book of Esther tells how the antisemitic plot was foiled.

Then came Artaxerxes, Ezra, and Nehemiah. Ezra returned from Babylon eighty years after Zerubbabel returned and fifty-eight years after the temple was finished. When Ezra arrived in his homeland, he was horrified by the low spiritual condition of the people and the laxity that could be seen everywhere, so he launched a vigorous, Bible-based, thoroughgoing reform.

Nehemiah, a highly-placed Jew in the Persian court, obtained a decree from King Artaxerxes in 445 B.C. that authorized the rebuilding of the walls of Jerusalem. Until then the walls had remained in their ruined condition. The Jews, exposed to the spite and malice of their foes, needed a man of iron will, resourcefulness, and zeal to take charge of rebuilding the walls, and God found such a man for them in the person of Nehemiah. Armed with the necessary documents, he arrived in Jerusalem in 444 B.C. He surveyed the enormous damage, organized the Jews, defied all opposition, and completed the task in only fifty-two days! He also joined Ezra in instituting religious reform. Nehemiah remained in Jerusalem as governor for twelve years, then returned to Persia in 433 B.C., where he served in the court until 420 B.C. It seems that he retired then and went back to Jerusalem.

Around 435–395 B.C. the last Old Testament prophet raised his voice. Malachi, appalled by the formalism, secularism, and hypocrisy into which the third generation of repatriated Jews had sunk, made one last appeal to God's people to repent. The dark night of the intertestamental period foretold in Daniel 11 was about to descend on the nation. God would not speak again for four hundred years.

Chapter 1

HOSEA

PROPHET OF THE BROKEN HEART

I. THE TRAGEDY IN HOSEA'S HOME LIFE (1:1–3:5)
  A. The Signs (1:1-11)
    1. The Challenge to the Prophet (1:1-2)
    2. The Children of the Prophet (1:3-11)
      a. The Nation Defeated: Jezreel
      b. The Nation Deported: Lo-ruhamah
      c. The Nation Discovered: Lo-ammi
  B. The Sins (2:1-23)
    1. The Personal Note (2:1-4)
    2. The Prophetic Note (2:5-23)
      a. Israel's Treacherous Lovers (2:5-7)
      b. Israel's True Lord (2:8-23)
        (1) Acting in Punishment (2:8-13)
        (2) Acting in Pardon (2:14-23)
  C. The Savior (3:1-5)
II. THE TRAGEDY IN HOSEA'S HOMELAND (4:1–14:9)
  A. The Polluted People (4:1–7:16)
    1. The Lord's Controversy with Israel (4:1-5)
    2. The Lord's Commentary on Israel (4:6-14)
    3. The Lord's Caution about Israel (4:15–5:15)
      a. Warnings Addressed to Judah (4:15-19)
      b. Warnings Applicable to Judah (5:1-15)
        (1) Israel's Determination (5:1-7)
        (2) Israel's Doom (5:8-15)
    4. The Lord's Compassion for Israel (6:1-11)
    5. The Lord's Contempt for Israel (7:1-16)
      a. The Throne (7:1-7)
      b. The Throng (7:8-16)

       (1) The Bakeshop (7:8-10)
       (2) The Barnyard (7:11-15)
       (3) The Battlefield (7:16)
B. The Punished People (8:1–10:15)
  1. The Trampled Covenant (8:1-14)
    a. Where Israel Sinned (8:1-6)
    b. What Israel Sowed (8:7-10)
    c. Where Israel Stood (8:11-14)
  2. The Tragic Consequences (9:1-17)
    a. Bewilderment (9:1-9)
    b. Barrenness (9:10-17)
  3. The Terrible Conditions (10:1-15)
    a. Israel's Detestable Religion (10:1-2)
    b. Israel's Departed Rulers (10:3-6)
    c. Israel's Deserted Ruins (10:7-8)
    d. Israel's Desired Repentance (10:9-12)
    e. Israel's Dreadful Reward (10:13-15)
C. The Pardoned People (11:1–14:9)
  1. Israel's Persistence (11:1–12:1)
    a. Her Destiny (11:1)
    b. Her Determination (11:2-7)
    c. Her Desolation (11:8-11)
    d. Her Deceptions (11:12–12:1)
  2. Israel's Past (12:2-14)
    a. A Message to Judah in the South (12:2-6)
       (1) Jacob's Birth
       (2) Jacob's Blessing
       (3) Jacob's Belief
    b. A Message to Israel in the North (12:7-14)
       (1) Jacob's Wages
       (2) Jacob's Wives
  3. Israel's Punishment (13:1-16)
    a. Spiritual Death (13:1-2)
    b. Sudden Deportation (13:3)
    c. Sure Disillusionment (13:4)
    d. Stubborn Defiance (13:5-6)
    e. Swift Destruction (13:7-8)
    f. Smitten Defenses (13:9-11)

     g. Sordid Depravities (13:12-13)
     h. Salvation Delayed (13:14)
     i. Successes Despoiled (13:15)
     j. Shocking Doom (13:16)
  4. Israel's Peace (14:1-9)
     a. The Plea (14:1-3)
     b. The Pledge (14:4-8)
     c. The Path (14:9)

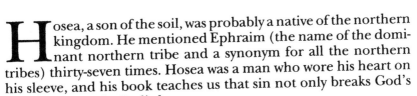

Hosea, a son of the soil, was probably a native of the northern kingdom. He mentioned Ephraim (the name of the dominant northern tribe and a synonym for all the northern tribes) thirty-seven times. Hosea was a man who wore his heart on his sleeve, and his book teaches us that sin not only breaks God's law; it also breaks God's heart.

A forerunner of the sob-choked Jeremiah of Judah, Hosea prophesied when memories of Elijah and Elisha were still fresh in the land. Hosea ministered for a long time—through the reigns of Uzziah, Jotham, Ahaz, and Hezekiah of Judah and Jeroboam II of Israel. Although Hosea's book reveals his intimate knowledge and love of the northern kingdom of Israel, most of his prophecies were directed against that apostate realm.

When God first called Hosea to the prophetic ministry, the vigorous dynasty of Jehu of Israel was still riding high under the direction of the powerful Jeroboam II. That military despot had recovered much of the territory Israel had lost to foreign powers during previous reigns. Yet Hosea foretold the downfall of Jehu's dynasty on the ancient battleground of Jezreel, where it had begun. (The valley of Jezreel in central Israel is the plain of Esdraelon that we often identify as Megiddo.) When Hosea made this prophecy, there were no outward signs that the days of the northern kingdom were numbered, but underneath the outward prosperity were religious corruption, social injustice, moral decay, and—after the death of Jeroboam II—increasing political anarchy.

The house of Jeroboam II still ruled during the first three chapters of Hosea's prophecy. From chapter 4 on there are few references to the lawless kings who rapidly succeeded each other.

I. THE TRAGEDY IN HOSEA'S HOME LIFE (1:1–3:5)

A. The Signs (1:1-11)

1. The Challenge to the Prophet (1:1-2)

As Hosea contemplated his nation's horrendous sins, his heart was deeply moved. How could the Israelites—a people who professed to be God's people, a people who had God's Word, a people to whom Elijah and Elisha had just recently ministered with power and miracles, a people who had every advantage—grovel in idolatry and sin? They were blood-kin to Abraham, Isaac, and Jacob and lived only a day's march from Jerusalem and the temple, yet they wallowed in superstition, indulged in every form of immorality and social injustice, and worshiped at the feet of graven images. Hosea must have thought, *Surely they have sinned away the day of grace. Could God still love such a people? To what lengths will His love go? Where is the line between God's mercy and His wrath?*

Into his musings and meditations broke the voice of the living God. No doubt it startled Hosea. The voice that rang in his soul had once commanded light to shine out of darkness. The voice that had communed with Adam in Eden, had commanded Abraham to leave Ur, and had recently spoken to Elijah, was now speaking to *him.* It is one thing to become aware that God is speaking to you from a specific passage of His written Word; it is something else to hear that voice speak directly to your soul. Comparatively few people have had that experience, which to Hosea was "the beginning of the word of the Lord" (Hosea 1:2). God's word took on such a new dimension, such a new distinctness in Hosea's soul, that he almost felt as if God had never spoken to anyone else but him.

If Hosea was surprised by this voice, he must have been equally startled by what it said. "The Lord said to Hosea, Go, take unto thee a wife of whoredoms and children of whoredoms." He could hardly believe his ears. Hosea was a young, God-fearing, idealistic, pure-minded, clean-living man, and the voice told him to marry a whore! *Is this* God *speaking?* he must have asked himself. *Or is it a demon? Would this kind of message come from the holy One of Israel, the One who is "of purer eyes than to behold evil" and before whose holiness the very seraphim hide their faces? Surely I must be mistaken.*

The plural in the phrase "a wife of whoredoms" is significant. Just as "men of bloods" (Psalm 5:6, literal translation) refers to men given over to murder, and "a man of sorrows" (Isaiah 53:3) reveals that the Lord's whole life and ministry were overshadowed by

sorrow, so "a wife of whoredoms" refers to a woman who is repeatedly guilty of sexual immorality. Perhaps she was a temple priest-
ess—one of the harlots (victims of a foul religion) kept by the vile
priests of Baal and Ashtoreth to service the lusts of the devotees of
the Canaanite shrines. Perhaps she was a "liberated" woman who
was thoroughly indoctrinated by the humanism of the day to think
that her body was her own, to do with as she pleased; passing from
one casual liaison to another was simply her lifestyle. Or perhaps she
was a common call girl who made her living by pandering to the
appetites of men. We can be sure Hosea never planned to marry a
woman like *that*.

After he was told to link his life with such a woman, he was at once
given the assurance he needed that the voice he had heard was
God's. The confirmation was in the explanation that followed the
command: "For the land hath committed great whoredom, depart-
ing from the Lord" (Hosea 1:2). The hateful word *whoredom(s)*
occurs three times in this verse, and at least fourteen times in the
book of Hosea, for the prophet compared the unfaithfulness of
Israel to marital infidelity. When speaking to Hosea, God deliberately likened idolatry to adultery.

2. The Children of the Prophet (1:3-11)

Hosea did as he was told. We do not know how the young prophet
met the woman he married. She was probably attractive and he
evidently gave her his heart and loved her.

The woman's name *Gomer* means "completion" and is parabolic,
as are other names in the book of Hosea. We hear echoes in *Gomer*
of the filling up of the measure of Israel's idolatries and apostasies.
Gomer was the daughter of *Diblaim*, whose name means "a double
clump of figs" and suggests sensual pleasure or the sweetness—the
parent of all wrongdoing—that we find in sin. *Hosea*, a name similar
to the one Jesus assumed when He came down to this world of sin,
means "salvation" or "the Lord saves."

a. The Nation Defeated: Jezreel

So Hosea married Gomer and she presented him with a son. God
told Hosea to call him *Jezreel*, a name that can mean "may God
scatter" (see Jeremiah 31:10) or "may God sow." Jezreel was the
name of a place, so the Lord explained, "For yet a little while, and
I will avenge the blood of Jezreel upon the house of Jehu, and will
cause to cease the kingdom of the house of Israel" (Hosea 1:4).

The place called Jezreel assumed special significance in the history of Israel during the time of Ahab and Jezebel, especially in the story of Naboth, the Jezreelite who owned a vineyard near the palace and refused to sell it to Ahab (1 Kings 21). Jezebel arranged for Naboth to be murdered so that Ahab could take possession of the vineyard he coveted. Elijah denounced the deed and foretold the doom of the guilty pair and their descendants, a doom that would overtake them at Jezreel, where Naboth had been killed.

God used Jehu to make a clean sweep of Ahab, his house, and the vile religious system that Jezebel had brought to Israel. God foretold that Jehu's dynasty would last for four generations (2 Kings 10:30) and when Hosea prophesied, the third generation was on the throne. Nothing could have looked less likely in the flourishing days of Jeroboam II than the overthrow of Jehu's dynasty and the kingdom of Israel, but that is what Hosea foresaw and that is why he named his son Jezreel.

The twofold meaning of *Jezreel* was prophetic. The strength of the kingdom of Israel was to be broken on the fateful, classic battlefield of Jezreel. Moreover the sufferings inflicted by the Assyrians there were to be a warning and foretaste of worse things to come at the time of the siege and sack of Samaria: God would scatter the ten tribes and sow them among the nations in an agelong exile.

b. The Nation Deported: Lo-ruhamah

Hosea settled down with Gomer, but she soon proved faithless to her marriage vows. With ever-deepening sorrow, Hosea faced the fact that the wife he loved, the mother of his little boy, had gone back to her evil ways. When she presented him with a second child, a daughter, Hosea had grave doubts that the little girl was his. Obeying the word of God, he called her Lo-ruhamah.

The word *lo-ruhamah* is rendered "not beloved" in Romans 9:25 and "had not obtained mercy" in 1 Peter 2:10. Used as a name, the word expresses deep yearning and means "she who never knew a father's love" or, more abruptly, simply "unpitied." Psalm 103:13 tells us that the Lord "pitieth his children," but through Lo-ruhamah's name God was saying, "I will no more have mercy upon the house of Israel; but I will utterly take them away" (Hosea 1:6).

Gomer must have eyed her husband with apprehension (or was it callous indifference?) when she heard him solemnly disown the child. As for Israel, her doom was sure. God had shown mercy time and time again. Jeroboam I had provoked Him with the installation of the golden calves and the corruption of the Hebrew faith. Ahab had provoked Him by installing the foul worship of Baal, Ashtoreth, and Moloch. Jehu had provoked Him when he instituted his religious reforms by reverting to calf worship instead of bringing the kingdom back to God. Now Jeroboam II was provoking Him by taking his military successes for granted and continuing the sins of Jeroboam I. God had shown mercy by sending Elijah, Elisha, Joel, and Jonah, but they had prophesied in vain. The day of mercy was over for Israel.

But Judah was to be spared. God said, "I will have mercy upon the house of Judah, and will save them by the Lord their God, and will not save them by bow, nor by sword, nor by battle, by horses, nor by horsemen" (Hosea 1:7). Judah, who had a good king and would have a succession of good kings, would be delivered from the fate that would overtake Israel. The Assyrians triumphed over Samaria, but when they came hammering at the gates of Jerusalem, they were overthrown—not by Hezekiah's army, but by God's direct intervention.

c. The Nation Discovered: Lo-ammi

Eastern women usually nursed their children for several years and when Gomer had weaned Lo-ruhamah, she bore yet another child. God said, "Call his name Lo-ammi: for ye are not my people, and I will not be your God" (Hosea 1:9). *Lo-ammi* means "not my people" or "no kin of mine."

Knowing that his wife was no better than a harlot, sad Hosea bluntly denied having any relationship at all to this poor little boy. In the same way that Hosea denied being Lo-ammi's father, God announced His determination to deny having any relationship to apostate Israel. The nation so greatly loved by God had repaid Him with indifference and contempt. She had shown her scorn by embracing the vile religions of the surrounding nations and cleaving to pagan gods with a devotion she never gave to Him.

No Biblical prophet ever pronounces only doom, so Hosea also spoke of a coming day when Israel will be forgiven, cleansed, and restored (Hosea 1:10-11). He prophesied that the tribes of Jacob will be gathered under one head and once more be God's people. "Great shall be the day of Jezreel," he said, referring to the battle of Armageddon, which will be fought on the ancient battleground of Jezreel. There Christ will rout the enemy and be installed as Israel's true Messiah.

The prophetic signs were written in tragedy and human heartache. Hosea's neighbors and friends who knew what was going on must have shaken their heads. "What does he see in Gomer?" they no doubt asked. "Why doesn't he divorce her and be done with it?" The angels too might well have wondered at the exceeding riches of God's grace. "What does He see in the human race?" they may have asked. "Why doesn't He make an end of them and be done with it?" God's answer is His love that will not let us go, His love that "suffereth long, and is kind" (1 Corinthians 13:4).

B. The Sins (2:1-23)

1. The Personal Note (2:1-4)

One wonders what happened to Gomer's children, especially the little girl and boy whom Hosea disowned. Hosea would have been within his rights to turn them out along with their faithless mother, but he did nothing of the kind. Instead of calling them Lo-ruhamah and Lo-ammi in daily life, he called them *Ammi* (which means "mine") and *Ruhamah* (which means "pitied one"). Reflecting the grace of God, Hosea wrapped those unfortunate children in the arms of his love. It was no fault of theirs that their mother had become a woman of the streets.

When the children were grown Hosea said to them, "Plead with your mother, plead: for she is not my wife" (Hosea 2:2). The children were old enough to understand the estrangement, Hosea's yearning, and their mother's shame. Hosea was begging them to urge Gomer to give up her evil life, for if she persisted in her wicked ways, he would have no choice but to resort to judgment, disown her, and disinherit the children born of her sin. Hosea's plea of course was parabolic. The adulterous mother was the nation of Israel; the children were the individuals who comprised the nation. God was pleading with the apostate nation to repent; otherwise severe judgment would come upon the land (2:3) and God would disown the people for centuries (2:4).

2. The Prophetic Note (2:5-23)

In Hosea 2:5-23 the lessons drawn from Hosea's unhappy home are applied to the apostate nation and its people.

a. Israel's Treacherous Lovers (2:5-7)

The nation of Israel had played the harlot with the pagan gods of surrounding nations. Her great sin was expressed by the prophet in Hosea 2:5: "She said, I will go after my lovers." False religion had not been forced upon Israel; with besotted persistence she had run after the licentious nature-gods and goddesses of the pagans. The people of Israel actually came to believe that Baal, Ashtoreth, Moloch, and the like could provide bountiful harvests and years of plenty.

Hosea 2:7 says, "She shall follow after her lovers, but she shall not overtake them." (The words translated "follow after" are emphatic and suggest intensive, diligent pursuit.) Throughout the long history of the scattered Hebrew people they have chased after false Christs and phantom ideals. What is the Talmud, for instance, but a vast, vain attempt to snare a ghost? The shaping of the Talmud after Israel's rejection of Christ was the attempt of a Christ-rejecting people to shape their destiny apart from Him. During the Middle Ages particularly, the Jews were easy prey for pseudomessiahs, and someday the Jews will fall for the blandishments of the beast, the devil's messiah. No people have been more diligent in their pursuit of religious ideals and they have pursued false ideals as diligently as they once pursued false gods—all to no avail.

Hosea foresaw the end of all such pursuits: "She shall not find them: then shall she say, I will go and return to my first husband; for then was it better with me than now." The utter waste, want, and worthlessness of her life will finally dawn on Israel, the wayward and prodigal wife. The fires of the great tribulation and the glorious appearing of the Lord Jesus will bring the nation to her senses at last.

b. Israel's True Lord (2:8-23)

In this section we see the Lord's twofold response to Israel's apostasy. First, in Hosea 2:8-13 we see Him *acting in punishment*. Note the divine "I wills": "Therefore will I return, and take away my corn....And now will I discover her lewdness....I will also cause all her mirth to cease....And I will destroy her vines....And I will visit upon her the days of Baalim." In these verses the prophet envisioned natural disasters, the devastation of the land by war, and the destruction of its people. Such are the results of sin. "She went after her lovers, and forgat me, saith the Lord" (2:13). The sinful soul does not merely forsake the Lord; eventually it forgets Him.

In Hosea 2:14-23 we see God *acting in pardon*. Man's miseries, even when they are deserved and brought on by divine judgment, awaken God's mercies. God extends His mercy to us not because we deserve it, but because we need it. Beginning in verse 14, note again the tramp of God's sovereign "I wills" marching down the corridors of time: "I will allure....And I will give...for I will take away the names of Baalim out of her mouth....And in that day will I make a covenant....And I will break the bow...and will make them to lie down safely. And I will betroth thee unto me for ever....I will hear....And I will sow....And I will have mercy....And I will say to them which were not my people, Thou art my people; and they shall say, Thou art my God."

In the midst of this account of the divine pursuit of mercy, Hosea paused in verse 16 to indicate what the response of poor, destitute Israel will be: "At that day, saith the Lord,...thou shalt call me Ishi; and shalt call me no more Baali." In other words, instead of calling God *my Lord,* Israel will call Him *my Husband.* Hallelujah, what a Savior!

What will bring about this change? The great tribulation, that terrible period which is also known as the "time of Jacob's trouble" (Jeremiah 30:7). What happens in "the valley of Achor" (the valley of trouble, Hosea 2:15) is what will change Israel. It was not until the New Testament prodigal came to the end of himself that he said, "I will arise and go to my father" (Luke 15:18), and not until the nation of Israel comes to the end of herself will she be ready for genuine conversion.

C. The Savior (3:1-5)

Chapter 3 picks up the story of Hosea's personal life. In the midst of the desolation of his heart and home, Hosea heard God say, "Go yet, love a woman beloved of her friend, yet an adulteress, according to the love of the Lord toward the children of Israel, who look to other gods" (3:1). It seems that Gomer, abandoning all pretense, had left her husband and was living in a sinful, adulterous relationship with another man. Now Hosea could no longer treat her as a wife, but he still treated her as a friend. God told him to love her, to act on the principle of divine love.

Wretched Gomer had come down in the world. Presumably she had sold herself as a slave to the man with whom she was living. He must not have cared that much about her, for he was quite willing to sell her back to Hosea. Evidently the man did not value her highly either, for he sold her for a paltry fifteen pieces of silver (half the price of a common slave; see Exodus 21:32) and a month's supply of barley (the food of the poor, the food usually given to animals).

Having paid the price of Gomer's redemption and being well aware of her history, Hosea explained the terms on which she could come home: "Thou shalt abide for me many days; thou shalt not play the harlot, and thou shalt not be for another man: so will I also be for thee" (Hosea 3:3). In other words, she was put on probation

for a considerable time during which she was to remain true to her
husband, as he would remain true to her. Hosea could hardly
demand less. Time had to do its healing as well as its revealing work.
    Here the story of Hosea's personal tragedy ends. We wish we
could visit the patient prophet from time to time, to see how he is
getting along. Does Gomer truly repent? Does she weep bitter tears
over her disgraceful life? What do the children think? Does Gomer
finally give her heart unreservedly to Hosea? How does she get
along with her gossipy neighbors? Does she ever get her good name
back? Do Hosea and Gomer live happily ever after? We like to think
the story has a happy ending, and perhaps it does, for the larger
story of Jehovah and Israel is to have a happy ending.
    Hosea made the application in 3:4: "For the children of Israel
shall abide many days without a king, and without a prince, and
without a sacrifice, and without an image, and without an ephod,
and without teraphim." This statement has been true of Israel and
Judah for centuries. Did they not reject their rightful King and say
to Pilate, "We have no king but Caesar" (John 19:15)?
    Hosea was speaking of a people without a temple and its services,
a people cured of idolatry. What a description of the Hebrew
people as they are today and have been for more than two millennia! But the end is in sight: "Afterward shall the children of Israel
return, and seek the Lord their God, and David their king; and shall
fear the Lord and his goodness in the latter days" (Hosea 3:5).
Hosea was anticipating the coming millennial reign of Christ.

II. THE TRAGEDY IN HOSEA'S HOMELAND (4:1–14:9)

From the beginning of chapter 4 until the end of the book, the
tragedy of Hosea's home life is swallowed up in the even greater
tragedy of Hosea's homeland. The society in which Hosea lived was
permissive and pornographic, so there must have been many
broken homes in Israel in his day. But the reason for Hosea's
marital problems was not to call attention to that fact alone. In the
Lord's eternal purposes, Hosea's broken heart was to be a mirror
reflecting to the world the broken heart of God.

A. The Polluted People (4:1–7:16)

1. The Lord's Controversy with Israel (4:1-5)

Chapter 4 begins with a list of sins, a catalog that has few equals
in Scripture—that is, before Romans 1, which presents God's court

case against the human race. Hosea 4 presents God's court case against the Hebrew race: "There is no truth, nor mercy, nor knowledge of God in the land. By swearing, and lying, and killing, and stealing, and committing adultery, they break out, and blood toucheth blood" (4:1-2). The use of the polysyndeton (for example, "and...and...and") is intended to focus our attention on each item in the indictment.

The next verse, beginning with "Therefore," illustrates the ancient law of cause and effect, of sowing and reaping: "Therefore shall the land mourn" (4:3). God's moral laws are as sure and certain as His material laws.

2. The Lord's Commentary on Israel (4:6-14)

Twice in this passage God refers to Israel as "My people." The amazing love of God will not let us go, will not let us down, and will not let us off.

In Hosea 4:6 God says, "My people are destroyed for lack of knowledge." Ignorance is never accepted as an excuse in a court of law. We are expected to acquaint ourselves with the law by which we will be judged. But Israel was not merely guilty of simple ignorance; she was guilty of studied ignorance—that is, she chose to be ignorant of God. She did not want to know God, so He said, "Thou hast rejected knowledge." As we say today, there are none so blind as those who will not see. God's verdict is in verse 9: "I will punish them."

The people saw corruption, covetousness, and carnality in their priests, modeled themselves after the priests' example, and used it as an excuse. *If such a lifestyle is good for the priests,* they rationalized, *it is good for us.* When a nation's priests and preachers are evil and her teachers, leaders, opinion-makers, and pace-setters are unprincipled, what hope is there for her?

The Russian people followed the lead of their secular "priests," Marx and Lenin, and became a nation of atheists and materialists. The Germans followed their militaristic, antisemitic "priests," Hitler and Goebbels, into persecution, war, and destruction. The Iranians followed their narrow-minded and ruthless "priest," Khomeini, into an Islamic revolution that clamped a rigid, intolerant, militant fanaticism on their nation. A nation's behavior, no less than an individual's behavior, is governed by its beliefs, and a nation rises no higher than its priests, be they secular or spiritual.

Israel's priests were evil. Jeroboam I chose them in the beginning from the lowest of the people. Only completely unprincipled people would have consented to be consecrated to his false religion.

It did not take them long to establish calf worship in the northern kingdom. Then Ahab and Jezebel imported into Israel an even fouler foreign religion, complete with a licentious, pagan priesthood. Soon the people were bowing at the feet of the cruel gods of Phoenicia and reveling in every form of sexual sin as part of their worship. Jehu attempted reform, but it suited his purpose to leave the old priesthood of Jeroboam in power.

Gomer had probably been one of the victims of those priests, and Hosea was indignant. With his heart broken by what the priests had done to his wife, he cried out, "Like people, like priest" (4:9). Then he summed up Israel's religious life in three words: "Whoredom and wine" (4:11). In a system where fornication, adultery, and sodomy were not only tolerated but also encouraged and where male and female prostitutes were available to help consummate worship at every shrine, to go "a whoring" (4:12) after strange gods was much more than a mere figure of speech. Yet God still called the Israelites "My people."

In Hosea 4:6, when God used the expression "My people," His emphasis was on their immorality. When He used the expression in 4:12, His emphasis was on their idolatry. "My people ask counsel at their stocks," He said. There is no greater folly than to pray to an idol made by man. Imagine taking a piece of wood or a slab of stone, carving it into the likeness of a man or a monster, painting it, putting it on a pedestal, and then praying to it! One might as well pray to the kitchen sink. Yet even today millions of people— Hindus, Buddhists, Shintoists, Roman Catholics—pray to graven images of one sort or another.

Idolatry is always demoralizing. Evil spirits that lurk behind the idols blind people's minds and lure them into sin. Hindu idolatry is often accompanied by the same kinds of moral decadence that characterized Israel's idolatry.

Gomer, ruined by the priests, had been unable to settle down to a regulated home life. As brokenhearted Hosea wrote his prophecy, he had visions of his wife plying her infamous trade under the direction and control of some filthy-minded priest.

3. The Lord's Caution about Israel (4:15–5:15)

a. Warnings Addressed to Judah (4:15-19)

Another vision rose up in Hosea's mind: a vision of Israel's sister-nation Judah, where a good king was spearheading a return to God. "Let not Judah offend," the prophet cried in an aside to that land

(4:15). He then likened his own nation to a "backsliding heifer" (4:16), a significant description since Israel's chief idol was a golden calf. Hosea, a country man, had seen many intractable, untamed animals pull back from the yoke when they could. If they could not avoid the yoke, they would pull sideways or backward. Israel was just like them. Judah had, in the mercy of God, been pulled back from the abyss, but let her beware of backsliding again!

Holding Israel up as an example to Judah of the end result of sin, Hosea made one of the most terrible statements in the Bible: "Ephraim is joined to idols: let him alone" (4:17). The nation was so besotted by its idolatry that no Holy-Ghost-inspired, God-breathed word, voiced either in tones of yearning love or in terms of boiling wrath, would make any difference. So God said, "Let him alone." When God gives up on an individual or a nation, all that remains is judgment.

How like Hosea's day is our day! How like Hosea's homeland is our homeland. He would probably describe our country the way he described his country: "Their drink is sour: they have committed whoredom continually: her rulers with shame do love [or, do love shame]" (4:18). Like us, Hosea lived in a pornographic society in which those who should have been on the side of Biblical morality and simple decency supported permissiveness and upheld every form of moral and religious decadence.

What hope was there? None! Israel had long since sown the wind and she was about to reap the whirlwind (see 8:7 and 4:19). All Hosea could see ahead was doom.

b. Warnings Applicable to Judah (5:1-15)

In this passage Hosea turned his attention back to Israel, but occasionally warned Judah. Two expressions in chapter 5 stand out: "I know" and "I will go" (5:3,15).

(1) Israel's Determination (5:1-7)

The Lord knew all about Israel's determination. "I know Ephraim," He said. "They will not frame their doings [what they do will not allow them] to turn unto their God" (5:3-4). The One who had experienced Israel's perfidy over and over again said, "They *will* not" (italics aded). The battle against evil always ends up as a battle of the will. The wicked should not say that they *cannot* overcome evil; the truth is that they *will not*.

Hosea prophesied that because of Israel's determination not to turn to God, "they shall go with their flocks and with their herds to seek the Lord; but they shall not find him; he hath withdrawn himself from them" (5:6). When at last they say, "We will," God will say, "No you won't." When the Israelites have sinned away the day of grace, they will bring flocks and herds for sacrifice in a last desperate move to avert their doom, but God will no longer be available. When He has knocked and knocked, and called and called in vain, He will go away.

The Israelites should have known what would happen, for they knew that God had withdrawn himself from King Saul. Saul sinned against God with a high hand, but the time came when he desperately needed God. However, no message came to him from God. Samuel was dead. David knew God and wrote Psalms, but Saul had driven him away. God had abandoned Saul. No more terrible state of soul can be imagined. In desperation he resorted to witchcraft—finding the door of Heaven barred, he went down and knocked at the door of Hell. God opened that door and let Saul fall through it into the darkness on the other side.

At the time of Hosea's prophecy, Israel had little time left: "They have dealt treacherously against the Lord....Now shall a month devour them" (5:7). A month, the symbol of a short time, is ruled by the moon. The moon is never still; it is ever moving on its ordained path and we can do nothing to stop it. The moon waxes and wanes, and darkness comes. Likewise Israel's doom was coming.

(2) Israel's Doom (5:8-15)

As we read Hosea's description of Israel's doom, we find an unexpected figure of speech in 5:12: God said, "Therefore will I be unto Ephraim as a moth, and to the house of Judah as rottenness." Unseen and unheard, a moth in a garment eats away at the fabric and destroys it. Likewise rottenness secretly eats away at wood, but more slowly. Israel's doom was coming swiftly; Judah's, more slowly. God was secretly undermining both countries because of their wickedness.

In 5:13 we find Hosea's first use of the dreadful word "Assyrian." Some saw it as a welcome patch of shade in the prophetic picture, but it was really the shadow of approaching night.

The forces of decay and destruction were already at work and God retired to Heaven to wait. He said in Hosea 5:15, "I will go and return to my place, till they acknowledge their offence, and seek my face." It has been a long wait and although God has revealed Himself in Christ, Israel still has not turned to Him.

4. The Lord's Compassion for Israel (6:1-11)

The prophet's mind tossed and turned as he thought of his beloved country, just as he had tossed and turned on his bed as he thought of Gomer before he redeemed her.

Prior to that purchase, when Hosea thought of his wife, one moment his love would rise and he would forgive all her sins and yearn over her in his innermost soul. He would think of her many woes and how she had been used and abused by the priests, and his heart would go out to her in pity and great longing. The next moment his mind's eye would see her running after a lustful man, smiling and laughing at his lewdness, and flinging herself at him. And Hosea would be furiously angry—angry at the way she had dishonored him, angry at the permissive society that condoned her lifestyle, angry at the wickedness of the priests, angry at the kind of religion that condoned her sins, angry at what her sin was doing to her children.

Hosea's pity struggled with his anger. During the day he would see Gomer's children growing up in a broken home and torn between two worlds. Near the temple of Baal he would see his estranged wife plying her shameless trade with a brazen face, and he would return home and have another bad night.

Now when Hosea thought of Israel's sins and her unspeakable shame, he would remember God's compassion and he would remember His wrath. Chapter 6 reveals how the prophet's thoughts jumped backward and forward, here and there. One moment he thought of the day of grace; another moment, the day of judgment. One moment he thought of the great tribulation; another moment, the millennial reign. Words flowed from the prophet's lips like molten lava from an erupting volcano. Indeed his thoughts seem so disjointed and chaotic to many readers that they have despaired of trying to see any kind of progressive outline in Hosea 4–14.

In 6:1 we stand with the prophet at the end of the great tribulation and hear prodigal Israel's latter-day cry of repentance and remorse: "Come, and let us return unto the Lord: for he hath torn, and he will heal us; he hath smitten, and he will bind us up."

In 6:2 we detect one of those vague references to time so characteristic of Old Testament prophecy: "After two days will he revive us: in the third day he will raise us up, and we shall live in his sight." Hosea prophesied in the eighth century B.C. and it is now near the end of the twentieth century of the age of grace; so if we apply Peter's famous formula—"One day is with the Lord as a thousand years, and a thousand years as one day" (2 Peter 3:8)—we could conclude that Israel has already passed two of the days and is now in the third. Soon the third day will end and the millennial age will dawn. Then Israel will indeed be healed and raised up, and the Jews will live under the approving eye of God.

In Hosea 6:4 the prophet returned abruptly to the subject of Israel's and Judah's sins. Sadly and soberly he pondered the sights he saw in Samaria and the surrounding countryside. He saw a robber band setting an ambush for a wayfaring traveler, and the highwaymen turned out to be a company of priests who were plotting murder and mayhem! He saw every form of exposure and indecency being paraded without blush or shame. Over much of what he saw he wrote the word "lewdness" (6:9). Hosea's pure heart recoiled. "I have seen an horrible thing," he said (6:10). The "horrible thing" that filled his righteous soul with loathing and disgust was the "whoredom" of Israel.

The whoredom of Israel was not just a flirtation that had gone too far. In such a case the guilty parties are often overwhelmed with a sense of uncleanness and shame. Nor was Israel's whoredom merely a sinful, unblessed union entered into without regard for the conventions of society or the laws of God. Nor was her whoredom simply a matter of adultery. The "horrible thing" was far worse.

True, unblessed unions have penalties, not the least of which is a grieved Holy Spirit. People indulging in such relationships will be haunted by their guilt and in the end their sin will find them out. And God's law imposed the death penalty for adultery in Old Testament times. Although unconventional liaisons are common today and adulterous behavior is practically laughed out of court, God's judgment is certain. He has an arsenal of weapons for punishing sexual sin. There are physical, psychological, medical, and spiritual consequences, as King David discovered.

But Israel would have to face even more severe consequences, for she was guilty, both literally and symbolically, of *spiritual* whoredom in her besotted idolatries. In her foul religion, union with a temple prostitute was considered the highest act of worship. Hosea saw such worship as whoredom and so did God.

No wonder 6:11 speaks of a "harvest." Hosea was addressing Judah, but Judah's judgment was to be postponed by a succession of good kings—Uzziah, Hezekiah, Josiah—and a galaxy of great prophets. Israel's doom was nearer—so near that here Hosea took it for granted.

5. The Lord's Contempt for Israel (7:1-16)

a. The Throne (7:1-7)

In the beginning of chapter 7 Hosea had the sins of Israel's throne particularly in view: "They make the king glad with their wickedness, and the princes with their lies" (7:3). Kings were surrounded by loose and unscrupulous nobles, a profligate court, adultery, drunkenness, and conspiracies. The lust, lawlessness, and licentiousness of the people was but an extension of their rulers' disorder and decadence.

Hosea went on to describe a disgusting court scene in which a king took pleasure in evil people who made him drink too much and he vomited in his drunken stupor: "In the day of our king the princes have made him sick with bottles of wine; he stretched out his hand with scorners" (7:5). The expression "the day of our king" probably refers to one of the many coronations that took place during Hosea's long ministry as one king after another fell to the assassin's knife. None of these kings had even a passing thought for God. Scripture says, "All their kings are fallen: there is none among them that calleth unto me" (7:7).

Murder had become the acknowledged way to the throne, the simplest and most satisfactory way to silence opposition. The red knife of the assassin was never far from the royal throat in Israel's latter years. During the dynasties of Omri and Jehu, the kings either left no sons or left them to be slain. Nadab, Elah, Tibni, Jehoram, Zachariah, Shallum, Pekahiah, and Pekah were all assassinated by their successors. Truly in those days it could have been said, "Uneasy lies the head that wears a crown."[1] Of all the kings of Israel, only eight died a natural death: Jeroboam I, Baasha, Omri, Menahem, Jehu, and the next three kings of Jehu's house.

b. The Throng (7:8-16)

With kings and courtiers so evil, no wonder the rank and file were evil. Hosea used three illustrations to describe how worthless Israel had become.

His first illustration is taken from *the bakeshop:* "Ephraim is a cake not turned" (Hosea 7:8). The picture is that of a pancake burned to cinders on one side and doughy on the other. Because the baker fell asleep (7:6), the cake is worthless. Nobody wants to eat either ashes or raw dough. The overdone side does not atone for the underdone side. What can be done with "a cake not turned"? It can only be tossed away. It is too late for the baker to do anything to make the cake edible.

Likewise when we are wiser and older, we cannot go back and undo the wrong things we did in our passionate youth. The opportunities we neglect disappear forever. Lives that because of our carelessness have been soiled or spoiled can never be reclaimed by any repentance on our part.

When Hosea wrote 7:8, all hope for Israel was gone. The prophet explained the reason in 7:9: "Strangers have devoured his strength, and he knoweth it not: yea, gray hairs are here and there upon him, yet he knoweth not." Time and opportunity had passed Israel by. It was too late.

Hosea's second illustration is taken from *the barnyard:* "Ephraim also is like a silly dove without heart" (7:11). An eastern proverb says that there is nothing more simple than a dove, and simple Israel thought she was sophisticated, clever, and able to handle her own affairs in a dangerous world. A poor pigeon of a people, Israel fluttered here and there, dabbling in international diplomacy. Hoping to be an international power broker and play off one world power against another, she flitted back and forth between Egypt and Assyria. "They call to Egypt," God said, "they go to Assyria....And they have not cried unto me" (7:11,14).

Hosea's third illustration is taken from *the battlefield:* "They are like a deceitful bow" (7:16). What more useless weapon could a man carry into battle than a crooked bow? No matter how carefully he aimed an arrow, it would always fly in the wrong direction. The best thing he could do would be to throw the bow away. Israel was to have been God's bow, His weapon against idolatry. Now it was warped and worse than useless, fit only to be destroyed.

B. The Punished People (8:1–10:15)

This passage of prophecy shows where Israel went astray and weighs the consequences of her misbehavior.

1. The Trampled Covenant (8:1-14)

a. Where Israel Sinned (8:1-6)

"They have transgressed my covenant," God said, "and trespassed against my law" (8:1). The northern kingdom was divinely ordained to be a protest against Solomon's gross idolatry. Jeroboam I had a marvelous opportunity to weld the ten tribes into a true theocracy—"one nation, under God, indivisible, with liberty and justice [and true religion] for all"—but he failed. Instead of bringing the Israelites back to God, he set up two golden calves and ordered the people to worship them—or rather, to worship Jehovah as represented by the calves. He turned the likeness of the invisible God, who at Sinai had sounded the warning trumpet against all images, into a golden calf.

One calf was set up at Dan for the benefit of the northerners; the other was set up at Beth-el to accommodate the southern Israeli tribes. Samaria was the capital where the king who supported this apostasy was enthroned. So God declared through Hosea, "Thy calf, O Samaria, hath cast thee off" (8:5).

b. What Israel Sowed (8:7-10)

Hosea 8:7 tells us, "They have sown the wind, and they shall reap the whirlwind." Israel had sowed the wind by courting the Gentiles and their gods, and would reap the whirlwind of invasion and deportation to Gentile lands (8:8). And as foretold, the Assyrian army, like a thundering tornado, descended on Israel, whose helpless people were caught up and whirled away into captivity.

In 8:9 Hosea used another powerful illustration: he called Israel "a wild ass alone by himself." The wild ass of the East is a headstrong, unruly, and obstinate animal that can outrun a horse. It is drawn in all directions by its lust, hunger, and thirst. It usually roams in bands, but sometimes one breaks away from the pack and becomes a prey to lions. Israel, in her fierce independence of God, became a prey to the Assyrian lion.

A person who is singularly obstinate and unruly is referred to as "a wild ass's colt" (Job 11:12). Ishmael was such a person (Genesis 16:12).

c. Where Israel Stood (8:11-14)

We read in Hosea 8:11, "Ephraim hath made many altars to sin." To have made many altars was bad enough—there was to be only one altar, the one in the temple in Jerusalem. But the real sting in this indictment lies in the words "to sin." God's evaluation of false religion is that it is sin. Altars erected to serve false religions are not altars to God at all; they are actually altars to sin.

2. The Tragic Consequences (9:1-17)

a. Bewilderment (9:1-9)

It seems that at a time when the land was relatively peaceful, Hosea saw the Israelites singing, dancing, and feasting. Apparently he put an abrupt end to the festivities, or at least poured cold water on their merriment, for he said, "Rejoice not, O Israel, for joy, as other people: for thou hast gone a whoring from thy God" (9:1). (Hosea must have been about as popular as a skunk at a Sunday school picnic!) Other nations derived joy from their pagan celebrations because they knew no better. Their sin was the sin of ignorance. They had not changed their gods as Israel had done.

Israel had no reason to rejoice, for judgment was on the way. With both Egypt and Assyria posing a threat to the Israelites, Hosea prophesied, "They shall not dwell in the Lord's land" (9:3). This statement is one of the numerous passages in Scripture that speak of the whole land of Israel being the Lord's. Judah and Israel were only tenants, who would be expelled if they ignored and defied the terms of the contract that allowed them to live in the land. The countdown to the day of judgment had begun. The peace and calm were only the lull before the storm. "The days of visitation are come," thundered the prophet (9:7).

Since the blind folly of the people was aggravated by their "prophets" and "spiritual leaders," Hosea added, "The prophet is a fool, the spiritual man is mad [or, raving mad is the man of the spirit]." The frantic prophetic ecstasy experienced in King Saul's day (1 Samuel 10:11-12; 19:20-21) had turned to delirium, fanaticism, and demonic utterance. That is why the New Testament hedges transitional gifts (such as prophesying and speaking in tongues) with strict rules, prohibitions, and warnings. Such ecstatic gifts are easily imitated by evil spirits, and when exercised apart from the Holy Spirit's restrictions, must always be highly suspect. They come from a counterfeit source.

Rather than doubt the inspiration of the lying prophets, however, the people of Hosea's day believed their lies to be divinely inspired. People today are the same; they crave extra-Biblical pronouncements, accept them uncritically, and are deceived. Listening to such messages only leads to bewilderment and confusion.

b. Barrenness (9:10-17)

Israel "went to Baal-peor," wrote Hosea (9:10). Baal-peor was the foulest of the heathen gods and his shrines were the first Canaanite shrines that the children of Israel had contact with. They immediately became embroiled in this filthy paganism (see Numbers 25) and as they began, so they continued. God patiently put up with their wickedness for hundreds of years, but long-delayed judgment was about to fall.

So terrible would the judgment be, that barrenness would be a blessing, not a curse. It would be a mercy to have no children. Those who had children would wish that they had never had them. "Ephraim shall bring forth his children to the murderer," prophesied Hosea, and he prayed, "Give them, O Lord...a miscarrying womb and dry breasts" (9:13-14). Surely those who lived to see what the Assyrian soldiers did to pregnant women and little children agreed that Hosea's prayer had come from a heart broken by certain foreknowledge of what lay ahead.

Hosea 9:15 and 17 refer to the survivors. "I will drive them out of mine house," the Lord said. And the prophet wrote, "They shall be wanderers among the nations."

3. The Terrible Conditions (10:1-15)

Everywhere Hosea looked, he saw the writing on the wall for Israel.

a. Israel's Detestable Religion (10:1-2)

The prophet likened Israel to "an empty vine" (10:1). Some translate the phrase as "a luxuriant vine," but if they are right, the vine had a profusion of leaves and no fruit for the divine husbandman.

Evidences of idolatry were everywhere. The more God allowed the Israelites to enjoy material prosperity, the more they ran after their idols. The word translated "images" in 10:1 suggests the *asherah*, upright pillars that advertised the vileness of their worship. The pillars were sex symbols fashioned from the stumps of living trees or artificially manufactured and set in the ground. Sometimes the pillars were made of stone and anointed with oil. Two such columns stood before every Phoenician temple. These symbols incited the worshiper to participate in all forms of impurity and obscene orgies. How Hosea hated the *asherah!* His wife had been debased by them.

b. Israel's Departed Rulers (10:3-6)

"Now they shall say," wrote Hosea, "We have no king" (10:3).

Perhaps he was referring to the assassinations that swiftly removed one king of Israel after another. More likely he was referring to the final catastrophe when the Assyrians came and made an end of the monarchy.

c. Israel's Deserted Ruins (10:7-8)

Graphically depicting the utter desolation of the land, the prophet wrote, "The thorn and the thistle [living symbols of the curse] shall come up on their altars" (10:8). Instead of being thronged with people every day, the busy thoroughfares, the well-tended altars, and the shrines dedicated to false gods would be overgrown with weeds. The Assyrians would do such a thorough job of destruction that the vile altars would decay and noxious growths would spring up to cover their shame. The moon would cast cold shadows and the owls would hoot over the haunted ruins.

d. Israel's Desired Repentance (10:9-12)

Israel would not repent until the full harvest of iniquity had been reaped, but for just a moment Hosea anticipated her repentance at the end of the age. "It is time to seek the Lord," he wrote (10:12). He pleaded with the Israelites to sow righteousness and reap mercy, but they would not be seeking the Lord for a long time—not until He came and rained righteousness upon them.

e. Israel's Dreadful Reward (10:13-15)

The nation's vice and vileness were about to be rewarded in judgment. All her defenses against the enemy would fail—with terrible consequences. Hosea reminded the Israelites of what had happened when Shalman (Shalmaneser) took Beth-arbel. The triumphant and calloused Assyrian soldiers had seized infants and, before the eyes of their horrified mothers, had dashed out their brains on the rocks. Then the soldiers had treated the mothers in the same way. Such terrible scenes were about to be re-enacted on a national scale.

Hosea added a detail at the end of the chapter: "In a morning shall the king of Israel utterly be cut off" (10:15). The prophet was referring to Hoshea, the last king of Israel. Without exception, all the monarchs who sat on the throne of the northern kingdom were bad. Never again will the ten tribes have a king—not until Jesus comes to reign.

C. The Pardoned People (11:1–14:9)

1. Israel's Persistence (11:1–12:1)

Beginning his final review of Israel's doom and destiny, Hosea considered the past, the present, and the prospects for the future. When he looked at the present—the days in which he lived—he could see only persistence.

a. Her Destiny (11:1)

This verse of Scripture states, "When Israel was a child, then I loved him, and called my son out of Egypt." The thought of the coming exile reminded Hosea of a past exodus, but at this point his vision soared far above the miasmas of Israel's present apostasy and far above the jubilation of the ancient exodus from Egypt. He uttered one of the mysterious prophecies that tower above the Old Testament landscape as commanding signposts pointing to Jesus.

Devout Jewish students must have often pondered this Messianic prophecy. *How can the Messiah possibly come out of Egypt?* they no doubt reasoned. *No way! It is the destiny of the Jewish people to bring the Messiah into the world. He is to be born in Bethlehem, of the tribe of Judah, of the house of David. He is to be a Nazarene. Galilee will be his home. This prophecy must refer to the nation of Israel, not to the Messiah.* Yet how simply and literally the prophecy was fulfilled (Matthew 2:15)!

As we ponder Hosea 11:1 we wonder whether the prophet realized that he had spoken words of such a high and noble order. Whether he knew it or not, the Holy Spirit knew it and treated it accordingly. However, that prophetic lightning flash blazed out amid an ever-darkening sky.

b. Her Determination (11:2-7)

God "loved," "taught," and "drew" Israel (11:1-4). And what was Israel's response? "They sacrificed unto Baalim....They knew not" (11:2-3). Israel responded with determination to go its own willful way. But who can match wills with God and win? He answered Israel's determination with His determination. As 11:5-6 indicates, God would make sure that Israel would reap what it had sowed: "[Israel] shall not return into the land of Egypt [an Egyptian invasion would be relatively benign], but the Assyrian shall be his king, because they refused to return. And the sword shall abide on his cities, and shall consume his branches, and devour them."

c. Her Desolation (11:8-11)

Israel's desolation broke the heart of God. "How shall I give thee up, Ephraim?" He asked (11:8). His question echoed in Hosea's heart. "How shall I give thee up, Gomer?" he must have often cried. Hosea let her go, but never stopped loving her and eventually bought her and brought her back. We see a similar resolution in the case of Israel. God said, "I will not execute the fierceness of mine anger" (11:9). If he had, the ten tribes would have been blotted out forever.

If a mere man like Hosea could temper justice with mercy in dealing with his loved but faithless wife, how much more could God in dealing with loved but faithless Israel! The prophet's blend of justice and mercy was a mere shadow. To see the substance we must go to God, who at last will take us to Golgotha.

And so Israel has been lost among the nations, but not lost to God. True, He summoned the Assyrians to sack Samaria, and they did a thorough and terrible job. But God Himself did not enter the city; He did not make an utter end of it, as He had Sodom. Instead He waited outside. Down through the ages He would stay with the scattered tribes—"the Holy One in the midst of thee"—to watch over their wanderings and preserve them from total assimilation and extermination.

Their long sojourn among the nations would not be wholly unproductive: "They shall walk after the Lord....The children shall tremble [come or hasten with trembling] from the west" (11:10). Here we have a hint of the gospel blessings that so many Jews (especially western Jews) have received; the harvest of Pentecost was but the firstfruits (Acts 2:5-11).

d. Her Deceptions (11:12-12:1)

Returning abruptly to the present, Hosea said: "Ephraim compasseth me about with lies, and the house of Israel with deceit....He daily increaseth lies." The prophet cited the example of Israel's faithlessness in its foreign relations as it tried in vain to wring advantages from Egypt and Assyria simultaneously. Men call such negotiating diplomacy; God calls it deceit. God does not bless international duplicity any more than He blesses individual duplicity.

2. Israel's Past (12:2-14)

The ten-tribe nation of Israel and the two-tribe nation of Judah had a common heritage, for they both descended from Jacob. In

12:2-6 Hosea addressed his prophecy to Judah and in 12:7-14 the prophet addressed Israel. In both cases Hosea used illustrations from the story of Jacob.

a. A Message to Judah in the South (12:2-6)

Hosea reminded Judah of *Jacob's birth:* "He took his brother by the heel in the womb, and by his strength he had power with God" (12:3). Then, leaping suddenly from the prenatal to the supernatural, the prophet reminded Judah of *Jacob's blessing* that the patriarch received on that dark night at the Jabbok when "he had power over the angel" (12:4). Finally Hosea reminded Judah of *Jacob's belief* memorialized at Beth-el, where he learned that there was a way back to God from the dark path of sin. Such was Judah's heritage. They were chosen and blessed even before they became a nation. They were to have power with God and they were to be in touch with Heaven.

God was still talking to Judah. The nation had a rich heritage, was not yet guilty of open apostasy, and had not yet filled up the measure of its sins. Yet God had "a controversy with Judah" (12:2). "Therefore," Hosea wisely advised, "turn thou to thy God: keep mercy and judgment, and wait on thy God continually" (12:6).

b. A Message to Israel in the North (12:7-14)

Hosea reminded Israel of Jacob's dealings with his Uncle Laban in Padan-aram. First there was the matter of *Jacob's wages.* "He is a merchant," wrote Hosea, "the balances of deceit are in his hand" (12:7). Jacob's name meant "cheat," but Jacob met his match in Uncle Laban. "[He] changed my wages ten times," Jacob cried to his wives when he decided to return to the promised land (Genesis 31:7). But wily Jacob paid his unscrupulous uncle back with counterfeit coin. There was crookedness and duplicity on both sides.

Then Hosea mentioned the matter of *Jacob's wives:* "And Jacob fled into the country of Syria, and Israel served for a wife, and for a wife he kept sheep" (12:12). Hosea's point was that in spite of all his craftiness, one thing in Jacob's life rang true: his love for Rachel. His love contained no cheap alloy, only purest gold. Hosea's love for Gomer and God's love for Israel were also of purest gold.

Surely the entire message to Israel in 12:7-14 is designed to contrast the difference between deceitfulness and devotedness. Israel was deceitful in her relationship to God, and God was loving in His relationship to Israel.

But God's love was not given at the expense of the law. "Ephraim provoked him to anger most bitterly: therefore shall he leave his blood upon him" (12:14). Hosea was saying, "Let Israel beware!" The blood she had shed was about to be required of her. Many innocent children had been sacrificed to the vile, vicious gods of Canaan. Not one drop of their blood or one moment of their agony had been overlooked by God. His long account with Israel was about to be paid in full. There would be judgment—but God's changeless love would be a rainbow in the face of the storm.

3. Israel's Punishment (13:1-16)

The crisis was on its way. On one side of the scale, Israel's sins multiplied and ripened for judgment. On the other side, portents of doom grew clearer. Already Assyria was on the march. So Hosea 13 is full of lightning flashes. Nearly every verse focuses on a different theme.

In 13:1 the prophet singled out the damning sin of Israel: "In Baal, he died." The vicious and vile worship of Baal affronted the holy One of Israel, demoralized the nation, and totally negated its calling and election.

"They sin more and more," sobbed Hosea in 13:2. His prophecy was falling on deaf ears, so he cried, "Let the men that sacrifice kiss the calves." Setting up the golden calves as objects of worship was Jeroboam's great sin and the ultimate source of Israel's woes. Hosea was saying in effect, "Let them go and kiss those foolish objects of worship and find out how much good it will do them!"

Hosea 13:3 is a picture of Israel's future: "They shall be…as the smoke out of the chimney." Like the early dew they would have a moment in the sun, and then they would be gone.

In 13:4 the living God said, "There is no saviour beside me." There was no savior in the golden calf, no savior in Baal, no savior in Moloch, no savior in any god worshiped by the nations surrounding Israel. Likewise there is no savior in Islam, Buddhism, or any eastern religion. There is no savior in the false cults of Christendom. There is no savior in a creed of good works. There is no savior in humanism or communism.

God beautifully illustrated both His love and His wrath when He said in 13:8, "I will meet them as a bear that is bereaved of her whelps." Nothing in nature is more tender than a mother in the wild. And nothing is more terrible than a bear that has been robbed of her cubs, especially a naturally fierce Syrian bear; she is the incarnation of fury and ferocity.

Continuing in 13:11 to speak of His wrath, God said, "I gave thee a king in mine anger, and took him away in my wrath." That king was Saul, whom the people chose when they rejected godly Samuel and the theocracy, and demanded a government like the monarchies the nearby pagan nations had. Saul was removed after many years of provoking God. It could be said of all of Israel's miserable kings that they were taken away in wrath.

Hosea 13:13 states, "The sorrows of a travailing woman shall come." Birth pains are sudden, irresistible, and often violent. A moment before they come, all is at peace, but the onslaught is inevitable, given the prevailing condition. When the pains come, they increase in intensity. If they fail to accomplish their purpose, the mother and baby may die (this was especially true in the days before the advance of medical science). Israel's death pangs were on the way.

"An east wind shall come," Hosea continued in 13:15. The east wind that blows across Israel comes from the Arabian desert. Hot and dry, this wind is destructive to vegetation and oppressive to man. Nothing can stop it. It is as certain as the seasons.

"Samaria shall become desolate," Hosea prophesied in 13:16. He added a number of gruesome details typical of what happened when the Assyrians captured a city that had stubbornly resisted a siege.

Judgment is prophesied, but the offer of pardon is included in 13:9-10: "O Israel, thou hast destroyed thyself; but in me is thine help. I will be thy king." Beyond the darkness lies the dawn of another day.

4. Israel's Peace (14:1-9)

a. The Plea (14:1-3)

The tide of denunciation had rolled its billows over Ephraim, and the last wave had poured its judgment flood over Samaria, the seat of power. The separate existence of the northern kingdom had turned out to be a curse rather than a blessing. As a nation, Israel's day was done, but the people remained and God's promises remained. So Hosea closed his prophecy with God's plea to the people of Israel to return to Him: "O Israel, return unto the Lord thy God" (14:1). The plea has thus far been ignored, but the day will come when Israel will cry, "Take away all iniquity, and receive us graciously" (14:2).

b. The Pledge (14:4-8)

Again and again God said, "I will...I will...I will." He promised, "I will heal," "I will love them," "I will be as the dew unto Israel" (14:4-5), for in the end "Ephraim shall say, What have I to do any more with idols?" (14:8)

c. The Path (14:9)

Hosea concluded: "Who is wise, and he shall understand these things? prudent, and he shall know them? for the ways of the Lord are right, and the just shall walk in them: but the transgressors shall fall therein." The prophet was indicating that the path to Israel's peace is the path of wisdom and prudence.

We know from history what happened to the wretched people and nation to whom Hosea preached. We know from prophecy, especially later prophecy, that one day the remnant of Israel will return, repent, be regenerated, and "live happily ever after."

But what about Hosea himself? Did Gomer emerge from her period of discipline a sadder, but wiser woman? Did she at last return Hosea's love? Did she in time become a model wife and mother? We can certainly hope that she did, so that Hosea too could "live happily ever after."

Chapter 2

JOEL

PROPHET OF THE PLAGUE

I. THE DAY OF THE LOCUST (1:1-14)
   A. Divine Displeasure Expressed (1:1-5)
      1. A Word for the Prophet (1:1)
      2. A Word for the People (1:2-5)
         a. The Descendants (1:2-4)
         b. The Drunkards (1:5)
   B. Divine Displeasure Expanded (1:6-14)
      1. Desecration (1:6-7)
      2. Desolation (1:8-12)
      3. Desperation (1:13-14)
II. THE DAY OF THE LORD (1:15–3:21)
   A. The Day of Assyria (1:15–2:32)
      1. A Day of Destruction (1:15-20)
      2. A Day of Darkness (2:1-10)
      3. A Day of Deliverance (2:11-32)
         a. A Call for Repentance (2:11-19)
         b. A Call for Rejoicing (2:20-27)
         c. A Call for Revival (2:28-32)
   B. The Day of Antichrist (3:1-16)
      1. The Gathering of the Hebrew People (3:1)
      2. The Gathering of the Heathen Peoples (3:2-16)
         a. A Gathering of the Wicked (3:2-8)
         b. A Gathering of the Warmongers (3:9-13)
         c. A Gathering of the World (3:14-16)
   C. The Day of Anticipation (3:17-21)
      1. A Wonderful Coming (3:17-18)
      2. A Woeful Contrast (3:19)
      3. A Welcome Conclusion (3:20-21)

————❦————

The day of the Lord"! "The day of the Lord"! "The day of the Lord"! Like the drumbeat of doom, the measured tread of marching feet, or the refrain of a song, this phrase occurs again and again in the book of Joel. "The day of the Lord" is Joel's signature tune, the dominant color on his canvas of catastrophe.

Joel loomed up mysteriously in the morning mists and vanished into the shadows. All he left behind was the sound of his voice and the echo of distant thunder. Beyond his name and his father's name, which distinguishes the prophet from a dozen other Joels in Scripture, his personal history is conjecture. Joel spoke familiarly of Zion and the children of Zion, and probably ministered in Jerusalem. Based on his interest in the temple, some scholars have speculated that he was a priest. While Hosea's message primarily related to the northern kingdom of Israel, Joel's message related to the southern kingdom of Judah.

There is wide disagreement about the date of Joel's prophecy. Some historians suggest that he prophesied during the last seven years of Zedekiah's reign—that is, the last seven years of the kingdom of Judah. If so, Joel preached when Ezekiel and Jeremiah were preaching. Other historians go to the other end of the political spectrum and suggest that Joel prophesied during the reign of Uzziah or even as early as the days of Elisha. The fact that the Hebrew Canon and the Septuagint group Joel with the early pre-exilic prophets supports the latter viewpoint.

Joel mentioned no king, but neither did Nahum, Micah, or Habakkuk. Joel did not mention idolatry, the prevailing sin of both kingdoms, but he was preaching to Judah where people at least nominally worshiped Jehovah and frequently reacted against idolatry. His brief book is remarkably free of prophetic denunciations.

He made no mention of Assyria, but neither did Amos. Joel did mention the Greeks as slavers, but even secular historians (in the Tell el-Amarna tablets for instance) made similar references to the Greeks.

Some of the scholars who assume an early date for Joel's prophecy argue that other Biblical writers borrowed freely from him, and some of the scholars who assume a late date for his prophecy argue that Joel borrowed freely from others. Both sides of the time debate estimate that twenty-seven phrases, clauses, or expressions in Joel's seventy-three verses have parallels in other Old Testament writings. The existence of parallel passages, however, does not prove that Joel quoted from other prophets or that other prophets quoted from Joel. The Holy Spirit—the ultimate author of all the books—had no need to quote from anyone.

Joel made no references to time because his burden of prophecy far transcended his own times. It transcended the times of the divided kingdoms of Judah and Israel, and even transcended the time of the reconstructed nation after the Babylonian captivity. His prophecy leaps across the ages to the endtime. His favorite expression "the day of the Lord" occurs five times in his book (1:15; 2:1,11,31; 3:14).

Far more formidable enemies than either the Assyrians or the Babylonians lurked on the distant horizon. Joel focused on these latter-day foes, particularly the ominous northern power that will invade Israel.

If Joel did indeed prophesy early (as the rabbis assumed), he was the first and the last: the first of the writing prophets in terms of time and the last of the writing prophets in terms of topic.

I. THE DAY OF THE LOCUST (1:1-14)

A. Divine Displeasure Expressed (1:1-5)

1. A Word for the Prophet (1:1)

"The word of the Lord that came to Joel." Thus the prophecy begins. Joel's book is not, as destructive critics assume, merely a summary of passages from previous prophets compiled after the Jews returned to their homeland in the days of Nehemiah. George Adam Smith summarized what one agnostic commentator said: "Joel gathered up the pictures of the Messianic age in the older prophets, and welded them together in one long prayer by the fervid belief that the age was near....There is no history in the book: it is all ideal, mystical, apocalyptic. That is to say, there is no real prophet or prophetic fire, only an old man warming his feeble hands over a few embers that he has scraped together from the ashes of ancient fires, now nearly wholly dead."[1]

What a scandalous view of the Holy Writ! Joel's prophecy is not a patchwork quilt stitched together from bits and pieces snipped from other people's prophecies. "The word of the Lord...came to Joel"! Joel did not originate this far-reaching prophecy; it came hot from the heart of God. The pen was Joel's, but the prophecy was the Lord's. The word of the Lord came to Joel out of eternity—from God's throne on high. The prophecy came from the One who gathers all the ages into the eternal present, who sees the end from the beginning. He sees tomorrow's distant day of the Lord as clearly as yesteryear's day of the locust.

Joel 1:1 is either the glorious truth or an outrageous falsehood. Either the prophecy was divinely inspired, or Joel was a liar and his book is an outright forgery.

2. A Word for the People (1:2-5)

a. The Descendants (1:2-4)

Having identified himself and his source of inspiration, Joel got right down to business. First he addressed the descendants: "Hear this, ye old men, and give ear, all ye inhabitants of the land. Hath this been in your days, or even in the days of your fathers? Tell ye your children of it, and let your children tell their children, and their children another generation" (1:2-3).

The land had been devastated by a locust plague of horrendous proportions: "That which the palmerworm hath left hath the locust eaten; and that which the locust hath left hath the cankerworm eaten; and that which the cankerworm hath left hath the caterpiller eaten" (1:4). In the Hebrew text, this summary of the plague is given in meter. There are three lines in the verse, each consisting of four words. The first and third of the four words are the same in each line. The fourth word of the first line becomes the second word of the second line, and the fourth word of the second line becomes the second word of the third line. Pusey illustrated this pattern for the non-Hebrew reader by presenting the verse in Latin:

> Residuum erucae comedit locusta
> Residuumque locustae comedit bruchus
> Residuumque bruchi comedit exesor[2]

The words are structured to provide a rhythmic beat for the ear and a precise order for the eye. Reinforcing the significance of the plague, this literary device helped impress the facts of that scourge on the minds and memories of succeeding generations. The English language cannot adequately convey the force of the original idioms, but they can be expressed as follows:

> Gnawer's remnant, swarmer eats;
> Swarmer's remnant, devourer eats;
> Devourer's remnant, consumer eats.

Joel used four descriptive words to depict the four stages of the locust. Note the italicized terms: "That which the palmerworm [*gazem*, the gnawer, the old locust] hath left hath the locust [*arbeh*, the swarmer, the newly hatched hopper] eaten; and that which the locust [*arbeh*] hath left hath the cankerworm [*yelek*, the devourer, the crawler, the pupa] eaten; and that which the cankerworm [*yelek*] hath left hath the caterpiller [*hasil*, the consumer, the mature flier] eaten." These four words show the completeness of the Almighty's destructive agents.[3]

Locust plagues are the scourge of agricultural communities. The worst in modern times struck the Middle East in the early 1950s. In Iran, Iraq, Jordan, and Saudi Arabia, every green thing in hundreds of thousands of square miles was destroyed. The desert locust, ranging a territory of some eleven million square miles, threatens nearly 20 percent of the world's land surface in all or parts of about sixty-five countries where 10 percent of the world's population live. Locusts have been called "the teeth of the wind" and, even more expressively, "the incarnation of hunger." Human intervention has never stopped a locust plague and probably never will. The only thing that can stop one is an equally terrible disaster: widespread drought.

When food is abundant, locusts begin to multiply until their numbers reach astronomical proportions. The more they eat, the more they breed. In a breeding area there can be five thousand eggs in a square yard. There are no compact or mapped breeding areas, so no continuous or systematic control measures are possible. At intervals females deposit their egg pods four inches deep in damp soil or sand where conditions are favorable for hatching. Each female will lay at least three hundred pods in her lifetime and each pod contains up to one hundred eggs.

Each pod remains in the ground from ten to twenty days. When the eggs hatch, usually after a rain, the hatchlings find their way to the surface, shed their first skin, and become hoppers. If they have adequate living space, they will remain in this solitary phase—developing, breeding, and dying where they were hatched—just as ordinary grasshoppers do.

However, if living conditions become crowded, the insects will enter a gregarious stage in which they seek each other's company and constantly touch one another. This change of behavior triggers a change in color from green to yellow, black, and red. Then the locusts form bands and begin to march. Small bands merge to form larger ones and all of them move forward together in the same direction.

Marching forward, feeding as they go, the locusts pass through five stages of growth, shedding their skins in each stage. They take short flights and then begin to migrate in swarms. A medium-sized swarm may comprise more than a billion locusts, and some swarms reach prodigious proportions with an estimated million million locusts extending over two hundred square miles. Having no maps, homing instinct, or control over where they go, locusts simply ride the prevailing winds. During its five or six months of life, each locust travels between two and three thousand miles, breeding as it goes.

The swarms move forward in a kind of rolling motion, some of the locusts always being on the ground as the rear ones pass on to the front. As the rear of the swarm passes over them, those on the ground resume flight. The period spent on the ground enables each locust to replenish its fuel supply for further flight.

Locusts look like well-armed horsemen and have incredible strength. With teeth like saws, they devour grass and leaves, fruit and foliage—everything green and edible; they attack the young branches of trees and the bark on trunks; they consume corn in the field and fall on vines, willows, and even bitter hemp; they strip palm trees bare.

Many observers have described locust plagues. One person saw the air eighteen feet above the ground filled with the insects. Reddish-brown in color with gauzy wings sparkling in the sunlight, they reminded him of dense snowflakes driven by a storm. He was awed by their numbers and said the strange sight would have seemed beautiful if he could have forgotten about the devastation the locusts were bringing.

Another person observed a plague that came like a living deluge on his village. The villagers dug trenches, kindled fires, beat drums, and flailed and burned locusts to death by the thousands, but their efforts were useless. The swarm rolled up the mountainside, poured over obstacles, and descended on crops and trees. It took days for the whole swarm to pass through the area. The roads were covered with locusts marching along like soldiers. The villagers broke their ranks, but the locusts closed rank again as soon as they passed the men.

Someone else who witnessed a locust plague said that hundreds of the insects sat on each bush and after eating the leaves, gnawed frantically at the woody fibers. The locusts invaded towns and houses and devoured food, linen, woolen garments, and leather belts.

Such a locust plague had devastated Judah in Joel's day. To the prophet the plague was both a parable and a prophecy. Although the scourge was past, Joel used it as a picture of worse things to come. The real locusts became symbols of real warriors who would invade the land in successive waves. Some people think that Joel was referring to the four world empires (later defined in Daniel's prophecy) whose armies successively invaded Judah.

Joel emphasized the importance of remembering the plague and its portents. He demanded that his warning, backed as it was by a drastic and dramatic demonstration of disaster, be handed on to posterity.

b. The Drunkards (1:5)

Next Joel addressed the drunkards. He drew on the portent of the plague to warn them about what the approaching disaster would mean to them. The locusts had stripped the vines that grew the grapes that turned water into wine, so Joel cried, "Awake, ye drunkards, and weep; and howl, all ye drinkers of wine, because of the new wine; for it is cut off from your mouth."

In a country where wine was the common table beverage, drunkenness was a problem. God, who is always against drunkenness, gave many severe warnings against inebriation. He always called drunkenness a sin, not a disease, because it is culpable behavior. It destroys character, home life, business performance, and national fiber and opens the door to crime and every other form of sin. The locusts were God's warning about the consequences of drunkenness and a harbinger of worse judgments to come.

B. Divine Displeasure Expanded (1:6-14)

1. Desecration (1:6-7)

The locust invasion was an illustration of the desecration of a real invasion: "A nation [symbolized by the locusts] is come up upon *my* land....He hath laid *my* vine waste, and barked [reduced to chips] *my* fig tree" (italics added). The Lord was reasserting His claim to the land of Israel.

Israel is His land. No resolution of the United Nations or conference of superpowers is going to change that. Nations that tamper with Israel are tampering with God's land and are put on notice as to the consequences. Moreover the Hebrew people are God's people—His vine, His fig tree—and their land is the land He has given them. Therefore any violation of the land or people of Israel is a desecration.

2. Desolation (1:8-12)

The locust plague brought such desolation that Joel likened Judah to a young bride who has been suddenly widowed. The offerings in the temple were cut off and even the worship in God's house was affected; no greater proof of the catastrophic dimensions of the plague could be cited. There was not enough corn or wine in the land for meal and drink offerings. Everywhere Joel looked he saw ravaged fields, farms, vineyards, and orchards.

3. Desperation (1:13-14)

As a result of the plague, conditions in the land were so desperate that the prophet urged the priests to call a special, solemn assembly of all the inhabitants to cry unto the Lord.

II. THE DAY OF THE LORD (1:15–3:21)

A. The Day of Assyria (1:15–2:32)

1. A Day of Destruction (1:15-20)

Joel did not use the name Assyria when he wrote of a super-power—symbolized by the locust plague—that would devastate Israel and Judah. But if we assign an early date to Joel's prophecy, we have difficulty avoiding the conclusion that Assyria was the enemy to be feared.

When Assyrian armies ravaged God's land again and again, they were utterly ruthless. Yet the Assyrian king was only a type of an even more sinister king who will rise to power during the last days. The shadow of this latter-day despot now lies heavy across the world.

For the first time in Joel's prophecy and for the first time in Scripture (assuming that Joel was the first of the writing prophets) the pregnant phrase "the day of the Lord" occurs in Joel 1:15. In this verse Joel rapidly shifted his focus, as the writing prophets often did, from a near future event to a distant future event—from something on the immediate horizon to something on the end-time horizon.

Then he moved from "the day of the Lord"—an end-time focus—to a further description of the locusts' devastation, which in turn provided him with a graphic illustration of the devastation his country would experience at the hands of both the Assyrians and the antichrist.

The expression translated "the day of the Lord" in Joel 1:15 occurs twenty times in the Bible—sixteen times in the Old Testament (Isaiah 2:12; 13:6,9; Joel 1:15; 2:1,11,31; 3:14; Amos 5:18 twice; 5:20; Obadiah 15; Zephaniah 1:7; 1:14 twice; Malachi 4:5) and four times in the New Testament (1 Thessalonians 5:2; 2 Thessalonians 2:2; 2 Peter 3:10; Revelation 1:10).[4] The expression is thus stamped by usage with the number four, which in Scripture refers to the world.

The Bible emphasizes various "days": man's day, the day of Christ, the day of the Lord (as in Joel 1:15), and the day of God.

Man's day, the day in which we live, is referred to in 1 Corinthians 4:3. The King James version reads "man's judgment," but "man's day" is a better translation of the original. Man's day is the day in which man is judging and God is silent; man is allowed to run the world his own way.

The day of Christ (Philippians 1:10, for example) is the day of the rapture, when Christ will come for His own.

The day of the Lord is a long period that begins right after the rapture, runs through the great tribulation and the battle of Armageddon, and continues into the millennium. This day, which embraces both judgment and glory, is the subject of extensive Old Testament prophecy, where it is also called "that day," "a day of wrath," "the day of vengeance," and so on. On the day of the Lord everything will be done to put man in his proper place and to exalt the Lord.

The final nuclear holocaust will take place on the day of God, which will become the eternal day. God will be "all in all" and there will be a new Heaven and a new earth (2 Peter 3:12-13; 1 Corinthians 15:28).

2. A Day of Darkness (2:1-10)

Again in 2:1 Joel used his newly discovered and highly original phrase "the day of the Lord," which he described as "a day of darkness" in 2:2. He went on to portray a country overrun by foreign troops—just as his country had been overrun by locusts. Probably his primary reference was to the Assyrian invasion (the subject of many later prophets), but since he used the phrase "the day of the Lord," we know that he was also referring to the terrible wars that will be fought during the days of the antichrist.

The Assyrian invasion, when it came, was a fearful scourge. As Joel had prophesied, the enemy was "a great people and a strong" with a scorched-earth policy: "A fire devoureth before them; and

behind them a flame burneth" (2:2-3). He had envisioned the
invaders moving swiftly, scaling the walls of besieged cities, and
their disciplined ranks marching inexorably forward to sack a city.
Israel and Judah would become all too familiar with such horrors.

The end-time application of Joel's prophecy involves darkness.
He wrote, "The sun and the moon shall be dark, and the stars shall
withdraw their shining" (2:10). Many other prophets spoke of
similar phenomena. Darkness, whether literal or symbolic, will be
a hallmark of apocalyptic times.

3. A Day of Deliverance (2:11-32)

a. A Call for Repentance (2:11-19)

We know from many Old and New Testament prophets that the
antichrist will take over the world in the day of the Lord. A number
of wars will be fought during the antichrist's rise to power, and
Israel will have a significant role in his strategy. Once the Jewish
nation and people have served his purpose, however, the antichrist
will turn against them and the blood bath of the great tribulation
will threaten to exterminate the Hebrew people completely. This
terrible persecution will purge Israel of radical unbelievers and the
stage will be set for the battle of Armageddon. By that time the land
of Israel will have been ravaged by foreign troops and thousands of
her people will be dying daily. When Israel is in her last extremity,
the Lord Jesus will return to rescue the beleaguered Hebrew
people from the final conflict at Megiddo.

Joel was the first prophet to catch a glimpse of this great climax,
which he described in 2:11: "The Lord shall utter his voice before
his army: for his camp is very great: for he is strong that executeth
his word: for the day of the Lord is great and very terrible; and who
can abide it?" We know from the Apocalypse that the One who will
execute the divine decree is the Lord Jesus. Followed by the armies
of Heaven, He will descend from the sky arrayed in great glory. A
sharp sword (the Word of God) will come out of His mouth, and
with it He will smite the nations (Revelation 19:11-21). One word
from Him and the battle will be over.

Moved by the sight, Joel appealed to latter-day Israel to prepare
for the Lord's return by fasting, weeping, mourning, and returning
to the Lord, who will be "gracious and merciful" (2:13). "Blow the
trumpet in Zion, sanctify a fast, call a solemn assembly," pleaded
the prophet (2:15). He urged the priests to take the lead in
intercession and pray, "Spare thy people, O Lord, and give not
thine heritage to reproach, that the heathen should rule over

them: wherefore should they say among the people, Where is their God?" (2:17)

When the Hebrew people finally return to the Lord in repentance and acknowledge Jesus as Messiah, Savior, and Lord, "then will the Lord be jealous for *his* land, and pity *his* people" (2:18, italics added). Note again whose land and people it is. At last, land and people will enter into the destiny God planned for them from eternity past (2:19).

b. A Call for Rejoicing (2:20-27)

In 2:20 Joel slightly shifted his focus and for the first time mentioned "the northern army." In his day the Assyrian invasion of his native land was still in the distant future. We know now how that event loomed as a dreadful threat to Israel and Judah, developed into a terrible reality, and finally brought about the end of the northern kingdom and the devastation of the southern kingdom. We know too how fully and fearfully God judged the arrogant, cruel invader before the gates and walls of Jerusalem. Joel's prophetic word came true: "I will remove far off from you the northern army, and will drive him into a land barren and desolate....Fear not, O land; be glad and rejoice" (2:20-21).

The Assyrian invasion, terrible as it was, by no means exhausted this prophecy concerning "the northern army" and many years later Ezekiel added substantially to Joel's predictions (Ezekiel 38–39). It will be helpful to put the still future events foretold by Joel and Ezekiel in sequence:[5]

Having risen to power in Europe and the West, the antichrist will be confronted in his bid for world supremacy by Russia, the great northern power of the endtimes. With the military, economic, and industrial might of the West at his command, the antichrist will sign a treaty with Israel that guarantees Israel's security and endorses the rebuilding of the temple. As the Jews begin to rebuild their temple on its ancestral site, the Arab-Muslim bloc will react violently and appeal to Russia for aid. The Russians, confronting a united West— truly a revived Roman empire headed by a Satan-inspired genius who knows exactly where he is going—will be forced to rally to the Arab cause if they do not want to lose their position as a global superpower. They will mobilize their military might, summon their satellites and sympathizers, and head for the heart of the Middle East: Israel. The West will mobilize too, but the swift and sure Russians will wreak terrible vengeance on the way to Israel and then blitzkrieg that little land. For the moment it will seem that "the northern army" has succeeded, but this godless power, which has defied the living God for decades and exported atheism and violence over the world, will have provoked God for the last time.

God will unleash His arsenal. Civil war will break out in the ranks of the Russian army and five-sixths of the military will be wiped out (Ezekiel 39:2). It will take the Jews seven months to bury the enemy's dead (39:12). Truly, "his stink shall come up" (Joel 2:20). The Jews will salvage enough fuel from abandoned war equipment to supply all their needs for seven years (Ezekiel 39:9)—the fuel will last well on into the millennial reign.

Both Joel and Ezekiel foretold the effect this deliverance will have on the Jewish people: "Ye shall know that I am in the midst of Israel, and that I am the Lord your God, and none else: and my people shall never be ashamed" (Joel 2:27; also see Ezekiel 39:22).

Throughout Joel's call for rejoicing (2:20-27) the prophet anticipated the millennium. He saw a land bearing fruit, barns full to bursting, and people enjoying annual rains. And he made his classic statement of the Lord's glorious promise: "I will restore to you the years that the locust hath eaten" (2:25). Although the statement is clearly millennial in context, by application it is one of those "exceeding great and precious promises" (2 Peter 1:4) that the believer can claim when he finally gets right with God.

c. A Call for Revival (2:28-32)

Now we come to Joel's great prophetic statement that we identify with the day of Pentecost:

> And it shall come to pass afterward, that I will pour out my spirit upon all flesh; and your sons and your daughters shall prophesy, your old men shall dream dreams, your young men shall see visions....And I will shew wonders in the heavens and in the earth, blood, and fire, and pillars of smoke. The sun shall be turned into darkness, and the moon into blood, before the great and the terrible day of the Lord come. And it shall come to pass, that whosoever shall call on the name of the Lord shall be delivered.

On the day of Pentecost, Peter quoted this prophecy. "This is that which was spoken by the prophet Joel," he said, explaining to the assembled crowds in Jerusalem the remarkable phenomenon of speaking in tongues (Acts 2:16). The church was born that day, but what happened then was only a partial fulfillment of Joel's prophecy, which is also clearly linked with "the great and the terrible day of the Lord" (2:31). The prophecy will be completely fulfilled during a revival after the rapture of the church.

The greatest spiritual revival of all time has not yet taken place. We learn about it in Revelation 7, which says that enormous multitudes will be saved as a result of the witness of the 144,000 Hebrew evangelists. These converts will not be in the church of course, but they will be in the kingdom. A fresh outpouring of the Holy Spirit will energize this revival and there will probably be a fresh bestowal of the sign gifts. If so, the restored gift of tongues will be identical to the gift bestowed on the day of Pentecost, when all the people heard the gospel preached in their native languages and local dialects. Such speaking in tongues is a far cry from the modern phenomenon, which is unscriptural and a counterfeit.

B. The Day of Antichrist (3:1-16)

Now Joel's prophecy turned squarely to the endtimes.

1. The Gathering of the Hebrew People (3:1)

Speaking idiomatically, Joel foretold the restoration of the Jewish people: "Behold, in those days, and in that time...I shall bring again the captivity of Judah and Jerusalem." The exiles and the saved remnant of Israel will be gathered in and millennial blessings—hinted at by Joel and expanded by Isaiah and many other Old Testament prophets—will burst upon the world. The Jewish people will take their place under Christ as the head of the nations. Today we see sobering indications that end-time events are about to take place: the rebirth of the state of Israel and the partial return of Jews from all over the world.

2. The Gathering of the Heathen Peoples (3:2-16)

a. A Gathering of the Wicked (3:2-8)

In this passage Joel described the last great assize before the millennium. Christ will gather the Gentile nations in the valley of Jehoshaphat for judgment (see the Lord's parable of the sheep and the goats in Matthew 25:31-46).

During the reign of King Jehoshaphat, the land of Judah was invaded by vast hosts from across the Jordan. In his fear Jehoshaphat appealed to God, who responded with a prophetic word: "Be not afraid nor dismayed...for the battle is not yours, but God's....Stand ye still, and see the salvation of the Lord" (2 Chronicles 20:15-17). The Lord caused the enemies to war among themselves and they slew each other. All Judah had to do was reap a rich harvest of spoils from the dead bodies. The fear of God fell on the surrounding kingdoms (20:29) and Jehoshaphat gathered his rejoicing people together in a valley to bless God for His deliverance (20:26). Doubtless Joel had this historical event in mind when he spoke prophetically of "the valley of Jehoshaphat."

That valley, the common burial place for the people of Jerusalem, was also the place where Asa, Josiah, and Hezekiah cast out and burned the idols that had defiled the land (1 Kings 15:13; 2 Kings 23:4,6,12; 2 Chronicles 30:14).

"The valley of Jehoshaphat" is the Kidron valley, which lies between Jerusalem and the mount of Olives—scenes of significant events in the life of Christ. At the time of the triumphal entry, the Lord halted on the mount of Olives to weep over Jerusalem. In the garden of Gethsemane on that mount, Judas betrayed Christ to His foes. After His resurrection Jesus led His disciples to the mount of Olives to witness His ascension. To that same mount He is coming again.

And in "the valley of Jehoshaphat" God intends to put an end to Gentile power and judge the Gentile nations for the way they— collectively and individually—have treated the Jewish people. Note how God identifies Himself with the Hebrews in Joel 3:2-5: "My people...my heritage...my land...my silver...my gold." He used the personal pronouns "my" and "me" ten times in these few verses.

In 3:4 Joel referred to Tyre and Sidon (modern Lebanon) and Philistia (the Gaza Strip; translated "Palestine" in the King James version) as particularly culpable. In Bible times these nations occupied the coastal territories of Israel and were known as the Philistines and Phoenicians. Joel accused these enemies of the Hebrew people of plundering God's land and selling His people into slavery. In our day these Arab countries have again come into prominence. They harbor some of Israel's most bitter and relentless foes, who doubtless will seize the opportunity, when Israel is beset by enemies (at the time of the Russian invasion and when the antichrist turns against the Jews), to rush in and indulge their antisemitic hate.

b. A Gathering of the Warmongers (3:9-13)

In Joel 3:9-10 we see God throwing down the gauntlet to the Gentiles: "Prepare war, wake up the mighty men, let all the men of war draw near....Beat your plowshares into swords, and your pruninghooks into spears: let the weak say, I am strong."

It seems that even after the returning Christ overthrows the world's armies at Megiddo, there will be a residual of hostility against Him. This is not surprising, for the God-hate and blasphemy of the antichrist will have infected the vast majority of mankind with a spirit of rebellion against God. The masses will not take kindly to the prospect of a reign of inflexible righteousness. But what can they do? Declare war on Christ? Mobilize against the mighty victor of Megiddo? God dares them to try: "Go ahead," He says in effect. "Prepare for war, crank up your munitions factories, mobilize your remaining men, and rally to your mighty ones!"

One way or another, the surviving Gentiles are drawn to Megiddo, for the Lord summons the nations to "the valley of Jehoshaphat" for judgment. The earth's population is greatly reduced by this time. Considering the wars, persecutions, upheavals, natural disasters, and plagues that ravage the earth during the judgment phase of the day of the Lord, it is a wonder that any people at all are still alive, but many are.

c. A Gathering of the World (3:14-16)

From earth's remotest bounds, people come for the judgment. They abandon the great cities and leave farms and fields unattended. Silence descends on all the haunts of man. In a vast migration people come across the seven seas from all five continents. None is able to resist God's call. He sees to it that everyone is there.

A human tide crosses the frontier of Israel from north, south, east, and west and jams the roads leading to Jerusalem. "Multitudes, multitudes in the valley of decision," Joel cried (3:14). Continuing his prophecy, he added, "The Lord also shall roar out of Zion....The heavens and the earth shall shake" (3:16). No longer the Lamb, Jesus is now the Lion. This judgment has not been convened to show mercy, but to weed out the wicked and consign them to the lake of fire. Thus the millennial age begins with a remnant of Jews and Gentiles who are genuine believers in Christ and have been regenerated by the Holy Spirit.

C. The Day of Anticipation (3:17-21)

1. A Wonderful Coming (3:17-18)

In the prophet's reference to the millennial Jerusalem in 3:17, the key word is "holy." "Then shall Jerusalem be holy," Joel cried.

We speak of Jerusalem as the holy city and one day she will be just that. People will make annual pilgrimages to the holy city to see the new temple and worship at the Lord's throne.

In the millennium the countryside will glow with new health and everything will be bountiful and beautiful. So the prophecies of Joel began with a land devastated by locusts and ended with a land flowing again with milk and honey.

2. A Woeful Contrast (3:19)

In contrast to the land flowing with milk and honey, "Egypt shall be a desolation, and Edom shall be a desolate wilderness." Egypt and Edom have been enemies of Israel through the ages. The prophet Ezekiel had many dire warnings of judgment for Egypt, which will be one of Israel's bitterest adversaries in the last days.[6] Obadiah joined Joel in warning Edom (modern Jordan) of judgment to come. The Arab-Islamic countries have been implacable foes of Israel from the beginning of the British mandate and the implementation of the Zionists' demands. Although these states have bitter antagonisms among themselves (witness the Iran-Iraq war), they are united in their intolerance of Israel. Scripture seems to indicate that both Egypt and Edom are going to be particularly desolated by the end-time wars of the antichrist. The Lord will arrange that as punishment for their violence against the Jewish people.

3. A Welcome Conclusion (3:20-21)

In contrast to Egypt and Edom, "Judah shall dwell for ever, and Jerusalem from generation to generation" (3:20). During the millennium, Jerusalem will become the capital of Christ's world empire. Moreover the heavenly Jerusalem—the celestial city that will be placed in stationary orbit over the earthly Jerusalem—will endure forever. Most likely the heavenly Jerusalem will be the center of all the starry empires that God will bring into existence when He creates a new Heaven and a new earth.

In Joel 3:21 we read some puzzling words: the Lord said, "I will cleanse their blood that I have not cleansed." The word translated "cleanse" is not the word for natural cleansing. It means "to pronounce innocent." During the terrible times preceding the millennium, the antichrist and his minions will shed the blood of many believing Jews after accusing them of heinous crimes. But during the millennium God will publicly proclaim the innocence of these people of His whose names have been besmirched. Possibly this vindication will include all of God's people who, down through the ages, have been falsely accused, maligned, and slain.

Joel concluded his prophecy saying, "The Lord dwelleth in Zion." The Lord will reside in Jerusalem during the millennial reign. His banner will fly over Zion. His personal presence will be the great fact of the age to come and will lend permanent stability to the kingdom.

What a prophet Joel was! When God told him, "Blow ye the trumpet" (2:1), he went up to the tower, put the trumpet to his lips, and blew such a blast that he awoke the echoes of the apocalyptic age.

Chapter 3

AMOS

THE COUNTRY COUSIN

I. INTRODUCTION (1:1-2)
II. THE VIGILANCE OF THE PROPHET (1:3–2:16)
  A. Lands Near to God's People (1:3–2:3)
    1. Those Always Considered as Gentile Foreigners by Israel (1:3-10)
      a. Damascus (1:3-5)
      b. Gaza (1:6-8)
      c. Tyre (1:9-10)
    2. Those Always Considered as Genetic Family by Israel (1:11–2:3)
      a. Edom (1:11-12)
      b. Ammon (1:13-15)
      c. Moab (2:1-3)
  B. Lands Native to God's People (2:4-16)
    1. The Doom of Royal Judah (2:4-5)
    2. The Doom of Rebellious Israel (2:6-16)
      a. The Formula (2:6a)
      b. The Facts (2:6b-12)
      c. The Future (2:13-16)
III. THE VOICE OF THE PROPHET (3:1–6:14)
  A. As to the Present (3:1-15)
    1. The Lord's Questions to Israel (3:1-9)
    2. The Lord's Quarrel with Israel (3:10-15)
  B. As to the Past (4:1-13)
    1. The Lord's Scorn (4:1-5)
    2. The Lord's Scourge (4:6-13)
  C. As to the Prospect (5:1–6:14)
    1. The Distress of the Lord (5:1-15)

2. The Day of the Lord (5:16-20)
3. The Disgust of the Lord (5:21-27)
4. The Determination of the Lord (6:1-14)
IV. THE VISIONS OF THE PROPHET (7:1-9:10)
   A. Judgment Restrained (7:1-6)
     1. The Devouring Locust (7:1-3)
     2. The Devouring Flame (7:4-6)
   B. Judgment Required (7:7-17)
     1. The Plumbline (7:7-9)
     2. The Priest (7:10-17)
   C. Judgment Restored (8:1-9:10)
     1. The Solemn Sign (8:1-3)
     2. The Sobering Sermon (8:4-14)
     3. The Startling Sight (9:1-4)
     4. The Sudden Stroke (9:5-6)
     5. The Sifting Sieve (9:7-10)
V. THE VINDICATION OF THE PROPHET (9:11-15)
   A. Israel's Privileges Restored (9:11-12)
   B. Israel's Prosperity Restored (9:13-14)
   C. Israel's Protection Restored (9:15)

There were only about thirty or forty years between the ministries of Elisha and Amos, but in that short span of time the whole world changed. A new superpower, Assyria, stalked onto the international stage. Rapacious, strong, and cruel, Assyria was as different from Egypt as night is from day. Egypt—the bumbling, benevolent giant of the South—had dominated world affairs from remotest antiquity. The Egyptians were a peace-loving people and had left other countries alone, except when new vigorous dynasties eager for fame and fortune came into power. But the Assyrians, who were about to threaten the Middle East, were driven by a lust for conquest and a thirst for blood. They were more ruthless and relentless than all who had gone before.

The emergence of Assyria changed everything for Israel and Judah. These two small sister-nations standing astride the caravan routes to Egypt were natural targets for warlike Assyria. The Jews desperately needed to get right with God because they had no other defense against this ominous northern power. Assyria's policy was to use terror and propaganda to soften up any opposition and to deploy its irresistible military might against all who offered even the slightest resistance. Participants in resistance movements were tortured to death in hideous ways and conquered peoples were forcibly uprooted and deported across the wide reaches of the Assyrian empire.

With the Assyrian star rising in the northern sky, it was imperative that voices ring out loud and clear to call Israel and Judah back to God. Moreover, since exile was certain if national repentance was not achieved, it was essential that God's messages be written down.

We can well understand those times. In our day the development of nuclear weapons, intercontinental ballistic missiles, and high technology has slammed the door irrevocably on the past and confronted the world with enormous, deadly perils. The rise of Assyria to world-power status and its awesome military might had the same effect on Old Testament civilization. The expansionistic Assyrians intrigued far and wide, took advantage of any hint of weakness in their enemies, and trampled on those whose strength was inferior to theirs. They were determined to control and exploit the Middle East. No alliances could save Israel (then and now) from ultimate invasion. God was her only defense.

A new breed of prophets was needed so God raised up the writing prophets. The miracle-working prophets, Elijah and Elisha, had pointed men to God's works. The new breed performed no miracles; instead they pointed men to God's Word.

When the first of the new breed appeared like new stars in the prophetic sky, the Hebrews did not even know it was getting dark. Their kings were strong, capable, and vigorous. Amos preached to a generation that had grown up never knowing defeat. Surrounding kingdoms such as Syria, Philistia, Ammon, Moab, and Edom had been put in their place and the borders of Israel and Judah were as secure as they had been in the palmy days of David and Solomon.

However, both nations were ill-equipped to face the Assyrian threat. Formerly the Hebrews had been fighting farmers, but they had experienced a cultural revolution; now they were citified, sophisticated, worldly-wise, cultured, proud, and—they imagined—safe. They had taken a giant step from an agricultural economy to an urban form of life.

Once before the Hebrew people had taken a giant step—from nomadic life in the wilderness to agricultural life in Canaan. That step had been fraught with peril, for it had brought the Jews into contact with the Canaanites' filthy nature-cults. God's answer had been *the temple*. The step to an urban economy was also fraught with peril because city life gave rise to a wealthy, aristocratic ruling class who cared nothing about the woes of the common people. God's answer this time was *the twelve* minor prophets and four other writing prophets.

The northern kingdom of Israel was particularly vulnerable during the days of the early minor prophets. The national religion was a corruption of the faith that was commenced with Abraham, codified by Moses, and celebrated by David. Jeroboam's cult was deeply entrenched among the ten tribes; the worship of a golden calf was lavishly supported by the throne and served by an apostate priesthood. Major idolatrous shrines—loathed by Jehovah—existed at Dan, Gilgal, Tabor, Carmel, and Penuel. The crafty Jeroboam had capitalized on sites that would evoke sacred memories. For example a pagan temple now stood at Beth-el, where Heaven had come down and filled the souls of Abraham and Jacob.

In the cities people were preoccupied with getting rich. Using money extorted from the poor, the grandees of the court were building mansions. Not even an earthquake could shake the pride of the wealthy. "The bricks are fallen down, but we will build with hewn stones: the sycomores are cut down, but we will change them into cedars," they boasted (Isaiah 9:10).

To such a society came Amos with his own brand of thunder. Amos was a rustic from that wild stretch of land way down south known as the wilderness of Judah. He was a herdsman, shepherd, and gatherer of sycamore fruit—in other words, a farmhand. What this country boy saw when he went to Beth-el and Samaria, made his blood boil. He had heard about the calf worship of the Israelites for years and now he saw it himself. Worse than that, he saw people snared in all the vileness of the Canaanite nature-cults. The immorality, drunkenness, and gross idolatry filled his soul with outrage. Deeply stirred, he denounced what he saw with an eloquence that drew its inspiration from farm, forest, and field. Wild beasts, starry skies, and threatening storms were the images of his wrath.

Try to imagine an untutored lad, fresh from the hills, clumping through the fashionable clubs of Washington and with rude speech denouncing (in God's name) the lifestyle of the urban elite. Such was Amos. The society ladies of Samaria must have shuddered when he called them cows—"ye kine of Bashan" (Amos 4:1).

I. INTRODUCTION (1:1-2)

There is a cold logic in the book of Amos that is altogether missing in the book of Hosea. Hosea spoke the language of love;

Amos spoke the language of law. Hosea spoke from the heart; Amos
spoke from the head. Hosea thought in terms of God's outreach;
Amos thought in terms of God's outrage. Hosea expressed fervor
and fire; Amos stated causes and conclusions.

It is hard to miss Amos's calm logic. When you go through his
book you will notice his mathematical bent. For instance the
formula "for three transgressions...and for four" occurs eight
times (1:3,6,9,11,13; 2:1,4,6). You will also notice his use of the
word "because" in those same verses and his use of the word
"therefore" in 2:14; 3:2,11; 4:12; 5:11,13,16,27; 6:7; 7:16,17. Amos
used repetition to hammer home what he discerned and deduced:
for example "Yet have ye not returned" occurs in 4:6,8,9,10; "Hear
this word" and kindred expressions occur in 3:1; 4:1; 5:1; 7:16; 8:4.
He piled up arguments, as in 8:7,9,10,11 where he kept repeating
"I will," and in 5:4,6,8,14 where he kept repeating "Seek." Amos was
also fond of using the word "though" to emphasize his points (see
5:22; 9:2,3,4).

In 1:1 Amos told us he came from Tekoa, located about six miles
from Bethlehem. Tekoa looked out on desolate wilderness; it was
a town on the edge of nowhere. Between it and the Dead Sea was
a veritable chaos of wild hills and valleys. The cold moon and
planets stared down at Tekoa at night and a burning, relentless sun
looked on the dreary world of Amos by day. At night the young
herdsman would often hear the howl of a beast of prey; he would
get a tighter grip on his stout staff and prepare to defend his flocks.
Tekoa was a cruel corner of the country, one that only grudgingly
yielded a living to its inhabitants.

The prophet made no effort to disguise his humble origins. For
instance in 7:14 he said he was "a gatherer of sycomore fruit."
Sycomore trees, which would grow in the parched, sandy soil of
Palestine, yielded a fruit similar to a small fig. This fruit was eaten
only by the very poor. The gatherers would pinch or bruise the
sluggish lumps of fruit to make them ripen, so Amos described
himself as "a pincher of sycomores"—not a very high-class profes-
sion. But "God hath chosen the weak things of the world to
confound the things which are mighty" (1 Corinthians 1:27). So
God chose Amos and although he was only a poor workingman, as
was our Lord, he had a great view of God.

Notice that Amos dated his prophecy: "in the days of Uzziah
king of Judah, and in the days of Jeroboam the son of Joash king
of Israel, two years before the earthquake" (Amos 1:1). We are not
absolutely certain about the date of the earthquake, but it must

have been a major catastrophe, for Zechariah mentioned it two hundred years later (Zechariah 14:5). (Josephus wrote that it coincided with the smiting of King Uzziah with leprosy, but for various reasons this notation is written off as a typical Josephus flourish.) In Amos 8:9 there is a reference to a total eclipse of the sun that, according to the calculations of astronomers, took place on June 15, 763 B.C.

Amos preached when Judah was led by a successful but proud king who sought in his own arrogant way to bring his people back to God, and while Israel was riding the crest of the last wave of prosperity and power. The twin kingdoms were enjoying political stability and success. But although wealth was abundant, poverty was widespread and at least in Israel pride and carelessness went hand in hand with licentiousness and religious apostasy. It was into the faces of people who did not care about God that the prophet flung his predictions of doom.

II. THE VIGILENCE OF THE PROPHET (1:3–2:16)

A. Lands Near to God's People (1:3–2:3)

1. Those Always Considered as Gentile Foreigners by Israel (1:3-10)

Amos directed his opening broadsides against three troublesome neighboring nations that had no blood ties with the Hebrew people.

a. Damascus (1:3-5)

Damascus was the capital of Syria, Israel's most persistent and implacable foe—today as well as in Bible times. When we review the history of the Jewish kings, we find that from the days of David, Syria was constantly at war with Israel. Adad was the Syrian king who fought against David. Adad's descendants, who reigned for ten generations, each took the name of the founder of the dynasty; thus the designation *Ben-hadad* originated, which itself means "son or worshiper of the idol Hadad [the sun]."

In Amos 1:3 we find the first occurrence of the expression "for three transgressions...and for four." This idiom does not mean that four transgressions are added to the first three. It means that one additional transgression—the straw that breaks the camel's back—makes judgment inevitable. With that final sin the hidden boundary between God's mercy and His wrath is crossed. So the fourth transgression of a nation was the one that tipped the scales.

The Syrians had filled up the measure of their iniquities by threshing Gilead (the territory of Israel on the east side of the Jordan) with iron threshing instruments. This atrocity had been perpetrated by Hazael, king of Damascus, during the days of Jehu and Jehoahaz (2 Kings 10:32-33; 13:3-7). Hazael tore and mangled the bodies of Israelites who fell into his hands. Such cruelty had been foretold by Elisha (2 Kings 8:12).

As the Syrians had sowed, so would they reap. Bloody war was decreed for Damascus; its fortified, ironbound gates would be broken down. An invader would capture Syria's valleys and cities and take her people into captivity. Amos did not name the foe who would trample out the vintage where the grapes of wrath were stored,[1] but we now know him to be the Assyrian conqueror Tiglath-pileser, whose policy was to uproot conquered peoples and deport them to prevent future uprisings.

b. Gaza (1:6-8)

Gaza was representative of all Philistia. After invoking his formula of doom, Amos quickly added the roll call of other prominent Philistine cities: Ashdod, Ashkelon, and Ekron. He omitted Gath, probably because King Uzziah had already thrashed that city (2 Chronicles 26:6). Whenever the five Philistine cities are mentioned together, Gaza always heads the list. Strongly fortified, Gaza was the first important town on the trade route out of Egypt toward Tyre and Sidon.

The crowning sin of the Philistines, who had been foes of Israel for centuries, was their rape of an Israeli settlement. They swept away the entire population—men, women, and children—and delivered their captives to the Edomites, from whom the Hebrews could expect no mercy. No doubt the Philistines made a handsome profit from the transaction. (Such a raid is recorded in 2 Chronicles 21:16-17.) God's just verdict was the decimation of the Philistine population.

c. Tyre (1:9-10)

Tyre of Phoenicia was one of antiquity's most powerful city-states. The Phoenicians were great traders and colonists. Their ships sailed down the Mediterranean, up the coast of Spain, and even as far as Britain. Cities like Carthage and Tarshish were jewels in their imperial diadem.

On the whole, relations between Tyre and Israel had been friendly from the days of David, whom Hiram (king of Tyre) greatly admired (1 Kings 5:1). Indeed it seems that an actual treaty of mutual friendship had been signed. But later Tyre reversed its traditional policy and chose to ignore the treaty.

The sin that filled up the measure of Tyre's iniquity was that of selling Hebrew prisoners of war as slaves. Like the Philistines, the Tyrians callously sold their Jewish captives to Edom. The crime was unprovoked; no Hebrew king had ever made war on Phoenicia. The punishment, Amos foretold, was that Tyre would be burned. The prophecy was finally fulfilled by the Chaldeans under Nebuchadnezzar.

We can imagine that by this time Amos had become popular in Samaria and Israel. People were spreading the news about the country fellow who was denouncing, in the name of God, Israel's hereditary foes. Perhaps they still sneered at him for his total lack of sophistication, but they applauded his message. Then Amos shifted his focus and his words hit a little closer to home.

2. Those Always Considered as Genetic Family by Israel (1:11–2:3)

Edom, Ammon, and Moab had genetic kinship to Israel. The Edomites descended from Esau, Jacob's twin brother; the Ammonites and Moabites descended from Lot, Abraham's nephew. Nevertheless these three nations had long opposed the Hebrews and had often been at war with them. All three held territory across the Jordan.

a. Edom (1:11-12)

Amos first denounced Edom. From the start, God had impressed on Israel its brotherhood relationship to Edom (Numbers 20:14; Deuteronomy 2:8). On no account was Israel at that time to tamper with Edom. Doubtless Moses hoped that good relations might eventually be established with that nation. The wars of Saul and David against Edom were defensive wars. Later Judah had to put garrisons in Edom (as a wild beast is held in a cage) so that the Edomites would not injure the Hebrews, but the Hebrews did not take the Edomites' land or expel them from it. As time went on, wars between Edom and the Jews increased in severity and generated considerable bitterness. Indeed there was outright malice on the part of the Edomites and no worse fate could befall a Hebrew captive than to be sold into Edomite hands.

Edom joined other nations surrounding Israel in their hatred of God's people. In the same way Arabs today—ever quarrelsome among themselves but rarely going to war with each other—are united in their hatred of Israel.

We find the crowning sin of Edom in Amos 1:11: "He did pursue his brother with the sword, and did cast off all pity, and his anger did tear perpetually, and he kept his wrath for ever." In reply to Edom's undying malice, God summoned the Assyrians and then the Babylonians to wage war on that haughty country and to leave its cities and strongholds in the dust. Edom's sin and its final doom was the special burden of Obadiah.

The Israelites must have rubbed their hands with glee when Amos uttered his prophecy of punishment for Edom (Amos 1:12). We can imagine them crowding around Amos, slapping him on the back, and encouraging him: "That's right, Amos. Give it to them! You have the right idea."

b. Ammon (1:13-15)

Both Ammon and Moab had shameful beginnings (Genesis 19:30-38) and neither country ever shook off the stamp of its origin. The people of these nations chose gods like themselves. The Ammonites, who indulged wanton ferocity (1 Samuel 11:1-3), chose Moloch, who had to be propitiated with the sacrifice of living children. The Moabites, who seduced Israel (Numbers 25:1-3), chose Chemosh and the degrading Baal-peor, who was worshiped with every form of licentiousness.

At one time the Ammonites, wanting to expand their holdings east of the Jordan, had invaded Gilead and performed horrible atrocities on pregnant women. The incident, which is not mentioned in the history books of the Old Testament, was recorded by Amos (1:13) along with his prophecy of punishment. When the prophet foretold invasion, destruction, and captivity for Ammon, he specifically mentioned the capital city of Rabbah, which is now Amman, the capital of Jordan.

c. Moab (2:1-3)

Although the fourth transgression of Moab was actually directed against Edom, not Israel, this crowning sin was denounced by Amos. Moab's sin revealed a spiteful state of soul that called for God's judgment. Indulging a spirit of revenge, Moab "burned the bones of the king of Edom into lime" (2:1).

This incident probably occurred during the war recorded in 2 Kings 3:26-27. Jehoram of Israel, Jehoshaphat of Judah, and the king of Edom had joined forces against Moab. It seems it was Edom's unusual alliance with the Hebrews that engendered the outburst of spite mentioned in Amos 2:1. Men and nations are often moved to hate a friend or ally who, for one reason or another, sides with a person or nation they hate or fear. The king of Moab directed his fury against the king of Edom and indulged in a revenge that did not stop at death—an implacable and insatiable revenge that impotently grasped for eternal retaliation. Unable to wreak continuing hurt, the king of Moab continued to show his hate by venting it on the corpse of the king of Edom. Even the grave cannot extinguish this species of hatred.

Because of Moab's display of unrestrained anger and hate, Amos prophesied that God would execute his righteous vengeance on Moab. God's judgment was finally carried out by Nebuchadnezzar, who did such a thorough job of thrashing Moab that it disappeared as a nation.

I cannot help feeling that Amos's prophecies against Israel's hostile neighbors have by no means been exhausted. The Arabs occupy these countries today and their implacable hatred of Israel is well-known. They are prepared to use any means—war, propaganda, terrorism, or alliance with God-hating Russia—to bring about an end to the Jewish state.

B. Land Native to God's People (2:4-16)

1. The Doom of Royal Judah (2:4-5)

We can imagine that the people of Israel, delighted as they doubtless were to hear Amos denouncing all their traditional enemies, were even more delighted when he turned his prophetic artillery on Judah, his native land.

The kings of Israel disliked Judah because Judah had the real thing. Judah had Jerusalem, the citadel of David, the temple, and the rituals of the true faith. All Israel had was a cheap imitation. Thus jealousy of Judah was never far away from the heart of any northern king—jealousy and fear. What if the ten tribes were to return to the true faith? What if they were to resume their annual pilgrimages to Jerusalem? What if they were to recognize in David's descendants who were still enthroned in Judah the legitimate royal line? What if a grass-roots movement to reunite the kingdoms became popular? To head off any such possibilities, Jeroboam I had invented his calf brand of Jehovah worship, but the ghost of a return to Jerusalem could never be finally laid to rest. So when Amos prophesied against Judah, the king of Israel must have applauded.

The crowning sin of Judah was worse than that of any of the surrounding heathen nations. Amos charged, "They have despised the law of the Lord, and have not kept his commandments" (2:4). Solomon had imported wholesale idolatry into Jerusalem. From time to time godly kings would try to root it out, but it always revived. Nothing could have more completely negated God's law. God had commanded: "Thou shalt have no other gods before me. Thou shalt not make unto thee any graven image" (Exodus 20:3-4). When God's people transgressed these commandments, they transgressed all His commandments. The fact that they turned to idolatry proved that they had rejected His law.

"Their lies caused them to err," thundered Amos. They turned their backs on God's truth and embraced falsehood. Then they believed the lies they had chosen. Liars always end up believing their own lies. What they once knew to be false, they soon believe to be true.

Turning against the truth was the source of Judah's subsequent sins, just as it is the source of our sins today. Like Judah of old, we have turned our backs on the Bible, the anchor of absolute truth. We have invented lies, propagated them, and then believed them.

God's answer to Judah's besetting sin was no different from His answer to the besetting sins of her pagan neighbors. That answer was judgment. In due time the Assyrians scourged Judah up to the walls of Jerusalem, but the judgment that Amos foresaw was staved off for several generations by a succession of godly kings. However, the foundations of national life were eroded by lies and neglect of God's Word and doom fell on Judah when the Babylonians came.

2. The Doom of Rebellious Israel (2:6-16)

As Amos delivered his prophecies, he encountered approving smiles everywhere in Israel. People would say to their friends, "You know that cowboy—what's his name? You should have heard what he said about Judah last night! He'll be in trouble back home when the *Jerusalem Post* gets hold of his statement. You should go to hear him, but be sure to sit at the back. The fellow has never learned the niceties of sophisticated people. He smells like a barn."

But when Amos turned his broadsides on the Israelites, they responded differently. We can hear them growl, "That fellow Amos should be locked up. Why, last night he denounced the temple in

Beth-el. The primate should report him to the king. The man's a troublemaker. He ought to be deported or stoned!"

Let us analyze his prophecy concerning Israel.

a. The Formula (2:6a)

The relentless formula, "for three transgressions...and for four," pealed out for the eighth time. Israel too had added a crowning sin to all her other crimes.

Sin among God's people is even more serious than sin among those who do not know Him. In fact 1 John 5:16 tells us that "there is a sin unto death" among the people of God. "God is no respecter of persons" (Acts 10:34).

b. The Facts (2:6b-12)

Injustice, immorality, idolatry, ingratitude, and intolerance were Israel's crowning sins that called for God's wrath. Amos spelled them out one after another.

"They sold the righteous for silver, and the poor for a pair of shoes," he charged (2:6b). In Israel the insolvent were sold for a song. So great was the oppression of the poor that the downtrodden people cast dust on their heads in mourning, as was the custom in the East (Job 2:12).

Society was so devoid of moral restraints that a man and his son would resort to the same harlot—probably one of the prostitutes available at a temple of the goddess Ashtoreth. God saw that sin as a profanation of His holy name. For sins such as this, God had driven out the former inhabitants of the land.

Even worse was the treatment that Nazarites and prophets received in Israel. When a young man, in protest against the lifestyle of the wicked, took a Nazarite vow of consecration to God, the people would try to seduce him to violate his oath by drinking wine. Moreover they told God's prophets to be quiet. The Israelites wanted to silence all testimony against themselves, whether it was expressed by the vow of the Nazarite or the voice of the prophet.

c. The Future (2:13-16)

With flashing eyes turning everywhere, the vigilant prophet saw sin tipping the scales in favor of judgment at home as well as abroad. What he saw burned into his soul, and out of his burning heart his mouth spoke.

From now on he would speak to erring Israel, for her peril was greatest; her doom was already on the horizon. Amos saw war in Israel's future and an invader before whom no one would be able to stand.

III. THE VOICE OF THE PROPHET (3:1–6:14)

A. As to the Present (3:1-15)

1. The Lord's Questions to Israel (3:1-9)

As we run our eyes down this segment of prophecy, questions stand out in bold relief. We notice the first question in Amos 3:3: "Can two walk together, except they be agreed?" When we read this verse, we think of two people who have agreed to meet with each other—they meet by appointment. Similarly, God had an agreement with Israel; they would meet by appointment. Israel's feast days ordained under the Mosaic law were appointments with God. With no other nation had God signed an agreement; Israel was unique. "You only have I known of all the families of the earth," God said (3:2).

But when two people meet and do nothing but quarrel as they walk together, what happens? They come to a parting of the ways. In the case of God and the ten tribes, the parting of the ways was very near. God had put up with the bad behavior of Israel for as long as He could. "I will punish you for all your iniquities," He said.

More questions follow. "Will a lion roar in the forest [thicket], when he hath no prey?...Can a bird fall in a snare upon the earth, where no gin [trap] is for him? shall one take up a snare from the earth, and have taken nothing at all?" (3:4-5) Here Amos was drawing on his experience in the wilds. He knew that a lion usually does not roar until it has found its prey, and that God only threatens when He is prepared to punish. Amos also knew that a snare only springs up from the ground when it has caught something, and that Israel must not imagine his prophecies to be idle threats.

Another question occurs in 3:6: "Shall a trumpet be blown in the city, and the people not be afraid?" In Amos's day a trumpet blast was an urgent signal of danger, as was the air raid siren in World War II. How well I remember, as a boy in Britain, being wakened at night by the screaming siren. The hideous shrieking meant danger. Within minutes bombers would indiscriminately unload their cargoes of death on factories and homes. We had no time to waste in seeking shelter. Our sense of urgency was like Amos's. He was sounding a siren to warn Israel that the Assyrians were mobilizing. Danger was on the way and careless Israel should be alarmed.

Amos was not speaking idle words or making meaningless threats. He was not guessing or drawing inferences. He knew what he was talking about. God had revealed His purpose to him, as to all His prophets. As Amos commented in 3:7, the Lord "revealeth his secret unto his servants the prophets."

Amos summoned Ashdod (one of the Philistine cities and a foe) and Egypt (a nation to which Israel would appeal as a friend) to come to the mountains of Samaria and witness God's wrath falling on the people of Israel, who had so sorely sinned against great light and privilege.

The city of Samaria was well chosen as a capital, embedded as it was in the mountains, off the usual caravan routes. It was built on a hill that stood alone in a valley that was about five miles in diameter. The valley was surrounded by higher mountains. God, who intended to turn the whole area into an amphitheater, invited pagan nations to behold the spectacle of Israel's punishment. Since Israel had for centuries given the pagan nations, to whom they should have been a testimony, a dreadful impression of God, He would be His own witness and vindicate His name before the watching nations.

2. The Lord's Quarrel with Israel (3:10-15)

"They know not to do right" was the Lord's final verdict (3:10). All moral sense was gone from Israel. The Israelites had indulged in so many lies for so many years that right was now wrong and wrong was now right. Nothing could be done except to punish them. So the Lord called for an adversary to destroy the palaces, which were the strongholds of robbery and violence. The robber barons imagined themselves to be safe from any uprising of the downtrodden poor, and no doubt they were. But their thick walls, iron gates, and uniformed troops would be powerless against the destroyer God was about to summon.

Amos graphically illustrated what lay ahead for Israel: "As the shepherd taketh out of the mouth of the lion two legs, or a piece of an ear; so shall the children of Israel be taken out that dwell in Samaria in the corner of a bed, and in Damascus in a couch" (3:12). The prophet, who was used to lying on the cold, hard, desert ground, looked with scorn on the pillowed couches and ivory-decorated lounges on which the pampered members of Israeli society stretched, yawned, and indulged themselves. If there was one thing that galled this country man from the harsh wilds of Tekoa, it was the luxury and ease in which the elite lolled. Well, he had news for these softies. When the lion (Assyria) was through with them, there would be nothing left but a few tattered, worthless leftovers.

What was coming was no ordinary ebb and flow of tribal or local hostility, such as the desultory wars that Israel had fought with Syria for years. The Assyrian was coming; like a lion he devoured people and left little behind. All that would be left of Israel would be the crumbs of the lion's meal: two shinbones and a piece of an ear.

"Hear ye," demanded the prophet (3:13). A day of visitation was coming when God would foreclose on the accumulated debt of Israel's sins. Particularly galling among these sins were the sacrifices made to the golden calf at the "altars of Beth-el" (3:14). Almost as offensive to God's prophet-ambassador were the winter and summer houses of the rich. It vexed Amos's righteous soul and outraged his sense of justice to think that the wealthy could have two or three palatial homes in which to escape the extremes of climate while the poor lived in hovels. This sinful lifestyle was going to be abruptly ended.

B. As to the Past (4:1-13)

1. The Lord's Scorn (4:1-5)

"Hear this word, ye kine of Bashan" (4:1). Thus the prophet, speaking as an oracle of God, described the socialites of Samaria. Bashan was a lush farming region east of the Jordan river, between mount Hermon and the hills of Gilead. The cattle of Bashan were renowned for their fine appearance and strength, and Amos likened the sleek, extravagant women of the capital to these cows. And he said that these women, who ground down the poor to indulge their expensive tastes, would be driven out like cows. Yet when Amos preached with passion to these people, he seemed to them to be as one that mocked. There appeared to be nothing to justify his threats. The ruling elite of Samaria looked about and saw only untroubled skies.

The Israelites were deluded by the national religion, which had been born of apostasy. Every animal sacrificed on the false altars at Beth-el and Gilgal was an affront to God. All false religion is an offense to God, especially when its devotees are so duped that they think they are pleasing Him with their rites and rules. The Israelites thought they were secure in the favor of Heaven because of their religious observances, so Amos tried to jolt them with sarcasm, urging them to sacrifice more and more. He told them to continue doing what they were determined to do anyway. In Amos 4:4-5 we catch an echo of Elijah's sarcasm on Carmel when he challenged the false prophets of Baal: "Cry aloud: for he is a god"! (1 Kings 18:27).

2. The Lord's Scourge (4:6-13)

In this passage Amos listed the various kinds of natural disasters that God had visited on the nation through the years. Again and again the recital is interrupted with these words: "Yet have ye not returned unto me, saith the Lord" (4:6,8,9,10,11). God had sent famine, poetically described by Amos as "cleanness of teeth" (4:6). God had sent "blasting and mildew" (4:9), the effects of the desert's searing east wind. God had sent locusts and other plagues like those He once called down on Egypt. Yet, pharaoh-like, the Israelites had hardened their hearts. God had sent devastating wars that decimated the male population and left battlefields heaped with rotting corpses. God had sent overturnings and judgments comparable to the overthrow of vile Sodom and Gomorrah. But all these natural and national disasters were in vain.

God's people continued to grovel before a molten image while the God of creation Himself banged on the tightly closed doors of their hearts. There was no hope for a nation that preferred to give homage to a golden calf rather than worship the true and living God—"he that formeth the mountains, and createth the wind, and declareth unto man what is his thought, that maketh the morning darkness, and treadeth upon the high places of the earth, The Lord, The God of hosts" (4:13).

Israel's obstinacy is so aptly summed up in the phrase "yet have ye not returned unto me." No matter what kind of disaster God sent in an attempt to reach the conscience of the nation, it made no difference. Israel was obdurate. False religion—appealing to the senses, indulgent of sin, served by a powerful priesthood, centered at popular shrines, and backed by the throne—had a firm grip on the nation. As the official religion for about two hundred years, it had acquired a certain spurious sanctity of its own and an authority that comes with age. To attack Israel's false religion in Amos's day was like attacking Rome's dogmas and traditions today; they have in like manner acquired a certain false sanctity from age.

Having hammered away at Israel in vain, Amos cried out, "Therefore...prepare to meet thy God, O Israel" (4:12). This is one of the monumental statements of Scripture, one of the sayings that loom like a grand peak above a plain. Such an arresting text so dominates its context that we can tear it out of context and, without doing any damage, use it in preaching the gospel. (Other examples include John 3:16, Romans 10:9, and Revelation 3:20.)

"Prepare to meet thy God"! This text appeals to the guilty consciences of sinners, saints, and nations alike. If we, like Israel, remain unrepentant in our sins, we will be unprepared to meet God. Amos's famous statement is threatening, in or out of context. It is freighted with warning and heavy with doom.

C. As to the Prospect (5:1–6:14)

1. The Distress of the Lord (5:1-15)

Now we hear a voice raised in lamentation. It is the voice of the Lord, crying over the people He loved, a people who would have nothing to do with Him. Warnings and wooings are mixed together in this segment of Amos's prophecy.

In his mind's eye the prophet saw a land already harvested by the Assyrians. The cities were empty. Where thousands of people once went about their business, where the sights were once kaleidoscopic, where voices once bargained in the marketplace and cheered at games, there were now only burned-out buildings. The handful of people that remained wandered around in sackcloth and ashes and sifted through rubble and ruins.

No doubt Amos himself was startled when the voice of the Lord broke in saying, "Seek ye me" (5:4). It abruptly brought him back to the present. "Seek not Beth-el...Gilgal...Beer-sheba," God commanded (5:5). Alas for those places once linked with Jacob, Joshua, and Abraham. Abraham had pitched his tent and raised his altar at Beth-el when he first entered the promised land. There Jacob had seen his vision of the ladder and been converted. At Gilgal Joshua had reinstituted the covenant seal of circumcision. There too his victorious troops had returned again and again for spiritual renewal during the conquest of Canaan. Abraham had dug his well at Beer-sheba. Israel should have been able to return to these places in gratitude to God, but they had become polluted centers of idolatry and rank heathenism disguised by the use of Biblical terms and forms. *If only the Israelites would seek God,* thought the prophet, *there would be hope.* "Seek the Lord, and ye shall live," burst out Amos (5:6).

There was so much guilt everywhere. Which illustration would the prophet choose? He remembered a visit to a court where he had witnessed a particularly callous demonstration of injustice against a poor defendant. The man could not afford to bribe the judge, so although he was clearly innocent, the judge decided against him. Amos fumed, "[You] turn judgment to wormwood" (5:7). Injustice is bitter indeed.

"Seek him that maketh the seven stars [Pleiades] and Orion, and turneth the shadow of death into the morning," continued Amos (5:8). He is the One with whom the godless ultimately have to deal—the God of creation, the One who can hurl stars into space, bind them into constellations, and bend them to His will. He is the One to seek. He can chase the dark shadow of death away and flood the blackness of the tomb with light. He can put out the sun or summon the sea to inundate the globe. Amos urged the Israelites to seek Him—not a senseless golden calf. Since the Israelites had almost forgotten who He was, the prophet reminded them, "The Lord [Jehovah] is his name" (5:8).

Years before, David had depicted God's foes sitting in conference and audaciously ruling Him out of His universe, just as communists and humanists seek to do today, but the psalmist had added, "He that sitteth in the heavens shall laugh" (Psalm 2:4). Likewise Amos said that God "strengtheneth the spoiled against the strong" (Amos 5:9), or as one translator put it, "maketh devastation to smile on the strong." In other words, the oppressors of Amos's day thought themselves to be strong, but their self-confidence only brought a grim smile to God's lips. There is something terrible about God's angry smile. It proclaims both the greatness of the anger and the ease with which the offender can be punished. The devastation God would summon to punish the oppressors, would smile at their fortifications and their supposed strength.

Standing in Samaria's gate where public business was transacted and the judges sat, Amos lifted up his voice to uphold righteousness. The rich, the powerful, and the king were there, as were the wretched poor. Amos preached to rich and poor alike. He felt the hatred and scorn of the ruling class when he boldly denounced them for treading down the poor and helpless. With their ill-gotten gains, the rulers were building great houses of stone, but they would never live in them. "I know your manifold transgressions," said God, breaking into Amos's rebuke (5:12). The living God saw bribes changing hands. He saw people prudently holding their tongues, afraid to speak out because evil was on the throne.

Amos, however, refused to hold his tongue. The country boy who had faced the roaring lion in the defense of his flock, boldly faced the entrenched establishment. "Seek good," he cried, as he tried to help the Israelites avert judgment (5:14). "It may be," Amos said, "that the Lord God of hosts will be gracious unto the remnant of Joseph [the collective name of the ten tribes]" (5:15). The uncertainty did not lie with the ever-gracious God, but with the wicked nation that was unlikely to turn from their evil ways just because an inspired farmhand told them to do so.

2. The Day of the Lord (5:16-20)

Amos picked up an echo from the preaching of Joel and twice employed Joel's famous phrase "the day of the Lord" (Amos 5:18,20). Amos graphically described the terror of that day. Taking his illustrations from his native wilds, he told his listeners that it will be "as if a man did flee from a lion, and a bear met him; or went into the house, and leaned his hand on the wall, and a serpent bit him" (5:19). What a picture of hopeless flight. Imagine a man running in terror from a lion lurking in the thickets of the Jordan. Somehow he manages to elude the lion, only to run into a bear. With a frantic yell he rushes off in another direction and manages to elude the bear. At last, exhausted and still shaking with fright, he arrives home, slams the door, leans his hand on the wall while he catches his breath, and is bitten by a poisonous snake; the snake bite proves to be fatal. In other words, in the day of the Lord there will be no escape, no place to hide, no refuge from the foe.

A dark day was coming for Israel. Sooner than they supposed, they would be faced with the Assyrian invasion, which would be the initial, partial, and illustrative fulfillment of Amos's prophecy. But the full and final enactment will not come until the day of the Lord, when God's judgment will fall on the whole world.

The darkness foretold by Joel and Amos is already beginning to close in. Storm clouds are gathering in our age, and our generation needs to hear these prophecies as the time for their end-time fulfillment draws nearer. The prophecies are not merely dry, dusty prognostications meant for a day and age long since departed. They are tremendously relevant to a people and a time poised on the brink of the day of the Lord.

3. The Disgust of the Lord (5:21-27)

"I hate, I despise your feast days," God said (5:21). Israel's entire sacrificial system was out of order. It claimed to be the worship of Jehovah, but was nothing of the kind. The people fondly imagined that their sacrifices earned them God's favor. Little did they know that their religious practices were an abomination to God. He wanted no part of them. He repudiated the altars of the Israelites and called their music "noise" (5:23).

Much that is done today in the name of religion is equally offensive to God. "No man cometh unto the Father, but by me," Jesus said (John 14:6). Religion without Christ is dead religion. It is cursed, as was the religion of Cain, which is the prototype of all false religion.

Cain was neither an atheist nor a worshiper of a false god. He was a false worshiper of the true God. Cain did not like God's rule, so he tried to approach Him in his own way. Cain's religion had elements of beauty and order; it was costly and involved much thought and hard work. But God rejected Cain's religion, as He rejected the false religion of Israel, and as He rejects much that is religious today.

God was about to judge Israel, partly because of the nation's false religion. Amos 5:25 gives the crux of the matter: "Have ye offered unto *me* sacrifices and offerings in the wilderness forty years, O house of Israel?" (italics added) After their miraculous exodus from Egypt, the Israelites offered a kind of half-service to God in the wilderness. They criticized and complained. They doubted Him and dared Him. Then they crowned all their other wrong-doings by making a golden calf and claiming that this image was the god that had emancipated them from bondage.

The idolatry of the wilderness was revived, as we have seen, by Jeroboam I, the first king of the separated ten tribes. His religion was also a kind of half-service to God. It was not wholly pagan, for it acknowledged Jehovah. And it was not wholly pure, for it was idolatrous, it was served by a false priesthood, and it was bolstered by a false religious calendar of events. Yet the kingdom of Israel trusted in this false religion. But the object of the Israelites' trust turned out to be the source of their trouble.

God did not say that they did not offer sacrifices; He said that they did not offer them to Him. The words "unto me" in Amos 5:25 are emphatic. Satan was the real source of their calf worship, the real author of their religion, the real explanation for the hold that it had on their hearts. There seemed to be no end to their religious follies, for Israel also succumbed to the worship of stars and fearful false gods such as Moloch.

It is astonishing what people will believe in the name of religion. In our day for instance some believe that a man who was a scoundrel and a public nuisance, who countenanced and practiced polygamy, was God's prophet. They believe that he received eighty golden tablets from an angel and that he translated these tablets from Egyptian hieroglyphics into King James English with the aid of magic stones!

Other people believe that there is no pain and death, that these concepts are errors of the mortal mind. Still others consult the stars or believe that babbling baby talk is speaking in tongues. The examples of false religion are virtually endless. People are the same today as they were in the days of Amos. They will believe anything but the truth and they imagine that they are doing God a service when they blatantly propagate Bible-denying, Christ-rejecting, God-dishonoring lies.

God's answer to Israel's persistent wickedness and vain trust in false religion was judgment: "Therefore will I cause you to go into captivity beyond Damascus" (5:27). Damascus was on the way to Assyria. The Lord's mind was made up.

4. The Determination of the Lord (6:1-14)

Again Amos showed his disgust with the pampered lifestyle of the Israelites and the false sense of security their false religion engendered. He challenged them to look at neighboring nations: Calneh (also spelled Calno or Canneh), one of the cornerstones of Nimrod's power (Genesis 10:10; Isaiah 10:9; Ezekiel 27:23); Hamath, a chief Syrian city on the Orontes river; Gath, a great Philistine city. All had succumbed to foes. "Does Israel imagine that she is better than these kingdoms?" Amos asked in effect.

The rugged prophet, used to a harsher life, was contemptuous of the luxury of the idle rich who put aside as unthinkable his warnings of judgment. Reading his graphic descriptions of their self-indulgence, we can picture them stretching themselves out on gilded couches, feasting to their heart's content, listening to enchanting music, drinking wine in abundance, and anointing themselves with rich perfumes. But drastic changes lay ahead for them: war, siege, and famine; the terror of a city sacked by bloodthirsty and licentious troops; the chafing of iron chains; the crack of the slave driver's whip; the agony of marching mile after endless mile, tormented by thirst, flies, and fatigue; the gnawing heartache over lost loved ones, many of whom were brutally butchered or tortured to death.

"Therefore now shall they go captive," wrote Amos (6:7). The Lord was determined to send the Israelites into captivity: "The Lord God hath sworn by himself, saith the Lord the God of hosts, I abhor the excellency of Jacob, and hate his palaces; therefore will I deliver up the city" (6:8). Samaria was strong; it resisted all the armed might of Assyria for three years and was the last city of Israel to fall. But fall it did.

Amos continued his prophecy:

> It shall come to pass, if there remain ten men in one house, that they shall die. And a man's uncle shall take him up, and he that burneth him, to bring out the bones out of the house, and shall say unto him that is by the sides of the house, Is there yet any with thee? and he shall say, No. Then shall he say, Hold thy tongue: for we may not make mention of the name of the Lord (6:9-10).

What a grim picture! The situation was this: Ten people lived in a large house. (Perhaps Amos was standing at its door in a day of prosperity when he foretold its future.) But as a result of war, famine, and plague, all but one of its inhabitants died, so a distant relative had to take care of the funeral arrangements. Probably because of fear of the plague, the dead bodies were to be burned, not interred according to standard Hebrew custom. The distant relative and the body burner, hesitant to search through the pestilence-ridden rooms of the ghastly house, called to the sole survivor who crouched in a dim recess, "Is there anyone else with you?" No one else was there and the survivor would soon become the final victim.

Perhaps the relative was cursing and taking God's name in vain because of the extent of the calamity—men often blaspheme God in such circumstances—for the survivor whispered, "Hush! You must not mention Jehovah." The desperate man feared that just as a noise can precipitate an avalanche on a steep slope of a mountain, the mere mention of God's name might precipitate another avalanche of His wrath.

"The Lord...will smite the great house with breaches," Amos cried (6:11). He could foresee the proud stone walls of the stately mansion being broken by the battering rams of the plunder-seeking foe.

Having delivered this ominous prediction, Amos returned to the cause of the coming catastrophe: Israel's sin. Gathering illustrations from the countryside, he wrote: "Shall horses run upon the rock? will one plow there with oxen?" (6:12) Both situations are pictures of the ridiculous. On rocks, a horse would slip and break its leg and a farmer would break his plow. The Israelites were just as ridiculous, for they were changing judgment into oppression and trusting in riches gained by extortion.

The Israelites were also boasting in their own strength because, under the vigorous leadership of Jeroboam II, their arms had been victorious everywhere. They had no thought of giving God the glory. During Jeroboam's reign Israel had no enemy west of the Euphrates and even ruled Damascus. From the entrance of Hemath, the pass between the Lebanons, to the southern boundary of the ten tribes, where the Jordan river falls into the Dead Sea south of Jericho, all was peace. But an enemy Israel would be unable to conquer was coming. The scene of triumph was to become a scene of woe. Within four or five decades Tiglath-pileser III would put an end to the peace.

IV. THE VISIONS OF THE PROPHET (7:1–9:10)

Amos saw five more pictures of woe: the devouring locust, the consuming fire, the probing plumbline, the basket of summer fruit, and the Lord standing ominously upon the altar. Because of the intercession of Amos, the first two chastisements stopped short of total destruction.

A. Judgment Restrained (7:1-6)

1. The Devouring Locust (7:1-3)

In this vision Amos saw the Lord making locusts "in the beginning of the shooting up of the latter growth...after the king's mowings" (7:1). It seems that the first mowing was given as a tax to the king. The farmer could keep the second mowing. (Hay harvest probably preceded corn harvest, so it is likely that the latter grass sprang up at the time of the latter rain.) It was this harvest, on which the people relied for their own needs, that would be threatened by a locust plague. In the vision the locusts consumed all the grass of the land. So Amos pleaded with God for restraint and his prayer was answered. "It shall not be, saith the Lord" (7:3).

2. The Devouring Flame (7:4-6)

In this passage the fire represents the relentless heat of the sun that burns fields black and heralds famine and drought. In Amos's vision the fire was so terrible that, poetically speaking, it "devoured the great deep, and did eat up a part" (7:4). "The great deep" refers to the sea, and "a part" refers to the part of the promised land that belonged to Israel. Amos was not one to gloat over the sufferings of

Israel, so again he pleaded for divine restraint, and again this godly intercessor saw God draw back His hand. "This also shall not be, saith the Lord" (7:6).

B. Judgment Required (7:7-17)

1. The Plumbline (7:7-9)

Next the prophet saw a vision of the Lord standing on a wall with a plumbline in His hand. The plumbline represented God's Word. The Lord was indicating that if Israel was out of plumb this time, His judgment could not be averted. God's Word contains His inflexible standard of right and wrong—spiritually, morally, nationally, and religiously. Because that plumbline unerringly revealed Israel's iniquities and inequalities, there was no hope for her. What hope would there be for our land if God were to hold that same plumbline over our nation, our institutions, and our shortcomings?

"And the high places of Isaac shall be desolate," God revealed, "and the sanctuaries of Israel shall be laid waste; and I will rise against the house of Jeroboam with the sword" (7:9). God called the nation "Isaac" to contrast Israel's behavior with the guileless, gentle piety of Isaac; He called the nation "Israel" to contrast Israel's falseness with the tried integrity of Jacob after his name was changed. The "sanctuaries" were the two chief idol temples at Dan and Beth-el; these were condemned to total destruction. "The house of Jeroboam" was ravaged by the sword in the next generation; the line of Jeroboam II was extinguished when his son and successor, the sensual Zachariah, was murdered by the conspirator Shallum.

Now Amos was cutting too close to the bone. He was becoming offensive to the religious and royal establishments, and opposition raised its threatening head.

2. The Priest (7:10-17)

The clergy at Beth-el, where Israel's false priests and prophets were trained, were becoming increasingly angry with this upstart prophet from Judah. It was not to be taken lightly that Amos was challenging the powerful and well-entrenched calf cult and bearding the old lion in its den at Beth-el.

Suppose today someone stood in the Vatican and loudly,

boldly, and persistently denounced Rome and her idolatry, shrines, relics, dogmas, intrigues, college of cardinals, and pope. For a while the establishment might consider it politically expedient to ignore the agitator, especially if he was obviously a nobody. But if he continued to protest, the clergy would soon have him arrested.

Likewise Amaziah, the high priest of the Beth-el temple, finally took steps to silence Amos. In a message to the king, the priest accused the prophet of high treason. Amaziah indicated that the prophet's plot was aimed at the religious heart of the nation, and argued that the country could no longer tolerate such sacrilege.

The priest added venom to the charge by saying, "Amos saith, Jeroboam shall die by the sword" (7:11). This statement was a false accusation, for Amos had predicted the fall of Jeroboam's *house* by the sword. Jeroboam, like the Roman emperors, was both prince and priest—king of Israel and *pontifex maximus* of the cult—so this charge was especially dangerous.

The indictment also stated that Amos had said, "Israel shall surely be led away captive out of their own land." Taking words out of context is of course a common way of incriminating a man. True, Amos had prophesied the coming captivity, but only in the context of Israel's guilt and God's offered grace.

Jeroboam seems to have left the handling of Amos up to his archbishop, for Amaziah turned on the prophet and said, "O thou seer, go, flee thee away" (7:12). In other words, "Go on home to Judah and play the prophet there." We can almost hear the high priest's voice rise as he continued, "But prophesy not again anymore at Beth-el: for it is the king's chapel, and it is the king's court" (7:13), and we catch the prelate's haughty tone. He, the confidant of kings, had nothing but contempt for this unpolished farmhand who was far beneath him in every way.

Amos, who scorned pretense, replied, "I was no prophet, neither was I a prophet's son; but I was an herdman, and a gatherer of sycomore fruit" (7:14).

William Carey was by all standards an ordinary workingman. But fire burned in his soul and he became the father of modern missions. What he accomplished in India just as a translator confirmed his genius. On board the ship that took him to India, he mixed with Britain's empire-builders—colonial officials, the military officer class, and haughty representatives of the nobility. Carey was not a popular figure in this high society. They looked askance at a man who was going to India to be a *missionary*. One evening a snobbish aristocrat tried to humiliate him when he was a guest at the captain's table.

"I understand, Carey," he said, "that before you decided to become a missionary you were just a shoemaker."

"No, sir," replied Carey, "I was not a shoemaker. I was only a cobbler. I did not make shoes; I mended them."

Amaziah received a similar answer from Amos. He was not a trained theologian. He had not attended the schools of the prophets. He was just a farmhand from the bottom of the social scale. But God has his own school for training men; He can, and often does, bypass Bible institutes and seminaries. He is not limited to finding His men in such places. Degrees are not nearly so important to God as they are to us.

Amos did not have a classical or theological education. He was not a polished graduate of an Ivy League school. He did not speak Hebrew with a cultured accent. However, as the false priest Amaziah was about to find out, Amos knew God.

Now Amos turned on the apostate Amaziah. There was nothing personal, nothing vindictive in what Amos said. He just spoke as a man who had his eyes open to the future, and he described it as though it were present. One suspects that there was no anger in his voice, just a sob over a lost soul. His words came out, however, with an authority and certainty that silenced the haughty priest.

We can paraphrase the prophet's response as follows: "Hear the word of the Lord! You tell me not to prophesy against Israel. You tell me not to go on and on like the dreary, endless dripping of the rain. Well, God summoned me when I was tending the flock and He said, 'Go, prophesy unto my people Israel.' I don't take my orders from you. And I have something else to tell you. The Lord says that your wife will become a harlot in the city; your children will be slain by a sword; you will die in a polluted land; and Israel will surely go into captivity."

Note the cause and effect indicated by the repeated use of the word "therefore" in Amos 7:16-17. Amaziah's personal doom was the direct result of his personal attack on God's accredited ambassador.

What a terrible statement Amos made! This visionary clearly foresaw and described the horrors of the Assyrian invasion. Israel would face defeat, defilement, death, and deportation. No doubt Amaziah was stunned. He suddenly knew he had heard from God. The priest had not heard from his foolish calf-god who could not speak at all; if the idol did seem to speak, the messages came through demons. Amaziah had heard from the holy One of Israel, whom Israel had abandoned.

C. Judgment Restored (8:1–9:10)

1. The Solemn Sign (8:1-3)

After Amaziah's brief interruption, Amos resumed his prophecy against the nation. Louder and more insistent than ever now that the opposition had been cowed, the prophet declared his visions.

The Lord showed Amos a basket of ripe summer fruit that would soon perish. "The end is come," He said (8:2). It seems that Amos was in the vicinity of the calf temple in Beth-el when he saw this vision; he could hear the choir singing a hymn, ostensibly to God but actually to one of the evil spirits that energize idolatrous religions and haunt pagan temples. So the Lord said through Amos, "The songs of the temple shall be howlings in that day" (8:3). The prophecy goes on to say that there would be corpses everywhere. The dead bodies would be carted away silently and even the howlings would cease.

2. The Sobering Sermon (8:4-14)

The prophet raised his voice again to address the careless profiteers who were making merchandise of the poor. Wrathfully Amos exposed the false weights and balances they used to defraud the impoverished people. He denounced the evildoers who trampled on the helpless and bought "the poor for silver, and the needy for a pair of shoes" (8:6). He denounced those whose greed for gain made them impatient during holidays when no business could be transacted.

The Lord broke in, saying "I will…" seven times in a row (8:7-11). In verse 7 He said, "I will never forget." What a terrible thing to have one's sins—whether individual or national—always before the mind of God.

In 8:8 Amos foretold an earthquake during which the land would heave and sink like the fluctuations of the Nile. But terrible as this and other arresting phenomena were, they were no substitute for the judgment to come.

In 8:9 Amos foretold an eclipse. This verse, which is a parable as well as a prophecy, indicated that instead of gradually declining into insignificance, the sun of Israel would plunge into darkness when it was at its meridian. And so it did. After Jeroboam II died, one military coup succeeded another, and the shadow of the eclipse began to move relentlessly across the face of Israel's sun.

When Pekah ascended the bloodstained throne, he brought some order back to government. However, he turned his hand against Judah by joining with Rezin (king of Syria) in the Syro-Ephraimitic alliance so that he could eliminate the royal Davidic line (Isaiah 7:6). Ahaz (king of Judah) in turn appealed to Assyria for help. At once the terrible armies of Tiglath-pileser moved south and subdued and deported the two-and-a-half tribes east of the Jordan. Hoshea murdered Pekah, and the Assyrians returned under Shalmaneser. The eclipse was complete.

Amos described the anguish that would accompany the Assyrian invasions in 8:10 and something worse than natural and national disasters in 8:11-12:

> Behold, the days come, saith the Lord God, that I will send a famine in the land, not a famine of bread, nor a thirst for water, but of hearing the words of the Lord: And they shall wander from sea to sea, and from the north even to the east, they shall run to and fro to seek the word of the Lord, and shall not find it.

Here the prophet's vision went far beyond the impending dispersal of the ten northern tribes to the age-long wanderings of the Hebrew people. He saw them enduring a spiritual famine and his prophecy has come true. The famine began with the rabbis' growing infatuation with tradition. In time, after the crime of Calvary and the Romans' destruction of Jerusalem, the Jews substituted the Talmud for the Word of God, and for thousands of years they have tried to feed their souls on religious husks.[2]

The reason for Israel's coming judgment was their infatuation with idolatry. So infatuated were they that they took oaths by "the sin of Samaria" (8:14). This phrase is doubtless a reference to the nearby calf at Beth-el, the center of Israel's idolatry, which was sanctioned by the king, whose capital was Samaria. Farther north, people praised the golden calf at Dan and swore "by the life of the god"—by the life of a lump of metal made to look like a cow! Amos had heard the oaths and seen "the manner [literally, way] of Beer-sheba," which some scholars think was a long avenue of idols leading to the central one. When the people said, "The manner of Beer-sheba liveth," they were implying, "The way of Beer-sheba is a living way!" Disgusted, Amos prophesied, "They shall fall, and never rise up again."

3. The Startling Sight (9:1-4)

Amos, who had heard God often, now saw Him, and what he saw chilled his blood: "I saw the Lord standing upon the altar" (9:1). Doubtless this was the high altar at Beth-el—the altar used by the king, the altar set up by his namesake, Jeroboam I, some two hundred years earlier. At that time God had sent a man to prophesy its overthrow. Now no mere man, but the Son of God, the Lord Himself, was about to make the final pronouncement of doom.

The position of the Lord above the altar is important. A true altar speaks of the mercy that is shown when a propitiatory sacrifice is interposed between the sinner and the fire of God's holiness. But since the false altar at Beth-el had never been recognized by God, it was a place of judgment, not mercy. Israel, in her blindness, had always imagined that that altar provided atonement and reconciliation, but it had actually been the focal point of her rebellion, and now was the focal point of God's wrath.

"Smite" was the Lord's command (9:1). The spurious altar that had been a snare to the ten tribes was to be so smitten by God that it would never be recognized again. With their semblance of worship smitten, the people would be exposed, shattered, empty, and defeated. They would have no hiding place. God's wrath would pursue them "though they dig into hell...though they hide themselves in the top of Carmel...though they be hid from [His] sight in the bottom of the sea...though they go into captivity" (9:2-4). Sinners would be willing to go to Hell if there they could escape God. Neither the earth nor the sea would hide them. God would even send His wrath to pursue the exiles in captivity. The persecution of the Jews throughout history testifies to the truth of this prophecy, and the book of Esther gives an example of the perils they have faced in Gentile lands.

4. The Sudden Stroke (9:5-6)

When the stroke comes from God, there is no hope. "The Lord God of hosts [one of Amos's favorite titles for God] is he that toucheth the land," cried the prophet, "and it shall melt" (9:5).

In 9:6 Amos gave a description of God's visible and invisible power. He portrayed God building story after story, realm after realm, in the heavens and founding "his troop [or arch] in the earth" (9:6). Perhaps Amos was referring to the sky—the visible heaven that overarches the earth. Then he added a reference to the flood, which is historical evidence of His power and illustrative of what happens when His wrath overflows.

5. The Sifting Sieve (9:7-10)

In their senseless, stubborn addiction to idolatry, the Israelites had become "as children of the Ethiopians" (9:7). They prided themselves on being the "children of Israel," but two centuries of persistent idolatry had changed that. They were as far from God as the pagan Ethiopians were. In God's sight they were "children of the Ethiopians," the descendants of Ham, not Abraham.

Did the fact that God had brought the Israelites into the land from Egypt make them the children of God? Of course not. God had brought "the Philistines from Caphtor, and the Syrians from Kir." Did that make *them* the children of God? Idolatrous Israel had about as much claim on God as the pagans whose religions they had imitated or imported wholesale and whose gods they had worshiped and served.

The sifting time was near: "I will sift the house of Israel among all nations, like as corn is sifted in a sieve, yet shall not the least grain fall upon the earth" (9:9). That sifting is still going on. The prophet Amos was quite right. The Hebrew people are literally found among all nations. And perilous is their lot. Antisemitism is endemic in all Gentile societies and from time to time becomes epidemic. Then the Jews experience a holocaust. The worst one still lies ahead—in the great tribulation. Through the centuries God has been sifting His ancient people, but not one grain of true wheat will perish. Even in judgment God always remembers mercy.

V. THE VINDICATION OF THE PROPHET (9:11-15)

The closing verses of Amos's prophecy form an epilogue that speaks of Israel's restoration.

A. Israel's Privileges Restored (9:11-12)

All was dark when Amos wrote. There was no future for Israel. There was more hope for the pagan Ethiopians than for the Hebrews. At least the Ethiopians had not sinned against great light and privilege.

There was no hope, but there was hope. In the end, Amos said, grace would triumph. The Hebrews who were "as children of the Ethiopians" would become God's people again. Later Hosea picked up this theme and wrote of Israel, "I will say to them which were not my people, Thou art my people" (Hosea 2:23). So Amos will be vindicated, but not until the end of the age.

"In that day," said Amos, leaping over the centuries and the intervening church age, "will [the Lord] raise up the tabernacle of David that is fallen" (Amos 9:11). With his prophetic eye straying for a moment toward his native land of Judah, Amos saw again the ruin of Judah, which in time would follow the downfall of Israel.

Note that he used the word "tabernacle" to describe Judah's condition. The Hebrew term translated "tabernacle" here literally means "a hut" and suggests a temporary shelter made of intertwined branches, such as watchmen erected in vineyards (Isaiah 1:8). The word might also refer to a cattle shed (Genesis 33:17), a rough shelter built by soldiers in the field (2 Samuel 11:11), or a temporary booth put up by the Jews when they kept the feast of tabernacles (Hosea 12:9).

The idea in Amos 9:11 seems to be that the fortunes of the royal house of David would fall, but God would rebuild it and restore its glory. The house of David was at a low ebb when Christ came: the surviving scion was a carpenter of Nazareth and the royal heir was a poor peasant girl. And David's line will be in a state of utter weakness and collapse when the King comes back to fulfill His promises.

Amos went on to prophesy that the old territory of Edom will fall into Jewish hands. The remnant of the Edomites (perhaps the Jordanian Arabs) will be blessed because of the restoration of the nation of Israel, which they have so bitterly hated. God promised that blessing to "all the heathen, which are called by my name" (9:12)—probably the Gentiles who survive the ordeal of the valley of Jehoshaphat.

B. Israel's Prosperity Restored (9:13-14)

No longer will locust, famine, drought, and pestilence plague Israel. So bountiful will be the harvests of the millennial reign that "the plowman shall overtake the reaper" (9:13). Before the farmers have finished garnering one season's bumper crops, it will be time to plow and plant again.

"I will bring again the captivity of my people of Israel," said the Lord (9:14). In other words, He will reverse their long exile and bring them back to the promised land. The beginning of the fulfillment of that promise is evident in our day in the rebirth of the state of Israel and the first ingathering of the exiles. What we see today, however, is only a tithe of the future final ingathering. Many Jews cannot return to Israel now because oppressive governments refuse to let them emigrate. Other Jews, such as many in America, do not return because they are too comfortable in exile.

C. Israel's Protection Restored (9:15)

"And I will plant them upon their land, and they shall no more be pulled up out of their land which I have given them, saith the Lord." Here Amos was referring to the millennium.

The Jews who have already gone back have shown great tenacity. Their Arab neighbors have launched war after war against them, yet the Jews have successfully fought their enemies to a standstill and increased their territorial holdings.

Israel still has to face Russia's attack that will be aimed at the annihilation of the Jewish state. And the antichrist will turn against Israel and will almost succeed where others have failed. But the Jews will be determined to stay in their land.

Dark days lie ahead for them because they persist in rejecting God's final revelation of Himself in Christ and bitterly disowning Him as Messiah and Savior. But when He comes back He will plant the Jews in the land in such a way that no power on earth will be able to dislodge them.

Chapter 4

OBADIAH

PROPHET OF EDOM'S DOOM

I. THE DOOM OF EDOM (1-16)
  A. The Doom Declared (1-2)
    1. The Name of the Prophet (1a)
    2. The Nature of the Prophecy (1b-2)
      a. Its Subject (1b)
      b. Its Substance (1c-2)
        (1) Battle (1c)
        (2) Belittlement (2)
  B. The Doom Described (3-9)
    1. Edom's Territory Subdued (3-4)
      a. The Hollowness of Edom's Pride (3a)
      b. The Height of Edom's Pride (3b)
      c. The Humbling of Edom's Pride (4)
    2. Edom's Treasures Stolen (5-6)
      a. The Indolent Greed of the Common Thief (5)
      b. The Insatiable Greed of the Coming Thief (6)
    3. Edom's Treaties Scorned (7)
      a. The Treachery of Edom's Allies (7a)
      b. The Triumph of Edom's Allies (7b)
    4. Edom's Troops Slaughtered (8-9)
      a. The Death of Her Sages (8)
      b. The Death of Her Soldiers (9)
  C. The Doom Deserved (10-14)
    1. Edom Encouraged Judah's Foes (10-11)
      a. Participating in the Spread of Violence (10)
      b. Participating in the Spoils of Victory (11)
    2. Edom Enjoyed Judah's Fall (12-13)

      a. Finding Pleasure in It (12)
      b. Finding Profit in It (13)
    3. Edom Enslaved Judah's Fugitives (14)
  D. The Doom Dated (15-16)
    1. A Fixed Day (15a)
    2. A Fearful Day (15b-16)
      a. A Partial Fulfillment:
        The Downfall of the Edomite Nation (15b)
      b. A Postponed Fulfillment:
        The Downfall of the End-Time Nations (16)
II. THE DELIVERANCE OF ZION (17-21)
  A. The Character of the Deliverance (17)
    1. Rescue (17a)
    2. Regeneration (17b)
    3. Recovery (17c)
  B. The Completeness of the Deliverance (18-20)
    1. Judah's Revenge (18)
    2. Judah's Revival (19-20)
  C. The Consummation of the Deliverance (21)
    1. Edom's Salvation (21a)
    2. Edom's Sovereign (21b)

————❦————

A certain married couple had twin sons. Unlike many twins, these boys were as different as night is from day. From birth it was obvious that they were dissimilar in appearance, appetite, and appeal. The older son was hairy; the younger son was smooth. The older craved sensual things; the younger was hungry for spiritual things. The older appealed to their father; the younger appealed to their mother.

The older boy was by instinct a killer. He liked to tramp the wild woods in search of prey. Nothing pleased him more than to bring down a deer with a well-aimed arrow, skin it, and bring the red meat back to camp. The younger boy was by instinct a keeper. He liked to roam the green pastures, sit beside still waters, and gather a flock around him. Nothing pleased him more than to mind sheep, breed them, care for their lambs, and bring strays back to the fold.

The father was a mild man—easily ruled, but given to appetite. He felt drawn to his older son, whose wildness probably fascinated him and whose daring doubtless met a need in his soul. In any case, the father, who liked to eat venison, encouraged his son's killer instincts.

The mother, a good cook, was clever and somewhat willful—not easily ruled and given to precipitous action. She felt drawn to her younger son, who was the wiser of the two boys. Perhaps he fascinated her because his disposition matched the keeper instinct in her soul.

The older son grew up to love this world. He did not care about God, the world to come, or the verbal traditions of truth that were his family's heritage. The younger son grew up to love the world to come. He cared about God, the family faith, the covenant, the things that spoke of Christ, and the pleasures that are at God's right hand for evermore.

As we might expect, the boys quarreled bitterly and to such an extent that bad blood stood between them. The enmity was so threatening that the younger son was sent away from home. He came back many years later—sadder, wiser, broken by God, and born from above. The older son strayed away and stayed away, growing ever wilder and bolder and partaking of the spirit of the age.

Both boys married. The older, Esau, who had a taste for the carnal, exotic, and sensual, chose a daughter of a local pagan Canaanite and a daughter of banished Ishmael. The younger, Jacob, chose his bride from among those who had some knowledge of the truth—a knowledge derived from the testimony of his godly grandfather.

Over time, two nations developed from the families of the two boys. The two families were related by blood, but riven by everything else. Little love was lost between the two peoples, just as little love had been lost between the two brothers.

Edom, the nation descended from Esau was wild and godless. Secure in inaccessible hills, it trusted in the power of its own might. Israel, the nation descended from Jacob, was chosen by God, secure in His love, and shepherded by the Most High in spite of its self-will and sin. Summing up the situation, God declared, "I loved Jacob, And I hated Esau" (Malachi 1:2-3).

Even before the twins were born, Esau sought to murder Jacob, and long after Esau died, Edom took pleasure in Israel's misfortunes. Esau and Jacob, Edom and Israel—they are locked together in history and prophecy. Obadiah told us how the two nations are linked in prophecy, for his book is a tale of two cities: Petra, the capital of Edom; and Jerusalem, the capital of Judah.

From the beginning the Edomites manifested an unbrotherly spirit toward the Hebrews (Numbers 20:14-21; Deuteronomy 2:1-8). David conquered Edom and put the country under tribute, thus making the elder serve the younger as prophesied (Genesis 25:21-23). The conquest of Edom might have seemed like a good policy at the time, but thereafter the Edomites nursed an ever-increasing bitterness and hatred against the Jews, and this hatred produced one Herod who tried to murder Christ at His birth and another Herod who mocked Him before His death.

A number of people in the Old Testament are named Obadiah, but none of them can be positively identified as the prophet. And no one knows for sure just when the prophet Obadiah preached. He has been grouped with the earliest prophets and placed among the latest. Some six hundred years divide the champions of one view from the champions of the other.

The dating of the book of Obadiah hinges on the interpretation of verses 11-14. Some scholars relate these verses to events in the days of Jehoram (2 Chronicles 21:16-17). Others relate the verses to events in the days of Ahaz (2 Chronicles 28:17). Still others link the passage with Jeremiah 49:14-16 and say that Obadiah and Jeremiah were contemporaries.

The prophecy of Obadiah contains many verbal parallels to Jeremiah 49:14-16. Does that mean that Jeremiah quoted from Obadiah, or that Obadiah quoted from Jeremiah? It is not necessary to assume that either prophet quoted the other. The Epistles of Jude and 2 Peter give us an example of how God inspired two men to give similar messages.

The book of Obadiah itself gives little help in dating the prophecy. It mentions neither the Assyrians nor the Babylonians. It raises no doctrinal issues and barely mentions the name of the prophet. We know nothing about him except that his name means "servant of Jehovah" and he prophesied to the southern kingdom of Judah.

Obadiah is placed with the early prophets in the Hebrew Canon, which was put in order about 200 B.C. This fact is often taken to be conclusive evidence of an early date for the prophecy, but the Jews may have been following a logical order rather than a strictly chronological order when they were arranging the Canon.

The background of the book of Obadiah is an invasion of the promised land. Four invasions of Jerusalem are recorded in sacred history. The first was by the Egyptian pharaoh Shishak, but since the Edomites do not seem to have been involved in it, that invasion can be discounted (2 Chronicles 12).

A joint Arab-Philistine invasion in the days of Jehoram greatly humbled the city of Jerusalem (2 Chronicles 21:16-17). A little earlier (21:8-10) the Edomites had broken away from Judah, so they might have exulted in the disaster that overtook Jerusalem and thus inspired Obadiah's prophecy. However, the text does not say so.

Second Chronicles 25 records the defeat of Amaziah of Judah by Jehoash of Israel, but there does not seem to have been any Edomite involvement in that invasion either.

Apparently the Edomites *were* involved in the overthrow of Jerusalem by the Babylonians (Ezekiel 35; 2 Kings 25:1-7; Psalm 137:7). Thus this invasion seems to be the one to which Obadiah referred. What he described was "not merely a disabled state, or a partially plundered capital...but a dismembered and dispossessed nation."[1]

The description in Obadiah 10-14 is vivid enough to be an eyewitness account. Some scholars consider this graphic writing to be an example of the prophetic future; that is, they believe that Obadiah saw the future so clearly that centuries before the invasion he could describe it as if he were in Jerusalem at the time it happened. Most likely, however, Obadiah prophesied at the time of the Babylonian invasion; it seems that he was a contemporary of Jeremiah and saw what Edom did to the fleeing Jews. Then, when the spirit of prophecy came upon Obadiah, he foretold Edom's certain doom.

The essential message of the book of Obadiah is that antisemitism eventually brings God's judgment. Nations that curse and persecute Jews will reap what they sow. They are attacking a people with whom God has a long-standing, unconditional, and irrevocable treaty (Genesis 12:1-3). Conversely, nations that harbor and protect Jews will enjoy God's blessing.

I. THE DOOM OF EDOM (1-16)

A. The Doom Declared (1-2)

1. The Name of the Prophet (1a)

The prophet Obadiah rose up like a phantom from the mists. His voice wailed out in a dire dirge of doom for Edom and then died away. Suddenly, as if to express an afterthought, he cried out again, but this time there was a note of triumph in his words. Then there was complete silence. The mysterious voice that had pronounced its last woe upon Edom and its last promise for Jerusalem had nothing more to say. The mists closed in and all that remained was a small pamphlet containing the shortest of prophecies, a memo that people hardly ever read anymore. But the prophecy of Obadiah was momentous enough to find its way into the eternal Word of the living God.

Who was this Obadiah? Was he the God-fearing and man-fearing steward who hid the Lord's prophets "by fifty in a cave" in the days of Elijah and Ahab (1 Kings 18:3-16)? Surely not. Was this Obadiah the law teacher whom Jehoshaphat sent into the cities of Judah to preach the Word (2 Chronicles 17:7-9)? Was this Obadiah the unnamed "man of God" who advised Amaziah not to allow the army of northern Israel to accompany him in an expedition against Edom (2 Chronicles 25:7)? Was this Obadiah one of the overseers of the temple repairs in the days of Josiah (2 Chronicles 34:12)? We do not know. All we know is Obadiah's name. He was simply a "voice of one crying in the wilderness" (Matthew 3:3).

2. The Nature of the Prophecy (1b-2)

Having seen a vision and heard God's voice, Obadiah affirmed the divine origin of his prophecy. "Thus saith the Lord," he wrote (1).

The prophecy was directed against Edom. This little country bordered Judah in the north, ran south all the way to the gulf of Aqaba, and bordered the desert in the east. Between twenty to thirty miles wide and about one hundred miles long, Edom was a wild, rugged, mountainous, and almost inaccessible land. Its central area was marked by red sandstone cliffs that towered as high as five thousand feet above sea level. Its deep ravines were easily defended. Its glens and flat terraces along the mountainsides were covered with rich, productive soil. Its major cities were Bozrah in the north, Teman in the south, and Sela (Petra) in the center.

No country was more bitter and constantly hostile toward Judah than Edom. Other enemies came and went. The Canaanites were succeeded by the Philistines, who were succeeded by the Syrians, who were succeeded by the Greeks. The Egyptians, Assyrians, Babylonians, Persians, Seleucids, and Ptolemies came and went, but Edom was always there—implacable, unmerciful, filled with hate. So in Obadiah's vision the Lord sent His ambassadors to stir up the nations to go to war against Edom. God summoned the Assyrians and then the Babylonians and their confederates to battle the Edomites.

And what was Edom's prevailing sin? It was pride—pride that had to be abased. Accordingly, in Obadiah's vision the Lord said to

Edom, "Behold, I have made thee small among the heathen: thou art greatly despised" (2). We tend to be easy on pride, but God never is. Pride turned glorious Lucifer into the devil (Isaiah 14:14). Pride is the sin of sins, the father of sins, and the original sin.

B. The Doom Described (3-9)

1. Edom's Territory Subdued (3-4)

a. The Hollowness of Edom's Pride (3a)

"The pride of thine heart hath deceived thee," Obadiah exclaimed. Edom was proud of its situation astride the trade routes between Syria and Egypt. One reason Judean kings such as Solomon, Jehoshaphat, Amaziah, and Uzziah warred against Edom was that they coveted control of the lucrative route that passed through Elath and Ezion-geber. But the Edomites were hard to subdue. They could sally out and wage war or hold up caravans and demand tribute, and no one could stop them, for their strongholds were virtually impregnable. So they became rich, insolent, and proud.

Before the *Titanic* left Southampton for her fateful maiden voyage, a passenger, Mrs. Albert Caldwell, asked a crewman if the ship really was unsinkable. "God Himself could not sink this ship," he told her.[2] A similar spirit prevailed in Edom. Believing that God Himself could not bring them low, the Edomites were deceived by their pride. How hollow was their boast!

b. The Height of Edom's Pride (3b)

Since Edom's pride towered as high as its rocky steeps, Obadiah exclaimed, "Thou that dwellest in the clefts of the rock, whose habitation is high; that saith in his heart, Who shall bring me down to the ground?"

The real stronghold of Edom was Petra, a city unknown to the modern world until 1812 when it was rediscovered by the Swiss explorer, Johann Ludwig Burckhardt. Petra's dwellings were hewn out of the rock of the purple mountains that run out from the Syrian desert for about a hundred miles. Esau's wild sons had clambered in those mountains and made them their own. They had perched on high shelves and hidden in caves at the end of deep gorges.

From mount Hor, Edom's summit, an observer can look down on a maze of mountains, chasms, rocky shelves, and strips of valley. On the east is the crested edge of a high, cold plateau that is covered with stones, except where there are stretches of cornfields and trees. On the west, black and red walls of rock rise steep and bare from the yellow floor of the desert. The interior is reached by passages so narrow that two horsemen can barely ride abreast. The sun is shut out from these travelers by overhanging rocks, and eagles and hawks are heard screaming in the sky above.

The main approach to Petra was a gorge that is now called "the valley of Moses." A rivulet threads its way along the entire length of the gorge. The valley with its branches is about 4,500 feet long and is flanked on all sides by precipitous sandstone cliffs. With incredible industry, the inhabitants of Petra tunneled into the hard rock, beautified its face with the sculptured lines of temples and palace tombs, and carved fortresses from the towering crags. An invading army would have had to creep down the narrow canyon and twist and turn through the mountains before they could have even seen the prize city. Because of the configuration of the passage, it would have been possible for a dozen determined men to hold Petra against an army. But what difference did rocks and mountains make to the One who made the canyon? Armies, already commissioned by the Almighty to humble Edom, were being summoned from afar.

c. The Humbling of Edom's Pride (4)

"Though thou exalt thyself as the eagle, and though thou set thy nest among the stars, thence will I bring thee down, saith the Lord." The eagle suggests soaring pride; the stars suggest settled pride. The eagle builds its nest in high places almost inaccessible to man. The Edomites were a race of eagles; they imagined themselves to be as secure as the stars. But today all that is left of Petra is its ruins. Edom's pride has been humbled to the dust.

The visitor to Petra emerges from a deep chasm—often so narrow that it is dark at noontime—into an arena that is more than a mile long and two-thirds of a mile wide. There he sees hundreds of rock-hewn mausoleums and, scattered all over the bottom of the city's site, the remains of a castle and the arches of a bridge. For centuries, even Edom's name was forgotten by all but biblicists and archaeologists.

2. Edom's Treasures Stolen (5-6)

The Edomites were middlemen between the Arabs and the Phoenicians. Holding a sword over the harbors of the gulf of Aqaba, the masters of Edom levied tribute on the Tarshish ships bearing the gold of Ophir. Sitting astride the roads that ran from Damascus to Memphis, Edom's customs agents halted merchant caravans from Arabia, Persia, the distant East, Egypt, Tyre, and far-off Greece. Either the traders paid taxes or forfeited everything. Thus the Edomites filled their caves with the wealth of both East and West.

Now it was Edom's turn to pay. All its treasures were to be plundered—and not by any ordinary robber band. If common thieves had penetrated Edom's rocky halls some dark night and stolen all they could carry away, much wealth would still have remained. "If thieves came to thee, if robbers by night...would they not have stolen till they had enough? if the grapegatherers came to thee, would they not leave some grapes?" (5) But the greed of the coming conqueror would be insatiable.

The Edomites had crossed the hidden boundary between God's merciful patience and His wrath. They had gone too far, indulging their antisemitism once too often. The enemy would harvest their accumulated riches and not leave even the leanest pickings. "How are the things of Esau searched out! how are his hidden things sought up!" (6)

3. Edom's Treaties Scorned (7)

The worst kind of treachery in the East is to betray a man whose bread one has eaten. Likewise a nation's destruction is always more bitter when former allies and confederates participate in it.

Through the years Edom had persecuted his brother Jacob, with whom he should have had friendly, peaceful relations. Now Edom's unbrotherly, unnatural hatred was to be returned to him. His friends and allies (probably Moab, Ammon, Tyre, and Sidon; see Jeremiah 27:3; Zephaniah 2:8; Ezekiel 25) with whom he had united to fend off Babylon and to persuade Zedekiah to rebel, would turn against Edom. "All the men of thy confederacy," Obadiah prophesied, "have brought thee even to the border: the men that were at peace with thee have deceived thee, and prevailed against thee; they that eat thy bread have laid a wound under thee" (7). Edom's treaties would prove to be worthless. The countries on which Edom thought he could rely would make peace with the invader.

Edom failed to recognize that his hostility toward the Jews was hostility toward God and that his antisemitic policies had sowed the seeds of his destruction. "There is none understanding in him," cried Obadiah. That was God's assessment of the situation.

Let the Arab and Muslim nations that surround Israel today

beware. These sons of Ishmael stand in Edom's shoes and are robed with Edom's mantle. Although they are blood kin, they hate the Jews with a passion equaled only by that of Edom of old. These antisemitic nations make alliances with one another, make common cause with Russia, and will even side with the antichrist against Israel. They do not understand that their bitter hatred of the Jews will bring them to grief.

4. Edom's Troops Slaughtered (8-9)

a. The Death of Her Sages (8)

"Shall I not in that day, saith the Lord, even destroy the wise men out of Edom, and understanding out of the mount of Esau?"

The deepest springs of the Edomites' hatred of the Jews were in their blood. Although Esau and Jacob were twins, they were opposites, as were the two peoples descended from them. The Jews were God's chosen people. They knew the true and living God. The Edomites, like Esau, were essentially irreligious and thoroughly profane. Rarely, if ever, do we read of Edom's gods in the Old Testament. Doubtless the Edomites had some gods, but religion was not their big preoccupation. Like Esau, they had no spiritual birthright, no faith in the future. They were dead to the unseen world and lived for power and plunder in this one.

In keeping with their freethinking, the Edomites gained a reputation for shrewdness and worldly wisdom. Eliphaz, chief of Job's friends and representative of worldly wisdom, was a Temanite (Job 4:1). The Herods—unprincipled statesmen known for cleverness, scheming, and lack of ideals—were Edomites. "That fox" was Jesus' estimate of Herod Antipas (Luke 13:32). The Edomites' shrewdness would do them little good. The wise men of Edom were destined for the sword.

Today's Russians with their carnal wisdom and political shrewdness are the spiritual heirs of the Edomites. Comparing American naiveté with Russian craftiness, someone said, "The Americans play checkers; the Russians play chess." But their craftiness will not help them in the end. Their materialism, hatred of God, and rabid antisemitism will bring them to the same doom that Edom experienced (Ezekiel 38–39).

b. The Death of Her Soldiers (9)

"Thy mighty men, O Teman, shall be dismayed, to the end that every one of the mount of Esau may be cut off by slaughter."

Thus Obadiah prophesied and, sure enough, along came the Babylonians. The rocky ramparts of Edom yielded to the military prowess of Nebuchadnezzar, the man to whom God symbolically gave the world (Daniel 2). Later, under John Hyrcanus of the Maccabean dynasty, Edom was further reduced. Under the Romans, the Edomites lost their national character altogether. Gone was Edom's boasted might. Gone were Edom's soldiers.

Neither sages nor soldiers could save Edom when God decreed that its domains would become a slaughterhouse. Obadiah could see it all: the marching troops of Babylon; the traitors within the gates of Edom; the people trapped at the end of their ravines; the plunder and slaughter. The prophet saw it, he told it, and so it was.

C. The Doom Deserved (10-14)

Edom had committed three unpardonable sins: encouraging Judah's foes, enjoying Judah's fall, and enslaving Judah's fugitives. Because of these sins, retribution was soon to be meted out.

1. Edom Encouraged Judah's Foes (10-11)

Obadiah said to Edom, "For thy violence against thy brother Jacob shame shall cover thee, and thou shalt be cut off for ever" (10). It is true that God's ancient people, like His people today, had many faults and sins and deserved chastisement. But they were still God's people and it was not Edom's place to urge on Judah's foes or actively side with the enemies of those who were dear to His heart. Whatever knowledge of God, salvation, true holiness, justice, mercy, and truth was to be found in the world, was deposited with God's people.

Terrible is the state of soul of those who rejoice to see God's people—however erring and backslidden they might be—attacked and harmed by their foes. Whose side are they on?

Edom was on the wrong side. "In the day that thou stoodest on the other side," added Obadiah, "in the day that the strangers carried away captive his forces, and foreigners entered into his gates, and cast lots upon Jerusalem, even thou wast as one of them" (11).

Consider what happened. It was the darkest hour in Hebrew history. The situation had been bad enough a century earlier when the Assyrians had carried the northern tribes into captivity and ravished Judah right down to the wall of Jerusalem. But now Jerusalem and the temple lay in ruins.

The northern tribes had never truly represented God's truth. They had worshiped the golden calf, and all their kings had been evil. So the northern kingdom had come to an end, while the preaching of Isaiah and the prayers of godly King Hezekiah had saved Jerusalem and the temple from the Assyrians. But now it looked as though "the light of the knowledge of the glory of God" (2 Corinthians 4:6) had gone out forever. It hadn't, of course. There was still a Jeremiah, an Ezekiel, and a Daniel.

The Edomites, who had encouraged Judah's foes, revealed their state of soul by rejoicing when the light of God on this earth was seemingly extinguished. They remind us that there are people who love darkness. There were people who rejoiced in the death of Christ and even mocked Him as He died. And today there are people who rejoice in the downfall of the church and in the disgrace of her ministers.

When the Chaldeans invaded Judah, "cast lots upon Jerusalem," carried off the spoil, and enslaved her people, Edom applauded and helped the conquerors. Obadiah was not the only prophet to react against this unbrotherly sin: see Psalm 137:7; 83:4-6; Ezekiel 35; Jeremiah 49:7-22; Isaiah 34; 63. The book of Obadiah is a divine commentary on Proverbs 17:5: "He that is glad at calamities shall not be unpunished."

2. Edom Enjoyed Judah's Fall (12-13)

Edom found both pleasure and profit in Judah's fall, and Obadiah's denunciation rang out again and again: "Thou shouldest not have…"

Here, incidentally, we come to the crux of the question, Was Obadiah speaking of the prophetic past or the real past? Scholars who believe that he was speaking of the prophetic past usually rephrase the words "Thou shouldest not have" as "Do not," "Look not," or "Gloat not." According to this view the words are a warning, not a woe; Obadiah was telling Edom not to gloat. However, even if strict translation calls for this rephrasing, Obadiah did not necessarily live long before the event. He could have been a contemporary and still have warned Edom not to play the wretched part it did. Or, if we stay with the King James text, he could have witnessed the sin of Edom (either actually or in a vision) and denounced it.

Note the things that Edom had done (or would do):

Thou shouldest not have looked on the day of thy brother in the day that he became a stranger; neither shouldest thou have rejoiced over the children of Judah in the day of their destruction; neither shouldest thou have spoken proudly in the day of distress. Thou shouldest not have entered into the gate of my people in the day of their calamity; yea, thou shouldest not have looked on their affliction in the day of their calamity, nor have laid hands on their substance in the day of their calamity (12-13).

We can picture the Edomites swarming down from their cliff homes when the tidings came that Nebuchadnezzar's army had breached the wall of Jerusalem and receiving the news with rousing cheers. We can hear the canyons echoing shouts of glee and the caves reverberating boastful words. "That will teach those despicable Jews a lesson," someone would have called out. Raising the flag of Edom in triumph, someone else would have cried, "Three cheers for Edom!" as if the Edomites had done the deed. "Come on, Edom!" another probably shouted. "What are we waiting for? Let's get in on the action. This is the day we've been hoping for."

Out of their rocky ravines the Edomites came—wild, fierce, exultant. Soon they were cheering the Babylonians, gloating over the captives, pouring into Jerusalem, and plundering the spoils. Their sin was unpardonable.

God had given Israel special instructions regarding Edom: "Thou shalt not abhor an Edomite; for he is thy brother....The children that are begotten of them shall enter into the congregation of the Lord in their third generation" (Deuteronomy 23:7-8). God expected the Hebrews to extend the olive branch to Edom, to evangelize the descendants of Esau and win them to Himself. The Hebrews never did, so they reaped the fruit of their failure. But their failure did not excuse Edom's behavior.

From the beginning Edom had hated the Hebrews and been jealous of them. That seed of hate had germinated and borne its bitter fruit of malice and revenge. The Edomites had progressed from indifference to Judah's fate, to active participation in the persecution of God's people, to rejoicing in their downfall.

Some professing Christians are like the Edomites. Instead of helping a brother when he falls, they delight in digging out the details and spreading the news. Feeling smug, they do not hesitate to add an extra kick or two to a man who is down. Obadiah warned against such wicked behavior.

3. Edom Enslaved Judah's Fugitives (14)

In verse 14 we read of Edom's final damning sin, the last malicious kick delivered to a fallen brother: "Neither shouldest thou have stood in the crossway [the fork in the road], to cut off those of his that did escape; neither shouldest thou have delivered up those of his that did remain in the day of distress."

We can picture a frantic mother who has somehow survived the horrors of the Babylonian siege of Jerusalem. Her husband is dead. She and her two small children have miraculously eluded the ravaging troops who are sacking the city and performing all the acts of horror expected of an invader. Through an unguarded hole in the wall, the three escape the city. *Maybe if we can get to the mountain pass, we will be safe,* the mother thinks, and she urges her children to be brave, to hurry, to run for their lives. Believing there will be some safety in numbers, she joins other desperate fugitives.

At last they reach the pass. The din of battle and the screams of the wretched people trapped in the city grow fainter and a prayer of thankfulness rises in the mother's heart. Hope revives—and then armed warriors, roaring with ill-begotten mirth, spring from ambush. Quickly they round up the fugitives and shackle young and old, women and children. The warriors are not Babylonians; they are Edomites! "Back you go," they mock. "We're handing you over to the Babylonians." The fugitives plead for mercy, but they might as well try to argue a tiger into giving up its prey.

D. The Doom Dated (15-16)

Having finished his indictment against Edom, Obadiah was about to pass sentence. At this point his prophecy was enlarged to embrace not only Edom, but also all the other countries that constitute themselves to be enemies of the Jewish people. Obadiah's vision carried him over the centuries to "the day of the Lord" (15), to the end-time fulfillment of many Old and New Testament prophecies. From God's point of view, that day was near.

Like so many prophecies, Obadiah's words would have a partial fulfillment for Edom and a later, postponed fulfillment for the end-time foes of Israel. The retribution pronounced on Edom follows the principle of all divine retribution: "As thou hast done, it shall be done unto thee: thy reward shall return upon thine own head" (15). Sin is like a boomerang. What we do to others comes back and is done to us. Obadiah's prophecy has its ultimate focus in "the day of the Lord," when all nations, including a latter-day Edom, will come up against the nation of Israel. Ancient hostilities will be back on center stage.

The rebirth of the state of Israel in our day heralds the approaching fulfillment of Obadiah's end-time prophecy. The ancient arena is fast becoming the modern arena. The old land of Edom is now part of the Arab country of Jordan, which joins with other Arab and Muslim nations in their hostility toward Israel. Jordan was created by the British government about the same time Britain was making plans to implement the Balfour declaration and the League of Nations' mandate. Hatred of Israel will cause embittered Arab nations to ally themselves with Russia, the antichrist, or anyone else who might make their dream of eradicating Israel and exterminating the Jews a reality.

God will see to it, however, that justice is done. The Middle Eastern Arab nations that are so vehement and unrelenting in their antisemitism will reap what they have sown: "As thou hast done, it shall be done unto thee." God's justice is poetic. The punishment parallels the offense, just as one line of a poem corresponds to another.

Historically, Edom's doom, although slow, was sure. Jeremiah foretold that Edom would be subject to Nebuchadnezzar (27:2-6), and after their captivity ended, Malachi bore witness to the fact that Edom had been made utterly desolate (1:2-3). Nebuchadnezzar no doubt conquered Edom when he marched against Egypt. He could not afford to leave behind him such a strong fortress of robber barons. He needed secure passage for men and materials, and the unsubdued Edomites sat astride his supply lines. It was the same passage that Edom had so spitefully denied to Israel centuries earlier when the Hebrews were marching from Egypt to Canaan. Moreover Nebuchadnezzar needed safe passage between the Dead Sea and the gulf of Aqaba. We can be sure that Nebuchadnezzar treated Edom the way he treated all conquered countries—with plunder, death, and captivity.

God's justice, however, is ever tempered with mercy. His judgments often are slow in coming, allowing time for repentance. Implacable Edom must have recovered at least some of its power during the years of Judah's exile because the repatriated Jews found Edomites plundering the Negeb in the south and ravaging as far north as Hebron. Malachi 1:4 records Esau's boast, "We will return and build the desolate places," and foretells further desolation.

Probably during the reign of Antiochus Epiphanes, who viciously persecuted the Jews, the Edomites took possession of the southern part of Judah and Hebron, which was just twenty-two miles from Jerusalem. Judah Maccabeus battled the Edomites at Arrabatene in Idumea and twenty years later Simon Maccabeus was still fighting them. Twenty years after that, Simon's son John Hyrcanus had to fight them again; he thoroughly thrashed them and forced them to accept circumcision, become Jewish proselytes, and accept Jewish law.

The Edomites' character, however, remained unchanged and Judah could not get rid of them that easily. In time Judah had to deal with the Herods and their opportunism, subservience to Rome, and insatiable cruelty. During the terrible siege of Jerusalem in A.D. 70 the Zealots made the fatal mistake of sending for the Edomites. The city was infiltrated by some twenty thousand Edomites, who only added further torment to the death pangs of Jerusalem. Then their name disappeared from history. Most of them perished during the dreadful extermination that accompanied the siege and sack of Jerusalem.

For Israel's end-time enemies, victory will be followed by revelry (Obadiah 16). The prophet could see, in vision, the victorious armies of the antichrist sweeping through Jerusalem, desecrating synagogues and shrines, plundering the already defiled temple, and toasting their successes in drunken orgies on the temple mount.

The antichrist will be the last of a long train of conquerors who have desecrated the holy city, "the city of the great King." Obadiah could see Edomites, Babylonians, Macedonians, and Romans in successive waves seizing Jerusalem and celebrating by drinking to the triumph of their gods over the God of Heaven.

But the victory of the heathen is temporary. Wine for wine! is the promise of verse 16. God has always triumphed in the end and the antichrist's doom is sure. Even as Jerusalem falls into his hands, the heavens will rend open and the rightful King will return.

II. THE DELIVERANCE OF ZION (17-21)

A. The Character of the Deliverance (17)

Notice the first word of verse 17: "But." Mark well the *buts* of the Bible. They are hinges on which great events and doctrines turn. "But upon mount Zion," Obadiah prophesied, "shall be deliverance, and there shall be holiness; and the house of Jacob shall possess their possessions." Edom could anticipate annihilation, but

Zion could look forward to restoration. Zion, a poetic name for
Jerusalem, was actually the stronghold of the city. In its millennial
context, Zion symbolizes the imperial power and universal rule of
Christ that will be centered at Jerusalem.

Obadiah saw the Hebrew nation resettled in the promised land.
Their sifting time over forever, the Jewish people will fully possess
the vast territory (from the Nile to the Euphrates) deeded by God
to Abraham. Holiness, the one thing no one can possess apart from
Christ and His indwelling Holy Spirit, will be established throughout the realm. The statutes of the sermon on the mount will
become the common law of Israel and the world.

B. The Completeness of the Deliverance (18-20)

1. Judah's Revenge (18)

As we have seen, Israel's ancient enemies will rise again. Today
the Arabs hold the lands that once belonged to Edom, Moab,
Ammon, Philistia, and Phoenicia. Syria and Egypt are again powers
in the Middle East. Iraq (ancient Babylon) and Iran (ancient
Persia) are also Middle Eastern powers; both harbor deep hostility
toward Israel.

In Obadiah's vision a united Jewish nation was back in its land.
The divided kingdom was a thing of the past. The prophet saw the
former territory of Edom raising its head against Israel. The nations
in that territory will continue to oppose Israel, support Israel's
enemies, and foment terrorism and war against Israel. In the end,
however, they will lose everything. The Jews will be God's chosen
instrument to punish them. Just as stubble burns in a fire, no
remnant of Edom will survive. "The house of Jacob shall be a fire,
and the house of Joseph a flame, and the house of Esau for stubble."

2. Judah's Revival (19-20)

Next Obadiah saw the restored Hebrew nation possessing the
territory of her former foes. Not even during the great days of David
and Solomon did Israel possess more than a tithe of the total land
grant that is hers under the Abrahamic covenant. But she will.
Israelites living in the southern part of the land will take possession
of mount Esau. Those dwelling in the lowlands toward the sea will
take what was once the land of the Philistines. The coastland and
the heartland will be securely Israel's. Obadiah foresaw it all.

During the terrible persecutions of the antichrist at the time of

the great tribulation, many Jews will be rounded up, herded into
concentration camps, and slated for death—as they were during
the dark days of the Nazis. But the returning Christ will liberate
them and install them at Zarephath, a town between Tyre and
Sidon. Thus modern Lebanon will become part of Israel's territory.
At present Lebanon is often used as a staging place for Palestinian
terrorists and as an outpost of Syria.

Scholars have made various conjectures concerning the location
of Sepharad (20). Some think the name refers to Spain or Sardis,
where the ancient Phoenicians sold their Hebrew slaves. Perhaps
the antichrist will establish concentration camps in various places
in Europe, and the liberated Jews from these death camps will head
for the promised land like homing pigeons, just as the survivors of
the Nazi holocaust did. They will settle, Obadiah said, in "the cities
of the south" (20)—in triumph over Edom.

C. The Consummation of the Deliverance (21)

"Saviours shall come up on mount Zion to judge the mount of
Esau; and the kingdom shall be the Lord's." Mount Zion will
become the center of all governmental control in Jesus' millennial
kingdom. "Saviours," or judges, will be in constant communication
with this power center and will exercise Christ's authority over the
most distant outposts of His world empire, including mount Esau
itself. Never again will Edom actually or representatively threaten
the Jewish people or anyone else.

"And the kingdom shall be the Lord's." With these words
Obadiah's prophecy ended. There was no more to be said, for
Christ is the King "against whom there is no rising up" (Proverbs
30:31). Obadiah turned our eyes toward Jesus and then put down
his pen.

Chapter 5

JONAH

THE REBELLIOUS PROPHET

I. THE WORD OF GOD (1:1-16)
   A. Jonah's Secret Rejoicing (1:1-2)
      The inescapable missionary challenge of:
      1. The Man (1:1)
      2. The Multitude (1:2a)
      3. The Message (1:2b)
   B. Jonah's Swift Rebellion (1:3-5)
      1. The Prophet Paying (1:3)
      2. The Pagans Praying (1:4-5)
         a. The Mariners Were Alarmed (1:4-5a)
         b. The Missionary Was Asleep (1:5b)
   C. Jonah's Sudden Realization (1:6-9)
      1. Jonah's Shame (1:6)
      2. Jonah's Blame (1:7-8)
      3. Jonah's Claim (1:9)
   D. Jonah's Stubborn Resolve (1:10-16)
      1. His Decision (1:10-12)
         a. The Sailors' Questions Asked (1:10-11)
            (1) Why? (1:10)
            (2) What? (1:11)
         b. The Sailors' Questions Answered (1:12)
      2. His Doom (1:13-16)
         a. What the Sailors Did (1:13)
         b. What the Sailors Desired (1:14)
         c. What the Sailors Discovered (1:15-16)
II. THE WORD WITH GOD (1:17–2:10)
   A. Jonah's Dreadful Prison (1:17)

B. Jonah's Desperate Prayer (2:1-8)
1. What Jonah Reaped (2:1-6)
a. A Feeling of Horror (2:1-3)
b. A Flash of Hope (2:4)
c. A Foretaste of Hell (2:5-6)
2. What Jonah Remembered (2:7)
3. What Jonah Realized (2:8)
C. Jonah's Dying Promise (2:9-10)
1. His Surrender (2:9)
2. His Salvation (2:10)
III. THE WORD FOR GOD (3:1-10)
A. Revelation (3:1-4)
1. The Prophet (3:1-2)
2. The Prophecy (3:3-4)
a. A Word about the Place (3:3)
b. A Word about the Proclamation (3:4)
B. Revival (3:5-10)
1. Faith (3:5)
2. Fasting (3:6-9)
a. Its Vast Extent (3:6-7)
b. Its Vital Expression (3:8)
c. Its Valid Expectation (3:9)
3. Forgiveness (3:10)
IV. THE WORD ABOUT GOD (4:1-11)
A. Jonah's Displeasure with God (4:1-9)
1. Jonah and His God (4:1-4)
a. Jonah's Rage (4:1)
b. Jonah's Resentment (4:2)
c. Jonah's Request (4:3-4)
2. Jonah and His Gourd (4:5-8)
a. His Decision (4:5)
b. His Discomfort (4:6)
c. His Dismay (4:7-8)
3. Jonah and His Grudge (4:9)
B. Jonah's Discovery about God (4:10-11)
1. An Appeal (4:10)
2. An Application (4:11)

———❦———

As a Hebrew and as a successful prophet, Jonah thought he knew God, but he did not know Him nearly as well as he thought he did. Jonah would have come under the apostle Paul's scathing indictment:

> Behold, thou art called a Jew, and restest in the law, and makest thy boast of God, And knowest his will, and approvest the things that are more excellent, being instructed out of the law; And art confident that thou thyself art a guide of the blind, a light of them which are in darkness, An instructor of the foolish, a teacher of babes, which hast the form of knowledge and of the truth in the law. Thou therefore which teachest another, teachest thou not thyself? (Romans 2:17-21)

Being of "like passions as we are," Jonah had problems. He did not know God well enough to grieve over sin the way God grieves. Neither did he know God well enough to rejoice over the repentance of sinners the way God rejoices. Jonah had great difficulty accepting the fact that God loved Gentiles just as much as He loved Jews and the fact that He loved the cruel and oppressive Assyrians just as much as He loved him.

Some scholars believe that Jonah, the first apostle to the Gentiles, was already an old man when he was called to preach to Nineveh. He lived in the northern kingdom of Israel and was a native of Gath-hepher, a Galilean town located three or four miles from Nazareth. Thus the Pharisees' sneering claim that "out of Galilee ariseth no prophet" (John 7:52) was simply not true.

Since Jonah is referred to as "the son of Amittai" in 2 Kings 14:25 as well as in Jonah 1:1, the identification is solid and the prophet's historicity is settled. Jonah was a contemporary of King Jeroboam II of Israel, who reigned from about 790–750 B.C.

The Lord Jesus believed that Jonah was an actual person and that his experience in the belly of the great fish was authentic (Matthew 12:40). Indeed he is the only prophet to whom Jesus directly likened Himself. He said that Jonah's experience was an illustration of His death, burial, and resurrection and that "as Jonas was a sign unto the Ninevites, so shall also the Son of man be to [His] generation" (Luke 11:30). (Jesus' generation was as grieved and angry over the faith and repentance of those to whom the resurrection of our Lord was proclaimed—especially when Gentiles began to respond to the gospel—as Jonah was over the repentance of the people of Nineveh.) Note also that the Lord referred to Jonah in the same context in which he referred to Solomon and the queen of Sheba, thus placing Jonah on the same level of historical fact (Matthew 12:42).

Since Christ took the book of Jonah literally, any attack on the book is an attack on the deity of Christ and is not to be countenanced by people who love the Lord. We need not trouble ourselves about the unbelieving theologians' contention that the book is a combination of allegory and myth.

To Jonah "the word of the Lord came"! This and similar expressions occur seven times in his book (1:1; 2:10; 3:1,3; 4:4,9,10). Again and again we read, "God said," but the liberal says He didn't. God speaks truth, and the liberal is a liar.

We cannot understand the book of Jonah without some knowledge of its historical setting. In the background looms the imperial, cruel, guilty city of Nineveh, capital of Assyria in the days of its glory. This metropolis was resplendent with terraces and storied palaces, arsenals and barracks, libraries and temples. Although Jonah could have walked past the temples and palaces in an hour, he would have had to tramp for days through endless warrens and mazes where the common people lived in order to cover the whole city with his message of doom.

Nineveh had massive embankments, extensive irrigation canals, and mighty gates fronting the Tigris river. Its high wall was so wide that several chariots could drive abreast along the top. The circumference of the city was about sixty miles, a three days' journey on foot. Beyond the walls, extensive suburbs sprawled along the east bank of the Tigris river, and other towns ran one into another for mile after mile. Dwellings set closely together on the plain seemed to form one immense complex of buildings.

This vast and growing city cast its long and heavy shadow on Jonah's book. In his day Nineveh, which already had a long history of aggression and atrocity, glowered over the ancient world. Given the fearful sins of Israel and the imperial lusts of Nineveh, Jonah was prophet enough to know that Nineveh meant destruction, deportation, and doom to Israel. Yet God sent Jonah to Nineveh.

When Jeroboam II came to the throne of Israel, his kingdom was weak because his people had been forced to pay tribute to Assyria ever since the days of his great-grandfather Jehu. But it was also a time of weakness for Assyria. So the vigorous Jeroboam II was able to capture Hamath and Damascus and restore to Israel all the

territory southward from Hamath to the Dead Sea—just as Jonah
had prophesied (2 Kings 14:25). Like everyone else in Israel and
the Middle East, Jonah would naturally have viewed with alarm any
revival of Assyrian power.

I. THE WORD OF GOD (1:1-16)

A. Jonah's Secret Rejoicing (1:1-2)

The book of Jonah records the greatest missionary success story
in history. Never, in all the annals of Israel and the church, has such
a monumental work been done for God on foreign soil, with a
Gentile people, in a single day (Jonah 3:4-5).

1. The Inescapable Missionary Challenge of the Man (1:1)

God could have evangelized Nineveh with angels, but that is not
His way. His desire is for man to evangelize man. God has given *us* the
ministry of reconciliation. We, not angels, are God's ambassadors to
the nations. So "the word of the Lord came unto Jonah" (1:1).
Jonah means "dove." Through the man bearing that name, God
wanted to send the Dove of Heaven to bring revival, not ruin, to the
lost city of Nineveh. But Jonah, an ardent patriot, was more like a
hawk than a dove. He was fierce, sullen, proud, angry, rebellious—
and brave.

Jonah was farsighted enough to know that the political successes
of Jeroboam II could not last. Israel's moral and spiritual condition
called for judgment, and the most likely instrument of God's wrath
was Assyria.

But at that time Assyria was in a state of decline. The brilliant reign
of Adadnirari (circa 810-780 B.C.) had come to an end. He had
conducted three expeditions against Israel and its environs. The
Hittites, Tyrians, Sidonians, Israelites, Edomites, and Philistines had
all paid him tribute. He had been the greatest of all the Assyrian kings
to date, but after his death, Assyrian ascendancy rapidly diminished.

More than anything else, Jonah hoped that Assyria would never
recover its superpower status. If God were to send judgment on
Nineveh, he believed, all would be well. Israel would be saved from
the Assyrian scourge.

Jonah's boldness was fanatical. He was willing to die rather than
help save Nineveh by warning that city of its impending doom. He
must be ranked with Moses, who prayed for Israel: "Oh, this people
have sinned....Yet now...forgive their sin—; and if not, blot me, I
pray thee, out of thy book" (Exodus 32:31-32). Jonah could also be

ranked with Paul, who wrote: "I say the truth in Christ, I lie not, my conscience also bearing me witness in the Holy Ghost....I could wish that myself were accursed from Christ for my brethren, my kinsmen according to the flesh" (Romans 9:1-3). Jonah was willing to die, to be blotted out of God's book, so that Israel might live.

God can use a man like Jonah far more than He can use a spineless, compromising one. "I would thou wert cold or hot," the Lord said to the Laodiceans (Revelation 3:15). In spite of his many faults, Jonah was just the man for Nineveh. Nobody else would do.

Likewise God can use us, no matter what our temperamental strengths and weaknesses might be. He has a place for all of us in His plan, whether we are impetuous like Peter, crafty like Jacob, meek like Moses, or headstrong like Jonah. But first He must extinguish our passions, which are too often set on fire by Hell, and then rekindle them with fire from on high. God does not try to make a Peter out of a Paul, a Samson out of a Samuel, or a Moses out of a Joshua. God takes people as He finds them, changes them, and then uses them. Jonah is the classic Biblical example of how God does His perfect work with an imperfect instrument.

2. The Inescapable Missionary Challenge of the Multitude (1:2a)

Jonah was to go to Nineveh, "that great city." God is interested in great cities! As we read through the Bible, we often find ourselves in man's great cities—Babylon, Damascus, Athens, Rome, Jerusalem, Nineveh, Tyre. It is estimated that Nineveh's population was over 1,000,000. The last verse of the book of Jonah tells us that infants alone numbered 120,000.

Truly the missionary challenge of reaching the multitudes has assumed gigantic proportions in our day. The world population is exploding. It has already passed the 5,000,000,000 mark. Every year about 85,000,000 people are added to the total. Every hour about 10,000 people are added. Two-thirds of these will never have enough to eat, one-third will grow up in communist lands and be indoctrinated with atheism, three-fifths will never learn to read, and two-thirds will never hear the gospel.

3. The Inescapable Missionary Challenge of the Message (1:2b)

God told Jonah to warn Nineveh of coming judgment: "Cry against it; for their wickedness is come up before me." Jonah's first reaction was one of undiluted joy. It was the best news he had ever heard: "Yet forty days, and Nineveh shall be overthrown" (3:4). He knew the reputation of Nineveh and the Assyrian people for raw savagery. He knew that Israel would welcome the permanent overthrow of Nineveh.

As Jonah thought about the doom hovering over Nineveh, he gleefully rubbed his hands. Instead of being dismayed by the thought of a million souls going to Hell, he was delighted with the news. He reacted to the message the same way many Christians react to Ezekiel 38–39. They derive comfort from these ominous chapters, which chronicle the coming catastrophic overthrow of Russia at the hands of the God it defies. Yet when Jesus contemplated the impending destruction of Jerusalem, He wept.

B. Jonah's Swift Rebellion (1:3-5)

1. The Prophet Paying (1:3)

Jonah wasted no time in making up his mind. He decided to run away. "Jonah rose up to flee unto Tarshish from the presence of the Lord." Cain, who had also gone away "from the presence of the Lord," was a marked man and soon Jonah too would have God's mark on him (see Genesis 4:8-16).

Instead of obeying God and finding a camel headed for Damascus, the Tigris, and Nineveh, the prophet "went down to Joppa; and he found a ship going to Tarshish: so he paid the fare thereof." There are no free rides in the devil's fairgrounds.

We can picture Jonah walking along the docks of Joppa, accosting various seamen, and asking where their ships were bound. He probably found ships headed for Antioch, Kittim, Egypt, and Carthage before he finally found one going to Tarshish.

Tarshish was a city named after one of the sons of Javan (Genesis 10:4). Scholars think that this Tarshish was a wealthy Phoenician merchant-city that traded in silver, tin, and lead. Located in Spain and known to the Greeks and Romans as Tartessus, the city was a colony of Tyre. Some have identified it as Seville. Tarshish was the westernmost point in the known world (unless the Biblical Tarshish was actually located in the New World). Since Nineveh was eastward, Tarshish suited Jonah's self-willed plan.

Jonah made his way to the shipping office to book passage to Tarshish and paid the fare with coins stamped with the image and superscription of Jeroboam II. However, as Alexander Whyte noted, no booking clerk could have told Jonah what it was actually going to cost him to get on board. Running away from God is always a costly business.

Jonah "went down," the Holy Spirit said—down to Joppa, down into the ship, down below the decks (3,5). Down! That is the only direction a person who is running away from God can go.

The Jews, who disliked the sea, left seafaring to the Phoenicians. But Jonah was so rebellious that he would rather brave the perils of the sea than go to Nineveh. *If the ship sinks,* Jonah probably thought, *that will put an end to it. I will drown, the sandglass of forty days will run its course, and Nineveh will be overthrown. I will have given my life as a ransom for many in my beloved native land. It would take God more than forty days to catch me.*

Soon Jonah was sound asleep—asleep to his call and commission, asleep to his duty, asleep to the perils that surrounded him. He might not have slept so soundly if he had been able to see through a few inches of planking—if he had seen what was swimming quietly along beneath the keel of the boat and keeping pace with its progress. Today's backslider would not sleep so well if he could see the unpleasant surprises that await him a little farther along the way.

We must not be too hard on Jonah. What would we do if one morning in our quiet time we were reading Ezekiel 38–39 and the Holy Spirit said, "Go to Peking, that great city, and cry against it, 'Yet forty days and China will be overthrown'"? Would you go? Would I? Probably not. Like Jonah, we would probably think that God's judgment on such a godless, ruthless nation was long overdue. Unlike Jonah, we would probably be afraid to go. Faith (misplaced and misdirected), not fear, sent Jonah to Joppa and out to sea.

2. The Pagans Praying (1:4-5)

Once free of the lee of the land, the vessel rose and fell with the swells of the mighty Mediterranean. Soon the coastline of Phoenicia and Philistia were out of sight. Then a howling storm raged over the sea, tossing the ship this way and that. The terrified sailors thought that it would burst apart at the seams.

When Jonah ran away from God, he upset the whole balance of nature. We are distinctly told that the bad weather was a direct result of Jonah's bad behavior. "The Lord," we read, "sent out a great wind into the sea" (1:4). Christ's disciples marveled, "Even the winds and the sea obey him!" but Jonah did not share their awe.

The panic-stricken sailors dumped the cargo and all the spare ropes and sails overboard. As they lightened the ship, they called on their heathen gods, but the wind still shrieked in the rigging and the angry waves still threatened to swamp the helpless ship at any moment. And all this time Jonah slept while the world around him was being torn apart.

C. Jonah's Sudden Realization (1:6-9)

1. Jonah's Shame (1:6)

Some texts in the Bible, as already noted, seem to tower above their surroundings. The preacher can hardly resist the temptation to lift them out of their contexts and use them in all their monumental grandeur to support great truths or causes. John 3:16 is such a text, as are Romans 10:9, Revelation 3:20, and Jonah 1:6.

Jonah 1:6 records the shipmaster's question, "What meanest thou, O sleeper?" What a text for a sleeping church! Today's world is being torn apart by drugs, drink, immorality, apostasy, and the menace of nuclear war—and the church sleeps. False religions and wicked philosophies are making giant strides—and the church sleeps. Abortion, pornography, syndicated crime, sodomy, and dreadful diseases threaten mankind—and the church sleeps. Friends, family, neighbors, and workmates grope in spiritual darkness—and the church sleeps. Two-thirds of the world's people will never hear the gospel—and the church sleeps. What a crime! A soldier caught sleeping on duty in a time of war faces a court martial and possibly death because his sleep placed other men in peril.

Jonah was asleep in the ship and its captain was enraged: "The shipmaster came to him, and said unto him, What meanest thou, O sleeper? arise, call upon thy God, if so be that God will think upon us, that we perish not." No doubt a brawny fist reached forth and hauled Jonah from his bed. For the first time the prophet felt the reel and plunge of the ship, saw the towering waves, and heard the wild screeching of the storm. The realization came home to his heart that his disobedience had imperiled the lives of innocent men.

But how could he call on his God when he had erected a barrier of deliberate disobedience, a disobedience he had no intention of abandoning? Jonah may well have been ashamed that he, a prophet and the only man on board who knew the true and living God, was not on speaking terms with Him. Jonah could hear the voice of God in the howl of the wind.

2. Jonah's Blame (1:7-8)

He was fully to blame for the crisis, but for the moment he stubbornly held his peace. So the sailors hauled Jonah up on deck, surrounded him, and cast lots to find out who was at fault. There

JONAH   144

was something supernatural about the storm. They had no doubt
that someone on board had offended the gods, and they were right.
"The lot fell upon Jonah" (1:7). The sailors eyed him accusingly
and demanded answers to questions. In effect the interrogation
was as follows:
"What is your occupation, stranger?"
"I am a preacher, a prophet of God."
"Where do you come from?"
"From the presence of the Lord. I am running away from God."
"What is your country?"
"I am from the promised land."
"Who are your people?"
"The people of God."
The sailors pumped answers out of him, and his answers terrified
them. Had they asked the questions before setting sail, they would
not have weighed anchor with Jonah on board.

3. Jonah's Claim (1:9)

At last Jonah confessed: "I am an Hebrew; and I fear the Lord, the
God of heaven, which hath made the sea and the dry land." It was
the testimony of a backslider whose sin had imperiled the lives of
those who had received him in their midst in good faith. The worst
kind of company a man can keep is that of a backslidden believer
like Jonah. He was a source of peril to everyone around him.

D. Jonah's Stubborn Resolve (1:10-16)

1. His Decision (1:10-12)

The only honest thing Jonah could have said next was, "Captain,
head back to Joppa or land me at Antioch on the way to Nineveh."
Such a statement would have indicated the prophet's repentance,
and the storm would have ceased. But Jonah had no such thought.
He stood back and let the sailors, even more afraid now than they
were before, struggle vainly against the storm.
"Why hast thou done this?" they demanded (1:10). Pagans
though they were, they knew enough to understand that a person
must not—indeed, cannot—run away from his God. The storm's
supernatural dimension, long suspected and now confirmed by
their scowling passenger, increased their terror. Scripture says,
"Then were the men exceedingly afraid." The original text can also
be rendered, "Then the men feared with a great fear."
Ceasing from their valiant but futile efforts to save the ship, the

sailors again confronted the silent prophet: "What shall we do unto thee, that the sea may be calm unto us?" (1:11) Jonah's answer revealed his determination to die rather than do what God demanded. "Throw me overboard," he said in effect. "It's all my fault."

2. His Doom (1:13-16)

The idea of deliberately throwing a man overboard horrified these pagan mariners almost as much as the storm. They desperately tried to row toward a hospitable shore, but their efforts were in vain. Exhausted, discouraged, and convinced, they soon abandoned the attempt and again surrounded their strange passenger. He was the only man on the ship who seemed to have no fear.

Earlier the captain had urged Jonah to call upon *Elohim*, the God of all creation (translated "God" as in 1:6). Now the sailors prayed to *Jehovah*, the living covenantal God of the Jewish people (translated "LORD" as in 1:10,14). Jonah had said he was fleeing from Jehovah and these desperate men learned fast. "O LORD," they cried, "O LORD." They implored Jonah's covenantal God to absolve them of guilt for what they were about to do.

Then, with their prayer still bantered by the wind, they seized the disobedient prophet and flung him into the sea. The result was miraculous and instantaneous. The sea, which moments before "wrought, and was tempestuous" (1:13), now "ceased from her raging" (1:15). Similarly when Jesus miraculously stilled the storm on the Galilean lake, the wind stopped blowing and the waves died down.

The sailors who threw Jonah overboard were awe-struck. There could be no mistaking the cause and effect. God had reached down from Heaven to erase the wrong impression of Himself that His prophet's misbehavior had created in their minds. "Then the men feared the LORD exceedingly, and offered a sacrifice unto the LORD, and made vows" (1:16).

II. THE WORD WITH GOD (1:17–2:10)

A. Jonah's Dreadful Prison (1:17)

The Holy Spirit assures us that "the Lord had prepared a great fish to swallow up Jonah," a fact that unbelievers have viewed with incredulity. The word translated "prepared" literally means "appointed" or "assigned," so the fish was not specially created for the occasion. In some translations of Matthew 12:40 we are told that a whale swallowed Jonah, but the Greek word rendered "whale," *ketos*, can refer to any large sea monster. The word *cetaceor*, which is related to the word *ketos*, signifies the mammalian order of fish.

Ignorant people have said that a whale could not swallow a man, but a giant sperm whale that certainly could have swallowed a man is exhibited in the Smithsonian Institute in Washington, D.C. Captured off Knight's Key, Florida, in 1912, this whale is forty-five feet long, has a mouth thirty-eight inches wide, and weighs thirty thousand pounds. A fish in its stomach at the time it was captured, weighed about fifteen hundred pounds.

Numerous stories of men being swallowed alive by whales—and surviving the ordeal—have been validated. In February 1891 the crew of the whaling ship *Star of the East* sighted a large sperm whale off the Falkland Islands. They harpooned the whale and in its death throes it swallowed a man named James Bartley. A day and a half later his shipmates, who thought he had drowned—found him unconscious in the whale's belly. Bartley lived to tell about it and his story was published in the newspapers. Describing his sensations as he slid into the innermost part of the whale, he said he could breathe easily, but the heat was unbearable. His whole appearance was changed by the ordeal, for his neck, face, and hands, which had been exposed to the whale's gastric juices, were permanently bleached to a livid whiteness. This story gives us an idea of what Jonah experienced when he was imprisoned in the "great fish."

Jonah was in his prison "three days and three nights" and much debate centers around whether or not he died while he was there. The Lord referred to Jonah's ordeal as a type of His death, burial, and resurrection. In Matthew 12:40 the parallel is exact: "As Jonas was three days and three nights in the whale's belly; so shall the Son of man be three days and three nights in the heart of the earth." A man who was miraculously kept alive for three days and three nights does not seem to be an exact parallel of the Lord, who was dead and buried for three days and three nights. So the likelihood is that Jonah died in the belly of the fish and was miraculously resurrected at the end of the third night. Probably Jonah uttered his prayer just before he lost consciousness. The Hebrew idiom translated "three days" can refer to parts of three days, but the expression translated "three days and three nights" must be taken literally.

B. Jonah's Desperate Prayer (2:1-8)

"Then Jonah prayed," records the Holy Spirit (2:1). On the deck of the storm-tossed ship he had stood stoically, watching the sailors call on their false gods and ignoring the captain's admonition to call on Elohim. And he had calmly contemplated a swift death by drowning. But now, horror of horrors, he had been swallowed alive by some dreadful denizen of the deep. A man would be less than human if he did not pray in a situation like that.

From Jonah's remarkable prayer we learn what he reaped, what he remembered, and what he realized.

1. What Jonah Reaped (2:1-6)

For a little while Jonah was allowed to reap what he had sowed. He had rejoiced at the thought of God's judgment being poured out on Nineveh. Now he found out what it was like to be under God's judgment. General Booth, founder of The Salvation Army, used to say that he wished all his soldiers could be hung over the environs of Hell for an hour so that they, having seen the torments of the damned, might have greater zeal for the salvation of men. God gave Jonah a taste of the horrors of Hell.

Jonah's prayer was evidently written in retrospect. "I cried.... He heard," the prophet recorded (2:2). "Thou hadst cast me into the deep, in the midst of the seas; and the floods compassed me about: all thy billows and thy waves passed over me" (2:3). We can sense *a feeling of horror* in his memories.

The prophet's prayer included a number of quotations from the Psalms. Parallels to Jonah 2 can be found in Psalms 3, 5, 18, 31, 42, 69, 77, 116, and 120. We see in dying Jonah a man whose soul was saturated with the Scriptures. The Lord Jesus also turned to the Psalms in His dying hours. Happy indeed is the person who has stored up the Word of God in his heart, for in the hour of death he has a rich treasury upon which to draw.

"I am cast out of thy sight," Jonah prayed despairingly, but as he hammered at the heart of God with verse after verse of Scripture, he had *a flash of hope.* He clung at once to what he was sure would carry weight with God. Remembering Solomon's prayer at the dedication of the temple, Jonah added, "Yet I will look again toward thy holy temple" (Jonah 2:4). Solomon had prayed:

> What prayer and supplication soever be made by any man, or by all thy people Israel, which shall know every man the plague of his own heart, and spread forth his hands toward this house: Then hear thou in heaven thy dwelling place, and forgive (1 Kings 8:38-39).

Jonah did not know where he was in relation to the temple in Jerusalem, but metaphorically he stretched out his hand toward it and had a sudden surge of hope that he would yet be able to "spread forth his hands" literally in the right direction.

Then he plunged back into the horror of what and where he was—a rebel in the hands of an angry God. He had *a foretaste of Hell:* "The depth closed me round about, the weeds were wrapped about my head. I went down to the bottoms of the mountains; the earth with her bars was about me for ever" (Jonah 2:5-6). That is what Jonah reaped. Having gloated over the nasty medicine that God had bottled for Nineveh, he was forced to take a large dose of it himself.

2. What Jonah Remembered (2:7)

"When my soul fainted within me I remembered the LORD: and my prayer came in unto thee, into thine holy temple." Jonah remembered the name for God that the benighted heathen sailors had so eagerly grasped: *Jehovah,* the God of the covenant, the great ever-present I AM.

"I remembered the LORD," wrote Jonah. God was not far away. He was "a very present help in trouble" (Psalm 46:1). He was with the prophet even in the belly of the whale. Jonah could have added Psalm 139 to his list of Psalms most applicable to his situation.

3. What Jonah Realized (2:8)

Jonah said, "They that observe lying vanities forsake their own mercy." The lying vanity to which he had paid court was his self-will displayed in his refusing the opportunity to be a channel of mercy for Nineveh. Like Solomon, Jonah now wrote "vanity of vanities" over his stubborn rebellion. He had been chasing the wind, and as long as he continued on that course, he was forsaking his own mercy. That is, as long as he was a candidate for God's judgment, what he needed more than anything else was God's mercy.

Now at last Jonah could see where his sinful pride and self-will had brought him, and he repented. At the end of his tether in that dark prison, he repented with his dying breath. He acknowledged his sin. He acknowledged God's justice that had given him just what he had wanted others to receive. He acknowledged that he had no hope other than the salvation over which God had an absolute monopoly. Certainly Jonah could not save himself.

C. Jonah's Dying Promise (2:9-10)

We read of *his surrender* in 2:9: "I will pay that that I have vowed." Jonah had evidently done what so many have done in their extremity: he had made a vow to God. "Lord, get me out of here," he had said in effect, "and I'll do anything you want me to do!" The Lord says to all such people, "Defer not to pay thy vows" (see Ecclesiastes 5:4). To give Jonah his due, he kept his word and paid his vow. He came to the place of surrender and offered thanksgiving, praise, and obedience to the Lord.

We also read of *his salvation.* Dredging up the words of David from somewhere in his reeling, failing mind, Jonah testified, "Salvation is of the Lord" (compare Psalm 3:8 and Jonah 2:9).

III. THE WORD FOR GOD (3:1-10)

A. Revelation (3:1-4)

1. The Prophet (3:1-2)

The fish spewed Jonah on the shore "and the word of the Lord came unto Jonah the second time" (3:1). This time the prophet discovered that the sandglass of forty days—the divine countdown to the day of Nineveh's doom—would begin to run, not from the day *he* received the message, but from the day *Nineveh* received it.

As soon as Jonah recovered, he headed directly toward that great Gentile city. Let's suppose someone struck up a conversation with him as he marched determinedly toward Nineveh. Let's also suppose that that person, having extracted from Jonah the secret of his mission, next asked the resolute prophet, "But aren't you afraid? It might be dangerous."

Jonah surely would have replied: "Dangerous? To go to Nineveh in the will of God? Let me tell you, sir, it is far more dangerous *not* to go to Nineveh. It is far more dangerous to be out of the will of God. Afraid to go? My dear sir, I'm afraid not to go!"

2. The Prophecy (3:3-4)

In due time Jonah arrived at *the place* where the prophecy was to be given. Nineveh was a widespread city for those days—about twenty miles across. The prophet entered the gates and began to make *the proclamation.*

Jonah's message was brief: "Yet forty days, and Nineveh shall be overthrown" (3:4). These eight words formed the shortest of all prophecies. Jonah added no padding or fancy illustrations and made no effort to be diplomatic.

His message was also blunt. The announcement was one of doom and gloom, yet Jonah made no attempt to dilute it. He did not promise alleviation of judgment in the case of national repentance. There was just one resounding threat (probably the only consolation Jonah derived from the whole business).

Jonah's message was blessed too. As a result of his one-man, one-day crusade, a massive revival broke out in the doomed city.

The prophet's most eloquent message was himself. He was a living epistle known and read by all men (see 2 Corinthians 3:2). The people of Nineveh listened to him and looked at him. The effects of his sojourn in the belly of the fish made him a horrifying sight to behold. "God punishes sin," they surely said. "Look at the man. He is livid." But the fact that Jonah was alive at all probably caused them to add, "God pardons sinners."

Jonah spoke with irresistible authority. Having been through death and burial, he was living in the power of resurrection life. He simply held up to Nineveh the ominous sandglass of forty days and preached judgment to come; he offered no glimmer of hope except that which he himself evidenced. God had punished him; God had pardoned him. In that, and that alone, the people of Nineveh saw a gleam of light.

B. Revival (3:5-10)

The Holy Spirit lingered long and lovingly over the effect of Jonah's preaching. There was faith, fasting, and forgiveness in Nineveh.

1. Faith (3:5)

"So the people of Nineveh believed God." After one day's preaching a million people turned to God. This was a genuine evangelical revival. The Ninevites were soundly saved—not just saved from national overthrow, but saved in a spiritual sense. They "believed God."

Paul told us that "the father of all them that believe"—that is, Abraham—"believed God, and it was counted unto him for righteousness" (Romans 4:11,3). If Abraham was saved when he "believed God," why should not the Ninevites have been saved when they "believed God"?

2. Fasting (3:6-9)

From the halls of the rich and powerful to the hovels of the poor and destitute—monarch and mendicant, gifted and retarded, landlord and serf, master and slave—one and all in Nineveh were caught up in an extraordinary fast.

Under the conviction of the Holy Spirit that their crimes and cruelties deserved the doom about to fall, the people of Nineveh cried out to God. The king "arose from his throne, and he laid his robe from him, and covered him with sackcloth, and sat in ashes" (3:6). Then he proclaimed:

> Let neither man nor beast, herd nor flock, taste any thing: let them not feed, nor drink water: But let man and beast be covered with sackcloth, and cry mightily unto God [Elohim]: yea, let them turn every one from his evil way, and from the violence that is in their hands (3:7-8).

What an astonishing demonstration of national repentance!

Several times during the dark days of World War II when Britain stood alone with her back against the wall, I can remember the king calling for a national day of prayer. But he never called for the kind of repentance that the king of Nineveh decreed. Had there been a national repentance, Britain might have remained a world superpower.

Even the animals were affected by Nineveh's fast—further evidence of the genuineness of the city's conversion. What a sight it must have been: bloodthirsty Assyrians covering their livestock with sackcloth and ashes! The inclusion of farm animals in the fast was a proof that a work of righteousness had been wrought in the people, for the Bible says, "A righteous man regardeth the life of his beast" (Proverbs 12:10).

When revival broke out in my homeland of Wales at the turn of the twentieth century, thousands of tough miners were converted. They were so changed by the mighty power of the Holy Spirit that when they returned to the mines to dig coal, they encountered an unexpected obstacle: the pit ponies would not work. Those unfortunate animals, taken down the shafts as young colts, toiled their lives away hauling heavy drams of coal from the seams to the shafts and were accustomed to being abused, kicked, and cursed by the miners. When the transformed men returned rejoicing in their new life in Christ, the ponies were confused. They did not know how to respond to kindness. They were not used to the language of redeemed lips. In a similar way, the repentance of Nineveh reached into barns and fields and affected helpless beasts.

After issuing his decree the king said, "Who can tell if God will turn and repent, and turn away from his fierce anger, that we perish not?" (Jonah 3:9) Again we see a remarkable parallel with Abraham, "who against hope believed in hope" (Romans 4:18).

3. Forgiveness (3:10)

"God saw their works, that they turned from their evil way; and God repented of the evil, that he had said that he would do unto them; and he did it not." Since God is immutable in His nature and will, one might wonder why Jonah wrote that "God repented." The expression is an example of a figure of speech that is common in the Bible. With this literary device human thoughts and feelings are attributed to God. The only way finite human beings can begin to comprehend the infinite is for God to use anthropomorphisms and clothe His person, thoughts, and ways in language suited to our ignorance.

God's sentence against Nineveh was conditional, as Jonah very well knew (see 4:2), although it seems that he did not tell the Ninevites that. God made His pronouncement in accordance with the principle recorded in Jeremiah 18:8: "If that nation, against whom I have pronounced, turn from their evil, I will repent of the evil that I thought to do unto them." God does not change, but He gives warnings so that men will have opportunity to change. His immutable holiness demands that sin be punished; His equally immutable love and justice demand that the repentant sinner be forgiven. This forgiveness was extended to Nineveh.

IV. THE WORD ABOUT GOD (4:1-11)

A. Jonah's Displeasure with God (4:1-9)

In chapter 4 the focus of the story returns to Jonah. We read of his wicked, ungracious reaction to Nineveh's repentance and revival.

1. Jonah and His God (4:1-4)

Jonah was furious because God's judgment did not fall on Nineveh. His reputation as a prophet was ruined—he had foretold imminent doom, and doom had not come. "It displeased Jonah exceedingly, and he was very angry" (4:1). His anger was not the petulant waywardness of a child, but the displeasure of a grown man for what seemed to him to be a good reason. Now that God had spared Nineveh, He could use Nineveh as His instrument to chasten Israel. There was no hint of any kind of national repentance in Israel—much less the kind of widespread repentance that had saved Nineveh.

The indignant prophet complained to God. "I knew it!" he said in effect. "I knew it all the time. That's why I ran away. I told you so right from the start."

Jonah 4:2 is arresting, for it tells us that in his anger and malice, the prophet voiced some of the most wonderful words about God in the Bible: "I knew that thou art a gracious God, and merciful, slow to anger, and of great kindness, and repentest thee of the evil." What a tremendous revelation about God! No heathen nation ever knew a God like Jonah's.

This truth about God, which should set joybells ringing in every human heart, actually filled Jonah with rage. He did not reveal this side of God's character to the Ninevites; they had to discover it for themselves. How terrible was his spiritual condition! How terrible is the spiritual condition of people today who know the truth about God and keep it to themselves! They are actually filled with envy and malice when they see God blessing others—especially those whom they dislike or with whom they disagree.

Jonah was so disgusted with the outcome of his preaching that he asked God to take his life. God, however, was as patient with Jonah as he was with Nineveh. "Doest thou well to be angry?" He asked (4:4). What wonderful proof that God is, as Jonah had just described Him, "gracious . . . and merciful, slow to anger, and of great kindness." A lesser god would have answered Jonah's prayer at once by slaying him on the spot.

2. Jonah and His Gourd (4:5-8)

Sick of the sight of sackcloth, the sullen prophet turned his back on Nineveh and went to the east side of the city. There he made a shack in which to wait for events to unfold. He thought that perhaps the desired judgment might yet fall.

The weather was hot and oppressive as it so often is in eastern lands, so the Lord took pity on the pouting prophet and "prepared a gourd" (4:6), just as He had previously "prepared" the great fish (1:17) and as He would later prepare the worm (4:7) and the "vehement east wind" (4:8). Worm, whale, or wind—all creation is at His command.

The Hebrew word translated "gourd," *kikayon*, occurs only here in the Old Testament. Some scholars think that the plant was the Syrian elkeroa, which is native to the sandy regions of the Middle East. The elkeroa has large leaves and grows to a considerable height in a few days. In any case, the gourd was "prepared" by God and adapted to throw a welcome shade over Jonah's hut. "Jonah was exceeding glad of the gourd" (4:6); literally, "Jonah rejoiced with great rejoicing."

But his contentment was not destined to last. "God prepared a worm when the morning rose the next day, and it smote the gourd that it withered" (4:7). Worse still, "God prepared a vehement east wind." The sultry weather sapped Jonah's strength and patience. "He fainted, and wished in himself to die, and said, It is better for me to die than to live" (4:8).

From Jonah's point of view everything was going wrong. He had been proved a false prophet. Nineveh had been granted a reprieve and that was the worst possible news for Israel. The little shrub that had given him such satisfaction had been killed by a miserable grub, and the enervating east wind had begun to blow.

What a pitiful spectacle Jonah presented. Yet some Christians are like him. They get more upset over a shrub in their garden that succumbs to blight than over the doom of millions of people—including their families and friends—who are heading for a lost eternity.

3. Jonah and His Grudge (4:9)

"God said to Jonah, Doest thou well to be angry for the gourd?" Something was wrong with his sense of values, for he replied, "I do well to be angry, even unto death."

In an Old Testament sense, Jonah was like the unmerciful servant in the Lord's parable. "O thou wicked servant," his master said, "I forgave thee all that debt, because thou desiredst me: Shouldest not thou also have had compassion on thy fellowservant, even as I had pity on thee?" (Matthew 18:32-33) Jonah was also like the prodigal son's elder brother. "As he came and drew nigh to the house, he heard musick and dancing....And he was angry, and

would not go in: therefore came his father out, and intreated him"
(Luke 15:25-28).

B. Jonah's Discovery about God (4:10-11)

The Lord's last word to His rebellious servant contained an
appeal and an application:

> Thou hast had pity on the gourd, for the which thou hast not
> laboured, neither madest it grow; which came up in a night,
> and perished in a night: And should not I spare Nineveh, that
> great city, wherein are more than sixscore thousand persons
> that cannot discern between their right hand and their left
> hand; and also much cattle?

Thus Jonah was suddenly silenced in the presence of God. Like
the elder brother in the Lord's parable, Jonah was hearing God's
voice, but his heart was not yet changed. We can only infer the rest
of the story.

Perhaps Jonah turned his back on his hut and the dead gourd,
cast one last look of dislike at Nineveh, picked up his staff, and
headed for home. But by the time he had crossed the Jabbok and
spent the night at Peniel, he—like the pilgrim Jacob—was ready to
go forward with God. He would pay his vow to the last penny.

We can picture Jonah arriving home and the men of Gath-
hepher congregating around him. We can hear them saying, "What
happened, Jonah? Why is your face so marred?" We can also hear
his reply:

> The word of the Lord came unto Jonah the son of Amittai,
> saying, Arise, go to Nineveh, that great city, and cry against it;
> for their wickedness is come up before me. But Jonah rose up
> to flee unto Tarshish from the presence of the Lord (1:1-3).

Jonah told the whole story, keeping nothing back, not even his
disgraceful behavior. Then he wrote it all down.

And so at last Jonah became a living epistle to his own unrepentant people, whose obduracy in rebellion against God was as
persistent and stubborn as his own.

Chapter 6

MICAH

A TALE OF TWO CITIES

I. THE PROPHECY OF RETRIBUTION (1:1–3:12)
  A. The Calamity (1:1-16)
    1. The Coming Forth of Jehovah (1:1-2)
    2. The Coming Focus of Judgment (1:3-16)
      a. The Salient Points of Focus (1:3-9)
        (1) The Sin of Samaria Was Spiritual (1:3-8)
        (2) The Sin of Samaria Was Spreading (1:9)
      b. The Subsidiary Points of Focus (1:10-16)
        (1) The Advancing Foe (1:10-15)
        (2) The Advertised Woe (1:16)
  B. The Cause (2:1–3:12)
    1. The People (2:1-13)
      a. The Robbers (2:1-5)
      b. The Revilers (2:6-7)
      c. The Resisters (2:8-9)
      d. The Repudiators (2:10-11)
      e. The Remnant (2:12-13)
    2. The Princes (3:1-4)
    3. The Prophets (3:5-12)
      a. The Lying Prophets (3:5-7)
      b. The Lord's Prophet (3:8-12)
        (1) His Claim (3:8)
        (2) His Courage (3:9-12)
II. THE PROMISE OF RESTORATION (4:1–5:15)
  A. Restoration Depicted (4:1-8)
    1. Exaltation of the Kingdom (4:1)
    2. Extent of the Kingdom (4:2)

3. Excellence of the Kingdom (4:3-5)
4. Exiles of the Kingdom (4:6-8)
  a. Restored in Weakness (4:6)
  b. Ruling in Power (4:7-8)
B. Restoration Delayed (4:9–5:6)
  1. The Times of Israel's Misery (4:9-13)
    a. The Babylonian Empire (4:9-10)
    b. The Beast's Empire (4:11-13)
  2. The Times of Israel's Messiah (5:1-6)
    a. The Insult (5:1)
    b. The Incarnation (5:2)
    c. The Interval (5:3)
    d. The Investiture (5:4-6)
C. Restoration Described (5:7-15)
  1. The Remnant (5:7-8)
  2. The Recovery (5:9)
  3. The Revival (5:10-14)
  4. The Revenge (5:15)
III. THE PLEA FOR REPENTANCE (6:1–7:20)
A. Israel's Sins (6:1-16)
  1. The Lord's Controversy with Israel (6:1-8)
    a. The Word of the Lord
      As Declared on the Hills (6:1-2)
    b. The Warmth of the Lord
      As Displayed to the Hebrews (6:3-4)
    c. The Will of the Lord
      As Discerned by the Heathen (6:5-8)
  2. The Lord's Condemnation of Israel (6:9-16)
    a. Sin's Deceptions (6:9-12)
    b. Sin's Disappointments (6:13-15)
    c. Sin's Distortions (6:16)
B. Israel's Sorrows (7:1-6)
  1. Blight (7:1-3a)
  2. Bribery (7:3b-4)
  3. Betrayal (7:5-6)
C. Israel's Savior (7:7-20)
  1. Israel's Forgiveness (7:7-11)

a. Revival (7:7-10)
b. Restoration (7:11)
2. Israel's Foes (7:12-17)
3. Israel's Future (7:18-20)

R evival rarely outlasts a generation and thus there is poetic significance in the fact that Micah follows Jonah. As the echoes of the book of Jonah die away, the Ninevites are in sackcloth and ashes, humbling themselves under the mighty hand of God. But by the time Micah writes his prophecy, the Assyrians have gone back to their warlike, wicked ways and the king of the north is on the march. The doom of Israel, suspected and feared by Jonah, is approaching. The Assyrian troops are about to terrorize the land with their atrocities.

For a hundred years the entire Middle East trembled before Assyria. Tiglath-pileser III meddled constantly in Judeo-Ephraimitic affairs, especially after Ahaz bribed him for help. The Assyrians besieged Samaria and captured it, thus terminating the kingdom of Israel. They also besieged Jerusalem and carried Manasseh into captivity, where he languished for at least a year. Nineveh had thrown off its sackcloth and ashes to become the tyrant and terror of the world.

When Micah picked up his pen, Samaria's doom was assured. Nor could godly King Hezekiah sufficiently stem the tide of apostasy in Judah to save his land entirely from the savagery of Assyrian invasion.

Micah was a younger contemporary of the great prophet Isaiah. While Isaiah was a courtier, Micah was a countryman. We know nothing about him except that he was a Morasthite and that he prophesied during the reigns of Jotham, Ahaz, and Hezekiah.

Micah was primarily a prophet to Judah, although Samaria fell briefly within his line of vision. He indicated that Samaria's doom was inescapable because "her wound [was] incurable" (1:9)—and her doom came, just as Micah had predicted. After his pronouncement about Samaria he concentrated on Judah. (He did not mention any kings of Israel; only the prophets who prophesied *in* the northern kingdom mentioned her kings.)

It was just a day's journey from Micah's hometown to Jerusalem, so he was aware of the sins of the capital as well as the sins of the countryside. Everywhere he looked he saw the sins of his people calling down inevitable judgment. Micah saw a godly descendant of David, aided and encouraged by Isaiah, fighting a losing battle against entrenched injustice, apostasy, and wickedness in high places. Micah could see that Judah, as surely as Israel, would come under God's lash, but his vision was not restricted to imminent retribution. In the dim and distant future he saw hope. Ruin was on the way, but so was redemption and the reign of a coming King.

In spite of King Hezekiah's efforts to reform the religious life of Judah, idolatry survived; it was the root of all the evil flourishing in the land. The nation's leaders remained proud, unscrupulous, and cruel. They were addicted to luxury and careless of the civil rights of the common people. Practical unbelief coexisted with the outward worship of Jehovah. Organized hostility to God's prophets was emerging. False prophets began to exert a disastrous influence, a trend that came to a head a century later in the days of Jeremiah. Micah himself suffered at the hands of the false prophets.

The prophecies of Micah were not readily accepted by many of his contemporaries, but later they were quoted as authoritative (Jeremiah 26:17-19). He began where he was—in a nation ripening fast for judgment. His themes were retribution, restoration, and repentance.

I. THE PROPHECY OF RETRIBUTION (1:1–3:12)

A. The Calamity (1:1-16)

1. The Coming Forth of Jehovah (1:1-2)

"The word of the Lord that came to Micah the Morasthite in the days of Jotham, Ahaz, and Hezekiah" (1:1).

The name *Micah* means "Who is like Jehovah?" The answer of course is that God stands alone. Between Him and the highest archangel of glory "there is a great gulf fixed" (Luke 16:26), a vast chasm that separates even the most exalted creature from the Creator.

Micah described himself simply as "the Morasthite"—that is, an inhabitant of Moresheth-gath, which some scholars think was a suburb of Gath. Moresheth was located in the plain between Judea and Philistia. Full of corn and cattle, the land was fair and lovely, with larks rising skyward and bees humming amid flowers. It was a place for big men, not big cities. It was far enough away from Jerusalem not to be too subservient to its ways and whims. The inhabitants of the plain loved the land and, because of hostile neighbors, were ever watchful.

Moresheth stood near the valley mouth that was the gateway to Egypt. There roads converged, travelers passed, and battles were fought. There Asia defeated Egypt, and there Vespasian (A.D. 67) and Saladin (A.D. 1187) camped as they prepared to attack Jerusalem. From his home Micah must have seen emissaries hurrying from the Jerusalem court to Egypt and rushing back with the empty promise that in the event of war with Assyria, Judah could count on Egypt.

Under Jotham, luxury reigned. His great ambition was to build palaces in Jerusalem and make the city impregnable. The fact that he accomplished his goals at the expense of the poor peasants did not concern him at all. Under Ahaz and his senseless foreign policy, Judah was forced to pay tribute to Assyria. Under Hezekiah, Jerusalem became a cauldron of intrigue. Some factions favored an alliance with Egypt; other factions advised abject submission to Assyria. Injustice was rampant and lust for money and power sapped the last vestiges of spiritual and moral values. Godly King Hezekiah could not stem the tide.

Into the midst of this scene of national chaos and confusion, Jehovah came forth. Or as Micah put it when he claimed divine inspiration for his prophecy, "The word of the Lord...came to Micah."

2. The Coming Focus of Judgment (1:3-16)

a. The Salient Points of Focus (1:3-9)

Micah first focused on Samaria and the northern kingdom of Israel, which had been founded on rebellion and apostasy and had never done anything but provoke God on high.

(1) The Sin of Samaria Was Spiritual (1:3-8)

Micah could hear the tread of terrible feet. What he heard was the Lord marching down the starways of the sky—coming out of eternity into time, coming from Heaven to earth, "trampling out the vintage where the grapes of wrath are stored."[1]

Micah could see the Lord's feet trampling "the high places of the earth" (1:3) where pride sat in the saddle. The "high places" in Israel and Judah were scenes of sin. There apostate people built groves, erected vile sex symbols and idols, and indulged in the

Canaanites' foul forms of worship (1 Kings 12:31; 14:23; Ezekiel 6:6). These evils even flourished in Jerusalem, especially toward the end (Jeremiah 32:35). Micah could see, beneath the tread of the Lord's holy feet, mountains melting and valleys splitting wide "as wax before the fire, and as the waters that are poured down a steep place" (Micah 1:4).

Micah could also hear the echo of that tread: the sound of the feet of marching men. The Assyrian legions were on the way. Micah's poetry was prophetic.

"What is the transgression of Jacob?" Micah asked. "Is it not Samaria?" A veritable spiritual cancer, Samaria was spreading its corruption and death throughout the whole body politic of the promised land. Even Jerusalem was infected. During the reign of Ahaz, the brazen altar of the temple was rudely pushed aside to make room for a new altar copied from a pagan Assyrian altar that Ahaz had admired in Damascus. That is how deeply the idolatries of Samaria had penetrated into Judah.

But for the moment Micah's prime concern was Samaria. The Assyrians would soon make short work of the city and its shrines. The wealth, luxury, and idolatry associated with Samaria would be swept away. "She gathered it of the hire of an harlot, and they shall return to the hire of an harlot" (1:7). That was true in a very literal sense, for worship associated with groves and high places centered around prostitution, as does much of Hinduism to this day. Young girls were taken into the temple and consecrated to a life of participation in immoral idolatrous rites. Liaison with one of these harlots consummated an act of worship.

Micah's statement about the harlot was true in another sense as well. Throughout the Bible, when God's people went after false gods, they were said to be involved in spiritual whoredom. Samaria had become the capital of that kind of apostasy.

Soon the harlot city would be robbed. Its temples and shrines, dedicated to spiritual harlotry, would be handed over to an even more notorious religious harlot.

Gazing northward, Micah could see, in his mind's eye, Samaria after the Assyrians had destroyed it. He could hear jackals ("dragons") howling over the haunted ruins (1:8). The sound was like the cry of an infant or the wail of a lost soul. The ostriches ("owls") were the image of bereavement, for they had a habit of forgetting their own eggs.

Let those who would turn our country toward the pursuit of false gods ponder well the sin of Samaria and the tramp of God's mighty feet.

(2) The Sin of Samaria Was Spreading (1:9)

"Her wound is incurable; for it is come unto Judah; he is come unto the gate of my people, even to Jerusalem."

Micah wrote the northern kingdom off. Because the prophets Hosea and Amos had been spurned and Israel's cancer had become inoperable, Micah became more concerned with Judah. The cancer had spread to Judah and Jerusalem, but the situation there was not hopeless yet. Surgery might effect a cure. Micah could see the great physician taking the sharp scalpel of Assyria and cutting away at Judah, right to the gates of Jerusalem. And in the days of Hezekiah, Assyrian armies did indeed ravage most of Judah and appear before the walls of Jerusalem. Micah's friend Isaiah, who lived in Jerusalem, described what happened in Isaiah 36–37.

b. The Subsidiary Points of Focus (1:10-16)

(1) The Advancing Foe (1:10-15)

Micah turned his attention to his native land, particularly a cluster of towns and villages that he had known since his boyhood days—including his own hometown. As each town came into focus, the Spirit of God enabled him to see it in the light of prophecy. Micah made puns out of the names of the towns, and each pun was a pungent prophecy.

Gath, Acco, Aphrah, Saphir, Zaanan, Beth-ezel, Maroth, Jerusalem, Lachish, Moresheth-gath, Achzib, Mareshah, and Adullam are just dull names to us. But these Hebrew names are alive with meaning to those who have the skill to understand the puns. Like thunder rolling across the Judean hills and plains, the names are ominous with doom. And just as Micah began his list with towns in the far west and moved steadily inland toward the capital, the storm of judgment moved on relentlessly. The prophecies embodied in the names can be summarized as follows:

- Baseness seen
    - (1:10a)   Baseness beyond telling
        Gath: "Tell it not in Tell-town."
    - (1:10b)   Baseness beyond tears
        Instead of the phrase "at all," some scholars render the original Hebrew *bakko* or *be-akko* as *Acco:* "Weep not in Weep-town."
- Brokenness seen
    - (1:10c)   *Aphrah:* "Roll in dust at Dust-town."

- Blight seen
  (1:11a)   *Saphir:* "beauty shamed at Beauty-town"
- Bondage seen
  (1:11b)   No more freedom
            Zaanan: "no going out from Out-town"
  (1:11c)   No more friends
            Beth-ezel: "no neighborliness at Neighbor-town"
- Bitterness seen
  (1:12a)   *Maroth:* "bitter tears at Bitter-town"
- Battle seen
  (1:12b)   Peace gone
            Jerusalem: "no peace at Peace-town"
  (1:13)   Power gone
            Lachish: "horsepower gone from Horse-town"
- Betrayal seen
  (1:14)   *Achzib:* "Falsehood reigns at False-town."
- Bankruptcy seen
  (1:15a)   *Mareshah:* "no possessions left at Possession-town"
            The Assyrians had been appointed by God to
            possess the land.
  (1:15b)   *Adullam:* "no testimony in Testimony-town"
            The nobility would flee to the well-known nearby
            cave, as David had done (1 Samuel 22:1).

These names, a vocabulary of human misery, spoke of all that
goes with war and the siege and sack of cities, and told of a nation
reaping the due reward of its deeds.

Micah could see the Assyrians triumphing over the backslidden
people of God, even in Judah. He certainly chose an original way to
describe the advancing foe, but there was more to his words than
pun and poetry. There was prophecy. When he stood on the roof
of his home and poured forth words of woe on every town in sight,
he did not curse in vain. Sennacherib (like other conquerors from
Vespasian to Saladin) shunned the expected northern approach to
Jerusalem and deployed his troops where those towns stood.

(2) The Advertised Woe (1:16)

"Make thee bald, and poll thee for thy delicate children; enlarge
thy baldness as the eagle; for they are gone into captivity from thee."
With these words Micah advertised the terrible doom that overshadowed the land. When other foes came, they despoiled, destroyed, and departed. But when the Assyrians came to conquer a

country, they deported entire populations. Now Judah might well adopt the customary heraldry of mourning—that is, the shaved head. In fact they should enlarge the bald spot so that it would be commensurate with the dimensions of the coming disaster.

B. The Cause (2:1–3:12)

1. The People (2:1-13)

Having pointed out national apostasy, Micah turned to the subject of national immorality. He called attention to social sins, the flagrant violations of justice that were so prevalent and that made such a mockery of the civil rights guaranteed under the Mosaic law.

a. The Robbers (2:1-5)

Among the people bringing on the calamity were those who at night lay awake making plans to do wickedness and in the morning bounded from their beds to execute those plans. No one had the power to stop them. Micah knew of such men. He knew men who coveted fields and houses, schemed to get the property by fair means or by foul, and succeeded in their nefarious enterprises.

While Isaiah was concerned about the corrupt politics of the capital, Micah was concerned about the social wrongs of the province. He knew avaricious landlords and oppressed peasants. He knew men like Ahab, who coveted Naboth's vineyard. He knew men who used the same oppressive, highhanded methods that Ahab and Jezebel used to rob the helpless of their heritage.

Anyone who studies the minor prophets must be impressed by God's hatred of social injustice and crime. Many of God's laws are designed to protect the poor, and Micah was quick to threaten His judgment on people who scorned those laws.

b. The Revilers (2:6-7)

There was an immediate reaction against Micah's prophecy of divine retribution. People in places of influence denounced him as a prating meddler and accused him of talking nonsense. Wrapped in their insular power and pride, they confidently believed that "it can't happen here." After all, they were of the house of Jacob. Their boast was that they were called Israel.

In a later age John the Baptist denounced the same spirit: "Think not to say within yourselves, We have Abraham to our father" (Matthew 3:9; also see John 8:39-40). John's point of course was that the boast was empty. Those who relied on their heritage as Abraham's children had long since ceased to be his children in spirit.

Likewise in contemporary society people imagine that because they mouth certain slogans or because they are heirs to the Judeo-Christian ethic, they are strong, when in fact their strength has been eroded by their departure from the spirit of the slogans and ethic. Prophets who expose the fallacy of such fond illusions are never popular.

c. The Resisters (2:8-9)

Micah turned on his critics and said in effect, "You are the foes of my people." Speaking as the voice of God, he accused them of beggaring folks and violently stripping off the coats and undergarments of peaceable citizens when they were off their guard. By oppressing the people, those in authority were actually declaring war on God. Particularly provocative to Him was the unscrupulous greed that resulted in women and children being thrown out of their homes.

d. The Repudiators (2:10-11)

Micah saw rich men twisting the law to suit themselves and quieting their consciences by relying on the words of hireling prophets who opposed him. These false prophets were telling the oppressors what they wanted to hear: namely, that God would not punish their wicked behavior.

Micah sarcastically referred to the lifestyle of these lying prophets in 2:11. The King James translation reads, "If a man walking in the spirit and falsehood do lie, saying, I will prophesy unto thee of wine and of strong drink; he shall even be the prophet of this people." The Revised Standard Version reads, "If a man should go about and utter wind and lies, saying, 'I will preach to you of wine and strong drink,' he would be the preacher for this people." These prophets, whose words were of the same value as a drunkard's babbling, were just what the wicked scorners of God's true messenger deserved.

e. The Remnant (2:12-13)

There was a godly remnant in Judah and the most prominent spokesman of this believing minority was King Hezekiah.

Contemplation of this remnant encouraged Micah to switch suddenly to a promise for the future. His vision leaped over the ages and he saw the end-time blessing of a regathered remnant of both Israel and Judah. Micah, who was fond of pastoral imagery, saw this remnant as "the sheep of Bozrah" (2:12), a district noted for its rich pasturelands (2 Kings 3:4). He heard the noise of a large crowd of people and saw, going before them, "the breaker" (2:13). The Messiah is the One who clears the way. Just as He marched ahead of His people when they came out of Egypt into the promised land, so He will march ahead of them in a coming day. He will clear out of their way the beast, the false prophet, and the massed armies of the world.

2. The Princes (3:1-4)

In his stirring book, *A Tale of Two Cities,* Charles Dickens described in many graphic passages the plight of poor Parisians on the eve of the French revolution. He also told of the wealth and extravagance of the idle rich, who had little or no pity for the poor. Some historians allege that when the queen heard how the poor begged for bread, she was astonished. "They cannot get bread?" she said. "Then let them eat cake!"

Conditions were the same in Russia at the time of the Bolshevik revolution. The czar and his court lived in a world of dance and daydream. The queen dallied with the mad monk Rasputin. As in Paris, the poor demonstrated in the streets and were shot down. The communists took terrible revenge when they had the fallen royal family in their power.

As for Micah, "pinched peasant faces peer between all his words."[2] He turned his angry gaze toward the capital where the "heads of Jacob" and the "princes of the house of Israel" (3:1) lived in the lap of luxury, on money sweat out of the poor. The prophet compared the princes to a cook who had a chicken in his hand. With deft fingers accustomed to the task, the cook stripped off the skin. Then with a sharp knife he cut off the edible meat. Not wanting to waste anything, he chopped up the bones and put them in the pot. Like ancient Shylocks, the princes wanted their full pound of flesh. They fleeced the poor and, scraping them to the bone, stripped away everything they had.

Micah could see that the scales of divine justice were already being tilted to redress these wrongs. He warned that retribution was on the way: "Then shall they cry unto the Lord, but he will not hear them" (3:4).

As in Micah's day, social injustice is now evident worldwide. The fabulously rich live in luxury by paying their employees minimal wages. In many countries sweatshops still grind the heart out of the masses. The gulf between the rich and the poor in much of the Third World has to be seen to be believed. No wonder communism sounds attractive to the poor (although it is deceptive and oppressive in practice).

3. The Prophets (3:5-12)

a. The Lying Prophets (3:5-7)

Wicked men can usually find a religion that will accommodate their sins. In Micah's day false prophets were willing to say whatever their patrons wanted to hear—as long as there was adequate remuneration. The establishment wanted to hear "Peace" (3:5), so the prophets said "Peace" even though Assyria, the superpower to the north, was eyeing Judah. These lying prophets have a legion of heirs in the world today.

They "bite with their teeth," wrote Micah. The word translated "bite" was generally used to describe the bite of a poisonous snake, so Micah was saying that the false prophets were as treacherous as serpents. What came out of their mouths was deadly poison.

As a result of listening to their lies, the land would face unrelieved darkness. Micah could see the approaching darkness and the prophets themselves groping blindly in it. The people who had been so fond of them would turn at last in utter desperation to God. But there would be "no answer of God" (3:7). There would be nothing but a terrible silence. God would ignore those who for so long had ignored and insulted Him.

b. The Lord's Prophet (3:8-12)

(1) His Claim (3:8)

The lying prophets had enjoyed the backing of rich, powerful men, but Micah was more than a match for them. He had the backing of God. "Truly I am full of power by the spirit of the Lord...to declare unto Jacob his transgression," he said.

John Knox was also "full of power." In Scotland during the days of Mary, Queen of Scots, he took a stand against the corruption of the age and the false faith supported by the queen. Powerful factions opposed him; persecution and arrest were his lot. But he braved the storm so boldly that the queen was forced to confess that she was more afraid of John Knox than all the armies of England.

(2) His Courage (3:9-12)

Micah boldly addressed the powerful men who were running the country: "Hear this, I pray you, ye heads of the house of Jacob...that abhor judgment, and pervert all equity" (3:9).

It is evident that Hezekiah, in spite of his herculean efforts to reform the nation's religion and morals, simply did not have the power to restrain the rich. The whole upper crust of society— nobles, princes, priests, and prophets—were mercenary. Corrupt judges had itchy palms ever open to receive bribes. Venal rulers were erecting lavish buildings in Jerusalem. What were they doing? According to Micah 3:10 they were building up Zion with blood.

The country was clearly in a deplorable state. Its leaders would not hear a case if they did not receive an adequate bribe. The priests refused to perform their religious function unless they were properly paid. The prophets would say whatever was expected of them, as long as they were suitably rewarded—and they backed up their lies by claiming to be divinely inspired. "None evil can come upon us," they claimed (3:11).

Micah, who could hear the marching of enemy troops, contradicted such false assurances. He was the first prophet to threaten Jerusalem with destruction: "Therefore shall Zion for your sake be plowed as a field, and Jerusalem shall become heaps, and the mountain of the house [the temple] as the high places of the forest [a jungle]" (3:12). Micah could see beyond Assyria to Babylon, and beyond Babylon to Rome.

II. THE PROMISE OF RESTORATION (4:1–5:15)

A. Restoration Depicted (4:1-8)

The first three verses of Micah 4 are practically identical to Isaiah 2:2-4. Did Isaiah quote from Micah? Or did Micah quote from Isaiah? Did both quote from a common earlier source? Or did the Holy Spirit inspire both men to give the same message? No one can resolve this question. God is sovereign and supreme and can repeat Himself if He so desires.

"The last days" (4:1) is the theme of the second section of Micah's prophecy. The pendulum has swung from predictions of impending doom to previews of the Messianic age.

1. Exaltation of the Kingdom (4:1)

"In the last days it shall come to pass, that the mountain of the house of the Lord shall be established in the top of the mountains, and it shall be exalted above the hills; and people shall flow unto it." Since Zechariah 14:9-10 and Ezekiel 47:1-12 confirm that there will be physical changes in the topography of Jerusalem, it is likely that Micah 4:1 refers to a change in the elevation of mount Moriah. However, the verse may also have spiritual, moral, and political implications, for Jerusalem will become the capital of the world and will be exalted above all nations.

2. Extent of the Kingdom (4:2)

Here we see the future nations of the earth making pilgrimages to the temple. They are saying, "He will teach us of his ways," and are promising, "We will walk in his paths." They will go to the holy city because "the law shall go forth of Zion"; that is, Jerusalem will be the legislative capital of the world.

An omniscient, absolutely righteous King will govern an empire stretching from pole to pole and from sea to sea. In that kingdom there will be no bribery or corruption, no inequitable laws, no heavy-handed or uneven administration of the laws. There will be universal peace, prosperity, and progress. No wonder the nations will flock to Jerusalem to see the beautiful, benevolent capital and its all-glorious King!

3. Excellence of the Kingdom (4:3-5)

The Lord's arm will reach to the remotest lands to enforce obedience to His laws. There will be no more war and all nations will be disarmed. Factories, built for the manufacture of military hardware, will be used for the production of consumer goods. Wrote Micah, "They shall beat their swords into plowshares, and their spears into pruninghooks: nation shall not lift up a sword against nation, neither shall they learn war any more" (4:3).

"They shall sit," the prophet continued, "every man under his vine and under his fig tree; and none shall make them afraid" (4:4). Both the vine and the fig tree form natural arbors, so the picture painted by Micah is one of security and prosperity. The communist vision—"to each according to his need; from each according to his ability"—will become a reality, not because an atheistic socialistic regime will be imposed on mankind, but because Jesus will reign and impose absolute economic equity on mankind. In the coming millennial age there will be perfectly equitable distribution of the world's wealth. The guarantee is that "the mouth of the Lord of hosts hath spoken it."

4. Exiles of the Kingdom (4:6-8)

Today the majority of Jews live outside the land of Israel. Some are prisoners of repressive regimes. Others are voluntary exiles, living in lands of freedom and opportunity. Micah could see the expatriated Jews restored in weakness and ruling in power.

a. Restored in Weakness (4:6)

Micah described the end-time Jews as lame, "driven out," and afflicted. They will be hated by all men. Indeed they already are hated by most people, even in lands where they are rich and influential.

b. Ruling in Power (4:7-8)

Micah went on to say that Israel will become "a strong nation." She will be invincible and no country will dare attack her. "The Lord shall reign over them in mount Zion from henceforth, even for ever" (4:7).

The "tower of the flock" in Micah 4:8 probably refers to Migdal-eder, the tower of Edar in Genesis 35:21. This tower was near Bethlehem, where David was raised. "The strong hold [Ophel] of the daughter of Zion" refers to the citadel where David reigned. By these references Micah was indicating that he anticipated the complete restoration of David and Solomon's empire.

B. Restoration Delayed (4:9–5:6)

1. The Times of Israel's Misery (4:9-13)

The vision of a gloriously restored and ruling Israel faded from Micah's view. In its place the mists rolled in. Through them he could discern present and future troubles for the nation. Alas, he saw the people of God—both in his day and in the last days—as not fit to govern themselves, much less the world. The present troubles would be brought to a head in the days of the Babylonian empire.

a. The Babylonian Empire (4:9-10)

Disaster did not fall until a century after Micah. Indeed in his day the idea of a Babylonian empire was remote, even ridiculed, because Assyria was at the zenith of its power and pride and ruled the world. But Micah's inspired vision was unerring.

He saw an empty throne and asked, "Why dost thou cry out aloud? is there no king in thee? is thy counsellor perished?" (4:9) Instead of a king and a counselor, he saw an anguished throng. "Be in pain, and labour to bring forth, O daughter of Zion, like a woman in travail," he told them, "for now shalt thou go forth out of the city...even to Babylon" (4:10). Boldly, in the face of all outward appearances, with unerring accuracy, Micah wrote down the word "Babylon."

That word conjured up thoughts of an unexpected thrill: "There shalt thou be delivered; there the Lord shall redeem thee from the hand of thine enemies." And the prophecy came to pass. Persistent, prevalent idolatry brought about Judah's downfall, but in Babylon, the ancestral home of idolatry, the Jews were forever cured of it. When the Babylonian captivity ended and the Hebrew people came back to the promised land, they were devoted to the Scriptures and looking for the Messiah.

b. The Beast's Empire (4:11-13)

Through the mists of time, the prophet saw the terrible days that would immediately precede the establishment of the Messianic kingdom. The Jews would fall into worse sins than idolatry and would have to endure a longer and more universal exile culminating in a condition of great peril. So Micah wrote about Israel in the days of the beast's empire: "Now also many nations are gathered against thee, that say, Let her be defiled" (4:11).

Antisemitism—hatred of the Jews—is endemic in all Gentile societies. From time to time the hatred becomes epidemic and the world witnesses a holocaust. The Jews have never been able to extinguish the fires of this universal hatred. It is part of the curse they pronounced on themselves in Pilate's judgment hall (Matthew 27:25).

Animosity toward the Jews and the reborn state of Israel rages throughout the Arab and Muslim worlds. This hatred is virulent and will one day bring Russia and her allies pouring across the frontiers of Israel (Ezekiel 38–39). The mantle of antisemitism will be worn by the antichrist, the one the Apocalypse calls "the beast."

He will gather all nations against Jerusalem, as Micah foresaw. (For more details see Joel 3 and Zechariah 12:8-9.)

One of the objectives of the antisemitic nations at the end of the age will be to defile Zion. They will want to pollute the land of Israel and slaughter its Jewish population, but they will be allowed to go only so far. "They know not the thoughts of the Lord," wrote Micah, "neither understand they his counsel: for he shall gather them as the sheaves into the floor. Arise and thresh, O daughter of Zion" (4:12-13).

The world's rulers will think that they are in control. Under the leadership of the antichrist they will set out to exterminate the Jews once and for all. Their aim will be to stamp out the lingering embers of the Judeo-Christian ethic. But Psalm 2:4 describes their failure: "He that sitteth in the heavens shall laugh: the Lord shall have them in derision." The Lord will bring the antisemitic world powers together to war against Israel so that through the power of the returning Christ, the Jews will triumph at last over all their foes. The nations think that they will thresh Israel, but Israel will thresh them.

2. The Times of Israel's Messiah (5:1-6)

a. The Insult (5:1)

Shifting his prophetic focus back to the downfall of Jerusalem at the hands of the Babylonians during the reign of King Zedekiah, Micah wrote: "Gather thyself in troops, O daughter of troops: he hath laid siege against us: they shall smite the judge of Israel with a rod upon the cheek." No greater insult could be offered to an oriental monarch than to smite him on the cheek. In the smiting of Zedekiah, Israel would be made to feel the burning shame to which her sins had brought her.

b. The Incarnation (5:2)

Again shifting his focus, Micah wrote, "But thou, Beth-lehem Ephratah, though thou be little among the thousands of Judah, yet out of thee shall he come forth unto me that is to be ruler in Israel; whose goings forth have been from of old, from everlasting." Whereas Isaiah 7:14 foretells the virgin birth of Christ, Micah 5:2 foretells the place where He would be born.

Bethlehem is about half a dozen miles southwest of Jerusalem. The name *Bethlehem* means "house of bread"; the name *Ephratah* means "fruitful." There David had been born and there Jesus would be born. Although Bethlehem was only a small place of little account, it would become world famous. It would assume an importance out of proportion to its size. In this little town the uncreated, self-existing second person of the godhead would step out of eternity into time and be incarnated as a child of Adam's race.

Many cities of the world, even in Israel, were more imposing and more influential than Bethlehem, but it was there that God would be manifested in flesh. There He would become a baby and be cradled in the hay. When God chose to become a man, He did not choose to be born in Athens, Alexandria, Babylon, Rome, London, Paris, or Washington, D.C.; He chose to be born in Bethlehem. Micah was the first person to realize this fascinating fact, and against all odds, he wrote it down.

c. The Interval (5:3)

"Therefore will he give them up, until the time that she which travaileth hath brought forth." In this verse Micah was saying that there was to be an interval between his time and the time of the incarnation. During that span Judah would lose its sovereignty. And so it did. First the Babylonians held the country, then the Persians, then the Greeks. Then it became a political football, kicked to and fro in the power struggles of Syria and Egypt. Finally the Romans came.

The house of David fell on evil times. The capital city of Jerusalem, where an Idumean usurper named Herod reigned, was no place for the Messiah's birth. Instead he was born in Bethlehem, the insignificant city of royal David's birth.

The woman Micah could see travailing in birth symbolized in a general sense the nation of Israel. In a more pointed and personal sense the woman symbolized the virgin Mary. In the interval foretold by Micah, the royal family of David would shrink in importance until it was represented by a peasant girl and a Nazarene carpenter.

d. The Investiture (5:4-6)

These verses evidently refer to the second coming of Christ. Having gone to Calvary as the great Shepherd of the sheep, He will retain His shepherd character when He returns. While the sheep was always slain for the shepherd in the Old Testament, in the New

Testament the Shepherd was slain for the sheep. As the hymn writer put it:

> When blood from a victim must flow,
> This Shepherd, by pity, was led
> To stand between us and the foe,
> And willingly died in our stead.[3]

And Jesus will reign as a shepherd. God's ideal Old Testament king was David, the shepherd king. In the Hebrew Scriptures the whole idea of kingship is wrapped up in the idea of a shepherd—one who pastors, protects, and provides. In Psalm 22 we see the suffering Shepherd, in Psalm 23 we see the sustaining Shepherd, and in Psalm 24 we see the sovereign Shepherd. Micah could see "our Lord Jesus, that great shepherd of the sheep" (Hebrews 13:20), standing and feeding His flock, with no one daring to interfere, "for now shall he be great unto the ends of the earth" (Micah 5:4).

"This man shall be the peace," Micah wrote, "when the Assyrian shall come into our land....And they shall waste the land of Assyria with the sword....Thus shall he deliver us from the Assyrian" (5:5-6). This reference to "the Assyrian" seems to point to the time just prior to the return of Christ and the establishment of the millennial kingdom. In Micah's day, Assyria was the great foe of mankind. The word *Assyrian* became a haunting synonym for war, cruelty, oppression, and terror to the hapless middle eastern countries that fell within the sphere of Assyria's imperialistic ambitions. So the Old Testament prophets seem to use the word as a title for the antichrist, who will wear Assyria's mantle of ruthlessness.

In his somewhat obscure reference to a latter-day Assyria, Micah may have had in mind the confederation of nations that will have as their common goal in the last days the extermination of the state and people of Israel. Or he may have caught a glimpse of the coming Russian invasion of Israel (Ezekiel 38–39).[4] In any case, Israel's Shepherd will be her protector during all the end-time troubles.

"Then shall we raise against him seven shepherds, and eight principal men [princes]" (Micah 5:5). The meaning of this statement is not clear, but the general idea seems to be that the Lord will raise up men who will be His instruments to effect or at least consolidate Israel's triumph over the latter-day Assyrian. Micah's way of using the numbers seven and eight reminds us of Amos's formula, "for three transgressions...and for four," and the Hebrew sage's phrase, "three things...yea, four" (Proverbs 30:15,18,21,29). Perhaps Micah used *seven* and *eight* in an idiomatic way to express the idea of enough and more than enough—seven being the number of completeness, and "eight principal men" being enough and more than enough to do the job. Or perhaps "seven" signifies completeness and "eight" signifies, as it often does, a new beginning. In any case, the Lord will raise up a latter-day contingent of Maccabees to conserve the fruits of the Assyrian's overthrow.

C. Restoration Described (5:7-15)

1. The Remnant (5:7-8)

The worldwide dispersal of the Jews today is part of God's judgment of their continued and outspoken rejection of Christ. Jews living in Gentile lands are both a bane and a blessing. They contribute much to their adopted countries. However, once they begin to prosper and exert influence, they often become arrogant. They bring pressure to bear to secure their own interests and to get their own way, thereby sowing the seeds of their own destruction. Their actions can at times fuel the flames of antisemitism. Hitler hated Jews because of the power and influence they exerted in Germany.

Exiled from their own land, Jews carry with them not only their greatness, but also their grudges, especially against Christ. They are often active in groups that oppose prayer in schools, the display of nativity scenes, and the free expression of Christianity. The Jews in the United States frequently espouse causes that are far too liberal to gain the support of much of the population.[5] Communism was born in the brain of an apostate Jew, and many early leaders of Bolshevism were Jewish.

Micah envisioned another dispersal of the Jews: "The remnant of Jacob shall be in the midst of many people as a dew from the Lord, as the showers upon the grass" (5:7). These Jews are those who will administer the blessings and benefits of Christ's millennial kingdom. Having served their apprenticeships in many lands, they will go back to those lands. Having been regenerated by the Holy Spirit, they will serve as the Lord's personal envoys, representatives, and viceroys. Their presence then will be an unmitigated blessing, like the dew and the rain.

Where their presence is resented, they will be "as a lion among the beasts of the forest" (5:8). They will have the full backing of the throne in Jerusalem. No one will dare to interfere with them because they will be "as a young lion among the flocks of sheep."

2. The Recovery (5:9)

When Micah prophesied, the Jews were facing the beginning of sorrows. The ominous Assyrians were already abroad. Micah did not know how many centuries of suffering the Jewish people would have to endure once the Assyrians hammered down the walls of Samaria and appeared at the gates of Jerusalem. He did not foresee the more than two-and-a-half millennia of suffering, but he did foresee the end-time recovery: "Thine hand shall be lifted up upon thine adversaries," he wrote, "and all thine enemies shall be cut off" (5:9).

3. The Revival (5:10-14)

First God will remove all the secular expedients in which the Jews trust. Then, when they have nowhere else to go but to God, He will send a spiritual awakening that will transform the Hebrew people. All forms of false worship will be rooted out of the nation, so that at last it will be an instrument for the Lord's hand.

4. The Revenge (5:15)

Then will come the turn of the Gentile nations to suffer, for the Lord will visit them with judgment. The massed military might of mankind will be overwhelmingly defeated at Megiddo (Revelation 16:12-21; 19:11-21) and the surviving Gentiles will be summoned to the valley of Jehoshaphat, there to be judged (Joel 3:2-16; Matthew 25:31-46).

III. THE PLEA FOR REPENTANCE (6:1–7:20)

A. Israel's Sins (6:1-16)

1. The Lord's Controversy with Israel (6:1-8)

Moving his focus from the dim and distant future, Micah abruptly brought the people back to the present.

a. The Word of the Lord As Declared on the Hills (6:1-2)

The Lord called on His people to explain their chronic misbehavior to the hills. This was not merely rhetoric. The prophets often expressed the thought that nature was involved in man's fall. Nature is the handmaiden of the Creator and the book of Jonah gives specific examples of the close connection between the sins of men and the storms of nature. So here in Micah, creation itself is called in as a witness of the Lord's controversy with Israel.

b. The Warmth of the Lord As Displayed to the Hebrews (6:3-4)

"O my people, what have I done unto thee? and wherein have I wearied thee? testify against me. For I brought thee up out of the land of Egypt, and redeemed thee." This is the language of love. The Lord loved the Israelites. Why did they turn their backs on Him? The Old Testament prophets repeatedly returned to the fact of His redemption of Israel from the land of Egypt, the house of bondage. How could He have demonstrated His love any better?

It is astonishing that we too neglect the Lord, as if He wearies us. He is the most fascinating, absorbing person in the universe. He is the Creator of the rolling spheres, full of wonders and inexhaustible in inventiveness. He is Lord of the universe, Master of galaxies, "pavilioned in splendor, and girded with praise."[6] Angels and archangels, cherubim and seraphim, gaze on Him with awe and fill all Heaven with His praise. Yet we yawn in His face and give our attention to our puny business matters and pitiful little pleasures as if they are more important to the universe. We are like the Israelites who found the golden calf of Egypt, the cursed gods and goddesses of Canaan, and the crude deities of Assyria and Babylon to be more to their liking than God. Such is the terrible bent of the human heart.

c. The Will of the Lord As Discerned by the Heathen (6:5-8)

The pagans were more easily instructed than God's chosen people. Micah emphasized his point by referring to a fragment of history. He mentioned an incident, hitherto unrecorded but evidently known, concerning Balaam (the hireling prophet of Mesopotamia) and Balak (the king of Moab), who offered Balaam a reward if he would curse the people of God (Balaam and Balak's story begins in Numbers 22). Sometime during their acquaintance Balaam and Balak engaged in the conversation recorded here by Micah. The dialogue may well have been part of the oral tradition of the Jews or it may have been revealed directly to Micah by the Spirit of God (see Jude 14-15 for another example of this kind of thing).

Speaking to the prophet on his payroll, Balak asked in effect, "What will the Almighty take in order to overlook my sins?" Then

like a man bargaining in an eastern marketplace, the king began to
make his bids: "Shall I come before him with burnt offerings, with
calves of a year old...with thousands of rams, or with ten thousand
rivers of oil [a Nile, a Tigris, a Euphrates of oil]? shall I give my
firstborn for my transgression, the fruit of my body for the sin of my
soul?" (6:6-7) Truly if salvation could be purchased or earned by
sacrifice or religious rites, Balak would have been saved.

In one of his mysterious flashes of genuine spiritual discern-
ment, the pagan Balaam swept the offers aside and said in effect,
"My lord king, God's salvation is not for sale. And even if it could
be purchased, it could not be bought with the currency you have
offered. If your majesty wants divine favor, try a different medium
of exchange."

Micah described a better currency: he told us what to do to please
the Lord. First, offer Him a life of transparent honesty. In Micah's
words, "Do justly" (6:8). Always do unto others what you would want
them to do unto you. Live a life beyond reproach. In every social
contact, be fair, good, and honest.

Second, offer Him a life of tender humanity. In Micah's words,
"Love mercy." Remember that the merciful will receive mercy. In
thought, word, and deed, always show mercy. As Shakespeare
reminded us:

> The quality of mercy is not strain'd,
> It droppeth as the gentle rain from heaven
> Upon the place beneath: it is twice bless'd;
> It blesseth him that gives and him that takes:
> 'Tis mightiest in the mightiest: it becomes
> The throned monarch better than his crown.[7]

Third, offer Him a life of true humility. In Micah's words, "Walk
humbly with thy God." Walk as Enoch and Noah did. Do not be
proud—like Lucifer. Always esteem others better than yourselves.

Returning to the conversation between Balak and Balaam, we
can hear Balaam continuing, "If salvation were by works, you would
earn your right to Heaven by offering God a life of transparent
honesty, tender humanity, and true humility. That would be His
irreducible minimum price. He would accept no less."

Micah 6:8 has been called "the greatest saying of the Old
Testament."[8] The context is Micah's pleading with the Jews to
repent and no statement could have been more calculated to bring
home to them their dreadful shortcomings and desperate need.

2. The Lord's Condemnation of Israel (6:9-16)

The Hebrew people were doing exactly the opposite of what God required. In condemning them for their sin, Micah spoke of sin's deceptions, disappointments, and distortions.

a. Sin's Deceptions (6:9-12)

The wealthy had accumulated their treasures by wicked practices such as plain theft ("the bag of deceitful weights" in 6:11) and telling barefaced lies. The rich did not even hesitate to resort to violence to secure what they wanted.

b. Sin's Disappointments (6:13-15)

Sin always brings retribution, so Micah warned that the wicked would be robbed of their health (6:13), their hopes (6:14), and their harvests (6:15). They could expect little good from their ill-gotten gains.

c. Sin's Distortions (6:16)

The Israelites had deliberately chosen Omri and Ahab as their religious mentors. Omri founded Samaria (soon to be destroyed) and a particularly wicked dynasty. Ahab took Israel much further into sin than Jeroboam had taken them. Ahab sponsored the establishment of vile, demonic fertility cults that found their way into the southern kingdom as well (2 Kings 16:3). Both Samaria and Jerusalem were tarred with the same dirty brush.

B. Israel's Sorrows (7:1-6)

Sin can never bring happiness. The stark tragedy of Israel's sinfulness overwhelmed Micah's soul. "Woe is me!" he cried (7:1). All Micah could see was civil strife, violence, bribery, and corruption. He looked in vain for a good man and said, "The judge asketh for a reward....The best of them is as a brier: the most upright is sharper than a thorn hedge" (7:3-4). The moral climate was so decadent that a man could not trust his friend, his counselor, or even his wife. All natural affection had been killed. "The son dishonoureth the father, the daughter riseth up against her mother," wrote Micah. "A man's enemies are the men of his own house"

(7:6). The most sacred ties meant nothing. How could a nation lacking even the basic elements of honor and decency expect to escape the consequences of its behavior?

C. Israel's Savior (7:7-20)

1. Israel's Forgiveness (7:7-11)

Coming to the closing stanzas of his prophecy, Micah fixed his eye on the Savior, who was his only ultimate hope.

a. Revival (7:7-10)

The prophet could see end-time Israel in the hands of her enemies. As George Adam Smith said, "Other nations have been our teachers in art and wisdom and government. But [Israel] is our mistress in pain and in patience."[9] In her suffering Israel at last will say, "I will look unto the Lord" (7:7). She will be like the prodigal son in the far country, who said when he came to his senses, "I will arise and go to my father" (Luke 15:18).

Micah could see Israel—besieged by foes, inundated by woes—telling the nations, "God will hear me. Rejoice not against me" (7:7-8). She will resolutely make up her mind to "bear the indignation [punishment] of the Lord....He will bring me forth to the light" (7:9). She will confess her sin and stake her all on His loving character. Her enemies will be confounded.

Thus in the extremity of the great tribulation, the Jewish people will belatedly turn to the Lord. This revival, which will be characterized by prayer, forbearance, and praise in adversity, will result in Israel's restoration.

b. Restoration (7:11)

With great patience, remarkable acumen, and resourcefulness in the face of constant opposition and harassment, the reborn state of Israel has in our day cleared marshes, irrigated deserts, built cities, established industries, and forged a nation. But it will all be swept away, for Micah could see ruins and rubble everywhere. The Russian invasion, the malignant enmity of the antichrist, wars, bombings, and terrorism will take their toll. However, there will be a final turn in the long lane of troubles. Zion will be rebuilt and her boundaries will be greatly enlarged.

2. Israel's Foes (7:12-17)

Micah could see the day when Assyria will come to Israel, not with warlike intent, but suing for peace. And Egypt will come—the river mentioned in 7:12 seems to be the Nile. Many nations will come "from sea to sea, and from mountain to mountain," all seeking to make peace with Israel and her mighty King.

The land of Israel will be a fertile garden. Carmel, Bashan, and Gilead (mentioned in 7:14) will again have rich pastures.

By drawing a word picture, Micah foretold that the nations will tread softly before Israel. He described a man putting his hand over his mouth because he was frightened that he might say the wrong thing, and putting his hands over his ears because he was frightened that he might be caught listening to something derogatory about Israel. Abject fear of Israel will possess the nations after the battle of Armageddon, the judgment in the valley of Jehoshaphat, and the inauguration of the new order. Micah 7:17 says of Israel's foes, "They shall lick the dust like a serpent, they shall move out of their holes like worms of the earth: they shall be afraid of the Lord our God."

3. Israel's Future (7:18-20)

Micah ended his prophecy with a eulogy of God's mercy. Unlike Jonah, who was angry because of God's mercy (Jonah 4:1-2), Micah rejoiced over it. "Who is a God like unto thee," he exclaimed. "He retaineth not his anger for ever, because he delighteth in mercy" (7:18). In one of his more famous statements, Micah added, "Thou wilt cast all their sins into the depths of the sea" (7:19).

When the old priest Zacharias indicated that his son's name was John, he regained his ability to talk. As he praised God and prophesied, he quoted Micah 7:20 (see Luke 1:72-73).

The prophecy of God's end-time mercy to Israel should fill our hearts with joy. What a marvelous God He is!

> Great God of wonders! all Thy ways
> Are matchless, Godlike, and divine;
> But the bright glories of Thy grace
> Above thine other wonders shine.
> Who is a pard'ning God like Thee?
> Or who has grace so rich and free?[10]

Chapter 7
NAHUM
GOODBYE, NINEVEH

I. NINEVEH'S DOOM DECLARED (1:1-15)
   A. The Lord's Patience (1:1-3a)
   B. The Lord's Power (1:3b-5)
   C. The Lord's Presence (1:6-8)
   D. The Lord's Purpose (1:9-14)
   E. The Lord's Protection (1:15)
II. NINEVEH'S DOOM DESCRIBED (2:1-13)
   A. The Siege of Nineveh (2:1-8)
   B. The Sack of Nineveh (2:9-13)
III. NINEVEH'S DOOM DESERVED (3:1-19)
   A. The Fierceness of Nineveh (3:1-3)
   B. The Filthiness of Nineveh (3:4-7)
   C. The Folly of Nineveh (3:8-10)
   D. The Fear of Nineveh (3:11-13)
   E. The Fall of Nineveh (3:14-19)

F or more than two hundred years the Assyrian city of Nineveh
had been the capital and curse of western Asia. She had set
the style in fashion and art and, to some extent, religion
among the Semitic nations. The world's trade routes converged at
Nineveh, so her streets were filled with a conglomerate of people.
Under Ashurbanipal, the last great king of Assyria, travel and
knowledge had increased until Nineveh was the acknowledged
leader in this world's wisdom.
   Situated on the eastern bank of the Tigris (opposite the present-
day city of Mosul), Nineveh was fortified by walls, towers, moats, and

forts. Her walls were between seven and eight miles in circumference and so thick that three chariots could have driven abreast on the top. People of the ancient world were as familiar with the size of Nineveh's walls and the height and strength of her towers as we are with the dimensions of Big Ben, the Eiffel tower, or the White House.

But Nineveh's inhabitants thought of her glories as Egypt's slaves must have thought of the pyramids they built or as China's slaves must have thought of the great wall. Nineveh was a monument to tyranny. The troops who manned her walls had tramped through every capital in the Middle East and were hated and feared by other nations. Nineveh had dashed their little ones against the stones. Their kings had been dragged in chains to the great city and hung in cages about her gates. Their gods had been hauled away to line the temples of Nineveh's gods. Year after year Nineveh had depleted the treasuries of other countries; their people had been starved and taxed to swell her coffers.

Then the Scythians came thundering out of the North. Like the later Mongols and Tartars, the Scythians lived in the saddle. They had no use for chariots or infantry. With a speed that was new to the world, they crossed the Caucasian mountains and traversed the plains. They swept southward as far as Egypt, then returned along the coastline of Philistia and over the fateful plain of Esdraelon to the steppes. The rising and receding of the Scythian tide was the first intimation to Assyria that there was a power that mocked her might. The paralyzed nations of the Middle East took fresh hope. Maybe the Assyrian empire would go the way of all others.

About 625 B.C. when word first leaked out that Nineveh's frontier fortresses had fallen to the Medes, a muted cheer went up. And in 612 B.C. when news came that Nineveh had fallen and Assyria was no more, there was universal relief and unrestrained rejoicing. The book of Nahum is the inspired essence of the whole world's sigh: At last!

For generations the people of Palestine and the Middle East had known nothing but an endless succession of Assyrian invasions. Shalmaneser III (859–824 B.C.) defeated Ahab and Ben-hadad (1 Kings 20:34; 22:1-3) and forced Jehu to pay tribute (1 Kings 19:15-17; 2 Kings 8:7-15; 9:1-6). Tiglath-pileser III (745–727 B.C.) forced Menahem to pay tribute and was bribed by Ahaz for help (2 Kings 15:19,28-29; 16:10-16; 1 Chronicles 5:6,26; 2 Chronicles 28:19-21; Isaiah 7:1-9:1). Then Shalmaneser V (727–722 B.C.) invaded Israel and besieged Samaria (2 Kings 17:1-3). Sargon II (722–705 B.C.) captured Samaria and terminated the northern kingdom of Israel (2 Kings 17:6; Isaiah 20:1-6). Then this warrior-king and city-builder invaded Egypt and conquered that country in the battle of Raphia. Sennacherib (705–681 B.C.) launched an attack on King Hezekiah and took a toll of much of Judah until he was supernaturally overthrown before the gates of Jerusalem (2 Kings 18:13–19:36). Esar-haddon (681–669 B.C.) put Manasseh under tribute, conquered Palestine and carried Manasseh into captivity (but later released him), and colonized Samaria (2 Kings 19:37; 21:13-14; 2 Chronicles 33:11; Ezra 4:2-9).

Ashurbanipal (669–633 B.C.), absolute monarch of Assyria and virtual ruler of Babylon for over forty years, forced Manasseh to pay tribute and in 664 B.C. destroyed the Egyptian city of Thebes (also known as No or No Amon) (2 Kings 21:2; 2 Chronicles 33; Ezra 4:2,9; Nahum 3:8-10). Two petty kings followed Ashurbanipal on the Assyrian throne, but by then the days of Nineveh were numbered.

For about two and a half centuries Assyrian rulers were connected with Bible history. Nearly all of them were cruel, allowing no considerations of pity to interfere with government policy. Not seeing much sense in placing expensive garrisons in conquered cities, these rulers used terror and deportation to ensure the submission of the inhabitants. The initial blood bath when a city was sacked was followed by fiendish cruelty inflicted on the leading men. Some had their tongues torn out by the roots. Others were flayed alive; their skins were stretched out on the city walls to terrify any who might entertain ideas of rebellion. Still others were impaled on sharpened spikes and left to scream away their last days and hours in excruciating torment. The kings of Assyria gloated over such torture in their inscriptions.

Ashurbanipal was exceptionally cruel and he boasted of the atrocities he committed. He tore the lips and limbs from conquered kings. He captured three Elamite kings, harnessed them like horses to his chariot, and drove them through the streets. He hung around the neck of one captured prince the head of his king. Ashurbanipal forced one Chaldean king to commit suicide, decapitated him, hung his head from a tree in his garden, then with the queen feasted beneath the grisly relic. The horror stories are endless.

When there was not a cloud on the Assyrian horizon, Nahum was given the assignment to preach the downfall of Nineveh. A century earlier Jonah would gladly have given his life for the task. Nahum's message must have made him the most popular prophet of all time. We know little about Nahum except for his name, which means "comforter." He was simply a voice crying in the wilderness that Assyria had made of the world.

In Nahum 1:1 he called himself "the Elkoshite," presumably a reference to his home. There are various conjectures as to where Nahum lived. Some scholars link the word *Elkoshite* with a small village about twenty-four miles north of Mosul, where to this day visitors are shown what is said to be Nahum's tomb. If this village was indeed his home, he belonged to one of the ten tribes carried into captivity by Tiglath-pileser III or Sargon II. Other scholars think that Nahum lived in El-kauzeh, a village to the east of Ramah. Still others think that the name *Capernaum* ("village of Nahum") is an echo of Nahum's residing in the area. Another conjecture is that when Esar-haddon repopulated Galilee and Samaria with a mixture of people from elsewhere in his domain, Nahum and many of his countrymen moved south to Judah. Still another thought is that Nahum lived in Elkese in the territory of Simeon, about twenty miles southwest of Jerusalem.

For generation after generation Nineveh had cracked the whip over the world, but now the city was to face utter destruction. Annihilation of a city was something new, for normally cities survive when empires fall. For instance the city of Babylon passed from the Babylonians to the Persians and then to the Greeks. But just as Nahum promised, Nineveh vanished into oblivion so completely that for centuries even the place where it had stood was forgotten.

I. NINEVEH'S DOOM DECLARED (1:1-15)

A. The Lord's Patience (1:1-3a)

Jonah preached revival to Nineveh; Nahum proclaimed ruin. When Jonah preached, Nineveh was in a trough between the waves of its influence on the world; when Nahum preached, the city was riding the crest of its triumphs.

The Ninevites had been God's chosen instrument for the siege and sack of Samaria, but they had gone too far and God was angry. Nahum declared, "God is jealous, and the Lord revengeth; the Lord revengeth, and is furious; the Lord will take vengeance on his adversaries, and he reserveth wrath for his enemies" (1:2).

Perhaps the Assyrian armies were still ravaging the land as Nahum seized his pen. Their atrocities were vivid in the prophet's mind. They had ruthlessly deported almost an entire population— young and old, rich and poor, bond and free, weak and strong—to the usual accompaniment of whip, terror, forced march, and callous treatment of those not able to keep up with the pace. Not content with the desolation they had imported wholesale into Israel, the Assyrians had also invaded the land of Judah where a godly king was seated on the ancient throne of David. They had seized Hezekiah's fortified cities and practiced their cruelties across the length and breadth of his land.

The Assyrians provoked God's jealousy and wrath because it was *His* land that they were ravaging and it was *His* name that they were despising. Nahum thundered out the name of the Lord three times in 1:2—the Lord Jehovah, Israel's covenant-keeping God. Jehovah had made an unconditional treaty with Abraham, pledging Himself to curse those who harmed Abraham's seed. As the Assyrians marched, they shouted the names and titles of their vile and vicious idol gods and took cities in the power and might of those names. What cared they for Jehovah, tribal God of the Jews?

When the Assyrian armies finally gathered around Jerusalem, they tried propaganda before resorting to assault. Rabshakeh, speaking for the invaders to the Jews, poured scorn on Judah's king, Judah's allies, and finally Judah's God:

> If thou say to me, We trust in the Lord our God: is it not he, whose high places and whose altars Hezekiah hath taken away, and said to Judah and to Jerusalem, Ye shall worship before this altar?...Beware lest Hezekiah persuade you, saying, The Lord will deliver us. Hath any of the gods of the nations delivered his land out of the hand of the king of Assyria? Where are the gods of Hamath and Arphad? where are the gods of Sepharvaim? and have they delivered Samaria out of my hand? Who are they among all the gods of these lands, that have delivered their land out of my hand, that the Lord should deliver Jerusalem out of my hand? (Isaiah 36:7,18-20).

Because of this blasphemous boast against the living God, the Lord smote the Assyrians at the gate (Isaiah 37:21-37).

When we read in Nahum 1:2 that the Lord "reserveth wrath for his enemies," we are reminded that Russia has provoked Him even more than Assyria did. In Ezekiel 38:18 He warns this atheistic nation that when its armies and those of its allies cross the frontier of Israel, that will be the last straw. "My fury shall come up in my face," He said.

Adding to the indictment against Nineveh, Nahum said, "The Lord is slow to anger" (1:3). (He was quoting Jonah 4:2 and Joel 2:13.) Today God's long patience with Israel's enemies aggravates the national sin of her foes. He acts so slowly that people come to the conclusion that either there is no God or if there is, He does not care. They think they can get away with their sins forever.

God waits and warns. This principle of divine patience was explained to Abraham when God first signed the Abrahamic treaty. God deeded the promised land to him immediately, but postponed actual possession for four centuries. The reason given was that "the iniquity of the Amorites [was] not yet full" (Genesis 15:16). God's calendar covers time spans far longer than ours.

Wicked nations misinterpret God's patience. They see only the silence of God and forget His sovereignty. But as Nahum said, "The Lord...will not at all acquit the wicked."

B. The Lord's Power (1:3b-5)

Nahum paused for a moment to think about the ever-present reminders of God's power: the thundering tornado, the angry storm, the terrifying earthquake, the erupting volcano, rivers drying and fertile lands wilting beneath the curse of drought. (Bashan, Carmel, and Lebanon, mentioned in 1:4, were renowned for their fertility and marked the eastern, western, and northern boundaries of the promised land as it was in Old Testament days.) The countries of the world have no grounds for discounting the power of God. Nature, the handmaiden of the Lord, has a score of ways of reminding us of our limitations. In a moment the forces of nature can overawe the power of even the mightiest nations.

C. The Lord's Presence (1:6-8)

The booted feet of Assyria's legions were stamping throughout the prophet's land. The invaders were like a flooding river carrying death and destruction everywhere. With a flash of insight Nahum saw another flood: he anticipated how God "with an overrunning [overflowing] flood" would "make an utter end" of Nineveh when His indignation came to a head (1:8).

There are three remarkable prophecies in Nahum's book. One deals with the impending sudden destruction of Sennacherib's armies. One deals with the death of the conqueror himself in the house of his god. One deals with the downfall of Nineveh, not by siege or famine, but by flood. Foreseeing the completeness of Nineveh's overthrow, Nahum referred to the "overrunning flood." The river that was the city's protection would be the means of its defeat.

God has many weapons in His arsenal, as Russia will one day discover to its dismay (see Ezekiel 38:19-22).

D. The Lord's Purpose (1:9-14)

"He will make an utter end," Nahum repeated (1:9). God's patience with Nineveh was exhausted. He had heard the cries of countless sacked cities. He had seen corpses piled high, their faces stamped with terror and torment. He had witnessed rapine and outrage. He had heard little children scream as they were dashed against the stones. He had watched the horrors of forced marches and seen impaled bodies lining the route. He had seen people kicked and whipped to death. He had seen lurking in the shadows the inevitable aftermath of the Assyrian mode of war: famine, pestilence, and bereavement. All this was going on and on, but the promise was "He will make an utter end."

The reason for the divine decision to make an end of Nineveh was its vain and boastful attitude toward the Lord. Nahum stated the charge against the Ninevites in the form of a question: "What do ye imagine against the Lord?" That is God's indictment against much of the world today, especially Russia, which has embraced atheism, taught two generations to disbelieve in God, and exported its atheism to country after country around the world. The God whom the Soviets deny demands, "What do ye imagine against the Lord?" (See Psalm 2.)

"Affliction shall not rise up the second time," said Nahum. It seems that he was referring not only to Nineveh's impending doom, but also to Jonah's proclamation many years before. God had spared Nineveh once, but never again would He relent. This time judgment would be swift and sure. And He would not have to take revenge a second time. Nineveh would come to "an utter end" indeed.

In 1:10 Nahum shifted his focus from the future back to his own day. He graphically described Sennacherib's invasion of Judah and the ignominious end of the campaign. Speaking derisively he likened the Assyrians to a bramble bush, a patch of tangled thorns that were harmful but vulnerable to fire. By attacking Hezekiah they were acting as stupidly as drunkards.

Addressing the enemy in 1:11, Nahum said, "There is one come out of thee, that imagineth evil against the Lord, a wicked counsellor." This wicked man was Rabshakeh, the chief political officer of the Assyrian army. He was the propaganda expert who, as we have seen, harangued the Jews of Jerusalem. He ridiculed Hezekiah, his allies, his religion, and his God. Some scholars think that Rabshakeh was a renegade Jew, a "counsellor" highly favored by Sennacherib. The fact that Rabshakeh addressed the Jews in Hebrew suggests more familiarity with the language than a typical Assyrian ambassador would have possessed. Moreover his words betrayed an unusual enmity toward Jehovah; he acted more like an apostate than a ordinary unbeliever.

In 1:12 Nahum noted the quiet calm of the Assyrian invaders. Generations of invincibility in war had made them arrogantly confident in their own strength, experience, and ability to capture a city as strong as Jerusalem. They had the advantage of numbers, their ranks were intact, and their siege artillery was in good repair. Time was on their side; they could sit down and wait if they wished, for eventually nerves would snap in the besieged city and famine and pestilence would do their work.

Yet the knowing Nahum declared, "Thus shall they be cut down, when he shall pass through." This prophecy was fulfilled in one night when the avenging angel slew 185,000 enemy soldiers camped expectantly before the walls of Jerusalem. The hand of the Lord has seldom been revealed the way it was that night. Utterly dismayed and alarmed, the Assyrians fled back to their own land (2 Kings 19:35-36; Isaiah 37:36-37).

Nahum turned to his own people, many of whom had already suffered at the hands of the invaders. The Assyrian scourge was disciplinary, but God's message for the Jewish people was encouraging: "Though I have afflicted thee, I will afflict thee no more." The prophet anticipated that Judah would enter wholeheartedly into Hezekiah's reforms and would no longer need to be chastised.

The Lord added, "Now will I break his yoke from off thee." The vassalage of Judah was over. The overthrow of Sennacherib was the beginning of the end for Assyria. Other Assyrians would rise to power, including the devilish Ashurbanipal, but Judah and Jerusalem would not need to fear this foe. He was firmly on the leash and his days were numbered. (What is a mere ninety years to God?) Assyria had started on its last lap and from the prophetic point of view the end was in sight.

Nahum briefly turned his attention back to Sennacherib, who had loosed his terrible dogs of war against Judah, and pronounced his personal doom:

> The Lord hath given a commandment concerning thee, that no more of thy name be sown: out of the house of thy gods will I cut off the graven image and the molten image: I will make thy grave; for thou art vile" (1:14).

This prophecy was probably given at the time of Sennacherib's invasion, about seventeen years before he died. His son Esarhaddon and grandson Ashurbanipal had already been born and would reign over Assyria, but no more of Sennacherib's vile seed would be sown to plague the world. His dynasty was facing extinction; so were his deities. The temples and idols of Assyria were doomed.

Many people groveled at Sennacherib's feet and glorified his throne and power, but in the eyes of God the man was vile. Just as Nahum's prophecy had implied, Sennacherib was murdered by his sons while he was worshiping his gods (2 Kings 19:37; Isaiah 37:38).

E. The Lord's Protection (1:15)

"Behold upon the mountains the feet of him that bringeth good tidings, that publisheth peace!" Nahum anticipated the delight with which the tidings would be received—tidings that Nineveh had been overthrown and the Assyrian threat was gone forever. He could see the messengers running from hill to hill to proclaim the welcome news: "Peace! Peace at last! Nineveh is no more!"

The mantle of God's protection was wrapped around little Judah: "O Judah, keep thy solemn feasts, perform thy vows: for the wicked shall no more pass through thee; he is utterly cut off." Hezekiah had reinstated the annual feasts, but the people of the land were hindered from going up to Jerusalem to keep the feasts because a number of Judean cities were in the hands of the enemy. It was neither possible nor safe to go on pilgrimages or even travel with so many fierce foreign troops everywhere. Besides, Jerusalem itself was besieged. But with the overthrow of Assyria, God's people would be able to show their gratitude by using their new-found freedom to attend to His worship.

The challenge to keep the feasts and perform vows was needed in Judah. Godly King Hezekiah's reforms, inspired and supported by Isaiah, had been thorough and widespread. Hezekiah had swept away most of the entrenched idolatry and reinstated Biblical Judaism in his country. But he had enforced his edicts with a heavy hand and when he died, there was an immediate, drastic, and widespread reaction against his reforms. His son Manasseh, a boy of twelve when he came to the throne, threw his influence wholeheartedly behind the counter-reformation.

Peace and prosperity seem to militate against a spirit of revival in all ages. Although a time of peace was always a time of danger for the true faith in Israel, Nahum envisioned a day when the wicked would no longer pass through his land. His words in 1:15 evidently soar far beyond the local situation and are millennial in their final focus.

II. NINEVEH'S DOOM DESCRIBED (2:1-13)

A. The Siege of Nineveh (2:1-8)

In this passage Nahum described, in a series of brilliant prophetic flashes, the events that would lead up to the capture of Nineveh.

Nahum 2:1 says, "He that dasheth in pieces is come up before thy face." This is a reference to Cyaxares and Nabopolassar and the armies of the Medes and Babylonians. Nahum picked up the prophetic story at the point where the Medes had already overrun the countryside of Assyria. He could see the old lion withdrawing to his den and making his last stand.[1] The suburbs of Nineveh were already full of enemy troops, and the city's massive walls and towers were surrounded. The combined Medo-Babylonian armies had moved toward Nineveh along the great roads that reached out in all directions from the city.

The well-fortified hills that drew a bow-shaped rampart around the city were already in enemy hands, but rivers, dikes, and moats helped strengthen Nineveh's defenses. The city had plenty of water, and walls within walls provided a triple line of defense, making Nineveh virtually impregnable. If the Assyrians were beaten in the suburbs, they could retire behind their mighty walls and hope that the attacking armies would finally wear themselves out in fruitless assaults and go away.

But Nineveh's time had come because the Lord had sufficiently judged His people. The "emptiers" (especially the Assyrians) had plundered Israel (2:2). So with elaborate irony, Nahum advised the city to "watch the way, make thy loins strong, fortify thy power mightily."

In his preview of the siege, Nahum could see that the military tunics of the attackers were red and their shields were dyed red— either they liked red or their shields were splashed with the blood of the Assyrians. He could see the bright steel of chariots reflecting the sunlight. Perhaps the chariots were scythed[2]—if so, they were terrible weapons indeed, especially when used against a demoralized foe. Even the caesars' legions were halted by the scythed chariots of the ancient Britons. Rushing to and fro, the chariots created havoc and panic in the streets of Nineveh.

Nahum could see the Assyrian king encouraging himself by

calling to mind his "worthies" (2:5)—his nobles and generals who in the past had made Assyria invincible. But the spirit had gone out of them. They stumbled as they marched to secure the walls. The walls were strengthened by some fifteen hundred awesome towers, each two hundred feet high, but Nahum's prophetic foresight told him that Nineveh's fortifications would prove to be a vain defense now that God had decreed the city's overthrow. God has weapons that can topple the strongest walls. The exact manner of Nineveh's fall is foretold in 2:6: "The gates of the rivers shall be opened, and the palace shall be dissolved."

Cyaxares the Mede and Nabopolassar of Babylon had signed a mutual assistance pact against Assyria, and the alliance had been strengthened by the marriage of Cyaxares' daughter to Nabopolassar's son. The Medes attacked the city from the north and at first suffered heavy casualties. The Ninevites, now doubly sure of themselves, celebrated this initial victory by a round of revelry. Their foe took advantage of this indiscipline to drive the Assyrians back behind their walls and inflicted serious losses on them.

For the time being, Nineveh itself was safe. It seemed impossible that any army, however resolute and strong, could breach its walls. But in the third year of the siege God directly intervened.

Heavy rains brought on a flood. The city lay on the east bank of the Tigris, the river Khasr ran through the city, and a manmade canal connected the Khasr and the Tigris. The flood would have caused these waters to rise. Presumably the "gates of the rivers" were the heavily fortified and guarded gates at the points where the rivers and canal came in contact with the walls. Any break in these gates would give a determined foe immediate access to the city. These gates were opened—either by the enemy, by traitors within the city, or by the flood waters. Possibly part of the walls, undermined by the flood waters, gave way too.

"And Huzzab shall be led away captive," Nahum prophesied (2:7). Some scholars think that "Huzzab" refers to the capture of the queen or the queen mother. Others think the word is a verb meaning "it is decreed." If the latter is true, Nahum's prophecy meant that Nineveh itself, stripped of all its fabulous wealth, would be helpless in the hands of an eager and vengeful foe.

B. The Sack of Nineveh (2:9-13)

This passage is a prophetic description of the sack of Nineveh. "Take ye the spoil," said Nahum (2:9). The spoils of countless cities overthrown by the Assyrians in centuries of war had flowed into

Nineveh. Now the invaders took all the treasures and apparently
carted much of the spoils off to Babylon.

Nahum described Nineveh as "empty, and void, and waste"
(2:10). The city was so completely ruined by the invaders that
Xenophon scarcely recognized the site. Alexander the Great
marched his men past the location "not knowing that a world
empire was buried beneath his feet." Gibbon confirmed that even
the ruins of Nineveh disappeared. It was not until Layard and Botta
identified the site in 1842 that the city was rediscovered by the
modern world.

"Where is the dwelling of the lions?" asked the prophet (2:11).
The lion, the lioness, the young lion, the lion's whelp—Nahum
mentioned them all. As a roaring and ravening lion, Assyria had
terrified and devoured the world. No one could tame the wild
beast. Nineveh's kings had boasted, "Where are the gods of Hamath,
and of Arpad? where are the gods of Sepharvaim, Hena, and Ivah?"
(2 Kings 18:34) But now the prophet demanded in effect, "Where
is Nineveh?" His contemporaries must have looked at Nahum in
astonishment, for when he prophesied there was not a cloud in the
Assyrian sky.

In Nahum 2:13 we read the Lord's words to Nineveh: "Behold,
I am against thee." God made an identical declaration against
Russia: "Behold, I am against thee, O Gog" (Ezekiel 38:3; 39:1).
God only sets His face against a people as a last resort and as a result
of long defiance and deliberate provocation. Russia, the Assyria of
our day, is equally determined to rule the world, equally ruthless in
war, equally boastful of its power and culture, equally antagonistic
to God and the Jew, and equally the eventual target of God's wrath.

III. NINEVEH'S DOOM DESERVED (3:1-19)

A. The Fierceness of Nineveh (3:1-3)

In his last chapter Nahum recapitulated his dirge of doom for
Nineveh. "Woe to the bloody city! it is all full of lies and robbery; the
prey departeth not" (3:1). Again much that is said of Nineveh can
be said of Moscow and the Kremlin. Who can count the millions of
people that have been killed to spread communism around the
world? What nation is more guilty of treachery in its treaty obliga-
tions than Russia? Assyrian promises were also notoriously untrust-
worthy and vengeance was on the way.

Transported into the future, Nahum could hear "the noise of a
whip, and the noise of the rattling of the wheels, and of the pransing

horses, and of the jumping chariots" (3:2). He could see the carnage and horror of battle as the cavalry hunted down the foe. Mounds of the dead littered the landscape, and the living tripped on the rotting corpses. Nineveh had become an abode of the dead.

B. The Filthiness of Nineveh (3:4-7)

Nahum described Nineveh as a harlot, for the city was full of whoredom and witchcraft. Idolatry was one of Nineveh's cardinal sins. The Assyrians waged religious wars: all their wars were fought in the name of one or another of their false gods. Wherever their victorious armies went, their gods went too. Conquered nations were compelled to pay their gods honor. And gross immorality always accompanies idolatry.

In 3:5 the living God again declared His opposition to this vile people. He warned that He would expose Nineveh's shame to the world and heap filth on the city's nakedness. The nations witnessing Nineveh's defilement would distance themselves from the disgraced city. Reaping the harvest of what it had sown, Nineveh would have no friends—none to pity, none to help, none to lament. One great universal cheer would go up at the news of its downfall.

C. The Folly of Nineveh (3:8-10)

Nineveh was asked, "Art thou better than populous No . . ?" (3:8) "No" refers to the city of No-Amon (No of the solar god Amon), also known as Thebes. In its heyday, Thebes was another Nineveh. The capital of upper Egypt, Thebes was renowned for its vast wealth, great size, and twenty thousand chariots. Its grandeur dated from the eighteenth dynasty, after the expulsion of the Hyksos (the "shepherd kings").

Its pharaohs were conquerors until the twentieth dynasty— about six hundred years (1706-1110 B.C.). They made Thebes the center of a great empire and marched victoriously from the Sudan to Mesopotamia. Thutmose III, in less than twenty years of conquest, raised the Egyptian empire to its pinnacle of power. He repeatedly attacked the most powerful nations of Asia. The people of Nineveh and Babylon felt the weight of his arm and the Armenians, Phoenicians, and Hittites were among those he subdued.

Various pharaohs sent their tax collectors into Asia to draw tribute to Thebes. Thutmose I carried countless slaves from Mesopotamia to Egypt, and Nubia was an almost inexhaustible source of wealth.

Thebes was a natural site for a great capital. It was located on a plain through which the Nile flowed. The city occupied most of the river valley, which was about ten miles wide. Chains of hills encircled the plain and beyond the hills were vast deserts. The only way an enemy could approach Thebes was down the long valley of the Nile. The city itself was strongly fortified.

For hundreds of years, successive pharaohs adorned the city with huge idol-temples, gigantic statues of the pharaohs, and massive pillars. Modern man cannot explain how eight hundred tons of granite could have been excavated, transported, and then set up at ancient Thebes—or how it could have been thrown down. Everything was colossal and in proportion. To this day we are awed at the ruins of Luxor and Karnak.

This Thebes—situated "among the rivers [the Nile and its canals]" and "whose rampart was the sea [the Nile]"—was the city to which Nahum directed the attention of Nineveh in 3:8.

In 3:9 the prophet focused on Thebes' sources of strength: Egypt and Ethiopia. The city's strength was "infinite," said Nahum. The might of all Egypt and Ethiopia was concentrated at Thebes. "Put and Lubim" were powerful confederate states to the south and to the west. They could be relied on to rally to the aid of Thebes, were she attacked. "Put" apparently referred to Punt, present-day Somaliland. "Lubim" referred to the neighboring country of Libya.

The one great weakness of mighty Thebes was her idolatry. Egypt was notorious for worshiping cows, cats, crocodiles, and a pantheon of animal-like gods and goddesses. As we have seen, the ancient name of Thebes was No-Amon, Amon being one of the chief gods of the Egyptians. This idol had a human body and a ram's head.

The final overthrow of pagan Thebes was foretold in Jeremiah 46:25 and Ezekiel 30:14-16, and some time before Nahum began to prophesy, Sargon captured the city. Under Sargon and Sennacherib, the Egyptian sun set, and the Assyrian star rose.

Nahum held up Thebes as an example to the Ninevites and other Assyrians. He let them read their own doom in the capture of Thebes. They knew what horrors accompanied an Assyrian invasion.

Nahum recalled the cruelties of the siege and sack of Thebes. Young children were dashed against stones. Panic-stricken people trying to escape were caught at every intersection. A slave market was set up in the fallen city and the victorious troops rolled dice to determine who would acquire this or that captive; Nahum 3:10 says, "They cast lots for her honourable men."

The folly of Nineveh lay in her presumption and pride. She

looked at her mighty walls and towers, her long record of conquests, her hardened veterans, and her possible rivals. "It can't
happen here" was her boast. But it had happened in Thebes, and
Thebes had been stronger and better defended than Nineveh, for
Thebes had had a vast, rich hinterland as well as mountains and
deserts encircling her. Thebes had also had loyal friends, and
Nineveh did not have a friend in the world.

D. The Fear of Nineveh (3:11-13)

Turning his attention from Thebes to the coming collapse of
Nineveh, the prophet warned, "Thou also shalt be drunken"
(3:11). This prophecy came true literally. Historians have described the last drunken orgy of Nineveh on the night the enemy
finally broke through, and artists have painted the scene. In their
paintings we see the effeminate king, surrounded by his women,
feasting, drinking, and toasting his useless gods as the slayers went
about their vengeful work. History books tell us that as a final
gesture of defiance, the king had himself burned alive in his palace.

But the drunkenness to which Nahum referred was doubtless
also figurative. The prophets often depicted doomed nations as
drinking the cup of God's wrath (Obadiah 16; Jeremiah 25:15-
17,27). People feeling the effects of judgment were shown to be
reeling like drunkards and staggering stupidly; such a comparison
indicated that they were overwhelmed by the onrushing force of
events over which they had no control and about which they could
neither think sanely nor come to proper conclusions.

Nahum described the ease with which Nineveh would be taken
by her foe. He pictured her people vainly trying to strengthen their
fortifications—only to have them fall like ripe figs. (Anyone can
cause figs to fall easily just by shaking the tree.) As the cheering
enemy burst through Nineveh's walls, her renowned shock troops
would become like women who were frightened out of their wits.

E. The Fall of Nineveh (3:14-19)

Scornfully Nahum called on Nineveh to prepare herself for her
coming fall. "Draw thee waters for the siege," he said. "Fortify thy
strong holds" (3:14). Since the city's walls were to be breached, he
advised the Assyrians to step up the production of bricks and
mortar so that they would have plenty of material to patch up the
holes! Their preparations would do them little good, for once a
nation has been weighed in the divine balances and found wanting,

NAHUM 198

no military maneuvers will avail. Nineveh seemed to be prospering when Nahum prophesied, but her day was done.

Many ancient cities had been torched by Assyrian troops and when Assyrian reapers had marched forth to war, they had harvested mountains of corpses. Now it was Nineveh's turn to suffer. Fire and sword would create havoc in the city. The prophet could see the metropolis stripped and as desolate as a landscape after a locust plague.

In 3:16 Nahum turned his attention to Nineveh's commerce. "Thou hast multiplied thy merchants above the stars of heaven," he said. Nineveh lay astride a great caravan route and the Tigris gave her access to the sea, so the wealth of the world flowed into her warehouses. For centuries she had been the capital of the earth's trade, but she would be left utterly despoiled.

In 3:15-16 Nahum pictured the Assyrians as the victims of locusts, but in 3:17 he likened the Assyrians themselves to locusts. Joel had done that, but with a different emphasis. Nahum focused on the fate of the locusts: "Thy crowned are as the locusts, and thy captains as the great grasshoppers, which camp in the hedges in the cold day, but when the sun ariseth they flee away, and their place is not known where they are." The Assyrian "locusts," who had descended on the world time and again, were themselves to be obliterated. Just as locusts become torpid in cold weather, the Assyrian military leaders would become paralyzed when the hour of Nineveh's crisis arrived. And just as a locust swarm vanishes at the mercy of the wind, the Assyrian army would melt away and Nineveh would vanish from the face of the earth.

"Thy shepherds slumber," said Nahum to the king of Assyria (3:18). The "shepherds" were the princes and counselors responsible for the safety of the state. The wisest counselor, the most astute nobleman is useless if he is asleep. Nahum was prophesying that the Assyrian cabinet, the joint chiefs of staff, the policy makers—all would be sound asleep to their nation's approaching doom. They would not be aware that the Medes and Babylonians could and would take Nineveh and sweep the mightiest empire on earth into oblivion. Nahum's prophecy was fulfilled half a century later when an alliance of Lydia, Media, and Babylonia brought Nineveh to its end in 612 B.C.

With one last look, Nahum saw the people of Nineveh "scattered upon the mountains." There was no one to aid, guide, or protect them. He said to the king, "There is no healing of thy bruise; thy wound is grievous" (3:19). Indeed the prophet foresaw the time when the news of Nineveh's downfall would be heralded to the

world. Still addressing the king of Assyria, Nahum said that all who
heard the tidings would "clap the hands over thee: for upon whom
hath not thy wickedness passed continually?" Cheers and applause
would be heard in every land.

In the Bible, Babylon represents Gentile political confusion, and
Nineveh represents Gentile religious apostasy. When Jonah
preached in the streets of Nineveh, there was immediate and far-
reaching revival and the city turned to God. But by the time of
Nahum, the city was wholly apostate. This apostasy, as C. I. Scofield
said, set Nineveh apart from all other ancient Gentile cities. And
this apostasy explains why Nahum did not call Nineveh to
repentance. He simply delivered a warning of a coming overthrow
without remedy. "He will make an utter end" was the keynote of his
message.

There is no remedy for apostasy—only judgment. God always
rewards apostasy with catastrophe. Thus Nahum's message to
Nineveh is a warning to the apostatizing world of today.

Chapter 8

HABAKKUK

PROPHET WITH A PROBLEM

I. THE PROPHET IS TROUBLED (1:1-17)
  A. The Crimes of Judah (1:1-4)
    1. A Personal Sorrow (1:1-2a)
    2. A Perilous Situation (1:2b-3)
    3. A Permissive Society (1:4)
      a. The Law's Power Was Curbed (1:4a)
      b. The Lord's People Were Careless (1:4b)
  B. The Coming of Judgment (1:5-17)
    1. Its Immense Extent (1:5)
    2. Its Impending Execution (1:6-11)
      a. The Success of the Chaldeans (1:6-10)
        (1) Their Coming (1:6)
        (2) Their Character (1:7-8)
          (a) Their Personal Traits (1:7)
          (b) Their Powerful Troops (1:8)
        (3) Their Cruelty (1:9)
        (4) Their Conquests (1:10)
      b. The Sin of the Chaldeans (1:11)
    3. Its Impossible Explanation (1:12-17)
      a. Revelation (1:12)
        (1) The Person of God (1:12a-b)
          (a) He Is Different from Man in His
              Existence—He Is Eternal (1:12a)
          (b) He Is Different from Man in His
              Essence—He Is Holy (1:12b)
        (2) The Purposes of God (1:12c-d)
          (a) God's Judgment Was Really Consistent
              (1:12c)

(b) God's Judgment Was Really Corrective (1:12d)
b. Reason (1:13)
(1) A Simple Declaration of God's Character (1:13a)
(2) A Seeming Denial of God's Character (1:13b)
c. Righteousness (1:14-17)
(1) The Fishing of the Foe (1:14-15)
(2) The Folly of the Foe (1:16)
(3) The Fate of the Foe (1:17)
II. THE PROPHET IS TAUGHT (2:1-20)
A. God's Righteousness on the Individual Plane (2:1-4)
1. The Eagerness of the Prophet (2:1)
a. His Receptive Attitude (2:1a)
b. His Responsive Attitude (2:1b)
2. The Enlightenment of the Prophet (2:2-4)
a. Regarding the Truth of God (2:2)
(1) To Be Recorded Simply (2:2a)
(2) To Be Relayed Swiftly (2:2b)
b. Regarding the Timing of God (2:3)
c. Regarding the Trustworthiness of God (2:4)
B. God's Righteousness on the International Plane (2:5-20)
1. The Wars of the Chaldeans (2:5)
2. The Woes of the Chaldeans (2:6-20)
The Lord will deal with:
a. Their Crimes (2:6-8)
(1) The Property They Had Stolen (2:6)
(2) The People They Had Slain (2:7-8)
b. Their Covetousness (2:9-11)
c. Their Cruelty (2:12-14)
d. Their Carousing (2:15-17)
e. Their Cults (2:18-20)
III. THE PROPHET IS TRIUMPHANT (3:1-19)
A. Faith Surrenders (3:1-2)
1. Habakkuk's Response to Revelation (3:1-2a)
2. Habakkuk's Request for Revival (3:2b)

B. Faith Sees (3:3-15)
  1. The Lord's Presence (3:3-5)
     a. The Region (3:3)
     b. The Resplendence (3:4)
     c. The Result (3:5)
  2. The Lord's Power (3:6-9a)
     a. Rending the World (3:6-7)
        (1) Methodically (3:6)
        (2) Mindfully (3:7)
     b. Riding the Waves (3:8)
     c. Remembering the Word (3:9a)
  3. The Lord's Progress (3:9b-15)
     a. Nature Trembled (3:9b-11)
        (1) Violent Storms (3:9b-10)
        (2) Visible Signs (3:11)
     b. Nations Trembled (3:12-15)
        (1) The Lord Saving Mightily (3:12)
        (2) The Lord Saving Majestically (3:13-14)
        (3) The Lord Saving Miraculously (3:15)
C. Faith Soars (3:16-19)
  1. Trembling (3:16)
  2. Trusting (3:17-19)
     a. Irreversible Judgment (3:17)
     b. Irrepressible Joy (3:18-19)

———❧———

Habakkuk has been called the doubting Thomas of the Old Testament. He seems to have been more concerned with solving a problem than with delivering a prophecy. Actually there was little need for another major prophet when a man of Jeremiah's stature was holding center stage. The prophecies of Jeremiah were passionate enough, persistent enough, and penetrating enough to suffice. But since God has declared that "in the mouth of two or three witnesses shall every word be established" (2 Corinthians 13:1), Isaiah was supported by Micah and Hosea, and Jeremiah was supported by Zephaniah, Habakkuk, and Ezekiel. Nahum had comforted Judah with the assurance that the

Assyrians would be overthrown, but Habakkuk joined Jeremiah in warning their countrymen of the coming of the Chaldeans to punish Judah for her sins. The rising power of the Babylonians filled Habakkuk's vision.

There is a wide difference of opinion about when Habakkuk ministered. The opinions range from as early as Manasseh to as late as Jehoiakim. About Habakkuk himself, we know very little. Some scholars think that the last verse of his book indicates that he was a Levite. The only other information we have about the prophet is his name, but that is certainly significant, for *Habakkuk* means "to embrace." His great ministry, as Martin Luther once observed, was to take the people of Judah into his arms and carry them to God. Habakkuk knew that his sinning, erring people were about to relive the horrors of invasion, battle, and siege and to experience the added torment of defeat and deportation.

The turning point in the history of the ancient world was the famous battle of Carchemish (605 B.C.) in which Nebuchadnezzar defeated Pharaoh Necho of Egypt and swung the balance of power in the Middle East to Babylon. The reformation of King Josiah (621 B.C.) was the turning point in the history of Judah. It had great potential to reverse the decline of Judah, but the revival proved superficial. In spite of Josiah's sincere attempt to restore and revive the worship of Jehovah, the reformation was really centered in the king; when he was slain the revival collapsed and the nation faced the inevitable judgment of God.

When Nineveh fell in 612 B.C. and the Medes and Babylonians divided the spoils, Babylon took Judah into its sphere of influence. In 609 B.C. Judah was invaded by Pharaoah Necho on his way to Carchemish, and King Josiah decided to oppose Egypt's advance. Judah had been sorely pressed by Necho for several years, but no reasons are given for Josiah's decision. He may have wanted to cement good relations with Babylon. More likely, he deemed the very present Egyptians to be a more serious threat to Judah than the distant Babylonians. Josiah's efforts were in vain. He fell in battle and Jehoahaz succeeded him.

It seemed that the future lay with Egypt. The victorious Necho apparently swept all the kings west of the Euphrates into his network of alliances. Acting with a high hand, he deposed Jehoahaz, set up Jehoahaz's brother Eliakim as king, and changed Eliakim's name to Jehoiakim.

Before Carchemish, people must have thought that Jeremiah

and his colleagues were preaching folly when they proclaimed the future successes of Babylon. Yet years before, Micah had warned about Babylon (Micah 3:12; 4:10) and so had Isaiah (39:6-7). For over twenty years Jeremiah hammered away relentlessly, warning of a coming Babylonian captivity (Jeremiah 6:1,22-25; 10:22; 34:3). Habakkuk too knew that God was about to punish His people by allowing the Chaldeans to overrun Judah.

Amidst the troubled politics of the times, Habakkuk wrestled with a twofold problem: Why did God allow the wickedness in his homeland to continue? And, even more perplexing, how could God allow His own nation, unrighteous though it was, to be punished by an even more unrighteous nation? The Babylonians were worse than the Jews. Faced with this seemingly insolvable problem, Habakkuk wisely took the matter to God. Other prophets addressed themselves to Israel, Judah, Nineveh, or Edom, whereas Habakkuk addressed himself to God.

The answer to the problem was that once the unrighteous instrument had served His purpose, God would destroy it too. As we learn from history, the Babylonian empire was really the creation of one man, Nebuchadnezzar, and was very short-lived, surviving for barely seventy years.

I. THE PROPHET IS TROUBLED (1:1-17)

A. The Crimes of Judah (1:1-4)

1. A Personal Sorrow (1:1-2a)

Habakkuk had a burden. Many of us know what it is to be burdened for an erring child, a lost loved one, or a bereaved friend; such sorrow does indeed weigh one down. It was the sins of the people of Judah that were a lead weight on Habakkuk's heart.

The mystery of the silence of God in the face of human suffering, despair, injustice, persecution, and woe added to this godly man's burden. "O Lord, how long shall I cry, and thou wilt not hear!" Habakkuk prayed (1:2a). The souls of the martyrs in the Apocalypse also cry, "How long?" (Revelation 6:10). This was the burden of the psalmist in Psalm 73 and this has often been the cry of the despairing saint. The silence of God has given many an ungodly sinner an excuse to blaspheme and many a weary believer the temptation to give up his faith. Habakkuk learned that when the saint asks, "How long?" God simply says, "Trust Me."

2. A Perilous Situation (1:2b-3)

Everywhere Habakkuk looked, he saw violence, civic injustice, and iniquity. The rich were oppressing the poor; the nobles were riding roughshod over the constitution; the land was filled with "strife and contention" (1:3). Such internal disorder augured ill for the nation. The earlier prophets had preached against the same sins. Now a century later the wickedness that had invited the Assyrian invasion was crying again to high Heaven for another visitation of wrath. The sinning seemed to go on and on, age after age, generation after generation. No wonder Habakkuk asked, "How long shall I cry?...Why dost thou shew me iniquity?" The prophet was sick of the sight of wrongdoing and fearful of what it would bring.

3. A Permissive Society (1:4)

The Mosaic law was the foundation of Jewish national life, but Habakkuk observed, "The law is slacked [benumbed, paralyzed], and judgment doth never go forth." The Hezekiah revival had been followed by a half-century of reaction and unbelievable wickedness during the dreadful days of Manasseh. During that time the temple fell into disrepair, the law of God was set aside, and every form of evil flourished. Society became so decadent that it permitted idolatry and immorality and even accepted sodomy as a lifestyle.

By the time Josiah came to the throne, the law of God had completely vanished. No one even had a copy of it. Then Josiah ordered the cleansing and renovation of the temple, and Hilkiah found "a book of the law of the Lord." The finding of that copy of the law was what spurred King Josiah to intensify his efforts to reform Judah (2 Chronicles 34:8-33). However, the results of his reforms were not long-lasting. He was killed while he was a comparatively young man and a counter-reformation followed, proving how little the revival had touched the conscience of the nation.

The law always becomes paralyzed in a permissive society, as we can see by simply looking around our own land. A permissive society redefines sin: today a drunkard is an alcoholic; a thief is a kleptomaniac; a murderer is a victim of society; adultery is merely having an affair; sodomy is an alternate lifestyle. Sins that would have outraged our fathers are tolerated in the name of personal and civil rights.

Today the law is emasculated. Criminals are coddled: the death sentence has been abolished in many places and judges slap repeat-offenders on the wrist. Pleas of temporary insanity can absolve perpetrators from the penalties for the most heinous crimes. Hardened criminals can play the appeals system for years and escape with punishments far lighter than their deeds deserve. Court cases are deferred until the memories of witnesses become hazy. Judges are inconsistent, often open to bribes, and frequently more concerned with protecting than punishing the guilty.

The absolute standards of morality mandated by God's law have given place to relative morality, which accommodates wickedness. The wholesale slaughter of unborn babies by abortion is condoned on the grounds of a woman's right to choose. Pornography flour-ishes under the guise of freedom of the press. Syndicated crime, drug trafficking, prostitution, child abuse, political corruption, and blind foreign policy contribute to the growing moral weakness of the nation.

Such is the permissive society we see, and such was the permissive society Habakkuk saw. He came to the conclusion that "the wicked doth compass about the righteous; therefore wrong judgment proceedeth." In other words the wicked outnumbered and out-voted the righteous. No wonder his nation was headed on a collision course with disaster.

B. The Coming of Judgment (1:5-17)

1. Its Immense Extent (1:5)

God answered Habakkuk at once: "Behold ye among the hea-then, and regard, and wonder marvellously: for I will work a work in your days, which ye will not believe, though it be told you." Paul quoted this verse to the unbelieving Jews of Pisidian Antioch when he shook off the dust of their city against them (Acts 13:41,51). The apostle was referring to the impending destruction of the Jerusalem temple in A.D. 70—and with it the last vestiges of Biblical Judaism.

Habakkuk was told to tell the people of his day to look at the heathen. The Jews had become as bad as the heathen, so God, who had once chosen the Jewish people, had chosen another people to be the instrument of their punishment. But the Jews would not believe what they were told. Judah stubbornly resisted the Babylonians to the bitter end and the Jews persecuted Jeremiah for telling them to submit to the Babylonians.

2. Its Impending Execution (1:6-11)

a. The Success of the Chaldeans (1:6-10)

Probably at the time of Habakkuk's prophecy the idea that Babylon could be a threat was ludicrous, for Egypt was the belligerent world power. But it was not Egypt that Judah had to fear; the Lord said it was the Chaldeans who would come. "Lo," He said, "I raise up the Chaldeans, that bitter and hasty nation" (1:6).

Habakkuk was invited by God to see with prophetic vision the Chaldeans marching triumphantly all over his native land. (Three successive Judean kings—Jehoiakim, Jehoiachin, and Zedekiah—saw the fulfillment of the prophecy when they witnessed the Babylonian armies advancing victoriously through their land.) The Chaldean conquerors whom Habakkuk saw were "terrible and dreadful" (1:7), ruled only by self-interest. Their horses were "swifter than the leopards" and "more fierce than the evening wolves" (1:8); their horsemen flew like eagles.

The Chaldeans would not be interested merely in conquest; they would be destructive. (They left Jerusalem and the temple behind them in utter desolation.) Their captives would be as numerous as the grains of sand. Habakkuk was also told that the Babylonians would "scoff at the kings" (1:10) and mock fortified cities that stood in their way as if they were sand castles.

b. The Sin of the Chaldeans (1:11)

"Then shall his mind change, and he shall pass over, and offend, imputing this his power unto his god."

Far from seeing the hand of God in their successes, the Babylonians would attribute their swift and astounding victories to their pagan idols. It would seem obvious to them that their gods were more powerful than the gods of the cities and nations they overthrew; otherwise those gods would have helped their devotees fight off the invaders. The Babylonians would apply the same logic to the God of the Jews. (Both Nebuchadnezzar and Belshazzar, the first and last great rulers of Babylon, had to be told by Daniel exactly who the God they had dishonored really was. See Daniel 2:27-30,47; 4:1-37; 5:18-28.[1])

3. Its Impossible Explanation (1:12-17)

a. Revelation (1:12)

Habakkuk had asked God how long He was going to tolerate all the sin in his country, where God's own people lived. God's answer was that He had already chosen the Chaldeans, a pagan and potentially warlike people, to thrash His erring children. To Habakkuk this was an impossible explanation. The Chaldeans were worse than the Jews and herein was the crux of his problem. Two wrongs did not make a right, or so it seemed to the puzzled prophet. Habakkuk expostulated in a verse pregnant with truth about the person and purposes of God (1:12).

(1) The Person of God (1:12a-b)

He began, "Art thou not from everlasting, O Lord my God, mine Holy One?" God is different from man in His *existence*—He is eternal. And God is different from man in His *essence*—He is holy.

God transcends time. He is not limited to our narrow view of time. He is not hampered by being locked into the succession of events as they occur. Habakkuk admitted that God's perspective was infinitely wider than his; the truth of God's eternal existence did not perplex him. But the thought that God's essence is holiness seemed to aggravate Habakkuk's problem. The prophet understood that God's holiness called for the punishment of sinful Judah, but he could not understand how a holy God could have dealings with the sinful Chaldeans.

(2) The Purposes of God (1:12c-d)

Habakkuk continued, "We shall not die. O Lord, thou hast ordained them for judgment; and, O mighty God, thou hast established them for correction." Like a lightning flash in his soul, a glimpse of the problem's solution came to the prophet as he wrote.

He saw that God's dealings with His people were *consistent*. If God was holy (and Habakkuk had just called Him "mine Holy One"), He would not permanently cast off the people with whom He had an irrevocable and unconditional covenant (Genesis 12:1-3; 15:5-21; 17:1-22). "We shall not die," he exclaimed. No matter what happened, God could not belie His own character.

Habakkuk also saw that God's dealings with His people were *corrective*, not merely punitive. What God had in mind was the correction of His people through disciplinary action.

The prophet addressed God with an unusual title, "O mighty God." A literal translation of the Hebrew is "O Rock." Nothing could change either His character or His immutable purposes concerning His people. There was some comfort in that thought for Habakkuk. But the core of his problem remained: Why did He choose the Chaldeans?

b. Reason (1:13)

Not satisfied with the revelation he had received, the prophet tried to solve his problem with reason. He rephrased his question: "Thou art of purer eyes than to behold evil, and canst not look on iniquity: wherefore lookest thou upon them that deal treacherously, and holdest thy tongue when the wicked devoureth the man that is more righteous than he?" A *simple declaration* of God's character (He is too pure to behold iniquity) is followed by a *seeming denial* of God's character (He plans to use a vile instrument). How could a holy God contemplate using people as treacherous as the Chaldeans? What fellowship does light have with darkness? Habakkuk's problem refused to go away. The prophecy made no sense.

c. Righteousness (1:14-17)

The prophet elaborated on the problem by reciting back to God what He had already revealed to him about the character of the Chaldeans. They treated men as though they were just fish in the sea to be caught and hauled away. Moreover the Chaldeans rejoiced over their successful "fishing." They did not care who suffered in the process. The angle, net, and drag mentioned in 1:15 were figures Habakkuk used to describe Babylonian implements of war. "They sacrifice unto their net," he went on (1:16). In other words their successes would not make the Chaldeans grateful to God. They would worship their own prowess in war.

In 1:17 the prophet asked if this cruelty and warfare would go on forever. The seemingly endless propensity of men to wage war is yet another problem. So Habakkuk was troubled. The whole first chapter of his prophecy is concerned with his ever-increasing perplexity.

II. THE PROPHET IS TAUGHT (2:1-20)

A. God's Righteousness on the Individual Plane (2:1-4)

1. The Eagerness of the Prophet (2:1)

Habakkuk was determined to wait upon God for some satisfactory explanation of his bewildering problems. He stood on his watchtower and said in effect, "I will wait and see." He intended to keep a lookout, to keep his eyes open. He also intended to keep his ears open so that he would not miss the answer that he was confident would come. And God did not disappoint His servant.

2. The Enlightenment of the Prophet (2:2-4)

When the answer came, it was threefold. The Holy Spirit spoke to His servant about the truth of God, the timing of God, and the trustworthiness of God.

a. Regarding the Truth of God (2:2)

Habakkuk was told to "write the vision, and make it plain upon tables [presumably tablets set in public places for all to read], that he may run that readeth it." Apparently the idea was that the message was to be written clearly and simply so that those reading it could swiftly relay it to others.

b. Regarding the Timing of God (2:3)

"The vision is yet for an appointed time, but at the end it shall speak, and not lie: though it tarry, wait for it; because it will surely come, it will not tarry." The immediate reference here seems to be not only to the coming of the Babylonians, but also to the end of the captivity. The principle involved in this verse applies to many divine prophecies. Their fulfillment often seems remarkably slow, giving scoffers ample time to exhibit their unbelief. But God's clock is much bigger than ours. Prophecies regarding the first coming of Christ took many centuries to be fulfilled, but in the end all of them were proven to be accurate to the letter.

Prophecy also often has an early, partial, illustrative fulfillment and a later, complete, detailed, literal fulfillment. Prophecies concerning the second coming of Christ have slumbered in the womb of time for thousands of years. Today they are stirring into remarkable life and end-time events will unfold swiftly when the time comes. It certainly seems that now His coming must be reckoned in terms of decades rather than centuries.

c. Regarding the Trustworthiness of God (2:4)

In 2:4a we find that the Lord knew all about Babylonian deceit and pride: "His soul which is lifted up is not upright," He said.

Historically the Babylonian star was just rising over the horizon, but prophetically it had already set.

Then in 2:4b we finally find the full answer to Habakkuk's question. The Lord's statement recorded there has echoed down the centuries. It put all divine-human relations on a higher plane: "The just shall live by his faith." This statement, which is quoted three times in the New Testament (Romans 1:17; Galatians 3:11; Hebrews 10:38), is the key to the book of Habakkuk and the key to God's dealings with men. God is simply saying, "Trust Me!"

The accents in the Hebrew place the emphasis on the words translated "shall live." To reflect this emphasis, Habakkuk 2:4b could be translated, "The just one by his faith shall live." In this word order the contrast is not between faith and unbelief, but between perishing and living forever (as in John 3:16). In the New Testament quotes the emphasis is different in each case. In Romans the emphasis is on "the just," in Galatians it is on "faith," and in Hebrews it is on "live."

Beyond the pages of the Bible, Habakkuk 2:4b made history with a vengeance, since it brought about the conversion of Martin Luther. He was seeking plenary indulgence for his sins by crawling on his knees up the *Scala Santa* (Pilate's staircase) in Rome and saying the required prayer to the virgin Mary on each step when this verse thundered in his soul. Luther was trying to earn salvation by works when it dawned on him that justification and life was by faith. He rose from his knees, dusted off his robe, stood upright, and marched back down the steps and out of the church of Rome. He took half of Europe with him.

B. God's Righteousness on the International Plane (2:5-20)

1. The Wars of the Chaldeans (2:5)

With astonishing clarity Habakkuk put his finger on one of the weaknesses of the typical Babylonian: he was addicted to alcohol. True, war was his trade—even his passion. Indeed the prophet described him as a man "who enlargeth his desire as [Hades], and is as death, and cannot be satisfied, but gathereth unto him all nations." But wine was his downfall. We know from Daniel 5 that on the night of Babylon's doom Belshazzar and his lords and ladies were in the midst of a carouse.

2. The Woes of the Chaldeans (2:6-20)

The Lord dealt with the crimes, covetousness, cruelty, carousing, and cults of the Chaldeans by pronouncing five woes upon them.

The woes would be severe enough to satisfy even Habakkuk, who had been so perplexed with God's choice of the Babylonians as His instruments to punish His people.

a. Their Crimes (2:6-8)

The Chaldeans had plundered the nations of the earth, so the prophet wrote, "Woe...to him that ladeth himself with thick clay!...Because thou hast spoiled many nations, all the remnant of the people shall spoil thee."

The reference to "thick clay" has been interpreted in several ways. Some think that Habakkuk was referring to the ill-gotten booty that would turn out to be a mass of pledges, a burden of debt to be paid one day with interest. Others think the prophet was referring to the worthlessness of the treasure accumulated by the Chaldeans; in the end it would only weigh the oppressors down. Still another view is that "thick clay" refers to the Babylonians as usurers who sought to increase their wealth even more by heaping up pledges from those they had plundered.

Regardless of the interpretation, the vast treasure in Babylon was the price of blood. "Because of men's blood" God pronounced the first woe.

b. Their Covetousness (2:9-11)

The second woe was punishment for the covetousness that had led to extortion and a strong commercial spirit in Babylon. (It was there that the Jews first developed a taste for business.) The Babylonians, secure in their wealth and power, imagined themselves to be as safe as an eagle in her lofty mountain aerie. But they were far from being immune to retribution. By committing many acts of plunder they had sinned against their own souls—they had guaranteed their own ruin. God warned that even inanimate walls and beams would witness against the rapacious Babylonians. Nothing militates more against spiritual life than materialism.

c. Their Cruelty (2:12-14)

The third woe is recorded in Habakkuk 2:12: "Woe to him that buildeth a town with blood, and stablisheth a city by iniquity!" The walls, gates, and streets of Nebuchadnezzar's Babylon were a tribute to the king's love of beauty and its magnificent hanging gardens were one of the wonders of the ancient world. But Babylon was built on blood; it was built on cruelty to conquered people and on plunder hauled away from vanquished cities, including Jerusalem. The builders of Babylon had labored "for very vanity," for in the end there would be a fire (2:13).

This prophecy leapt far beyond the fall of the Babylonian empire. The gorgeous capital fell intact into the hands of the Medes and Persians and continued to occupy an important place in history for many centuries, well on into the Christian era. The focus of Habakkuk 2:13 is found in the Apocalypse. We gather from Revelation 18 that Babylon will be rebuilt; it will become the commercial capital of the antichrist's world empire and then be destroyed. John's vision of the overthrow of this future Babylon agrees exactly with Habakkuk 2:13 and Jeremiah 51:58.

Habakkuk's next words are clearly millennial: "The earth shall be filled with the knowledge of the glory of the Lord, as the waters cover the sea" (2:14). The day is coming—after the destruction of Babylon and the subsequent defeat of the antichrist at Megiddo— when Christ will set up His kingdom and fill the world with the knowledge of God. Incidentally this is the fifth and last occurrence of this wondrous prophecy (Numbers 14:21; Psalm 72:19; Isaiah 6:3; 11:9; Habakkuk 2:14).

d. Their Carousing (2:15-17)

In recording the fourth woe, Habakkuk gave us one of God's strongest warnings against strong drink: "Woe unto him that giveth his neighbour drink, that puttest thy bottle to him, and makest him drunken also, that thou mayest look on their nakedness!" (2:15)

In verse 16 the prophet went on to describe the immorality that so often accompanies drunkenness and the disgusting vomiting of those who cannot hold their liquor. "The cup of the Lord's right hand" signifies the terrible cup of retribution, the cup of God's wrath that He will force all rebels and rebel nations to drink; their glory will thus be turned into shame.

According to 2:17 the Lord's case against Babylon was its violence not only against men, but also against the forests of Lebanon. This is an extraordinary example of foresight, for Nebuchadnezzar, who had not yet come to power in Habakkuk's day, was fascinated by the great cedars of Lebanon and felled many of the magnificent trees. He shipped the beautiful wood to Babylon for his numerous building projects.[2]

God accused the Babylonians of violence to men, cities, countries, animals, and trees, but apparently their prevailing sin was

drunkenness. We learn from Habakkuk 2:15 that the curse of God
rests not only on the Babylonians, but also on those who sell strong
drink and serve it to others today. God's point of view is based not
on the glowing advertisements and catchy commercials, but on the
appalling toll of alcohol in wrecked homes and lives.

The damage done by liquor is immeasurable. While under the
influence of strong drink, people have lost their virtue and their
honor. In fact there are some evil individuals who make people
drunk in order to take advantage of them while their defenses are
down. Hopeless alcoholics roam the slums of our cities. They pawn
their babies' shoes and sell their daughters into prostitution for
drink. Social drinkers drape the cursed custom with glamour and
respectability without being concerned about starting others down
the road to habitual, enslaving alcoholism. Yet our legislators are
too often soft on drunkenness. God knows about the whole business and in the end He will settle accounts with those involved.

Surely no conscientious Christian can serve strong drink. The
Bible may not actually teach total abstinence, but it comes very
close to it. Some cite the Lord's miracle at Cana as an excuse for
using and serving alcohol, but there is no proof there was any
alcohol in that "good wine" Jesus made. I believe a person could
have drunk gallons of that wine and not have become drunk.[3]

e. Their Cults (2:18-20)

In 2:18 Habakkuk laid the groundwork for the fifth woe by
asking, "What profiteth the graven image that the maker thereof
hath graven it...?" Then the prophet recorded the curse: "Woe
unto him that saith to the wood, Awake; to the dumb stone, Arise,
it shall teach! Behold, it is laid over with gold and silver, and there
is no breath at all in the midst of it" (2:19).

Ancient Babylon was the home of all idolatry. There it had its
roots and its rise. From Babylon idolatry spread to all parts of the
world. The Babylonian mysteries in time found a new capital at
Pergamos and from there they moved to Rome. The reigning
caesar was not only emperor, but also *pontifex maximus* of the pagan
idolatries. In Rome the infection spread to the church, and the
worship of images—especially those of the virgin Mary—became a
major part of worship. The bishop of Rome eventually inherited
the whole Babylonian system and the title "sovereign pontiff."

God's curse rests upon the worship of images, no matter where
they are or with what sanctity they are endowed. Graven images are
made of dead wood and dumb stones, as Habakkuk so scornfully

said. But behind them lurk evil spirits who divert the praise and prayers of the worshipers to Satan. The evil spirits also fasten themselves on the lives of those who bow before idols.

III. THE PROPHET IS TRIUMPHANT (3:1-19)

The third chapter of Habakkuk is a poem apparently written in a time of national crisis, as was chapter 1. The poem is a hymn, an anthem of praise. From the repetition of the word "Selah" (3:3,9,13)—so common in the Psalms—we gather that the hymn was designed to be sung in public worship. The land was threatened by invasion, but the song was triumphal.

A. Faith Surrenders (3:1-2)

Now, in response to God's answer to his problem, the prophet gave in. As at the beginning of chapters 1 and 2, Habakkuk bared his heart in 3:1-2. The word "Shigionoth" in 3:1 is the plural of "Shiggaion" (Psalm 7), which signifies a loud cry in a time of danger or joy. David used the word in a time of great danger. Habakkuk, the only other Biblical writer to use the word, employed it at a time of pain and praise.

Habakkuk acknowledged that he had heard from God and tasted fear. Many Old Testament saints had the same reaction when they heard God's voice or were made aware of His awesome presence (Exodus 14:31; Isaiah 6:5; Daniel 10:5-8).

In the presence of the Lord, Habakkuk had only one prayer: "O Lord, revive thy work in the midst of the years, in the midst of the years make known; in wrath remember mercy" (3:2). The expression "in the midst" occurs some 273 times in Scripture, but only here does it refer to time. Time, like an ever-flowing stream, was hurrying on its way. Somehow Habakkuk felt that he was "in the midst of the years" between the flood and the apocalypse. And so he was. About 3000 B.C. Enoch was translated and Noah was born—in round figures, 2400–2500 years before Habakkuk lived. From Habakkuk's day to ours are about 2500–2600 years and there is every indication that the apocalypse is imminent.

There "in the midst of the years" Habakkuk stood with time swirling past him and the timeless One making him aware of His presence. There he prayed for mercy and a revival that would avert judgment. If the Josiah reformation was already in progress when Habakkuk prayed, the prophet must have suspected that, noble as it was, it was too little and too late. He prayed for a revival that would go deeper and touch the heart of the nation. Such an awakening was Judah's only hope just as now it is the world's only hope. Three alternatives loom ahead of us today: ruin, revival, or rapture.

B. Faith Sees (3:3-15)

1. The Lord's Presence (3:3-5)

Habakkuk said, "God came from Teman, and the Holy One from mount Paran. Selah" (3:3). Teman was the southernmost large city of Edom, and Paran was the wilderness region in the east central part of Sinai, so the words "Teman...Paran" embrace the whole district south of Judah, including Sinai. Habakkuk saw the Lord's glory coming from the south. It covered the mountains, and the whole earth was "full of his praise." Blinding rays of light seemed to flash forth from His hand, and the brightness concealed His power (3:4). "Before him," wrote the prophet, "went the pestilence" and fire (3:5).

There can be little doubt that this vision is apocalyptic; it marches in step with the kind of end-time truth we find in the book of Revelation. The Lord is seen coming from the far south of Judah and stepping on Edom (Teman), the archetype of Israel's antagonistic neighbors. Edom represents the hostile Arab nations that today surround the state of Israel; they would love to push the Jews into the sea and take possession of their little land.

As Habakkuk prophesied, the Lord's coming in glory will be preceded by pestilence and fire—instruments God uses to reduce His human foes to nothing. Nations in the Middle East are already toying with chemical and bacterial weapons. Iraq used them in its war with Iran, and Libya has a factory for their production. Diseases such as AIDS are spreading since medical science offers no cure. The whole world is trembling on the verge of pestilences such as the Apocalypse describes. The rider on the pale horse (Revelation 6:8) is preparing to mount his steed.

2. The Lord's Power (3:6-9a)

Next Habakkuk saw the Lord rending the world, riding the waves, and remembering the Word.

a. Rending the World (3:6-7)

The prophet saw nature convulsing as the Lord drove His plow through the nations. "The tents of Cushan [were] in affliction: and the curtains of the land of Midian did tremble" (3:7). "Cushan [Cush]" refers to Ethiopia, and "Midian" refers to the area of

Arabia opposite Ethiopia, so we know that the Ethiopians will be numbered among the enemies of the Jews in the last days. They will side first with Russia (Ezekiel 38:5) and then with the antichrist (Daniel 11:43).

In recent years we have seen this hostility building up in the Middle East as the Islamic states have become increasingly antagonistic toward Israel. The Lord will deal with these inveterate enemies of His Hebrew people.

b. Riding the Waves (3:8)

Habakkuk saw God's wrath displayed against the rivers and the sea. Perhaps there is an echo in 3:8 of what happened when the Lord dried up both the Red Sea and the Jordan to get His people out of Egypt and into Canaan. No combination of Gentile nations could keep Israel from its land then.

The setting of Habakkuk's vision is the future. The battle of Armageddon is threatening and the antichrist's troops are already wreaking havoc in the streets of Jerusalem. Habakkuk saw the Lord riding His chariots of salvation to hasten Israel's deliverance from her terrible and final extremity in the last days.

c. Remembering the Word (3:9a)

"Thy bow," wrote Habakkuk, "was made quite naked, according to the oaths of the tribes, even thy word. Selah." He was referring to the oaths—the promises of God—sworn to the fathers of the tribes of Israel: Abraham (Genesis 12:1-3), Isaac (Genesis 26:1-5), and Jacob (Genesis 28:11-15). God has a treaty relationship with the nation of Israel. Let all antisemitic peoples beware.

3. The Lord's Progress (3:9b-15)

The magnificent vision continued. The rampaging Assyrian, the distant Babylonian, the interfering Egyptian—all these "petty" matters of the moment were forgotten. Habakkuk was transported far, far way. He was no longer "in the midst of the years." He was at the end of the age. The prophet saw that as the Lord made progress, nature and nations trembled.

a. Nature Trembled (3:9b-11)

We can hardly imagine what the world will be like at the end of the apocalyptic judgments. Wars, famines, pestilences, earthquakes, and tornadoes will leave the world a shambles. There are hints of nuclear war in the book of Revelation, and ecological disasters of global magnitude can be inferred from various passages. Climatic changes are already heralding what is to come. The earth will need to be renewed and only the Creator can do that.

Habakkuk saw all creation convulse with birth pangs as a new millennial age was born. He saw mountains trembling, upheavals in the earth, and changes in the sky. "Thou didst cleave the earth with rivers," he wrote in 3:9b.

b. Nations Trembled (3:12-15)

At the actual time of the Lord's return to reign, the whole world will be gathered in hostile armies at Megiddo. East and West will glower at one another, determined to decide once and for all who will rule the world. However, both sides will have one thing in common: a hatred of both the Jews and those who would join the great company of martyrs mentioned in Revelation 7 and 6:9-11. The Lord will break through the clouds and annihilate the millions massed against Him at Megiddo. Seeing the future as though it were already in the past, Habakkuk exclaimed, "Thou didst march through the land in indignation, thou didst thresh the heathen in anger" (3:12).

The prophet continued, "Thou wentest forth for the salvation of thy people" (3:13). He was indicating that the Lord will return just in time to rescue beleaguered Israel—just when the Jews are at the end of their resources and facing extermination.

In what seems to be a clear reference to the antichrist, Habakkuk cried, "Thou woundedst the head out of the house of the wicked." This lawless one will be destroyed by the Lord at His return (2 Thessalonians 2). Habakkuk saw Him "discovering the foundation unto the neck." In other words, the Lord will overturn the antichrist's empire from top to bottom. He will turn it upside down, thus putting an end to it. By adding "Selah" (for the third and last time), Habakkuk was saying, "There! What do you think of that?"

Habakkuk 3:14 tells us that those who come "as a whirlwind" to destroy the defenseless will be destroyed by their own weapons. "His staves" means "his own weapons." "The head of his villages" means "leaders." "The poor" here refers to the beleaguered nation of Israel.

The idea behind verse 14 seems to be that the ragtag motley armies ordered to Megiddo will have little in common, no matter which side they are on—the side of the antichrist and his ten kings or the side of the conglomerate kings of the East. National hatreds and rivalries will march along with the various armies, and quarrelsome nations will turn on each other. Still seeing the future as though it were already past, Habakkuk looked back on all the tumult and exclaimed, "Thou didst walk through the sea with thine horses, through the heap of great waters" (3:15).

C. Faith Soars (3:16-19)

When the ecstatic apocalyptic vision faded, the prophet was left weak and shaken: "When I heard, my belly [body] trembled; my lips quivered....Rottenness entered into my bones, and I trembled in myself" (3:16). He had come back down to earth, back to the present, back to a land that was still a pawn in the chess game of the superpowers, back to a land that was weakened by its own sins. Habakkuk now knew that his homeland was to be overrun by the Chaldeans. But trust in the promises of God banished terror. The prophet prayed that he "might rest in the day of trouble" when the invasion takes place.

Habakkuk had seen the havoc that would be wrought by the enemy—vineyards, olive groves, and fig trees destroyed and farms emptied of livestock. Yet he was able to say, "I will rejoice in the Lord, I will joy in the God of my salvation. The Lord God is my strength, and he will make my feet like hinds' feet, and he will make me to walk upon mine high places" (3:18-19). All his doubts had been removed. His problem had been swallowed up by praise. God was still on the throne!

One of the best ways to instill a truth into the heart, soul, and conscience of an individual or a nation is to set that truth to music, to incorporate it into a great hymn. So Habakkuk set his poem to music, dedicated it "to the chief singer," and picked up one of his own "stringed instruments" to help raise the song of praise.

Chapter 9

ZEPHANIAH

THE ROYAL PROPHET

I. THE DETERMINATION OF THE LORD (1:1-6)
  A. The Prophet's Pedigree (1:1)
  B. The Prophet's Perspective (1:2-6)
    1. The Lord's Decision (1:2-4a)
      a. The Devouring Flame (1:2-3)
        (1) Consuming (1:2-3a)
        (2) Cleansing (1:3b)
        (3) Conquering (1:3c)
      b. The Divine Focus (1:4a)
    2. The Lord's Discrimination (1:4b-6)
      a. Immorality (Baal Worship) (1:4b)
      b. Astrology (Worshiping the Hosts of Heaven) (1:5a)
      c. Insincerity (Swearing by the Lord) (1:5b)
      d. Cruelty (Sacrificing to Moloch) (1:5c)
      e. Apostasy (Turning Back to Sin) (1:6a)
      f. Infidelity (Not Seeking the Lord) (1:6b)
II. THE DAY OF THE LORD (1:7–3:8)
  A. The People (1:7-13)
    1. The Summons (1:7)
    2. The Sacrifice (1:8-13)
      a. The Royal Rebels (1:8)
      b. The Sin-Seekers (1:9)
      c. The Money-Makers (1:10-11)
      d. The Leisure-Lovers (1:12-13)
  B. The Period (1:14-18)
    1. Its Nearness (1:14)
    2. Its Nature (1:15-18)
      a. To Fulfill Prophecy (1:15-16)

b. To Finally Punish (1:17)
c. To Fully Purge (1:18)
C. The Places (2:1–3:8)
1. The Country of Judah (2:1-3)
a. Warned (2:1-2)
b. Wooed (2:3)
2. The Conquerors of Judah (2:4-15)
a. To the West: Philistia (2:4-7)
(1) Its Towns Given Over to Judgment (2:4-6)
(2) Its Territory Given Over to Jews (2:7)
b. To the East: Moab and Ammon (2:8-11)
(1) Their Policy (2:8)
(2) Their Punishment (2:9)
(3) Their Pride (2:10-11)
(a) Racial (2:10)
(b) Religious (2:11)
c. To the South: the Ethiopians (2:12)
d. To the North: Assyria (2:13-15)
(1) Ruin Predicted (2:13-14)
(2) Rejoicing Predicted (2:15a)
(3) Reviling Predicted (2:15b)
3. The Capital of Judah (3:1-8)
a. Its Pollutions (3:1-4)
(1) The People (3:1-2)
(2) The Princes (3:3)
(3) The Prophets (3:4a)
(4) The Priests (3:4b)
b. Its Punishment (3:5-8)
(1) No Regard for God's Presence (3:5)
(2) No Response to God's Patience (3:6)
(3) No Repentance at God's Persistence (3:7)
(4) No Realization of God's Purpose (3:8)
(a) To Assemble the Nations for Judgment (3:8a)
(b) To Assail the Nations in Judgment (3:8b)
III. THE DELIVERANCE OF THE LORD (3:9-20)
A. Israel's Responsibility (3:9-10)

1. The Conversion of the Nations (3:9)
2. The Cooperation of the Nations (3:10)
B. Israel's Repentance (3:11-13)
1. A New Humility (3:11-12)
2. A New Holiness (3:13)
C. Israel's Rejoicing (3:14-15)
1. A Merry People (3:14)
2. A Messianic Presence (3:15)
D. Israel's Redeemer (3:16-20)
1. The Climax of the Lord's Blessing (3:16-17)
2. The Context of the Lord's Blessing (3:18-20)
a. Gathering Israel (3:18)
b. Guarding Israel (3:19a)
c. Glorifying Israel (3:19b-20)

------❦------

Zephaniah prophesied during the days of Josiah, the last godly king of Judah. We must remember that throughout Josiah's reign the Assyrian still brooded over the distant horizon and for the first third of that reign the dangerous Ashurbanipal continued to hold court at Nineveh. The lion was getting old, but it could still growl. The Medes and Persians were watching, but were not yet ready to beard the lion in his den. Besides, they did not trust each other. It was not until near the end of Josiah's reign that they came to terms and turned on the tyrant on the Tigris together.

The victorious Cyaxares and Nabopolassar, their Babylonian ally, divided the spoils, and one small segment of the Babylonian share was Judah. Thenceforth Babylonian power and influence had to be reckoned with in Judah even though Babylon was not yet sure enough of itself to be a threat. Indeed when Pharaoh Necho made a bid to seize Babylon's share of the spoils, Josiah mobilized his forces against Egypt. Josiah, still a comparatively young man, was slain by the Egyptians at Megiddo.

It is not clear exactly why Josiah decided to take on the formidable pharaoh. Probably Josiah was determined to conserve the reforms he had introduced in Judah. He may also have wanted to prevent Egypt from robbing him of his cherished dream of cashing in on the recent fall of Assyria; he longed to gather back to the throne of David the territory of the banished ten tribes who had been in exile for a century. But Josiah made a tragic miscalculation and he was cut down in the midst of his days.

Some idea of the terrible state of the country when Josiah came to the throne can be gathered from 2 Kings 23. Every form of religious wickedness and every kind of moral perversion were practiced. Josiah even had to break down the houses of the Sodomites "that were by the house of the Lord" (23:7). There were shrines to the sun, moon, and stars. Men swore by the queen of heaven and sacrificed their children to Moloch. Josiah's earnest and well-intentioned reforms, like those of Hezekiah, touched only the surface of Judah's decadence.

Josiah's only wish was to reform Judah, but revival cannot be legislated. The people went along with what they were required to do, but their hearts were not in it. The princes were skeptical (their skepticism was encouraged by Josiah's untimely death—could not God have protected His own zealot?) and the common people were wedded to their wicked ways.

The preaching of Zephaniah may have helped spark the revival, but he himself was not interested in it. He was of royal blood and the reform party was headed by the king, so we might have expected him to endorse the revival—to call for it and urge it on when it came. We might have expected him to do what he could to clean up the nation, put the Bible back into the schools, oppose pornography and sodomy, improve the legal system, and march for civil rights, stricter marriage laws, and the protection of children. But Zephaniah ignored the reforms, for his mission was not to reform the nation.

Zephaniah stood up to preach in Jerusalem at a critical time. Judah was cynically ignoring the doom of the northern tribes who had long since vanished. The sins of Manasseh had pushed Judah over the hidden boundary between God's mercy and His wrath, so her doom was now fixed. Zephaniah's mission therefore was not to the whole nation, but to the remnant who would flee from the wrath to come. The mantle of Isaiah, Amos, Joel, and Hosea had fallen on Zephaniah.

Zephaniah and Habakkuk prophesied around the same time, although Zephaniah seems to have come first. Habakkuk's prophecy was subjective; he had a problem to ponder. Zephaniah's prophecy was objective; he had a punishment to proclaim. Habakkuk and Nahum were occupied with the great international event that overshadowed the period: Nahum concentrated on the impending fall of Nineveh, and Habakkuk concentrated on the next major power that Judah must fear after the Assyrians were defeated (that is, Chaldea). Zephaniah had a larger view, and perhaps this is why his book was placed after Nahum and Habakkuk in the Old Testament. Zephaniah picked up Joel's "day of the Lord" and invested that day with apocalyptic values.

I. THE DETERMINATION OF THE LORD (1:1-6)

A. The Prophet's Pedigree (1:1)

. In his opening statement Zephaniah told us that he was "the son of Cushi, the son of Gedaliah, the son of Amariah, the son of Hizkiah [Hezekiah], in the days of Josiah the son of Amon, king of Judah." It is not common to carry a genealogy back four generations. The reason Zephaniah did so seems to be to establish the fact that the illustrious King Hezekiah was his great-great-grandfather. The Bible only names one son of Hezekiah: the notoriously wicked and long-reigning Manasseh. But that does not prove that Hezekiah did not have other sons after the birth of his heir. The name *Zephaniah*, which means "Jehovah has hidden," may be a clue to the circumstances surrounding the prophet's birth. Perhaps Manasseh would have slain him if he had not been hidden.

We can also conclude from 1:1 that Zephaniah was a distant cousin of King Josiah. The prophet seems to have been very young when he was called to his ministry.

B. The Prophet's Perspective (1:2-6)

1. The Lord's Decision (1:2-4a)

"I will utterly consume....I will consume....I will consume" (1:2-3). So the prophecy begins. Zephaniah started with the Lord's declaration of wholesale destruction, because in his vision the prophet saw the fires of God's wrath burning everywhere. Neither man, nor beast, nor fish, nor fowl could escape.

God had visited the world with universal judgment before, notably in the days of Noah, and He could do it again. But Zephaniah's perspective was clearly apocalyptic. The impending Babylonian invasion was to be but a shadow of the end-time judgments.

"I will consume...the stumblingblocks with the wicked" (1:3). Here in recording "the word of the Lord" (1:1) Zephaniah used the figure of speech *metalepsis*, which is a double metonymy. (*Metonymy* is a figure of speech in which one noun is used in place of another related noun.) The word translated "stumblingblocks" is "put first for the idols and idolatry, and then idolatry is put for the ruin brought about by them."[1]

The Lord continued to reveal His decision to Zephaniah: "I will also stretch out mine hand upon Judah, and upon all the inhabitants of Jerusalem" (1:4a). Not even Josiah's vigorous attempts to clean up the capital had sufficed to avert the punishment God was determined to inflict on His own people. God does not condemn sin in the sinner and then condone it in the saint.

By the time the Babylonians were finished with Jerusalem, the city was a heap of ruins and the temple was a smoking mass of rubble, but the focus in Zephaniah 1:4a is on the distant future. The chief architect of the universal worship of the antichrist, the one who will set the beast's image in the temple and his mark on most of mankind, will be the false prophet—and he will be a Jew (in Revelation 13 the beast "out of the sea" is a Gentile, and the beast "out of the earth" is a Jew). So God's wrath will find its focus in Jerusalem and the land of the Jews.

2. The Lord's Discrimination (1:4b-6)

One of Judah's problems in Zephaniah's day was the prevalence of idolatrous priests and practices. The same problem had led to the downfall of the ten northern tribes.

Priests have always exerted enormous influence on society. They can help draw a nation to God or they can hasten its destruction. Often their power rivals that of the throne. Israel's "constitution" forbade the union of "church" and state by restricting priests to the tribe of Levi and the family of Aaron, and kings to the tribe of Judah and the family of David. This wise provision protected the country from total abuse of power by either class.

The presence of pagan priests dedicated to the spread of Canaanite cults was corrupting the land of Judah. In the Lord's discriminating eyes, these idolatrous priests were at the heart of all the nation's woes. He called them "Chemarims" (1:4b), which means "black-robed or cassocked"; no doubt He was referring to their distinguishing sacerdotal dress.

The religious offenses prevalent in Judah were listed by Zephaniah. Beginning with *immorality,* he spoke of "the remnant of Baal," for Baal worship was licentious in the extreme. The religion of Baal was a fertility cult and its adherents climaxed their worship with temple prostitutes. (Hindu practices are much the same in the temples of India.) God promised to root the vile religion out of the land once and for all.

In 1:5 the prophet denounced those who practiced *astrology:* "Them that worship the host of heaven upon the housetops." The worship of the sun, moon, stars, and planets is an ancient form of paganism, and so is astrology, which accompanies it. Those who rely on horoscopes for guidance foolishly imagine that the stars influence or determine our destiny. Worshiping the stars is just another way of serving the creature rather than the Creator. Astrology dishonors God and deludes men. Its practice was widespread in Zephaniah's day and the flat roofs were conducive to this form of worship.

Then Zephaniah gave an example of the *insincerity* in the land. He spoke of "them that worship and that swear by the Lord, and that swear by Malcham [also called Milcom and Moloch]." They were hypocrites and compromisers; they wanted a foot in both camps, the best of both worlds. The Lord promised to cut them off.

The reference to Moloch is also an indication of the people's *cruelty.* Moloch was the fierce Ammonite god to whom little children were sacrificed. Imagine trying to swear by both the Lord and Moloch!

In 1:6 Zephaniah spoke of the *apostasy* of "them that are turned back from the Lord." They once knew God but then deliberately turned their backs on Him.

Outright *infidelity* was also prevalent. There were "those that have not sought the Lord, nor enquired for him." These unbelievers had no interest in God whatsoever. The Lord promised to make a clean sweep of all such unbelief. He will do so fully and forever in the end-time purgings of this planet.

II. THE DAY OF THE LORD (1:7–3:8)

The prophet picked up Joel's classic phrase "the day of the Lord." Zephaniah used it primarily to refer to a day of judgment.

A. The People (1:7-13)

1. The Summons (1:7)

Evidently Zephaniah was transported in spirit to the endtimes. He saw the future as an observer present at the scene, and he heard a call for silence: "Hold thy peace at the presence of the Lord God."

There is a similar silence in the Apocalypse when the seventh seal is opened (Revelation 8:1). The preliminary judgments have run their course with the breaking of the first six seals during what Jesus called "the beginning of sorrows" (Matthew 24:8). The world has been reduced by human folly and sin to a state of total chaos. The 144,000 witnesses have been sealed and their mission has been described. The trumpet judgments are about to begin. The devil's antichrist is soon to come on stage and take over the earth, thus precipitating the outpouring of God's wrath in the vial judgments. The angels of the trumpets are about to sound their notes of doom. But first there is a pause and a solemn silence intervenes.[2]

In Zephaniah's vision the crisis hour apparently had arrived. The events to follow were so sobering, so severe, that a pause was needed for reflection. Then we read, "The day of the Lord is at hand: for the Lord hath prepared a sacrifice, he hath bid his guests." God had rejected all the sacrifices, even the Biblical sacrifices, that had been offered without repentance, for as Proverbs 15:8 tells us, "The sacrifice of the wicked is an abomination to the Lord." So He was about to make a sacrifice of His own, and a terrible one it was.

2. The Sacrifice (1:8-13)

Here Zephaniah described the sacrifice that the Lord had prepared. "In the day of the Lord's sacrifice" (1:8) the royal rebels, the sin-seekers, the money-makers, and the leisure-lovers would face God's wrath.

a. The Royal Rebels (1:8)

The Lord said, "I will punish the princes, and the king's children, and all such as are clothed with strange [foreign] apparel." The primary reference here is to the time of the Babylonian invasion when God actually consecrated Nebuchadnezzar and his armies to offer this sacrifice. The ruling caste would pay for their infatuation with foreign attire, customs, values, and religion. God would give them their fill of foreigners.

The weight of judgment would not fall on the king, for Josiah was a godly man. He would be spared the horror by a premature death. The weight would fall on other members of the royal family, who after Josiah's death would go right back to indulging in all the nation's religious and moral sins. And just as Zephaniah foretold, they did not escape punishment (2 Kings 25:7; Jeremiah 39:6-7).

b. The Sin-Seekers (1:9)

"In the same day also will I punish all those that leap on the threshold, which fill their masters' houses with violence and deceit." The picture here is of an unscrupulous man leaping over the threshold in his eagerness to injure an innocent person. Doubtless Zephaniah had seen men who were avid to perform wicked deeds. They rushed out of their masters' homes, rushed into their victims' homes, and rushed back laden with the spoils of deceit and violence. Who was to stop them when the overlords of crime were the nobles of the land?

c. The Money-Makers (1:10-11)

The whole city of Jerusalem was embraced in Zephaniah's vision of doom. He saw "all they that bear silver" being cut off (1:11) and wrote that as they face the wrath of God, "there shall be the noise of a cry from the fish gate, and an howling from the second [the new city], and a great crashing from the hills" (1:10).

"The fish gate" was located in the north wall toward its eastern extremity. Probably fish from Joppa and Jordan were brought into the city through this gate. The north side of the city was the weakest in terms of defense, and Nebuchadnezzar entered through this gate.

"The second" refers to Jerusalem's newer district. It stood on the hill Acra to the north of the older quarter (Zion). Huldah the prophetess lived in this newer section (2 Kings 22:14 says that "she dwelt in Jerusalem in the college [second district]"), and so did the rich. Zephaniah heard howls coming from "the second" because the enemy who breached the fish gate would enter this quarter of the city first.

Those who lived on mounts Zion, Moriah, and Ophel might congratulate themselves for choosing to reside in the older and stronger part of the city, but their complacency would not last long, for Zephaniah heard the noise of "crashing from the hills."

The "inhabitants of Maktesh" would howl too (1:11). The name *Maktesh* means "mortar." Some scholars think that Maktesh was the name of the merchants' quarter in the Tyropoeon valley west of Zion. Others think that "Maktesh" is an ordinary noun and that mortar could be symbolic of the pounding the people of Judah would receive from their enemies.

The word translated "merchant people" literally means "people of Canaan." Zephaniah used this contemptuous term to refer to the businessmen who had become so iniquitous that they were acting like heathens. The Phoenicians particularly were notorious for their dishonesty and unscrupulous practices.

d. The Leisure-Lovers (1:12-13)

God said, "I will search Jerusalem with candles, and punish the men that are settled on their lees: that say in their heart, The Lord will not do good, neither will he do evil." New wine was left on its lees only long enough to fix its color and body. If the wine was not then drawn off, it became thick and syrupy. Likewise men who were "settled on their lees" would be slothful and indifferent.

During the cruel days of Manasseh and Amon, hope had been kept alive by constant stirring, straining, and emptying from vessel to vessel. Hope was clear and sparkling when Josiah came to the throne, but no miracle happened. In spite of his reforms, the court was still full of foreign fashions and every night people on their housetops bowed to the stars. We can readily sympathize with Josiah. He might as well have been trying to liquidate the Roman Catholic Church, outlaw the Jesuits, and uproot Mormonism in the United States today.

The reformation was slow to take root and disappointment set in. The untimely death of Josiah at Megiddo caused men to become despondent. *If the good die so young,* they reasoned, *why bother about God? If His threatenings are anything like His patronage, we can take them with a grain of salt.* God is totally irrelevant. Many of them settled back into lethargy. But woe betide those who were so lazy and indifferent. God would search for them as a man searches his house with a candle. God was going to be feared.

What a picture of his people Zephaniah saw! In the twilight on the flat roofs of the city they were doing obeisance to the stars. Pagan priests were dressed in black robes, and the nobles in the latest Babylonian fashions. The rich lived in new suburbs near the dangerous fish gate, and unscrupulous cheats and indifferent idlers filled the heights and hollows. Above the whole scene thunderclouds of wrath were gathering.

History tells us that judgment has already fallen on Judah, but Zephaniah's picture can also be seen from the perspective of the end-time "day of the Lord," which is still future, but drawing ever nearer.

B. The Period (1:14-18)

1. Its Nearness (1:14)

"The great day of the Lord is near, it is near, and hasteth greatly." Zephaniah saw that each successive calamity in the wretched reigns

of Josiah's sons was another nail in the coffin of Judah's monarchy
and independence. The prophet realized that the Chaldeans
would come speedily and even the mightiest warriors would be
panic-stricken and cry out in terror.

Again the focus of his prophecy lingered briefly on the Babylonian
invasion and then hurried on to the endtimes when events will take
place rapidly. There will only be three and a half years between the
time the antichrist signs his treacherous treaty with Israel and the
beginning of the great tribulation, and only three and a half years
between the beginning of the great tribulation and the return of
Christ. Already the countdown to the rapture is accelerating, and
the rapture is the catalyst that will trigger the onslaught of end-time
events.

2. Its Nature (1:15-18)

To describe the day of the Lord, the prophet piled up words and
phrases expressing doom and gloom and crowded them into one
sentence:

> That day is a day of wrath, a day of trouble and distress, a day
> of wasteness and desolation, a day of darkness and gloominess,
> a day of clouds and thick darkness, A day of the trumpet and
> alarm against the fenced cities, and against the high towers
> (1:15-16).

In the day of the Lord everything will be dark and nobody will be
safe. Alarms will be sounded everywhere, but people will not be able
to find refuge in cities and high towers, for no defenses will be
strong enough to withstand the onslaught. God's wrath will be
unleashed against a world that murdered His Son, spurned His
Holy Spirit, scoffed at the Scriptures, and persecuted His saints.

The blindness of modern man to divine revelation is evident
everywhere. This blindness will increase after the rapture and
people will stumble from one foolish decision to another. The Lord
warned, "I will bring distress upon men, that they shall walk like
blind men, because they have sinned against the Lord" (1:17).

The world says that whom the gods would destroy they first make
mad. We could say the Biblical principle is that whom God would
destroy He first makes blind, either physically or spiritually. The
classic example is the blinding of the men of Sodom (Genesis
19:11).

In the days of the apocalypse the blood of evil men "shall be poured out as dust, and their flesh as the dung." The flesh and blood of the godless people of the earth will be treated as we treat filth, for in God's sight the lives and behavior of wicked men will be utterly worthless.

Zephaniah 1:18 indicates that nothing will be able to avert the prophesied judgment. The whole land will be swathed in flames to fulfill God's purpose of making "a speedy riddance" of all his enemies. The prophet's language is clearly apocalyptic in scope and character.

C. The Places (2:1–3:8)

1. The Country of Judah (2:1-3)

The promised land is always central in Biblical geography. Everything is north, east, south, or west of Israel. During the millennial age the promised land will be the focal point of world geography as well. The final horrors of the great tribulation will be centered in the land of Israel, the setting of the battle of Armageddon will be Israel, and the Lord will return to the mount of Olives in Israel.

The land of the Israelites loomed up foremost in Zephaniah's vision of the day of the Lord. Then all nations will be judged according to their treatment of the Jew and his land (Genesis 12:1-3; Matthew 25:31-46). But for the moment Zephaniah saw the Lord chastening Judah.

The Lord *warned* His people, "Gather yourselves together, yea, gather together, O nation not desired…before the fierce anger of the Lord come upon you" (Zephaniah 2:1-2). The word translated "gather" here is the one commonly used in reference to gathering sticks for a fire. The repetition of the verb reinforces the statement. In our day we can see the initial stages of the gathering process— a prelude to the coming judgment—as Jews from all parts of the world are returning to the promised land.

The phrase translated "not desired" in the King James version is rendered "unchastened" in the Septuagint. Judah is thus depicted as having no desire to amend its ways. Even today there is no national Jewish repentance—just the same age-long bitter antagonism to Christ. Zephaniah saw the nation's sins ripe for judgment in terms of his own time and also in terms of the endtimes.

After warning His people, the Lord *wooed* them: "Seek ye the Lord, all ye meek of the earth, which have wrought his judgment….It may be ye shall be hid in the day of the Lord's anger" (2:3). The Lord appealed to the "meek of the earth," not just the Israelites. We know from Revelation 7:9 that there will be Gentiles saved during the judgment age. Many will be massacred by the antichrist, but some will "be hid." Believing Jews will heed the Lord's warning concerning the antichrist's seizure of the rebuilt temple in Jerusalem and they will flee (Matthew 24:14-22). Perhaps they will find refuge at Petra. We know that the Lord will hide some from the coming holocaust because Zephaniah's name ("Jehovah has hidden") is a promise that not all believers will be exterminated by the antichrist's Gestapo.

2. The Conquerors of Judah (2:4-15)

Judah was encircled by its hereditary foes. The prophet foresaw that the nations surrounding Judah would take sardonic satisfaction in seeing the hated Jews being carried off into captivity and their country being reduced to a heap of rubble by Nebuchadnezzar. But Zephaniah's vision focused primarily on the situation in the endtimes and today the scene is being set for the further and final fulfillment of his prophecy. The reborn land of Israel is encompassed with foes just as in ancient times, and the territories mentioned by Zephaniah are now in the hands of antisemitic nations.

In Zephaniah 2:4-15 we see the prophet searching in all directions and finding foes everywhere.

a. To the West: Philistia (2:4-7)

Taking in the coastland, Zephaniah wrote, "Gaza shall be forsaken, and Ashkelon a desolation: they shall drive out Ashdod at the noon day, and Ekron shall be rooted up" (2:4). Here the prophet addressed four of the five great Philistine cities. The fifth, Gath, had been made a fifedom of Judah by both Uzziah and Hezekiah (2 Chronicles 26:6). The vision of Ashdod being driven out at noon is interesting. Noon was the hottest time of day, the customary time for a siesta, not a likely time for an invasion of an ancient oriental land. So the reference to "the noon day" must have indicated that disaster would fall on the enemy when least expected.

Zephaniah continued: "Woe unto the inhabitants of the sea coast, the nation of the Cherethites! the word of the Lord is against you" (2:5). The name "Cherethites" (Cretans) refers to the Philistines who occupied the southern part of the country. The Philistines are thought to have originated in Crete. Zephaniah saw this southern part of Philistia stripped of its warlike people and converted to pastureland for a peace-loving people.

The prophecy was that the troublesome Philistines would be permanently removed and the Jews would come back and possess their land: "The coast shall be for the remnant of the house of Judah...for the Lord their God shall visit them, and turn away their captivity" (2:7). All this had an initial fulfillment in the wars of Nebuchadnezzar and the return of the Jews after their seventy-year exile in Babylon. There can be little doubt, however, that the vision will be re-enacted in the endtimes.

Modern Israel now controls the ancient territory of the Philistines. One area of the coastline, the Gaza Strip, was held by the Arabs until 1967, but it was seized by the Jews during the Six-Day War. But the Arab states are not reconciled to Israel's control of the Gaza Strip. Old hatreds still slumber and the so-called occupied territories are held by Israel under simmering protest and defiance.

b. To the East: Moab and Ammon (2:8-11)

Turning to Moab and Ammon, Zephaniah accused them of "reproach" and "revilings" (2:8). Both words are cutting, emphatic terms signifying blasphemy. Historically Moab and Ammon (descendants of Lot) were bitter enemies of the Jews, and now their pride and self-importance increased as they observed the fall of the northern kingdom, the deportation of the ten tribes of Israel, and the growing weakness of Judah's kings. Moab and Ammon mocked God's people and took every opportunity to expand their own territory. "Therefore as I live, saith the Lord of hosts, the God of Israel, Surely Moab shall be as Sodom, and the children of Ammon as Gomorrah" (2:9). The prophet saw their land given over to nettles and salt pits. Because they reviled and opposed His people, God would humble Moab and Ammon by making their land "a perpetual desolation." Moreover the remnant of the Jewish people would possess their territory.

Zephaniah's prophecy regarding Moab and Ammon has been partially fulfilled. They tried to lure the gullible Zedekiah into an alliance with themselves, Tyre, and Sidon against Babylon, but soon made their peace with the powerful Nebuchadnezzar. They championed his cause and danced for joy at the downfall of Judah (Jeremiah 48:25-27). Later they conspired again against Nebuchadnezzar. Baalis, king of the Ammonites, was linked by Jeremiah with Ishmael, the murderer of Gedaliah, the Babylonian governor of Jerusalem (Jeremiah 40:14–41:10). It seems that Moab was also involved because Nebuchadnezzar took vengeance on both countries. Thus the two nations that had escaped at the time of Jerusalem's destruction were destroyed by Nebuchadnezzar five years later.

When the Jews came back from their exile in Babylon, two men united in opposing the rebuilding of Jerusalem: Tobiah (an Ammonite) and Sanballat (a Horonite—that is, a Moabite). These individuals were filled with envy and venom over the return of the Jews from captivity (Nehemiah 2:10; 4:1-9). In the endtimes the ancient hatred of Ammon and Moab toward Israel will be revived.

Today the territory of Ammon and Moab lies within the boundaries of the state of Jordan. The Hashemite kingdom of Jordan was a British creation. Under the terms of the mandate, the League of Nations gave Britain the administration of the old land of Palestine on both sides of the river Jordan. Britain's instructions were to develop a homeland for the Jews. One of her first acts was to partition the country along the line of the river: the territory to the west was to be a homeland for the Jews; the territory to the east was to be an Arab kingdom. The plan never did work. All Britain succeeded in doing was to create the state of Jordan out of the old territory of Moab and Ammon. Thus Jordan is heir to the mantle of Moabite and Ammonite hatred of the Jews.

If Jordan is now pursuing a moderate course, the reason is that through hard experience she has developed a healthy respect for Jewish military prowess. When the endtimes arrive, Jordan will again become an active foe of Israel—and all Zephaniah's predictions will have their final fulfillment.

c. To the South: the Ethiopians (2:12)

The Lord said to the enemies to the south, "Ye Ethiopians also, ye shall be slain by my sword." The general consensus seems to be that Ethiopia was included in this prophecy because they were allied to Egypt. From time to time Egypt was ruled by Ethiopian dynasties. There may have been Ethiopian regiments in Pharaoh Necho's army that killed King Josiah, for Ethiopians were numbered in Necho's army when Nebuchadnezzar smote the Egyptians at Charchemish (Jeremiah 46:9). Nebuchadnezzar invaded Egypt (at the same time he subdued Moab and Ammon) presumably to punish the Egyptians for giving asylum to the Jews who fled there after the murder of Gedaliah.

True, Egypt was a hereditary foe of Israel, and Egypt received retribution at the hands of Nebuchadnezzar. But this prophecy of

Zephaniah was directed against Ethiopia, not Egypt, and its focus is apocalyptic. We know from Ezekiel 38–39 that Ethiopia will be an ally of Russia when Russia invades Israel.[3] And we know from Daniel 11:43 that Ethiopia will be an ally of the antichrist in his final wars. This persistent foe of Israel will reap the vengeance of God.

d. To the North: Assyria (2:13-15)

When Zephaniah's eagle eye turned toward the north, he saw Assyria and confirmed its coming overthrow: "He will stretch out his hand against the north, and destroy Assyria; and will make Nineveh a desolation" (2:13).

After Egypt successfully revolted against Assyria and Ashurbanipal did nothing about it, a breath of hope must have rustled through the nations of the world. There was not a man alive who had known Assyria as anything but a menace. A century had passed since the Assyrian army had swept away the northern kingdom of Israel and brutalized most of the land of Judah. For nearly three hundred years Assyrian armies had marched out to sow destruction and torment. Now Assyria's turn to suffer was coming.

Zephaniah picked up Nahum's exultant theme. Assyria was to be left dry as a desert. Her imperial highways would be overgrown with grass and become rank pastureland where beasts would make their home. The "cormorant" (pelican) and "bittern" (probably hedgehog or porcupine) would "lodge in the upper lintels" (2:14). The pelican was a symbol of uncleanness and its Hebrew name suggests vomiting. The doleful singing of birds would sound from the windows of ruined palaces and homes. Carved cedar would be laid open to the destructive elements.

Nothing is more desolate than an abandoned house with windows broken, roof collapsed, wallpaper peeling in ribbons, mildew and other fungi growing over the floor, rats scurrying, and spider webs festooning the corners. Such utter desolation was predicted for "the rejoicing city that dwelt carelessly, that said in her heart, I am, and there is none beside me" (2:15)—words that belong only to God (see Isaiah 45:21-22). For this arrogance Nineveh and Assyria were to be overthrown. Nineveh, once the scourge of the world, would become the scorn of the world: "Every one that passeth by her shall hiss, and wag his hand."

Russia has taken the place of Assyria as the great northern power of end-time prophecies. Ezekiel 38–39 foretells the doom coming to this proud, cruel, God-hating, antisemitic nation.

3. The Capital of Judah (3:1-8)

a. Its Pollutions (3:1-4)

Zephaniah turned his attention back home to Jerusalem. He spared the king, but denounced the ruling classes and pronounced woe upon the city. "Woe," he said, "to her that is filthy and polluted, to the oppressing city!" (3:1) He traced Jerusalem's troubles to her people's rejection of God's Word and their departure from the Lord. What happens to a nation that has been founded on Biblical principles when it abandons the gold standard of the Word of God? Ample illustrations can be found in our own land.

Zephaniah likened Judah's nobility to roaring lions, and her judges to ravening wolves gnawing their prey to the very bone. He characterized her prophets as "light [reckless] and treacherous" (3:4). They were false prophets—empty boasters, claiming to have the gift of prophecy, pretending to speak from God. Judah's priests, he said, "have polluted the sanctuary, they have done violence to the law."

Thus people, princes, prophets, and priests were ripe for judgment—in spite of the fact that their king was desperately eager to bring them back to God.

b. Its Punishment (3:5-8)

Zephaniah was painfully aware that the Lord was present in Jerusalem. The visible token of God's presence was the shekinah glory cloud that rested between the cherubim on the mercyseat on the sacred ark, which was behind the veil inside the holy of holies in the temple. That cloudy pillar hovered over the temple precincts and did not leave the temple and the city until just before judgment fell (Ezekiel 10 describes the departure of the shekinah). Oh, the patience of God! He stayed so long in the midst of moral decadence and religious apostasy, and departed so reluctantly, leaving the city defenseless before the advancing foe!

Still present when Zephaniah prophesied, the Lord was not without His witness in the wicked city. The prophet warned, "He will not do iniquity" (3:5). Day by day He gave reminders that He must either destroy the sin or the sinner, but He was ignored. The wicked were not even ashamed of themselves.

Through His prophet, the Lord reminded the erring city of His judgments of other nations: "I have cut off the nations: their towers are desolate....I said, Surely thou wilt fear me...but they rose early, and corrupted all their doings" (3:6-7). The deportation of the ten northern tribes had brought the fact of God's judgment close to home. And the people of Jerusalem did not have to go far to see how close they themselves had come to judgment. The Assyrians had ravaged towns and villages a few miles north.

In His grace, the Lord had given Judah a godly king. With Josiah on the throne, the country had escaped troubles that had afflicted others. When the Scythians had made a swift, short, but sobering incursion in western Asia, they had passed Judah by. But neither proofs of God's wrath nor proofs of His mercy made any difference. The obdurate nation continued on its downward course.

In 3:8 the prophet's vision turned suddenly to the endtimes:

> Therefore wait ye upon me, saith the Lord, until the day that I rise up to the prey: for my determination is to gather the nations, that I may assemble the kingdoms, to pour upon them mine indignation, even all my fierce anger: for all the earth shall be devoured with the fire of my jealousy.

Now Zephaniah was focusing on the wicked empire of the antichrist, his merciless persecution of the Jews, and his blasphemous, daring challenge to God (2 Thessalonians 2:3-4). The Lord's answer will be to turn the counsels of the antichrist to foolishness and set the stage for the battle of Armageddon and the personal return of Christ to destroy His foes.

III. THE DELIVERANCE OF THE LORD (3:9-20)

A. Israel's Responsibility (3:9-10)

God always intended that the people of Israel should be a blessing to all nations. It was because Israel failed to minister the truth and grace of God to the nations, that evil kingdoms rose up and went on the rampage. But God has His own agenda, and when Israel fails to live up to its spiritual responsibilities, He pursues His own program anyway.

God plans to cleanse the speech of the Gentiles in the endtimes: "Then will I turn to the people a pure language, that they may all call upon the name of the Lord, to serve him with one consent" (3:9). Some people think Zephaniah envisioned the nations speaking a common language during the millennium—possibly Hebrew.

In his vision the prophet saw the Gentiles "from beyond the rivers of Ethiopia [the Blue and White Niles]" (3:10). We can infer that Jews living as far away as Ethiopia will be brought—by the Ethiopians—to their rightful homeland in Israel and that the Gentile Ethiopians will thus be bringing a kind of offering to the Lord.

While the prophecy in Zephaniah 3:9-10 is millennial, there has been a provisional fulfillment of it in the outreach of the gospel to the nations of the earth during the present church age. The stubborn, deliberate, persistent rejection of Christ by the Jews, as recorded in the Gospels, the book of Acts, and several Epistles (see Romans 9–11), did not hinder God from pursuing His purpose of saving a host of Gentile people.

B. Israel's Repentance (3:11-13)

Zephaniah saw a vision of a cleansed and restored Israel. He revealed that *a new humility* will characterize the Hebrew people in the endtimes: "In that day...thou shalt no more be haughty because of my holy mountain. I will also leave in the midst of thee an afflicted and poor people, and they shall trust in the name of the Lord" (3:11-12). Israel's former wickedness will be purged. The pride of race and religion, so characteristic of the Jews down through the centuries, will be a thing of the past.

During the period of the great tribulation, a large number of Jews will perish. The survivors will be converted at the return of Christ and these remarkable, able, and dynamic people will take their place in the millennial kingdom. Their terrible sufferings— and the belated realization that Jesus was indeed the Christ they rejected so long—will give birth to their new humility.

A *new holiness* will also characterize the Jews who enter the millennium: "The remnant of Israel shall not do iniquity, nor speak lies" (3:13). Prosperity and peace will attend this new heart condition of God's ancient people.

C. Israel's Rejoicing (3:14-15)

"Sing, O daughter of Zion; shout, O Israel," wrote the prophet (3:14), for the millennial age will be one of joy unspeakable and full of gladness and glory. We have a God who is happy as well as holy. He loves to hear us sing. One of the greatest books of the Bible is Psalms, the Hebrew hymnbook; it is full of joyful song. Only a redeemed people can really sing. The first song in Scripture was sung by Israel when, having been put under the blood and brought through the water, they stood on the other side of the Red Sea, which had swept their old enemies away; Exodus 14:30–15:1 records, "Thus the Lord saved Israel....Then sang Moses and the children of Israel."

In the millennial kingdom Israel—redeemed, regenerated, and regathered home—will sing. Oh, how they will sing! The sobs and anguish of centuries will be swept away in song. They will rejoice because the enemy is gone. The beast and the false prophet will have been cast into the lake of fire. The devil will have been incarcerated in the abyss. And the Lord will be enthroned in Jerusalem. "Thou shalt not see evil any more," wrote Zephaniah. "The Lord thy God in the midst of thee is mighty....He will joy over thee with singing" (3:15,17). What a day of rejoicing that will be!

D. Israel's Redeemer (3:16-20)

"In that day it shall be said to Jerusalem, Fear thou not: and to Zion, Let not thine hands be slack" (3:16). Antisemitism will be banished from the earth. The Jew will no longer be persecuted, fearful, hunted, and haunted by the possibility of betrayal and brutal treatment. He will no longer be characterized as "the wandering Jew."[4] The King of the Jews will reign with a rod of iron over all the nations of the earth. Jerusalem will be His all-powerful capital and Jews will be His ambassadors to all the countries and administrators of His empire. All nations will know Deuteronomy 7:21 to be a sober fact: "The Lord thy God is among you, a mighty God and terrible." Zephaniah 3:17 confirms the millennial dimension of Moses' words.

Zephaniah took one last, lingering look at the endtimes. He saw the Lord *gathering Israel:* "I will gather them that are sorrowful for [the cessation of] the solemn assembly" (3:18). True Israelites—the believing remnant who will have been scattered, hiding, living in fear for their lives during the days of the antichrist, and grieving over the termination of the temple services—will be gathered home.

He also saw the Lord *guarding Israel:* "At that time I will undo all that afflict thee: and I will save her that halteth, and gather her that was driven out" (3:19a). Israel's afflicted people will be like a flock of lame and footsore sheep, but their Shepherd will come to guide them home. When He comes, the Jews will be able to sing Psalm 23 as it has never been sung before.

Finally Zephaniah saw the Lord *glorifying Israel:* "I will get them praise and fame in every land where they have been put to shame" (3:19b). There is hardly a country on earth where Jews have not been insulted, vilified, hated, and persecuted. But in the millennial age, their management of public affairs will be so brilliant, their love for the Lord will be so personable and convincing, their influence and power will be so obvious, and their wisdom, insight, and skill will be so beneficial that all nations will hail them and welcome them—especially the nations that have cursed them and ridiculed them most.

The Lord said, "At that time will I bring you again, even in the time that I gather you: for I will make you a name and a praise among all people of the earth, when I turn back your captivity before your eyes" (3:20). When Zephaniah wrote this prophecy the ten northern tribes had been in captivity for a century and the two southern tribes would be deported to Babylon within forty years. A remnant would come back, but Zephaniah's vision was of the full and final regathering of God's people in time for the millennial golden age. At long last the promise to Abraham (Genesis 12:1-3) and the glowing promises of the prophets will be fulfilled.

The book of Zephaniah begins with a king and ends with a King. The prophet referred to a past king (his kinsman Hezekiah), a present king (his distant cousin Josiah), and a promised King. Hezekiah and Josiah were both good kings and both had bad fathers and evil sons; both failed, in spite of their sincere efforts, to bring the Hebrew people back to God. Hence the Hebrews needed another King, a King of kings, not just another king of the Jews. Earnestly hoping for the coming of this King, Zephaniah put down his pen; and earnestly hoping that this King will come soon, we ponder what Zephaniah penned.

Chapter 10

HAGGAI

FIRST THINGS FIRST

I. THE CALL TO BUILD (1:1-15)
   A. The Background (1:1-2)
      1. The Period (1:1a)
      2. The Prophet (1:1b)
      3. The Problem (1:2)
   B. The Burden (1:3-11)
      1. Its Context (1:3-4)
      2. Its Content (1:5-11)
         a. The Jews' Condition Exposed (1:5-6)
         b. The Jews' Condition Explained (1:7-11)
            (1) The Cause (1:7-9)
            (2) The Consequences (1:10-11)
   C. The Blessing (1:12-15)
      1. The Response (1:12)
      2. The Reassurance (1:13)
      3. The Revival (1:14-15)
         a. The Truth (1:14)
         b. The Time (1:15)
II. THE CALL TO BEHOLD (2:1-9)
   A. The Present (2:1-3)
      1. A Special People (2:1)
      2. A Struggling People (2:2)
      3. A Sorrowing People (2:3)
   B. The Past (2:4-5)
      1. An Application of Covenant Position (2:4)
         a. Be Strong (2:4a)
         b. Be Sure (2:4b)
      2. An Appeal to Covenant Principle (2:5)

C. The Prospect (2:6-9)
   1. The Lord and His Power (2:6-7a)
     a. Shaking All Nature (2:6)
     b. Shaking All Nations (2:7a)
   2. The Lord and His Presence (2:7b-c)
     a. In Grace (2:7b)
     b. In Glory (2:7c)
   3. The Lord and His Possessions (2:8)
   4. The Lord and His Peace (2:9)
III. THE CALL TO BEHAVE (2:10-19)
  A. The Blessing That Was Wanted (2:10-14)
   1. The Principle of the Law (2:10-13)
     a. Virtue Cannot Be Caught (2:10-12)
     b. Vileness Cannot Be Contained (2:13)
   2. The People of the Lord (2:14)
     a. Unclean in Their Souls (2:14a)
     b. Unclean in Their Sacrifices (2:14b)
  B. The Blessing That Was Withheld (2:15-17)
   1. The Neglected House (2:15)
   2. The Niggardly Harvests (2:16-17a)
   3. The Negligent Heart (2:17b)
  C. The Blessing That Was Waiting (2:18-19)
   1. The Ground of Blessing (2:18)
   2. The Greatness of Blessing (2:19)
IV. THE CALL TO BELIEVE (2:20-23)
  A. God Will Manifest His Power (2:20-22)
   1. By Shaking the Elements (2:20-21)
   2. By Shattering the Enemy (2:22)
  B. God Will Magnify His Prince (2:23)

———❦———

The casual reader may not realize that when he moves from one book of the Bible to the next, he may be passing over a century of time. That is the case, for example, when he moves from Isaiah to Jeremiah, or from Zephaniah to Haggai. The years between Zephaniah and Haggai were not silent, though, for Jeremiah, Ezekiel, and Daniel kept the prophetic witness alive.

In the intervening years the world changed. When Zephaniah preached, Assyria had not yet fallen. By Haggai's day, another world empire—Babylon—had come and gone. Judah had partaken of the bitter fruit of exile, and many Jews had acquired a taste for it. Those who at first had hung their harps on the willows and wept by the rivers of Babylon had been captivated by the bright lights and business opportunities of Babylon. Many had taken too literally Jeremiah's caustic advice to settle down and make the most of things because they were going to be in Babylon for seventy years. A new generation had arisen; born and bred in Babylon, they were accustomed to its lifestyle and indifferent to the promised land and the Scriptures. Here and there a daring Daniel refused to be seduced by all the glitter and glamour, but such men were few. If the captivity had lasted another generation, the Jews might well have been totally assimilated and their light extinguished.

Then came Cyrus, the Persian conqueror. Babylon passed into new hands and change was in the air. Cyrus's policy was to secure the goodwill of the gods of the kingdoms he ruled by supporting their worship. Accordingly he reversed the policy of the Babylonians and issued a decree that not only allowed the Jews to return to their ancestral home, but also encouraged them to return (538 B.C.). A small contingent of Jews responded—fewer than fifty thousand altogether (Ezra 2:64-65). Full of bright hope and rosy visions, they arrived in Jerusalem and, undaunted by the rubble, laid the foundation for their new temple (536 B.C.)

The mixed multitude of foreign colonists who called themselves Samaritans viewed the Jews' endeavors with cautious interest and offered to help. These colonists, who had been settled in central Palestine by the Assyrian conquerors, had evolved a kind of bastard Judaism—a mixture of Jewish and pagan rites and beliefs. The leaders of the Jewish expedition (Zerubbabel the governor and Joshua the high priest), not wanting to compromise, categorically refused the Samaritans' offer. This refusal, not unnaturally, stirred up bitter resentment among the Samaritans, who then set out to oppose the reconstruction of the temple by every means in their power. They appealed to the Persian court and were successful in bringing the work to a halt. Cyrus had lost interest in the project, so for the remainder of his life, no work was done on the temple. Neither was anything done during the reigns of his successors Cambyses and Smerdis nor in the beginning of the reign of Darius Hystaspes.

The zeal of the Jewish pioneers was dampened. Things were not as they had imagined they would be. They had pictured a land eagerly awaiting them, a land ready to blossom as a rose. Instead they found a land grown sterile and overrun with weeds through lack of cultivation; they found hostile neighbors, ruined cities, and shortages of life's amenities. So when official word came that the work must stop, the Jews tamely acquiesced. They looked with a kind of gloomy complacency on the weeds sprouting from the temple's new foundation. And since they could do nothing about the restraining order, they turned their attention to personal business.

In 521 B.C. Darius Hystaspes removed the usurper Pseudo-Smerdis, who had reigned for only seven months, and took the government of Persia into his own hands. When Darius came to the throne, the empire was in considerable disarray. His predecessors Cyrus and Cambyses had been chiefly occupied with wars of expansion and had given scant attention to the consolidation of the empire. A polyglot of peoples had been swept into what was at least a nominal subjection to Persia, but many of these were restless and rebellious. Darius had his hands full. Twenty-three provinces (Susiana, Media, Assyria, Armenia, and Parthia, for instance) were giving him problems and his whole empire was shaking.

Darius thought of a way to secure the goodwill of at least the Jews. (By this time they formed a considerable and influential body in the far-flung provinces of the empire.) He would lift the ban on the rebuilding of the temple. So Darius reversed the interdict and thus the way was cleared to finish the project.

But the repatriated Jews had acquired other interests in the interim. Hence a prophet was needed; indeed two prophets were needed to stand shoulder to shoulder, preaching in concord so that out of the mouth of two witnesses every word might be established. Haggai and Zechariah met that need. Haggai had only one concern: the speedy completion of the temple. Zechariah had a broader vision, one that took in the world, especially the world at the time of the end.

Haggai's burning desire was to stir his people out of their lethargy and materialism so that they would resume their work on the temple. It was obvious to him that Jewish spiritual life could not survive the pressures of the contemporary environment or the pressures of coming events without this great anchor for the faith. How right he was! Once Alexander the Great loosed Hellenism on the world, the Jews would need all the help they could get to prevent extermination and assimilation from destroying them. If they could not withstand mere materialism, how could they hope to withstand fierce persecution and fascinating philosophies? If they could not be victorious over the footmen, how could they battle with horsemen? Haggai had enough sense to see that they could not. First things first was the essence of his message.

I. THE CALL TO BUILD (1:1-15)

A. The Background (1:1-2)

1. The Period (1:1a)

Explaining the background of his first prophecy, Haggai began by telling us the date: "the second year of Darius the king, in the sixth month, in the first day of the month," which on our calendars would be August 29, 520 B.C. Darius was the king who reaffirmed the right of the Jews to rebuild their temple and ordered his officials to provide financial aid for the project from the tribute money of the province. The people were accustomed to gathering for public worship on the first day of the month, so they were assembled when the voice of the prophet broke the silence.

2. The Prophet (1:1b)

Zerubbabel, the civic leader, was there and so was Joshua, the high priest. Zerubbabel, whose name means "born in Babylon," was the grandson of King Jehoiachin. Cyrus had appointed Zerubbabel to be the governor of the new colony in Judea. Joshua was the son of Jehozadak ("Josedech"), whose father had been the high priest in Jerusalem at the time of the Babylonian invasion.

But our attention is drawn to the prophet who that day stabbed the consciences of his people. His name *Haggai* means "festive." Some scholars think that the prophet was born during one of Israel's annual festivals. Jerome said that Haggai "sowed in tears that he might reap in joy."

It has been conjectured that Haggai was a very old man when he prophesied and that he had seen Solomon's temple in all its glory before it was destroyed by Nebuchadnezzar's troops. Elaborating on the known facts, Jewish tradition has made Haggai a member of "the great synagogue" (the forerunner of the Sanhedrin) and assigned him to honored burial in the sepulcher reserved for priests.

3. The Problem (1:2)

Barely mentioning himself, Haggai immediately addressed the problem: "This people say, The time is not come, the time that the

Lord's house should be built." For sixteen years the work of rebuilding the temple had stood still, but this statement needs to be put into perspective. To do that we need to review the dates of the captivity and consider the attitude of the Jews toward prophecy.

We generally speak of the seventy-year captivity of the Jewish people in Babylon, but actually there were two periods of seventy years that overlapped: "the servitude" (605–536 B.C., Jeremiah 29:10) and "the desolations" (590–520 B.C., 2 Kings 25:1; Ezekiel 24:1-2). The servitude began with Jehoiakim's original submission to Nebuchadnezzar and ended with the decree of Cyrus. The desolations began during the reign of Zedekiah on the day Nebuchadnezzar surrounded Jerusalem with his armies for the third and last time. The fact that the book of Kings gives year, month, and day for only this date shows its historical importance. The period ended on "the four and twentieth day of the ninth month, in the second year of Darius," the very day Haggai uttered his third great prophecy: "From this day will I bless you" (Haggai 2:10-19). And that same day Haggai received his fourth and final message from the Lord (2:20-23).

One of the causes of Jewish apathy about completing the temple was a wrong attitude toward prophecy. The people seem to have erroneously inferred from prophecy that the temple could not be rebuilt until the desolations had run their course. Using prophecy as an excuse for inaction, they said, "The time is not come." For them prophecy had become a narcotic instead of a stimulant. Haggai sharply recalled them to their duty.

B. The Burden (1:3-11)

1. Its Context (1:3-4)

The word of the Lord came to Haggai and he promptly passed it on to the people: "Is it time for you, O ye, to dwell in your cieled [paneled] houses, and this house lie waste?" (1:4)

The early pioneers had thrown up rough houses to shield themselves from the elements, then turned their attention to the temple. They immediately cleared away the rubble and laid the foundation, but when the work was halted by a court order, they meekly gave in. Most of these people, born and bred in Babylon, had grown up surrounded by a sophisticated civilization. They were accustomed to the arts, sciences, and refinements of a cultured people. In the promised land they were suddenly reduced to a primitive lifestyle. Professional people, statesmen, poets, and idealists had to plow, plant, hoe, reap, quarry stones, and do sentry duty. It is no wonder that as soon as possible they abandoned their volunteer work on the temple and devoted their time to improving their own living conditions.

Not content with the improvements, they began to build elaborate, wainscoted, ornately decorated houses while they said, "The time is not come, the time that the Lord's house should be built." With more than a touch of sarcasm Haggai turned their own argument against them and said in effect, "Is it time for you to dwell in ornate houses while God's house is a heap of rubble?" Haggai's point was well made. Their sense of values was all wrong.

Haggai's words in 1:4 are a fitting retort to all those who have time for anything and everything except building the Lord's house in this present evil world. They have room for pleasure and business, time for family and friends. They willingly devote long hours every day to the study of secular subjects in order to achieve their ambitions in art, science, or industry. But they have no room, no time to devote to the kingdom of God.

2. Its Content (1:5-11)

a. The Jews' Condition Exposed (1:5-6)

Because of the law of cause and effect, the apathetic repatriates were not prospering. Haggai said:

> Now therefore thus saith the Lord of hosts; Consider your ways. Ye have sown much, and bring in little; ye eat, but ye have not enough....He that earneth wages earneth wages to put it into a bag with holes.

The harder the people worked, the less they seemed to have. The Law of Moses spoke directly to their condition (Deuteronomy 28:38-39; Leviticus 26:18-26). If they had heeded God's Word, they would have recognized the symptoms. It is a basic economic principle in both Old and New Testaments that if we are niggardly toward God, He will be niggardly toward us. We cannot neglect the spiritual dimension and then expect God to bless the secular dimension.

The relationship between spiritual prosperity and secular prosperity—the law of sowing and reaping—was particularly discernible in the Old Testament. There God was dealing with an earthly people. The Old Testament blessing was "the blessing of the Lord

[that] maketh rich, and he addeth no sorrow with it" (Proverbs 10:22). Incidentally, Job's friends judged him by the criterion of the law of sowing and reaping; there were other factors in the equation though, as the book of Job demonstrates.

This criterion is modified in the New Testament since there God is dealing with a heavenly people and He wants us to set our affection on things above, where Christ sits at the right hand of God (see Colossians 3:1-2). That is why the so-called prosperity gospel— so fondly preached by both liberals and charismatics—is false. God is not handing out brochures offering health, prosperity, and worldly success to those who are saved. The New Testament blessing is embodied in the beatitudes (Matthew 5:1-12), which sound strange to worldly and carnal ears.

Haggai's task was to awaken a people sunk in spiritual apathy to a sense of true spiritual values. This apathy was nothing new. It was spiritual apathy that had bred apostasy in the days of the kings. Because of widespread indifference, only fifty thousand of the millions in captivity were willing to return to the promised land. Even those who should have been especially dedicated to the Lord were uninterested. Of the twenty-four orders of the priesthood, only four returned; of the thousands of Levites, only seventy-four responded to the call (Ezra 2:36-40). Haggai challenged the spiritually lethargic people in Judea to consider their ways.

b. The Jews' Condition Explained (1:7-11)

If the repatriates were apathetic partly because of fear of the Samaritans and Persians, they must have forgotten that their God was the Lord of hosts. His host in the promised land was small, but there were countless armies on high well able to protect His little flock from the interference of neighbors and superpowers. So God said, "Go up to the mountain, and bring wood, and build the house; and I will take pleasure in it, and I will be glorified" (1:8).

Haggai urged the people to build the temple with their own resources and forget their vain hopes for imperial patronage. He exhorted them to get down to plain, hard work—go to the mountain, cut down trees, saw them into timbers, haul them to the site, set them securely in place—and see what would happen once God saw that they meant business. Many a work for God has languished because those with the vision are waiting for some millionaire to come along and finance the project. We must do what we can; then God will do what we can't.

With the law of cause and effect still in mind, Haggai came back to the main issue. The pioneers' hardships were a direct result of their neglect of God's house—a neglect more inexcusable because of their diligence in taking care of their own houses. "Therefore," wrote Haggai, "the heaven over you is stayed from dew, and the earth is stayed from her fruit" (1:10). The widespread drought was an indication of God's displeasure with His people. Haggai did not hesitate to draw the conclusion that the bad weather was linked to the people's bad behavior. He had Biblical warrant for saying so. The terms of the Palestinian covenant (Deuteronomy 27–30) plainly revealed the link.

C. The Blessing (1:12-15)

1. The Response (1:12)

Haggai's words, backed by God's written Word and delivered in the power of the Holy Spirit, rang true. What the prophet said was convincing to everyone but the most stubborn humanists. Zerubbabel, the secular leader, and Joshua, the spiritual leader, saw the connection between bad weather and bad behavior right away. They may have suspected it before, but now it was obvious.

All that the people needed was the voice of a prophet to stir them up. No other prophet ever enjoyed such a warm and wholehearted response to his preaching. "Then Zerubbabel...and Joshua...with all the remnant of the people, obeyed the voice of the Lord their God."

2. The Reassurance (1:13)

We learn from the parallel account in the book of Ezra that the new attempt by the Jews to rebuild their temple was immediately opposed by the local Persian government (Ezra 5:1-3). However, when the case came before the Persian court, it was resolved in favor of the Jews. The original order of Cyrus was found at Ecbatana ("Achmetha"), the capital of ancient Media, and this time the famous "law of the Medes and Persians, which altereth not" (Daniel 6:8,15) worked on behalf of the Jews. Darius Hystapses confirmed the order of Cyrus and commanded that funds from the royal treasury be contributed to the project (Ezra 6:1-13).

However, at the time the work was first recommenced, the Jews were taking a step of faith in the face of frowning circumstances. None of the dangers or difficulties had gone away. The people needed some kind of reassurance and it was swift in coming. "Then spake Haggai the Lord's messenger in the Lord's message unto the people, saying, I am with you, saith the Lord" (Haggai 1:13).

3. The Revival (1:14-15)

It was not the bluntness of Haggai's message that wrought the desired result. It was not the appeal to the cold facts of blighted harvests and empty wallets. It was not even the application of the Holy Scriptures to the situation. It was a direct work of the Holy Spirit.

Here was an appeal not just to the conscience, intellect, emotions, and will. It was an appeal to the spirit by the Spirit. "The Lord stirred up the spirit of Zerubbabel...and the spirit of Joshua...and the spirit of all the remnant of the people" (1:14). As a result of this Holy Ghost revival "they came and did work in the house of the Lord." In less than three weeks the work was recommenced. The date is given: "The four and twentieth day of the sixth month, in the second year of Darius the king" (1:15).

We can use all the reasoning and psychology we want on people, but it is the Holy Spirit who, by working in the human spirit, revives the work of God's house.

II. THE CALL TO BEHOLD (2:1-9)

A. The Present (2:1-3)

A month later God spoke again, on the twenty-first day of the seventh month. This was the seventh day of the joyful annual feast of tabernacles (Leviticus 23:39-44), the final feast of ingathering—Israel's harvest festival. It was a great time for God to speak again.

We do not know how much the reconstruction team had accomplished in a month, but evidently enough had been done to give the people a general idea of what the new temple would be like. The timber frame looked inferior to the dressed stone of the temple the Babylonians had destroyed. Some of the older generation remembered the first temple and the comparisons they made caused discouragement.

Exposing this new peril, Haggai asked, "Who is left among you that saw this house in her first glory? and how do ye see it now? is it not in your eyes in comparison of it as nothing?" (2:3) Disinterest had been overcome, but now discouragement threatened the project. Old people are sometimes prone to dwell on the past and make disparaging comments about the efforts of younger people to do something for God. The elderly think of the revivals or preachers or enterprises of their youth and throw cold water on what seem to them to be the small, inferior, inadequate endeavors of the present.

Solomon's temple had been one of the unsung wonders of the world. The temple glistened with precious stones and the whole house was overlaid with gold, including the altar, the cherubim, the floor, the front porch, and the holy of holies. Six hundred talents of gold were used to overlay the holy of holies alone. The inner altar was of gold and so were the table, the lampstand, the various utensils, and the nails. The nails alone weighed fifty shekels. (See 1 Kings 6:22-35; 7:48-50; 2 Chronicles 3:4-9.) If we say that a talent was the equivalent of about 140 pounds and the price of gold is three hundred dollars an ounce, the value of the gold used in the holy of holies would be in the neighborhood of four billion dollars today!

No wonder the older people looked with dismay, if not outright disdain on the new temple. Yet *they* could not take credit for building Solomon's temple. The sacrifices that made it possible were David's, not theirs. In fact their generation had polluted the temple. But they were critical, and God was not impressed with their comments. He was pleased with this new beginning. The enemy always attempts to minimize any genuine work for God.

B. The Past (2:4-5)

"Be strong" (2:4)! That was Haggai's response to any discouragement the disparaging remarks might have sowed in the hearts of the young who had been shouting for joy on that feast day. He took them back to a time when Israel had no temple at all, back to the exodus when God was content to dwell in a tent in the wilderness.

"Be strong," he said three times. "Be strong, O Zerubbabel, saith the Lord; and be strong, O Joshua...and be strong, all ye people...for I am with you." That was what mattered. He who had sat enthroned between the golden cherubim on the mercyseat on the ark within the holy of holies, behind the veil in the lonely grandeur of Solomon's temple, had once wrapped Himself in a fiery, cloudy pillar and marched with His people out of Egypt, across the Red Sea, and all along the wilderness way. Surely a God who was willing to do that would not desert His people now, just because they were poor and had no gold or jewels with which to garnish His new house.

"I am with you." They were reassuring words, but they were linked to the past. "I am with you, saith the Lord of hosts: According to the word that I covenanted with you when ye came out of Egypt, so my spirit remaineth among you: fear ye not." The covenant referred to here in Haggai 2:5 is the covenant at Sinai. Even after the Israelites sinned by worshiping the golden calf, and Moses became the mediator when God threatened to cast the Hebrew people off, God said, "My presence shall go with thee" (see Exodus 6:7; 19:5; 33:12-14). And even if there was no visible shekinah glory in Judah after the captivity, God's presence was still with the remnant in the land. The absence of the visible token of His presence was a step along the road to a more spiritual faith.

C. The Prospect (2:6-9)

1. The Lord and His Power (2:6-7a)

"Thus saith the Lord of hosts; Yet once, it is a little while, and I will shake the heavens, and the earth, and the sea, and the dry land" (2:6). This prophecy of the Lord's *shaking all nature* is clearly apocalyptic in scope. In both the Olivet discourse and the Apocalypse there are confirming prophesies of natural disasters providing a background of chaos for the closing scenes of the drama of the last days (Matthew 24:7; Revelation 6:12-17). Haggai, in 2:7a, added a prophecy of the Lord's *shaking all nations*. The word translated "shake" means "to shake violently" as in Psalm 46:3; 77:18; Jeremiah 10:10.

There was a "mild" shaking going on in the Persian world at the time of Haggai's prophecy. The Greeks were beginning to make their presence felt in the West. The beginning of Darius's reign was a period of upheaval (521–519 B.C.). Then although a dozen revolts had threatened his empire, especially to the north and east, Darius was forced to move westward in 518 B.C. And an expedition to Greece had to be cut short because of the hostility of the Greeks. But these troubles were nothing compared with what Haggai and other Old Testament prophets predicted for the endtimes.

The shaking to which Haggai referred is the great tribulation (Matthew 24:29-30). There are to be wars under the seals (Revelation 6:3-4), under the trumpets (8:8; 9:13-21), and under the vials (16:12-16). There is to be a massive Russian invasion of Israel (Ezekiel 38–39) and finally the terrible battle of Armageddon is to take place (Revelation 19:17-21). Violent shaking indeed!

Certainly a people in the care of a covenant-keeping God who is able to shake all nature and all nations with equal ease, need have no fear.

2. The Lord and His Presence (2:7b-c)

"The desire of all nations shall come: and I will fill this house with glory, saith the Lord of hosts." A great deal of controversy has centered on the expression "the desire of all nations" and various alternate renderings have been suggested. In spite of arguments to the contrary, "the desire of all nations" is probably Christ. Whether people consciously recognize it or not, He is the One for whom the human heart yearns. All creation groans and travails in longing for Him (Romans 8:19-22).

The first temple was resplendent in silver, gold, costly woods, and gorgeous fabrics. The new temple had little or nothing of these—and no shekinah glory. Five things were said to be lacking in this second temple: the ark of the covenant, the sacred fire, the shekinah, the urim and thummim, and the spirit of prophecy.

But the second temple had a glory that was denied Solomon's. It had Christ. It was to the second temple that He was brought as a baby to be offered to God. It was there that as a boy He sat in the midst of the doctors. It was there that He sat and taught and revealed things hidden from the foundation of the world. It was that temple that the money-changers defiled and Jesus cleansed, claiming that it was *His* Father's house. He was the Word made flesh, of whom John wrote, "We beheld his glory, the glory as of the only begotten of the Father" (1:14).

3. The Lord and His Possessions (2:8)

"The silver is mine, and the gold is mine, saith the Lord of hosts." Solomon's temple was encased in gold, covered with it as if gold were as cheap as paint. But what need did God have for gold? All the gold on earth was His. If He wanted to, He could create whole galaxies of gold. The presence or absence of gold was wholly immaterial to God. Its value was determined by the sacrifice and devotion of those who gave it. Those who did not have gold but gave what they had out of love and gratitude pleased God just as much as the wealthy who gave their gold.

Zerubbabel's temple was extensively rebuilt, enlarged, and embellished by Herod. He was a wicked man whose whole life was a scandal and a crime, and the Lord ignored his innovation.

4. The Lord and His Peace (2:9)

"The glory of this latter house shall be greater than of the former, saith the Lord of hosts: and in this place will I give peace, saith the

Lord of hosts." Here Ezekiel's millennial temple is seen as heir and successor of Zerubbabel's temple. The millennial temple will be built after the shaking of Haggai 2:6. While the Lord came in grace to the courts of Zerubbabel's temple, Ezekiel's temple will be connected with the glorious era of peace that will bless the world when Jesus reigns as both King and Priest in Jerusalem.

III. THE CALL TO BEHAVE (2:10-19)

A. The Blessing That Was Wanted (2:10-14)

About a month later—on "the four and twentieth day of the ninth month, in the second year of Darius" (2:10)—Haggai received two more messages for the pioneering remnant in the promised land. (The first of these two messages is recorded in 2:10-19 and the second in 2:20-23.) Blessing had been withheld from the pioneers because of disobedience. Now the blessing that was wanted could be bestowed because the people were putting first things first.

In explaining why blessing had been withheld, Haggai reminded the remnant of *the principle of the law* by asking two questions.

> Thus saith the Lord of hosts; Ask now the priests concerning the law, saying, If one bear holy flesh in the skirt of his garment, and with his skirt do touch bread, or pottage, or wine, or oil, or any meat, shall it be holy? And the priests answered and said, No. Then said Haggai, If one that is unclean by a dead body touch any of these, shall it be unclean? And the priests answered and said, It shall be unclean (2:11-13).

In other words, holiness is not catching, but uncleanness is. A healthy person cannot pass on his good health to a sick person, but a sick person can pass on his infection to a healthy person.

Haggai applied this principle to *the people of the Lord:* "So is this people, and so is this nation before me, saith the Lord; and so is every work of their hands; and that which they offer there is unclean" (2:14). Even though the people had been neglecting the temple, they had been offering sacrifices on the restored altar in Jerusalem. These offerings were far from acceptable to God. He had refused the sacrifices and as a result the land was impoverished. The Jews thought that the restored ritual would make their offerings holy, but their disobedience polluted even their sacrifices.

B. The Blessing That Was Withheld (2:15-17)

Neglect of the Lord's house had resulted in niggardly harvests, which were the proof of God's displeasure. With the blessing of God withheld, twenty measures had been reduced to ten. When fifty vessels of wine were expected from the press, the net yield was only twenty. Wastage, spoilage, and shrinkage devoured all the profits. Great expectations came to nothing. But these reproofs did not produce repentance or revival. What was needed was a fresh word from God, and the Lord challenged His people to "consider"—the word occurs five times in the book of Haggai (1:5,7; 2:15,18 twice).

Haggai wrote, "Consider...I smote you with blasting and with mildew and with hail in all the labours of your hands; yet ye turned not to me, saith the Lord" (2:15-17). It seems that judgment only hardens; it rarely produces repentance. What finally touches the negligent heart is God's word. Maybe that is why Elijah had to learn that God was not in the wind that rent the mountains or in the earthquake or in the fire, but in the still small voice (1 Kings 19:11-12).

C. The Blessing That Was Waiting (2:18-19)

Again the Lord pointed to the date: "the four and twentieth day of the ninth month" (2:18) or as we would say, December 24. It was three months after the work on the temple had been resumed and the Jews were in danger of fresh discouragement. They had worked for three months and the tide of misfortune had not yet turned, or so it seemed. There was no seed in the barn, for the harvest had been blighted by their past disobedience. The fruit trees had been stripped by hail before the close of the sixth month, when they resumed their work. The good influence of their new good intentions had not overcome the bad influence of all their previous preoccupation with themselves. Haggai was afraid that hope deferred might sap their resolve.

Repentance and new-found zeal do not immediately change one's material circumstances. Evil's blighting power is not always broken by holy living. The natural effects of past sin may remain; if they are removed, it is often slowly. The converted alcoholic may still have to suffer from severe damage to his liver; the person saved from a life of promiscuity may still have a diseased body. God does not always remove the consequences of sin, although He forgives the guilt and gives grace to live with the abiding thorn. David was forgiven for his sin with Bath-sheba, but the sword wrought havoc in his house for years thereafter. Nevertheless he grew in grace and increased in the knowledge of God through all his experiences and as a result wrote some of his most precious and helpful Psalms.

If the repatriates in Judah were expecting a miracle as a result of their newborn resolve, they were disappointed. No miracle came— but God gave them something better. He gave them His word: "From this day will I bless you" (2:19). Resting in that word, the people could take courage. God's word is His bond. What better guarantee could they have than the pledge of the living God? If they would plow and plant and prune, God would keep His promise in His own good time and way.

At first Haggai was restrained by God from promising anything. He was simply to set before the people the consequences of their neglect of God's house. They were to face the facts. They were to put first things first. They were to show God they meant business. They were to take appropriate steps to remedy their wrong attitudes and behavior. After three months Haggai was allowed to make a promise, but no miracles or rewards of any kind accompanied the new steps of faith and obedience.

Invariably that is the way God develops in us a maturing trust. He does not offer glittering prospects as the immediate reward of obedience. The present-day hankering after signs, miracles, and healings is infantile, to say the least. It is contrary to God's normal dealings with a soul. It is often Satanic and nearly always detrimental to proper spiritual development.

IV. THE CALL TO BELIEVE (2:20-23)

A. God Will Manifest His Power (2:20-22)

The same day that God entrusted Haggai with a promise for His people, He told him to "speak to Zerubbabel, governor of Judah, saying, I will shake the heavens and the earth; And I will overthrow the throne of kingdoms" (2:21-22). Zerubbabel was a scion of the tribe of Judah and the royal house of David. As we have noted before, he was the grandson of Jehoiachin, next to the last king of Judah. The message Haggai received was directed to Zerubbabel personally, but the prophet's vision was apocalyptic.

Haggai 2:21-22 could not have referred to events during Darius's reign. True, Darius had been forced to fight to secure his throne, but all of his battles had been far away from Judah and none of them had been of great consequence. The Persian empire was vast, covering some two million square miles. Once the usurper had been put down, the central stability of the empire had never been seriously threatened. In Haggai's day no foreign enemy was seriously challenging Persia. The Jews knew from Daniel's prophecies that the empire was to continue on for at least one more reign. It was the fourth king of Persia who was to stir up the enmity of Greece (in the end Greece became a terrible and triumphant foe). Darius was only the third king, reigning after Cambyses and Pseudo-Smerdis. The fourth, Xerxes, had not yet come to power (Daniel 11:1-2) and the empire would continue intact for several reigns after his.

Darius put down revolts in Babylonia and Media with ease. The Persian army merely had to appear to convince the rebels in Susiana to submit. Haggai's prophecy that the earth would be shaken could not have referred to these upheavals, for Darius subdued them in four years—before the Jews completed the temple. And there were no catastrophic convulsions of nature to provide an immediate literal fulfillment. So although Haggai's final message was addressed to Zerubbabel, who was the legal living representative of the throne of David, the prophetic focus of the message looked far beyond Zerubbabel and his times to Christ and the time of the end.

God's promise to "overthrow the throne of kingdoms" refers to the throne of the antichrist. For a short while his empire ("kingdoms") will be global, supported by the ten kings of the revived Roman empire in the West and by the temporarily cowed and submissive kings of the East. The chariots and horsemen in Haggai 2:22 refer to the military might of the antichrist and his confederates. God, however, is not impressed with the power of human kings. It is a small matter to Him to overthrow an empire.

Eventually the first five vial judgments will weaken the power structure of the antichrist so that he will lose his grip over the eastern half of his empire (Revelation 16:1-12). The kings of the East will throw off the tyrannical sway of the antichrist and mobilize against him. Pouring westward, they will cross the Euphrates and deploy in the plain of Megiddo. By then the antichrist will have other revolts on his hands as well (Daniel 11:40-44). He will deal with them in summary fashion and hasten on to Megiddo to confront his major opponent, the eastern foe that has so often haunted the minds of western statesmen. Even the most complacent of them fear what will happen when Japanese technology is united to the manpower of China, India, and the rest of the East.

Haggai 2:22 tells us that the heterogeneous forces will fight among themselves; they will "come down, every one by the sword of

his brother." But the final overthrow of the antichrist and all the
millions massed against God at Megiddo will be accomplished by
Christ personally (Revelation 19:11-21).

B. God Will Magnify His Prince (2:23)

"In that day, saith the Lord of hosts [Haggai's favorite name for
Christ], will I take thee, O Zerubbabel, my servant, the son of
Shealtiel, saith the Lord, and will make thee as a signet: for I have
chosen thee, saith the Lord of hosts."

The curse of God rested on Jehoiachin (also called Jeconiah).
Zerubbabel's ancestry therefore is only taken back one generation
to his father Shealtiel, who was a son of the disgraced and disowned
Jehoiachin. Jeremiah, who had contemptuously called Jehoiachin
Coniah, had written:

> As I live, saith the Lord, though Coniah...were the signet
> upon my right hand, yet would I pluck thee thence....Write ye
> this man childless, a man that shall not prosper in his days: for
> no man of his seed shall prosper, sitting upon the throne of
> David, and ruling any more in Judah (Jeremiah 22:24-30).

Jehoiachin was not childless in the sense that he had no sons, for
he had seven or eight[1] (1 Chronicles 3:17-18), but he was childless
in the sense that none of his sons ever sat on the throne. The signet
ring was precious to an eastern monarch, who would never part
with it, except when he gave it to someone who was temporarily
being entrusted with royal authority (Genesis 41:42; Esther 3:10).
So when God said that if Jehoiachin were a signet ring on His
hand, He would take the ring off and throw it away, He was
indicating how worthless the man was.

The curse was partially lifted from Zerubbabel because of his
obedience. Bestowing on him a special mark of honor and trust,
God called Zerubbabel His "signet." Indeed his name appears in
both genealogies of the Lord Jesus: in the regal line through
Solomon (Matthew 1:13) and in the natural line through Nathan
(Luke 3:27). Zerubbabel was one of God's chosen vessels.

The prophecy in Haggai 2:23, however, is surely Messianic.
God's true "signet" is Christ. He is the One who is the executor of
the divine will on earth. He is the One who is coming back to reign.

After Zerubbabel, the Jewish nation fell into a decline, in spite of
the brief revival under Nehemiah. The promised land became a

pawn in the struggles between Syria and Egypt, and as political power moved westward into Europe, Judea became just a small province in the Roman empire. The Jews fell into an obscurity that lasted for centuries.

Then God sent His "signet" into the world. He was born of a woman of the royal family of David. The circumstances of the royal family had been so reduced that one branch was represented by a peasant woman living in a despised provincial town and its other branch was represented by an unknown carpenter. So the world did not acknowledge God's "signet." His own people gave Him a cattle shed in which to be born and the world gave Him a cross on which to die. God's "signet" returned to Heaven, but He's coming back. "In that day" He will impose all the authority of His throne on this world.

Chapter 11

ZECHARIAH
LOOKING AHEAD

Woven into Zechariah's prophecy are ten distinct visions and symbols. Circled numerals (❶ - ❿) indicate where they occur in the outline. See page 274 for a complete list.

I. REVELATIONS CONCERNING ISRAEL'S FUTURE (1:1–6:15)
   A. The Voice of the Prophet (1:1-6)
      1. The Man (1:1)
      2. The Message (1:2-6)
         a. The Lord's Wrath (1:2)
         b. The Lord's Will (1:3-5)
         c. The Lord's Word (1:6)
   B. The Visions of the Prophet (1:7–6:15)
      1. God Sees (1:7-21)
         a. The Four Horses (1:7-17) ❶
            (1) The Imperialist Powers (1:7-11)
               (a) Their Coming (1:7-8a)
               (b) Their Character (1:8b)
               (c) Their Commission (1:9-10)
               (d) Their Complacency (1:11)
            (2) The Impassioned Plea (1:12-17)
               (a) The Plight of Jerusalem (1:12)
               (b) The Pledge of Jehovah (1:13-17)
                  i. The Lord's Command Exceeded (1:13-15)
                  ii. The Lord's Coming Explained (1:16-17)
         b. The Four Horns (1:18-21)
            (1) Gentile Power Displayed—Their Conquest (1:18-19) ❷

      (2) Gentile Power Destroyed—The Carpenters
          (1:20-21) ❸
  2. God Speaks (2:1–4:14)
      a. The Matter of Israel's Restoration (2:1-13) ❹
         (1) A Question of Perspective (2:1-5)
             (a) Jerusalem—About to Be Measured (2:1-2)
             (b) Jerusalem—About to Be Magnified (2:3-5)
                 i. Her Dimensions (2:3-4)
                 ii. Her Defenses (2:5)
         (2) A Question of Priorities (2:6-7)
             (a) The Jews and Their Past Captivity (2:6)
             (b) The Jews and Their Present Complacency (2:7)
         (3) A Question of Punishment (2:8-9)
             (a) The Lord's Heart (2:8)
             (b) The Lord's Hand (2:9)
         (4) A Question of Privilege (2:10-13)
             (a) A Call to Sing (2:10-12)
                 i. The Lord's Presence with His People
                    (2:10-11)
                 ii. The Lord's Portion in His People
                    (2:12)
             (b) A Call to Silence (2:13)
      b. The Matter of Israel's Righteousness (3:1-10)
         (1) The Converted Priest (3:1-7) ❺
             (a) The Adversary (3:1)
             (b) The Advocate (3:2-7)
                 i. Joshua Changed to a New Man
                    (3:2-5)
                 ii. Joshua Challenged with a New Ministry
                    (3:6-7)
         (2) The Coming Prince (3:8-10) ❻
             (a) Coming as the Servant (3:8)
             (b) Coming as the Stone (3:9-10)
                 i. A Vision of Holiness (3:9)
                 ii. A Vision of Happiness (3:10)
      c. The Matter of Israel's Revival (4:1-14)
         (1) The Testimony Restored to Israel (4:1-7) ❼
             (a) Why the Prophet Could See (4:1)

(b) What the Prophet Could See (4:2-7)
    i. The Lampstand (4:2-3)
    ii. The Lesson (4:4-7)
(2) The Temple Rebuilt in Israel (4:8-10)
    (a) The Lord's Servant Commended (4:8-9)
    (b) The Lord's Servant Criticized (4:10a)
    (c) The Lord's Servant Cautioned (4:10b-c)
        i. The Builder (4:10b)
        ii. The Beholder (4:10c)
(3) The Tribulation Reviewed for Israel (4:11-14) ❼
    (a) Why the Prophet Was Troubled (4:11-12)
    (b) What the Prophet Was Told (4:13-14)
        i. The Angel's Astonishment (4:13)
        ii. The Angel's Answer (4:14)
3. God Stirs (5:1–6:15)
  a. Implicitly to Convict (5:1-4) ❽
    (1) The Mystery of the Flying Roll (5:1-2)
      (a) Discerned by the Prophet (5:1)
      (b) Described by the Prophet (5:2)
    (2) The Ministry of the Flying Roll (5:3-4)
      (a) Its Curse (5:3)
        i. Against Those Who Steal
          (A Sin against Man) (5:3a)
        ii. Against Those Who Swear
          (A Sin against God) (5:3b)
      (b) Its Commission (5:4)
        i. To Detect the Houses of Those Who
          Sin (5:4a)
        ii. To Destroy the Houses of Those Who
          Sin (5:4b)
  b. Impartially to Condemn (5:5-11) ❾
    (1) The Container (5:5-6)
      (a) A Familiar Symbol (5:5-6a)
      (b) A Further Statement (5:6b)
    (2) The Cover (5:7a)
    (3) The Contents (5:7b-8)
      (a) Revealed (5:7b-8a)
      (b) Concealed (5:8b)

(4) The Carriers (5:9-11)
    (a) Their Form Revealed (5:9a)
    (b) Their Function Revealed (5:9b-11)
  c. Imperially to Conquer (6:1-15)
    (1) The Timely Coming of the Chariots (6:1-8) ❿
      (a) Description (6:1-3)
        i. A Vision of the Heights (6:1)
        ii. A Vision of the Horses (6:2-3)
      (b) Delineation (6:4-5)
        i. The Prophet's Ignorance Displayed (6:4)
        ii. The Prophet's Ignorance Dissolved (6:5)
      (c) Destination (6:6-7)
        i. Those with Marked Geographic Aims (6:6)
        ii. Those with More General Aims (6:7)
      (d) Determination (6:8)
    (2) The Typical Crowning of the Christ (6:9-15)
      (a) The Delegation (6:9-10)
      (b) The Demonstration (6:11)
      (c) The Declaration (6:12-15)
        i. The Messiah (6:12a)
        ii. The Mission (6:12b-13a)
        iii. The Monarch (6:13b)
        iv. The Memorial (6:14)
        v. The Movement (6:15a)
        vi. The Message (6:15b)
II. REVELATIONS CONCERNING ISRAEL'S FASTS (7:1–8:23)
  A. The Question Asked (7:1-3)
    1. The Month (7:1)
    2. The Men (7:2a)
    3. The Mission (7:2b-3)
  B. The Question Argued (7:4-14)
    1. Their Hearts Exposed (7:4-7)
      a. Their Fasting Examined (7:4-5)
      b. Their Feasting Examined (7:6)
      c. Their Failure Examined (7:7)
    2. Their History Explained (7:8-14)

a. The Simple Requirement (7:8-10)
  (1) Simple *Dos* (7:8-9)
  (2) Simple *Don'ts* (7:10)
b. The Stubborn Refusal (7:11-12)
c. The Solemn Request (7:13-14)
C. The Question Answered (8:1-23)
  1. Israel and Her Needs (8:1-19)
    a. The Prologue to the Answer (8:1-17)
      (1) No More Fury (8:1-2)
      (2) No More Falsehood (8:3)
      (3) No More Fear (8:4-6)
      (4) No More Flight (8:7-8)
      (5) No More Faltering (8:9)
      (6) No More Famine (8:10-12)
      (7) No More Foreboding (8:13)
      (8) No More Forgetting (8:14-17)
    b. The Proclamation of the Answer (8:18-19)
  2. Israel and Her Neighbors (8:20-23)
    a. The International Pilgrimage to Jerusalem (8:20-22)
      (1) Whole Communities Will Come (8:20-21)
      (2) Whole Countries Will Come (8:22)
    b. The International Prestige of Jews (8:23)
      (1) The Reality of It (8:23a)
      (2) The Reason of It (8:23b)
III. REVELATIONS CONCERNING ISRAEL'S FOLLY (9:1–14:21)
  A. The Coming of the King (9:1-17)
    1. The Grecian Age (9:1-8)
      a. Greece Devours the Land (9:1-6)
        (1) News from the North (9:1-2)
        (2) Wars in the West (9:3-6)
          (a) Phoenicia (9:3-4)
          (b) Philistia (9:5-6)
      b. God Draws the Line (9:7-8)
        (1) God's Power to Change Hearts (9:7)
        (2) God's Power to Change History (9:8)
          (a) The Immediate (9:8a)
          (b) The Ultimate (9:8b)
    2. The Gospel Age (9:9)

3. The Golden Age (9:10)
   a. World Disarmament (9:10a)
   b. World Dominion (9:10b)
4. The Godless Age (9:11-17)
   a. The Blood (9:11-12)
   b. The Battle (9:13-16)
      (1) Israel Confronting the Foe (9:13)
      (2) Israel Conquering the Foe (9:14-16)
         (a) The Lord Descends in Power (9:14)
         (b) The Lord Delivers His People (9:15-16)
            i. Shattering the Foe (9:15a)
            ii. Shepherding the Flock (9:15b-16)
   c. The Blessing (9:17)
B. The Call of the King (10:1-12)
   1. To a Concerned People (10:1-2)
      a. Their Future Prayer (10:1)
      b. Their False Prophets (10:2)
   2. To a Conquering People (10:3-8)
      a. The Visitation (10:3-4)
         (1) The Prophet Sees Judgment Coming (10:3)
         (2) The Prophet Sees Jesus Coming (10:4)
      b. The Victory (10:5-8)
         (1) No More Defeat (10:5)
         (2) No More Division (10:6a)
         (3) No More Dispersion (10:6b-8)
            (a) How the Lord Regathers Them (10:6b)
            (b) How the Lord Rejoices Them (10:7)
            (c) How the Lord Redeems Them (10:8)
   3. To a Converted People (10:9-12)
      a. A Ministering People (10:9)
      b. A Mighty People (10:10-11)
      c. A Mindful People (10:12)
C. The Crucifixion of the King (11:1-17)
   1. The Coming Invasion (11:1-3)
      a. Its Scope
      b. Its Severity
   2. The Crowning Insult (11:4-14)
      a. The Messiah's Ministry Declared (11:4-6)

      (1) The Flock Fed (11:4-5)
         (a) The Nature of the Flock (11:4)
         (b) The Nature of the Foe (11:5)
      (2) The Flock Forsaken (11:6)
    b. The Messiah's Ministry Depicted (11:7-14)
      (1) The Taking of the Staves (11:7)
      (2) The Breaking of the Staves (11:8-14)
         (a) The Resolve (11:8-9)
         (b) The Result (11:10-11)
         (c) The Reason (11:12-13)
         (d) The Rift (11:14)
  3. The Cursed Idolater (11:15-17)
    a. The Coming of the Antichrist (11:15)
    b. The Career of the Antichrist (11:16)
    c. The Collapse of the Antichrist (11:17)
D. The Curse of the King (12:1-14)
  1. A Time of War (12:1-9)
    a. What the Nations Forget (12:1)
      (1) To Look Up at the Heavens (12:1a)
      (2) To Look Around at the Hills (12:1b)
      (3) To Look Within at the Heart (12:1c)
    b. What the Nations Find (12:2-3)
      (1) Something That Makes Them Tremble (12:2)
      (2) Something That Gives Them Trouble (12:3)
    c. What the Nations Face (12:4-9)
      (1) Their Forces Are Incapacitated (12:4-5)
      (2) Their Foes Are Invincible (12:6-8)
         (a) Judah (12:6-7)
         (b) Jerusalem (12:8)
      (3) Their Fate Is Inescapable (12:9)
  2. A Time of Woe (12:10-14)
    a. Israel Convicted by the Spirit (12:10)
      (1) Salvation (12:10a)
      (2) Supplication (12:10b)
      (3) Sorrow (12:10c)
    b. Israel Confessing to the Savior (12:11-14)
      (1) The Example of Israel's Sorrow (12:11)
      (2) The Extent of Israel's Sorrow (12:12-14)

        (a) The Highest (12:12)
        (b) The Holiest (12:13)
        (c) The Humblest (12:14)
E. The Compassion of the King (13:1-9)
  1. Causes Removed (13:1-5)
    a. The Removal of Personal Defilement (13:1)
    b. The Removal of Prophetic Deception (13:2-5)
      (1) No More False Worship (13:2a)
      (2) No More False Witness (13:2b-5)
        (a) Parental Conviction (12:2b-3)
        (b) Personal Confession (13:4-5)
  2. Calvary Remembered (13:6-7)
    a. The Scars of the Shepherd (13:6)
    b. The Scattering of the Sheep (13:7)
  3. Crisis Rementioned (13:8-9)
    a. Those Slain in the Endtimes (13:8)
    b. Those Saved in the Endtimes (13:9)
F. The Coronation of the King (14:1-21)
  1. Jerusalem Ravished (14:1-3)
    a. The Siege of the City (14:1-2a)
    b. The Sorrows of the City (14:2b)
    c. The Salvation of the City (14:3)
  2. Jerusalem Rebuilt (14:4-8)
    a. A New Valley in the Vicinity (14:4-5)
      (1) The Return of the Lord in His Power (14:4-5a)
        (a) The Feet of the Returning Jesus (14:4)
        (b) The Flight of the Remaining Jews (14:5a)
      (2) The Return of the Lord with His People (14:5b)
    b. A New Day in the Darkness (14:6-7)
    c. A New River in the Region (14:8)
      (1) Living Water Supplied (14:8a)
      (2) Lasting Water Supplied (14:8b)
  3. Jerusalem Rescued (14:9-15)
    a. The Lord's Enthronement Reviewed (14:9-11)
      (1) The Lord (14:9)
      (2) The Land (14:10-11)
        (a) Renovated (14:10)
        (b) Repopulated (14:11)

b. The Lord's Enemies Removed (14:12-15)
  (1) The Scourge (14:12)
  (2) The Slaughter (14:13)
  (3) The Spoil (14:14-15)
    (a) The Booty Deposited in Piles (14:14)
    (b) The Beasts Destroyed by Plague (14:15)
4. Jerusalem Restored (14:16-21)
  a. God and the Heathen Nations (14:16-19)
    (1) The Remnant of the Nations (14:16)
    (2) The Rebellions of the Nations (14:17-19)
  b. God and the Hebrew Nation (14:20-21)
    (1) Holiness in the House of the Lord (14:20)
    (2) Holiness in the Houses of the Land (14:21)

———❦———

Two prophets stood shoulder to shoulder: Haggai, an old man with the single burden of the temple; and Zechariah, a young man with a much wider view that included the long ages ahead. The visions of Zechariah soared far beyond his own day. He saw the coming of the Greeks and Romans, the crucifixion of Christ, the rescattering of the Jewish people, the rise of the antichrist, the end-time horrors that await Jerusalem, and the return of Christ to set up a righteous kingdom on earth.

The name *Zechariah,* which means "the Lord remembers," was common among the Jews; more than twenty people in the Old Testament bore the name. This Zechariah called himself "the son of Berechiah, the son of Iddo" (1:1), and Ezra called him simply "the son of Iddo" (5:1; 6:14). It is likely that the father of Zechariah died young and for that reason he was linked directly with his grandfather in genealogies.

Iddo was one of the priests who returned from Babylon with Zerubbabel and Joshua (Nehemiah 12:4). So Zechariah was born a priest, but was called to the prophetic ministry before he was consecrated to the priestly office. It is generally accepted that Zechariah was quite young when he was called to preach. He began his prophetic ministry about two months later than his colleague Haggai.

According to Jewish tradition, Zechariah became a member of "the great synagogue" and also had a share in arranging the temple liturgy. It is likely that he saw the finished temple. He is said to have lived to a ripe old age and to have been buried in a tomb near Haggai's. The marked difference between the style of the early chapters of the book of Zechariah and the style of the later chapters probably indicates that chapters 9–14 were written by the prophet at a much later date.

The outline at the beginning of this chapter of commentary gives an idea of the scope and complexity of Zechariah's prophecies. Such a lengthy structural analysis is essential to understanding his book. The outline is given in full, but the commentary does not include a detailed exposition of every verse because that would call for a separate volume on Zechariah. This study, as part of a work on all the minor prophets, deals with the salient points of the outline and traces the prophet's themes. With the help of the outline, the student will be able to probe the more intricate parts of the prophecy for himself.

I. REVELATIONS CONCERNING ISRAEL'S FUTURE (1:1–6:15)

A. The Voice of the Prophet (1:1-6)

1. The Man (1:1)

We have already noted that Zechariah was a priest as well as a prophet. All too often in Israel's history the prophets had to take issue with the priests. Even the best and most sincere of God's anointed priests had a tendency to become absorbed with ritual; formalism was their besetting sin. The prophet's voice was needed to cut through the priestly preoccupation with outward forms and ceremonies to the heart of their religion. After all, tabernacle and temple, sabbaths and sacrifices, feasts and fasts, high days and holy days—however sacred and Scriptural—were but the trappings of the faith. The prophet's task was to emphasize the spiritual and the eternal; all the rites were only picture-book illustrations of the reality. It is therefore refreshing to find a priest who was also a prophet, a prophet who was also a priest.

Zechariah said he received his first prophecy "in the eighth month, in the second year of Darius" (1:1), which was sixteen years after Cyrus's decree. Haggai had already given his first two messages (Haggai 1:1-11; 2:1-9) and would soon give his last two (2:10-19; 2:20-23). Work on the second temple had recommenced and Haggai had promised that although it seemed that the new temple would be inferior, its glory would be greater than the glory of Solomon's temple. At this juncture the voice of Zechariah rang out.

Haggai had prophesied about the end-time shaking of the nations, but Zechariah's voice was new, young, and strident—much different from the mild but persuasive voice of his aging colleague.

2. The Message (1:2-6)

Vast numbers of Jews had ignored God's invitation to come back home to the promised land. They were scattered all over the rest of the civilized world. Long ago they had ceased to regard their exile as deportation; it now seemed to them to be a very profitable dispersion. They were getting on in the world and making a lot of money. During the reign of the next Persian king (Xerxes), Haman figured he would be able to pay the king's treasury ten thousand talents of silver from the spoils he expected to take from the Jews he planned to exterminate (Esther 3:9). That was an enormous sum, estimated to be the equivalent of two-thirds of the annual revenue of the empire.

On the other hand, the Jews who had returned to the promised land were poor, weak, and discouraged. Most of the repatriates were young and middle-aged men. There were few children and very few old people in the Jewish colony. Nearly all of the people had been born in Babylon.

The zealous young Zechariah preached to his fellow Jews in the Holy Land. "Your fathers...your fathers...your fathers," he thundered, "where are they?" (1:2-5) Emphasizing God's wrath, he cried, "The Lord hath been sore displeased....Be ye not as your fathers." Verse 2 can be rendered, "Wroth was the Lord against your fathers with wrath." Indeed, so great had been His wrath that He had allowed the Babylonians to reduce Judah to rubble and completely destroy the temple. Yet now God called the pioneers back to Himself.

In Babylon the Jews had finally acknowledged the justice of God's dealings with them. "They returned and said, Like as the Lord of hosts thought to do unto us, according to our ways, and according to our doings, so hath he dealt with us" (1:6). Like Haggai, Zechariah was fond of the title "the Lord of hosts." The title occurs fifty-three times in the book of Zechariah, forty-four of those occurrences being in his first eight chapters.

B. The Visions of the Prophet (1:7–6:15)

Included in this part of Zechariah's prophecy are the following ten visions and symbols:

❶ The Four Horses (1:7-17)
❷ The Four Horns (1:18-19)
❸ The Four Carpenters (1:20-21)
❹ The Man with the Measuring Line (2:1-13)
❺ Joshua the High Priest (3:1-7)
❻ The Branch (3:8-10)
❼ The Lampstand and the Olive Trees (4:1-7,11-14)
❽ The Flying Roll (5:1-4)
❾ The Ephah (5:5-11)
❿ The Four Chariots (6:1-8)

The commentary on Zechariah 1:7–6:15 will follow the structural outline, but will include annotations on these visions and symbols.

1. God Sees (1:7-21)

God's eye was on His people. He allowed His prophet to see what He Himself could see.

a. The Four Horses (1:7-17)

Zechariah received his first apocalyptic vision on the twenty-fourth day of the eleventh month of the second year of Darius's reign. That was three months after he was first called to preach and exactly five months after work on the temple was resumed. This vision and the next seven visions show Israel dispersed among the nations and the Gentiles in control of world affairs; in these end-time scenes the Lord is about to intervene on behalf of Jerusalem.

In his vision of the four horses, Zechariah saw a man on a red horse standing among the myrtles of the glen. Other horses of various colors were behind the red horse, but the prophet's attention was drawn to the red horse and its rider, who was the Jehovah angel (the Messiah in one of His preincarnate appearances). The other riders were ordinary angels. Riding "to and fro through the earth" (1:10), the horsemen found Jerusalem trodden down of the Gentiles and the nations "at rest" (1:11), quite unconcerned about the plight of the Jewish people.

The myrtle trees symbolize Israel. The glen speaks of Israel's humiliation. The area where the riders patrolled cannot be limited to the Persian empire, vast though it was, stretching from the

Hellespont to the Indus and from the Caucasus to Egypt. They rode throughout the whole world.

The angel asked, "O Lord of hosts, how long wilt thou not have mercy on Jerusalem?" (1:12) (That is still the great question. The delay has now lasted twenty-five hundred years.) The answer was comforting: Jerusalem would yet be crowned with mercy. The Lord, who had been "sore displeased" with the Jews, was now "very sore displeased" with the nations because of their treatment of the Jews (1:2,15). Focusing on the endtimes, Zechariah prophesied, "The Lord shall yet comfort Zion, and shall yet choose Jerusalem" (1:17). God loves Jerusalem.

b. The Four Horns (1:18-21)

Next Zechariah saw four horns, and his curiosity prompted him to ask the interpreting angel for an explanation. Often symbols of power, horns derive their significance from the horns of bulls and wild beasts. The four horns in the vision, then, symbolize the four world powers that over the centuries participated in the scattering of Israel (Daniel 2:31-45).

These powers turned out to be Babylon, Medo-Persia, Greece, and Rome. The Jews suffered under all four empires. The Babylonians deported them, the Persians at Haman's instigation planned to exterminate them, the Greeks (especially under Antiochus Epiphanes) persecuted them mercilessly, and the Romans uprooted them and scattered them with typical savagery. To this day millions of Jews remain in Gentile lands. Their suffering down through the centuries has been horrendous, and the revived Roman empire under the leadership of the antichrist will inaugurate a Jewish holocaust more terrible than any other in history.

Next Zechariah saw four "carpenters" (1:20)—that is, ironsmiths—and again he requested an explanation. The "carpenters" symbolize those who would be raised up to "fray [terrify]" the world powers responsible for terrifying the Jews through the centuries (1:21). In the vision the Jews were so maltreated "that no man did lift up his head." The Lord showed Zechariah that God has His own instruments for cutting even superpowers down to size. The repatriated Jews were living proof. The Babylonian empire, which had deported them, had collapsed like a house of cards. God eventually pulls down all nations that persecute or ill-treat the Jews.

2. God Speaks (2:1–4:14)

a. The Matter of Israel's Restoration (2:1-13)

The vision of the man with a measuring line prompted the prophet to deal with questions of perspective, priorities, punishment, and privilege.

(1) A Question of Perspective (2:1-5)

Zechariah saw the "man with a measuring line in his hand" starting out "to measure Jerusalem" (2:1-2). Jerusalem was very small compared to Babylon, which was still a resplendent city on the Euphrates. Its broad boulevards, hanging gardens, and magnificent palaces had once inspired Nebuchadnezzar to boast, "Is not this great Babylon, that I have built?" (Daniel 4:30) The Jews, who remembered Babylon, looked at Jerusalem from the perspective of their day and only saw streets cluttered with debris, walls and gates lying in ruins, and a once-magnificent temple being replaced with a much humbler structure.

The man started out, but before he could begin measuring, an angel gave him this message: The Jerusalem of his day might be small enough to be measured quickly, but in a coming day the city would spread out far beyond its present boundaries. And indeed it has.

(2) A Question of Priorities (2:6-7)

The Lord warned the Jews who were still at ease in their dispersion to reorder their priorities. "Flee from the land of the north," He said (2:6). Babylon was called "the land of the north" because the Babylonian invasions had come from that direction.

(3) A Question of Punishment (2:8-9)

The Lord said that the nations that touch the Jewish people, touch the "apple of his eye" (2:8). The Jewish people are precious to God, and woe betide any nation that harms them.

(4) A Question of Privilege (2:10-13)

The prophet foresaw the privileges God's people would enjoy and called for song: "Sing and rejoice, O daughter of Zion: for, lo, I come, and I will dwell in the midst of thee, saith the Lord. And many nations shall be joined to the Lord in that day" (2:10-11). Viewing a scene that was evidently millennial, Zechariah called for silence: "Be silent, O all flesh, before the Lord; for he is raised up out of his holy habitation" (2:13). The whole human race is to be hushed before God. The fact that He will reside in Jerusalem will be enough to sober even the most exuberant.

b. The Matter of Israel's Righteousness (3:1-10)

Millennial blessings lie ahead for Israel, but her restoration cannot be realized apart from righteousness. Her righteousness is clearly related to a Priest and a Prince. The prophet had visions of both.

(1) The Converted Priest (3:1-7)

In the first vision Zechariah saw Joshua, the high priest, clothed in filthy garments and standing before the Lord. Satan was there to make accusations against Joshua, but a divine advocate came forward to take his case and was so successful that the priest was given new garments and a new ministry.

This vision is highly symbolic and highly significant. The filthy garments indicate that we have no righteousness of our own. The great accuser delights to slander us and parade our faults and failures before God. But "we have an advocate with the Father, Jesus Christ the righteous" (1 John 2:1). He makes His righteousness our righteousness. Whenever Satan tries to raise the issue of our sin, our Advocate simply raises His nail-scarred hands to silence him. God wills out of existence the sins of those who are washed in the blood of the Lamb.

What is true of the Christian believer today was made symbolically true of Joshua in Zechariah's day and will be made spiritually true of Israel in a coming day. The vision anticipated the glorious day when the nation of Israel will undergo a spiritual rebirth and will be given a spiritual ministry to the nations, as indicated by Joshua's "fair mitre" (Zechariah 3:5), which was symbolic of his new and effective ministry. The very name "Joshua" *(Yeshua)* was significant, for it was the Old Testament form of the name *Jesus.* He is the One who will remove Israel's national sins, just as He removes our individual sins.

(2) The Coming Prince (3:8-10)

The Lord Jesus will be both a Priest and a Prince, "a priest for ever after the order of Melchizedek," who was a priest and the king of Salem.

We have already considered Zechariah's vision of the priest. The companion vision was of the "Branch" (3:8), one of the Old Testament titles of Christ. There are twenty-three words translated "branch" in the Old Testament. One of these, which occurs twelve times, is used specifically of the Messiah in four notable ways: (1) in Jeremiah 23:5-6 and 33:15 where the "Branch" refers to Christ as King, as in the gospel of Matthew; (2) in Zechariah 3:8 where the "Branch" refers to Christ as Servant, as in the gospel of Mark; (3) in Zechariah 6:12 where the "Branch" refers to Christ as Man, as in the gospel of Luke; and (4) in Isaiah 4:2 where the "Branch" refers to Christ as Jehovah, as in the gospel of John.

c. The Matter of Israel's Revival (4:1-14)

(1) The Testimony Restored to Israel (4:1-7)

Zechariah saw a vision of two olive trees feeding a golden candelabra with a ceaseless, living supply of oil. The symbolism here points to the day when the nation of Israel will experience a spiritual awakening that will make her a light to all mankind. The revival will come "not by might, nor by power, but by my spirit, saith the Lord of hosts" (4:6).

The world had a foretaste of Israel's revival on the day of Pentecost, when there was a partial fulfillment of Joel's prophecy (Acts 2:16-21; Joel 2:28-32). After the rapture of the church there will be another Pentecost that will produce the astonishing revival associated with the ministry of the two witnesses of Revelation 11 and with the preaching of the 144,000 of Revelation 7 during the tribulation. (The language used in the description of the witnesses in Revelation 11 is reminiscent of the description of Zechariah's vision.) However, both of these outpourings of the Holy Spirit, one giving birth to the church and the other to the tribulation revival, are only precursors of the universal spiritual awakening—the one described by Zechariah—that will inaugurate the millennium.

(2) The Temple Rebuilt in Israel (4:8-10)

The prophetic focus turned for a moment to Zerubbabel and the Jerusalem of Zechariah's day. The Lord told the prophet that the half-built temple would be finished, and in 516 B.C. it was. The new temple was dedicated four years after Zechariah gave the message recorded in 4:9 (see Ezra 6:15). It was a "day of small things" (Zechariah 4:10) and many despised it, but not God. He looked beyond that occasion to a future day when a greater than Zerubbabel would have the plummet in His hand. Every line will be true when the Lord rebuilds the earth. No evil will dare raise its head then, for the eyes of the Lord will "run to and fro through the whole earth."

(3) The Tribulation Reviewed for Israel (4:11-14)

The two olive trees and the lampstand again attracted Zechariah's attention. He was told that the two olive branches symbolized "the two anointed ones, that stand by the Lord of the whole earth" (4:14). The reference seems to be to the two witnesses who will confront the antichrist in the coming tribulation age (Revelation 11:3-13).

3. God Stirs (5:1–6:15)

a. Implicitly to Convict (5:1-4)

The "flying roll" was a large scroll—so large that it had the same overall dimensions as the holy place of the tabernacle. In Zechariah's vision the scroll flew over the land and pronounced a curse as it went because of Judah's sins against God and man.

In Scripture a scroll often symbolizes God's written Word, so this vision pictured the rebuke of sin by the Word of God. The Lord mentioned transgressions against both tables of the law, for theft is a sin against man, and swearing is an attack on the reverence due to God. The fact that the flying scroll was pronouncing a curse shows that the law can only curse.

b. Impartially to Condemn (5:5-11)

The ephah, a little over a bushel, was the largest dry measure among the Jews. A basket that could hold an ephah of grain was large enough to hold a small person. Such a container appeared in Zechariah's next vision. In this container sat a woman and she was sealed in by a cover that weighed a talent, the heaviest measure of weight among the Jews. Two women with stork-like wings "lifted up the ephah between the earth and the heaven" (5:9). Zechariah was told that the winged creatures were taking the container to the land of Shinar, where a house would be built for the woman inside.

To understand the immediate application of this vision, we need to keep in mind some facts about the exile. The Jews had been deported to Babylon as a punishment for their sins, especially the

sin of idolatry. There, where all idolatry began, idolatry was burned
out of the Jewish soul. But that sin was replaced by a commercial
spirit—and that spirit has been with the Jews to this day. Before the
exile the Jews as a pastoral people had been strangers to commercialism.

The ephah and the woman symbolize the commercial spirit,
which was contrary to the Mosaic law and out of place in God's land
and among God's people. The woman was cast into the ephah and
carried back to where she came from: Babylon. That is where
commercialism belonged. So the vision indicated God's judgment
of the Babylonianism that His people had brought with them when
they returned from exile.

In the prophetic application of the vision, the woman Zechariah
saw can be identified with the woman in Matthew 13:33 and the
scarlet woman in Revelation 17. She represents all that is incorpo-
rated in Romanism: pomp, secular power, idolatry, materialism,
false doctrine. Apparently, after the antichrist destroys the Roman
religious system (17:16), the spiritual uncleanness it has harbored
will be carried back to rebuilt Babylon (18:2), where it will meet its
final doom.

c. Imperially to Conquer (6:1-15)

(1) The Timely Coming of the Chariots (6:1-8)

In the last of the ten visions, Zechariah saw four chariots coming
out from between mountains of brass. Horses were harnessed to the
chariots. The first horses were red, the next were black, the next
were white, and the last were dappled and strong. The prophet was
told that the chariots and horses depicted "the four spirits of the
heavens, which go forth from standing before the Lord of all the
earth" (6:5). The black horses were sent northward and the white
horses followed them. The dappled horses were sent southward.
The "bay" or "strong" horses were sent "to and fro through the
earth" (6:7). Zechariah heard a voice ring out, "Behold, these that
go toward the north country have quieted my spirit in the north
country" (6:8).

The interpretation of most apocalyptic visions is difficult and
this one is not easy. It would seem, however, that the chariots are
war chariots. The colors depict war (red), victory achieved by
means other than war (white), famine and death (black), and
various judgments (spotted and strong). In Scripture, brass is a
symbol of judgment, so the mountains of brass stand for judgments

that have been accumulating for a long time. The horses are spirits sent from God to achieve His purpose on earth. The terrifying ministry of these angelic beings embraces all the earth, but the North is especially deserving of God's judgment. His Spirit has been particularly provoked by something in that area.

Many commentators take the expression "the north country" as a reference to Babylon and look for a fulfillment of the vision in Babylon, Greece, and Rome. Other scholars, who are probably closer to the mark, match the colors in the vision with the four horses of the apocalypse. The number *four* is the number of the earth: four seasons, four points of a compass, four elements (earth, air, fire, and water). Four angels imprisoned in or near the Euphrates are to be released under the sixth trumpet. Four angels rule the four winds of heaven. (See Revelation 6:1-8; 9:14; 7:1.)

Whatever the correct interpretation may be, the focus of the vision is surely on the endtimes. The special emphasis on the North probably relates to Russia and its role in end-time events. Its militant atheism, global ambition, ruthless persecutions, and vicious antisemitism lead me to believe that perhaps no other nation has so greatly provoked God. Indeed, He says that when Russia invades Israel in the last days, "My fury shall come up in my face" (Ezekiel 38:18). This invasion most likely takes place under the sixth trumpet after the four spirits imprisoned at the Euphrates are released.[1] God's spirit will be "quieted" after Russia has been judged.

Since the antichrist will inherit Russia's land and her uncompromising hatred of God, the prophecy of the chariots may have a further fulfillment in the events that lead to the downfall of the antichrist.

Some scholars think that "the north country" is Babylon. If so, the end-time fulfillment of the prophecy will be the overthrow of rebuilt Babylon, which will be the antichrist's economic capital. There will be rejoicing in Heaven over the destruction of both the Babylonish city and the Babylonish system (Revelation 18:2; 19:1-7).

(2) The Typical Crowning of the Christ (6:9-15)

Zechariah's ten visions were concluded. In them God had reconnoitered the earth, viewed Gentile world power, and revealed His ability to trim it down to size. He had surveyed His purposes concerning Jerusalem, the coming of His own Priest-King, and the millennial ministry of a redeemed Hebrew people. He had seen wickedness being returned to Babylon, from whence it came (Genesis 11), and His end-time judgments resulting in the universal destruction of His foes. But one thing remained undone: He had not crowned His own King.

Hence Zechariah 6 reveals the symbolic crowning of Joshua—not Zerubbabel the prince, but Joshua the high priest. It was not God's intention in Zechariah's day to reconstitute the Davidic monarchy. Besides, Zerubbabel was a son of Jehoiachin, whose sons were barred from the throne by divine decree. Let me emphasize that the crowning of Joshua was purely symbolic. In the Old Testament priests were not crowned and kings were not mitered. The functions of prince and priest were not to be united in one person, as Uzziah discovered at great cost. Zechariah 6:11 points to "the crowning day that's coming by-and-by"[2] when Jesus will be given the double crown of King and Priest.

The prophetic incident was sparked by the arrival in Jerusalem of certain Jews from Babylon; "them of the captivity" they are called. They were Jews of the now-voluntary dispersion who had not responded to the call to return to the promised land as pioneers to prepare it for the coming of Christ. Still wanting some share in the restoration, they brought a gift of gold and silver. Because they had chosen the dispersion, they were not sure they would be welcome, but they were hospitably received.

Zechariah was instructed to take the gold and silver "and make crowns [or one composite crown]" (6:11). Since silver stands for redemption and gold stands for royalty, the crown symbolically united the royal and priestly offices. Zechariah was to place this gold and silver crown on the head of the high priest. This act would point to the coming investiture of the Lord Jesus as King-Priest, "after the order of Melchizedek" (Genesis 14:18-20; Psalm 110:4; Hebrews 5:10; 6:20–7:17). Zechariah was to address Joshua with words that can only rightly belong to Christ:

> Behold the man whose name is The BRANCH....He shall build the temple of the Lord; and he shall bear the glory....He shall be a priest upon his throne....And they that are far off shall come and build in the temple of the Lord (Zechariah 6:12-15).

The symbolic event anticipated the day when Christ, having subdued His foes, will be owned by the restored, redeemed, and repentant nation of Israel, and the cry will ring out, "Behold the man" (6:12). That was Pilate's cry when he tried to persuade obdurate Israel to lay aside their hatred of Jesus. How the words must have resounded in the ears of Caiaphas and his crowd! They were listening to a pagan governor, who was unfamiliar with the Scriptures, use the prophetic words of Zechariah as he pointed to Jesus: "Behold the man!" (John 19:5) In a coming day the Holy Spirit will say, "Behold the Man!" to a nation ready at last to acknowledge Jesus as both King and Priest.

A King-Priest; Jews coming from afar with gifts; a divine title; a double crown; a temple being rebuilt; the crown placed in the temple "for a memorial" (Zechariah 6:14); a charge to "diligently obey the voice of the Lord" (6:15); God's pledge that "this shall come to pass"—all these were types and shadows that will be literally fulfilled at the second coming of Christ. Ezekiel's temple will be built. The King-Priest will reign. People will come from the ends of the earth to bring tithes and tributes to Jerusalem and worship in the temple.

Thus ended Zechariah's first round of prophecies.

II. REVELATIONS CONCERNING ISRAEL'S FASTS (7:1–8:23)

A. The Question Asked (7:1-3)

After a lapse of two years the prophet was given his next series of revelations. Zechariah 7:1 gives the exact date: the fourth day of the ninth month of the fourth year of King Darius—that is, December 4, 518 B.C. The constant repetition of the fact that Darius was king was a tacit acknowledgment that "the times of the Gentiles" were in full force. The temple was now half-finished. A delegation from Bethel (some think from Babylon) had just arrived at Jerusalem with a question for the priests and prophets.

Note that the returned exiles all seem to have gone back to their ancestral cities, and many of the repatriates were originally from Bethel (Ezra 2:28; Nehemiah 7:32). Bethel, once a chief site for the idolatry of Jeroboam, had in the past tried to compete with Jerusalem as a worship center, but now it acknowledged the primacy of Jerusalem.

The urgent question on the minds of the delegates and the rest of the people had to do with fasts. Since the downfall of Jerusalem in 586 B.C. the Jews had observed four annual fasts to commemorate recent tragic events: (1) the taking of Jerusalem by Nebuchadnezzar in the fourth month (Jeremiah 52:6); (2) the burning of the temple in the fifth month (52:12); (3) the murder of Gedaliah the governor in the seventh month (41:1-2); (4) the siege of Jerusalem in the tenth month (2 Kings 25:1). With the rebuilding of the temple progressing so well, the Jews wanted to know if it was still necessary for them to "weep in the fifth month" to commemorate the burning of the original temple (Zechariah 7:3).

B. The Question Argued (7:4-14)

The word of the Lord came to the prophet in response to the query. Dealing first with the hearts of the people, He asked them a question: "When ye fasted and mourned in the fifth and seventh month, even those seventy years, did ye at all fast unto me, even to me?" (7:5) In other words, "*Why* did you fast on the anniversary of the burning of the temple and on the anniversary of the murder of Gedaliah? Were you heartbroken over what these tragedies meant to *God?*"

The fasting and mourning, though severe enough, had been motivated by the people's selfish preoccupation with their own loss and fate. So the Lord sent them back to the Bible. What was important was to keep the things that God "by the former prophets" had enjoined on them (7:7). The people were concerned with an empty ritual; the Lord referred them to divine revelation. He also reminded them of the happy days when Judah and Jerusalem enjoyed the blessing of the Lord.

The Lord dealt next with the history of the people. Disaster had overtaken the country because before the exile the nation had refused to obey Him. The returned remnant were in danger of lapsing into the same old sins. The desolation of the land was an eloquent reminder of the consequences of ignoring God's Word.

C. The Question Answered (8:1-23)

1. Israel and Her Needs (8:1-19)

The basic problem with any merely religious duty is that it becomes a burden and a chore. In a moment of enthusiasm or despair it is easy to make a pledge from the heart, but to keep the pledge in the same spirit may be difficult. That is why the New Testament does not impose rituals on believers.

Evidently the question about fasts touched a raw nerve and in answer Zechariah read his people a lecture. "Thus saith the Lord," he cried ten times in chapter 8.

The Lord first reminded the Jews of His "great jealousy" over Jerusalem (8:2). Although the city had so often been unfaithful to Him, she would become a global center of truth and holiness and the Lord's home.

Millennial Jerusalem will be filled with very old men and women, for during the golden age people will live as long as Methuselah. "And the streets of the city shall be full of boys and girls playing in the streets thereof" (8:5). The streets will be playgrounds, not danger zones as in so many cities today. The reference to the old and young may indicate the absence of both among the repatriates.

Flocking into Jerusalem from East and West, oriental and occidental people will meet in happy harmony. The widespread unemployment resulting from God's judgments will be replaced by boundless prosperity.

It can be argued that Israelites away from the promised land have not always had a positive influence; Marxism for instance was born in the brain of a Jew, and so was Freudian psychology. But Israelites restored to the land and redeemed by the Lord will be a blessing to all mankind. "As ye were a curse among the heathen...ye shall be a blessing" (8:13).

Since the Lord intended "to do well unto Jerusalem" (8:15), Zechariah urged the people to be honest and peaceable—in short, good neighbors.

Having read his sermon, Zechariah turned to the question of the fasts. God had never ordained the fasts at issue. These irksome observances were galling chains the Jews had forged for themselves. God did not care whether they kept those fasts or not. What mattered to Him was whether or not they kept the Word *He* had given them. All their national calamities stemmed from their failure to obey God's laws and His prophets. The Jews should do what God required instead of trying to salve their consciences by keeping rules and regulations He did not make. Practical application of the moral law was far more important than mere rituals.

In the millennial age feasts will forever replace fasts.

2. Israel and Her Neighbors (8:20-23)

Viewing another millennial scene, Zechariah saw people from all over the world making their *pilgrimage to Jerusalem:*

> The inhabitants of one city shall go to another, saying, Let us go speedily to pray before the Lord....Yea, many people and strong nations shall come to seek the Lord of hosts in Jerusalem, and to pray before the Lord (8:21-22).

The risen Lord will be enthroned in Jerusalem. No wonder people will want to go there!

The prophet also saw the future international *prestige of Jews:* "Ten men shall take hold out of all languages of the nations, even shall take hold of the skirt of him that is a Jew, saying, We will go with you: for we have heard that God is with you" (8:23). Never have the Jews been that popular with the rest of mankind.

III. REVELATIONS CONCERNING ISRAEL'S FOLLY (9:1–14:21)

The rest of the prophecies of Zechariah were probably written considerably later than chapters 1–8. In general the burden of chapters 9–14 relates to the first and second comings of Christ. However, chapters 9–11 deal with nearer events as well. Thus in chapters 9–10 we see Israel under Greek dominion and in chapter 11 we see Israel under Roman domination. In the remaining chapters we see the nation of Israel in the last days.

A. The Coming of the King (9:1-17)

1. The Grecian Age (9:1-8)

During the reign of Darius Hystaspes, Greece was just getting ready to come on stage. He campaigned against Greece and was defeated at Marathon (490 B.C.). Then Xerxes threw the weight of the Persian empire against Greece and was defeated at Salamis (480 B.C.). Still Greece waited in the wings.

Then came Philip of Macedon (359–336 B.C.), who extended his power over the Greek states. He died and was succeeded by Alexander (336–323 B.C.), who consolidated and expanded his power. His victory at Granicus (334 B.C.) was quickly followed by his victory at Issus (333 B.C.), which opened up Syria and Palestine to his conquests. Tyre, Gaza, and Egypt fell to the conqueror in 332 B.C. He destroyed what was left of Persian power at the battle of Gaugamela (331 B.C.) and reached India in 326 B.C. Alexander died in 323 B.C. at the age of thirty-three.

Zechariah, who must have been familiar with Daniel's prophecies concerning Greece, added some revelations of his own. He prophesied that the armies of Greece would take Hadrach, Damascus, and Hamath. And as foreseen by Zechariah, judgment was inflicted on these key cities by Alexander the Great after the battle of Issus.

Tyre and Sidon also fell. Tyre, a strong city built partly on the mainland and partly on an island about half a mile offshore, defied Alexander's utmost efforts for seven months. Finally the

Macedonians built a mole from the mainland to the island and subdued, punished, and plundered Tyre. Sidon submitted to Alexander without a struggle. Zechariah had foretold, "Tyrus, and Zidon...Behold, the Lord will cast her out, and he will smite her power in the sea" (9:2-4).

The prophet, clearly foreseeing Philistia falling to the conqueror, gave details city by city: "Ashkelon shall see it, and fear..." (9:5). Zechariah mentioned four of the five prominent Philistine cities. He omitted Gath (as did Amos in 1:6-8 and Zephaniah in 2:4). Gath seems never to have recovered from its destruction by Uzziah (2 Chronicles 26:6).

Zechariah's vision soared for a moment to the endtimes when the Philistines would become a choice and elect remnant in Israel (9:7). He compared the future incorporation of Philistia into Israel to David's incorporation of the Jebusites into his kingdom after he took Zion from them (2 Samuel 5:6-9; Joshua 15:63).

Zechariah foretold that although the heathen nations would suffer at the hand of the Macedonian, Judah would escape (9:8). Thus it was that Alexander bypassed Judah on his way to Egypt. On his return he was met, according to Josephus, by the Jewish high priest Jaddua and a train of priests and citizens in white robes. Jaddua conducted the conqueror into Jerusalem. When Alexander was shown references to himself in Daniel's prophecy, he granted special empire-wide privileges to the Jews.

2. The Gospel Age (9:9)

"Rejoice greatly, O daughter of Zion; shout, O daughter of Jerusalem: behold, thy King cometh unto thee: he is just, and having salvation; lowly, and riding upon an ass, and upon a colt the foal of an ass." In this verse (which is the basis for Matthew 21:4-5) Zechariah foretold the first coming of Christ and His triumphal entry into Jerusalem, when the first sixty-nine weeks of Daniel's prophecy would be terminated (Daniel 9:24-26).

Zechariah put an unerring finger on the salient features of Christ's first coming and His formal presentation of Himself to Israel as her long-promised Messiah. The prophet revealed the uniqueness of His person, purpose, position, and power.

Christ was to be a uniquely "just" person—that is, justified, vindicated, acceptable to God as sinless, declared righteous. Christ's purpose was revealed in the words "having salvation." As the children's chorus simply states:

He did not come to judge the world,
He did not come to blame,
He did not only come to seek,
It was to save He came.[3]

Christ's position was to be "lowly." Here on earth we will never really appreciate how lofty He was. He was "high and lifted up" and the cherubim chanted before Him their ceaseless song (Isaiah 6:1-3). Yet He became "lowly" (Matthew 11:29). He was born in a cattle shed and raised in a provincial town where He worked as a carpenter. He was "despised and rejected of men" (Isaiah 53:3).

Zechariah truly revealed the uniqueness of Christ's power when he prophesied that He would come "riding upon a colt the foal of an ass." In the prophet's day, conquerors were accustomed to ride fiery war horses or emblazoned chariots. But our Lord's power did not need that "outward adorning." "He might have built a palace with a word; yet, at times, He had not where to lay His head." He had power over the raging elements, and twelve legions of angels marched unseen beside Him as He made His way to Calvary. But the only power He normally displayed was the power to heal and save and bless. The Jews had no use for such a King. Even as the multitudes waved their palm leaves and shouted hosannas, the leaders of the nation demanded that He silence them and plotted His death.

Unknown to this remarkable prophet Zechariah, there would be a gap between 9:9 and 9:10. God would stop the Jewish clock and between the two verses insert an age of grace. He would give birth to the church, an entity of which the Old Testament prophets never dreamed even in their most inspired raptures.

3. The Golden Age (9:10)

Zechariah knew nothing of Pentecost or the birth of a New Testament canon or the marvelous story of the church. He knew nothing of the mystery of men, women, boys, and girls of all nations, tribes, and tongues being washed in the blood of the Lamb. He knew nothing of people being baptized into a mystical body, of their being created anew as sons and daughters of the living God, of their being made joint heirs with Christ, of their being seated with Him in heavenly places above principalities, powers, thrones, and dominions. Blind to all this, the prophet leaped over the centuries and moved from the triumphal entry to the triumphant enthronement.

Zechariah envisioned God cutting off the enemies of His people at what we now recognize to be the battle of Armageddon. Once that war is over and His enemies are judged, He will "speak peace unto the heathen." The remnant of the Gentiles—those who survive the judgment in the valley of Jehoshaphat—will be blessed. They will join the remnant of the Jews in repossessing and repopulating the millennial earth. "And his dominion shall be from sea even to sea, and from the river even to the ends of the earth."

4. The Godless Age (9:11-17)

Having described the first and second advents of Christ, the prophet presented a picture of the future sufferings of the Jewish people. In the foreground is the prospect of blood, battle, and blessing during the later Greek period, and in the background is the prospect of end-time events.

a. The Blood (9:11-12)

Zechariah saw the blood of the covenant. Presumably the reference in 9:11 is to the covenant of Sinai, which was ratified by blood (Exodus 24:4-8). At Sinai God pledged deliverance and help to the nation of Israel if they met His conditions. However, His earlier pledge to Abraham was unconditional and it was also ratified by blood (Genesis 12:1-3; 15:1-21). The prophet saw the Jewish people, under the terms of God's covenant, being liberated from Gentile oppression.

In the foreground of Zechariah's vision was the struggle of the Maccabees against the diabolical Antiochus Epiphanes. The prophet called the fearless Maccabean warriors "prisoners of hope" (9:12) because the hope for a free nation and a coming Messiah had taken firm hold of them.

In the background was Israel's end-time struggle against the antichrist and its outcome. As the firstborn of the nations, Israel will receive the firstborn's double portion in the coming kingdom (Exodus 4:22; Deuteronomy 21:15-17). "I will render double unto thee" is the promise in Zechariah 9:12.

b. The Battle (9:13-16)

Zechariah saw the sons of Zion fighting the "sons" of Greece— that is the Greek empire in its later stages under the Seleucid dynasty. This vision was obviously a prophecy of the wars with

Antiochus, which are revealed in greater detail in Daniel 11. Zechariah also saw the Lord going forth to war on behalf of His beleaguered people. Only divine inspiration and revelation could have enabled Zechariah to foretell the rise of Greece and to prophesy that the empire would become the bitter enemy of the Jewish people.

The prophecy is so clear that we can picture the desperate struggle of the Maccabean warriors against the organized and disciplined armies of the Seleucids. We can see bows being bent and arrows darkening the sky. We can see the air full of stones hurled by slings. We can see blood flowing freely. We can hear the din and noise of war and above it all, the Lord's trumpet. Victory is assured.[4]

Zechariah's vision of the battle can also be applied to the terrible wars and woes that will overtake the Jewish people just prior to the second coming of Christ. The Russians will invade Israel and the antichrist will occupy the country, defile it, and wreak savage atrocities on its people. The land of Israel will be the focal point of the world's last battle and Jerusalem will be in its death throes when Christ returns.

c. The Blessing (9:17)

But at the end of the battle will be blessing. Men will be enraptured by the beauty of the King. His goodness will be the cornerstone of the coming kingdom. Zechariah prophesied universal prosperity and good cheer: "How great is his goodness, and how great is his beauty! corn shall make the young men cheerful, and new wine the maids."

B. The Call of the King (10:1-12)

1. To a Concerned People (10:1-2)

For a moment the prophet came back to his own day. He had done well to look thousands of years into the future and rhapsodize about the millennial age, but now he was inspired to apply prophetic truth to present needs. His people, who were pressing on with the task of rebuilding the temple, were suffering hardship as a result of successive years of drought. "Ask ye of the Lord rain in the time of the latter rain," Zechariah said. The latter rain, which was essential to swell the maturing grain, usually came at the time of the vernal equinox. The early rain normally came at the time of the autumnal equinox. Both rains were considered to be marks of God's blessing (Deuteronomy 11:14; Isaiah 30:23; Jeremiah 5:24).

Zechariah was concerned for his people, but he did not hesitate to re-emphasize the fact that the nation's troubles stemmed from its earlier idolatry and later indifference. He summarized their problem in 10:2: "There was no shepherd." Israel's monarchs were supposed to be shepherds like David, God's ideal king. David with his shepherd heart and spiritual nature was able to write Psalm 23. But Judah's later kings were false shepherds. Even Zerubbabel and Joshua had not been concerned for the flock. It took the voices of two prophets to restore concern to the leaders and the people.

2. To a Conquering People (10:3-8)

After giving brief attention to the current situation, Zechariah returned to the future—to the struggles preceding the golden age.

a. The Visitation (10:3-4)

Focusing on the tribulation, the prophet wrote, "The Lord of hosts hath visited his flock" (10:3). The purpose of the Lord's visit will be to transform His people from sheep into war horses. Our generation has had a preview of this transformation as Israel has emerged as a powerful military democracy. The world has been astonished because for centuries it has seen the Jews as meek people bowing supinely to every tyrant that came along. Under the Nazi regime, Jews from all over Europe were lined up to be herded like sheep into boxcars; with little struggle or protest they were shipped off to concentration camps. "Never again!" says the modern Israeli Jew.

Today's Israelis have transformed themselves into war horses by building the toughest, most advanced, and most disciplined fighting force in the Middle East. Thrashing the Arabs again and again, the Jews have served notice to the world that they do not intend to be pushed around anymore. They have the weapons, technology, and willpower to make any tampering with them a very costly undertaking. In the endtimes when the Russians invade Israel, the Jews will give them a severe mauling. Israel now has nuclear weapons and in an extremity would not hesitate to use them.

True, Zechariah saw judgment coming and the Jews armed to fight their foes, but he also saw Jesus coming: "Out of him came forth the corner, out of him the nail, out of him the battle bow, out of him every oppressor together" (10:4). In this verse the prophet used the phrase "out of him" three times to describe the Messiah and once to describe those the Messiah will cast out. The Messiah is "the corner," the cornerstone (see Isaiah 28:16; Matthew 21:42); "the nail," the vital peg or stake that holds a tent in place; and "the battle bow," the defense against aggression. These three symbols point to Israel's future stability and security under the returning Messiah. As for the oppressors, out they will go.

b. The Victory (10:5-8)

When the Messiah returns, there will be *no more defeat*. God's people will be "as mighty men, which tread down their enemies in the mire" (10:5).

When the Messiah returns, there will be *no more division*. God promised, "I will strengthen the house of Judah, and I will save the house of Joseph" (10:6a). The Hebrew nation will no longer be divided into the rival kingdoms of Israel (Joseph) and Judah. The repatriated Jewish people of the last days will form one united nation.

When the Messiah returns, there will be *no more dispersion*. God said of the Hebrews, "They shall be as though I had not cast them off" (10:6b). There will be nationwide rejoicing among the redeemed Jewish remnant and, basking under the smile of God, their numbers will greatly increase.

3. To a Converted People (10:9-12)

God said to Zechariah, "I will sow them among the people: and they shall remember me in far countries" (10:9). In the millennial age the Jews will be the Messiah's ambassadors who will uphold the laws of the kingdom. The conditions of their dispersal will be different from the conditions of the exile. They will not be carried off as captives; the Messiah will send them as His ministers. The nations that oppressed the Jews—Egypt and Assyria for example—will have no Jewish citizens or slaves. The Hebrew people will all be citizens of the reborn millennial state of Israel.

The present revival of the state of Israel is only preliminary and partial. Many Jews are still in Gentile lands, either as unwanted and persecuted minorities or as contented citizens of the lands of their adoption. To bring them back to their land, God will perform miracles, as He did in the exodus, and humble the pride of Israel's enemies. Zechariah likened these end-time enemies to Egypt and Assyria.

The Jews will be blessed in that their salvation and their shield will be the name of the Lord. No one will dare tamper with God's earthly people Israel as they go about their duties throughout the world. "They shall walk up and down in his name" (10:12).

C. The Crucifixion of the King (11:1-17)

Zechariah's vision suddenly changed, showing him the terrible episode when Israel's apostasy was displayed in the rejection of the promised Messiah.

1. The Coming Invasion (11:1-3)

This episode was to be preceded by another invasion of the promised land. "Open thy doors, O Lebanon," the prophet cried (11:1). The "doors" of Lebanon were the mountain passes through which invaders from the north would march. Zechariah did not name the new conquerors, but briefly depicting their line of march, mentioned the fertile land of Bashan and the banks of the Jordan. Thus the prophecy seems to refer to Israel falling into the hands of the Romans.

2. The Crowning Insult (11:4-14)

In this passage God addressed Zechariah and told him to act out a parable. The prophet was to assume the role of the shepherd of a flock destined for slaughter.

The Lord portrayed the actual shepherds of Israel as men so lacking in integrity that they were more concerned with accumulating riches than with caring for the flock. Such was the case in the days of Jesus. The leaders of the nation, Pharisees and Sadducees alike, were hypocritical and avaricious.

The Lord said, "I will no more pity the inhabitants of the land" (11:6). He foretold the factional strife that would come to a terrible head during the Roman siege of Jerusalem in A.D. 70 and revealed to the prophet that the land of Israel would be delivered "into the hand of his king [caesar]." The truth of the prophecy was confirmed when Pilate presented Jesus to the Jews as their King: they shouted, "We have no king but Caesar" (John 19:15).

The Lord continued, "They shall smite the land, and out of their hand I will not deliver them." These words suggest a picture of something being beaten to pieces with repeated blows of a hammer. And as foretold the land was subjected to heavy-handed pounding by the Romans at the time of the fall of Jerusalem and at the time of the Bar Kokhba rebellion.[5]

In Zechariah 11:7 the Jews are again referred to as "the flock of slaughter," a description indicative of their sufferings under Antiochus, Herod, and the Romans. Half a million people perished during the war of A.D. 70 and over a million Jews were slaughtered when Jerusalem fell.

Zechariah now began to carry out his instructions to enact a parable. He described how he played the role of a shepherd. In the East a shepherd carried "two staves"—one a heavy club to defend his flock against predators, the other a crooked staff for recovering fallen sheep from inaccessible places (Psalm 23:4). So Zechariah took "two staves." One he called "Beauty [literally Graciousness]" to depict the Good Shepherd's care for the flock. The other he called "Bands" to depict the oneness of the flock, a oneness only the Good Shepherd could ensure.

Next God's loathing for false shepherds is reviewed. Zechariah 11:8 states, "Three shepherds also I cut off in one month; and my soul lothed them, and their soul also abhorred me." The thought behind this verse seems to be the swift and certain judgment of Israel's false shepherds. That they "abhorred" the Lord Jesus is all too evident in the Gospels and in their bitter and unrelenting efforts to get rid of Him. Zechariah 11:9 continues, "I will not feed you." In other words, because of the false shepherds the Good Shepherd would abandon the flock to its doom, as threatened in the Law (Deuteronomy 31:17). One terrible aspect of this doom was noted by Zechariah: "Let the rest eat every one the flesh of another." This prophecy was fulfilled during the terrible Roman siege of Jerusalem.

In 11:10 we read that Zechariah, in his role as shepherd, broke "Beauty" to depict graphically and symbolically the withdrawal of God's grace and protection from His people. The actual breaking of the staff took place when Jesus pronounced His woes against the Jewish people (Matthew 23). A faithful few believed the prophet's message and, more important, a faithful few believed Jesus. The believing remnant of the nation became the nucleus of the Christian church on the day of Pentecost (Acts 2).

The reason for the rejection of the Jewish nation is given in Zechariah 11:12-13:

> And I said unto them, If ye think good, give me my price; and if not, forbear. So they weighed for my price thirty pieces of silver. And the Lord said unto me, Cast it unto the potter: a

goodly price that I was prised at of them. And I took the thirty
pieces of silver, and cast them to the potter in the house of the
Lord.

Acting out the role of the Good Shepherd, Zechariah asked the
people to put a financial value on his pastoral labors among them.
They gave him a paltry thirty pieces of silver, an affront so great that
they might as well have given him nothing. It was the price of a slave
gored by an ox. (Exodus 21:32). Such was Israel's contemptuous
evaluation of an inspired ministry. The prophet took the insulting
payment (sarcastically called "a goodly price" in Zechariah 11:13)
and threw it to a "potter in the house of the Lord." A potter was a
lowly worker whose products could be bought for a paltry sum. To
throw something to a potter was the equivalent of throwing it away.

We read about the fulfillment of this prophecy in Matthew 27:3-
10. The blood money was given to Judas to secure his betrayal of
Jesus. When Judas saw the terrible result of his treachery, he flung
the cursed coins on the temple floor. The priests, with even less
conscience than Judas, gathered up the thirty pieces of silver and
used the money to buy a potter's field.

Zechariah performed one more symbolic act in his portrayal of
the Good Shepherd. He broke the other staff, "Bands," thus
foretelling the total dissolution of Jewish national life.

3. The Cursed Idolater (11:15-17)

Ignoring the intervening church age, the prophetic vision
changed its focus to the endtimes and the coming, career, and
collapse of the antichrist. Having rejected the Good Shepherd
(and having persisted in this rejection for some two thousand
years), the Jews will be easily deceived by the evil shepherd.

Zechariah was instructed to take again the various accouter-
ments of a shepherd and portray this time "a foolish [worthless]
shepherd" (11:15). Then God made a pronouncement. He would
"raise up" a terrible shepherd, one who had no use for the flock or
love for the sheep; he would tear the sheep to pieces and devour the
flock.

In this new role Zechariah revealed the character of the coming
antichrist. Verse 17 calls him "the idol shepherd," perhaps because
his image is to be set up in the temple (Revelation 13). As head of
the revived Roman empire he will sign a seven-year treaty with the
state of Israel, but the treaty will mask his secret purpose. His real
objective will be to lull the Jews into a false sense of security. He will

get their temple built so he can desecrate it and then turn on them with a program of persecution of unprecedented proportions.

D. The Curse of the King (12:1-14)

"In that day." These words ring out time and again in Zechariah 12. For the most part, the focus is once more on the endtimes. The rise of the antichrist has already been mentioned and now the wars and woes of the period are described.

1. A Time of War (12:1-9)

a. What the Nations Forget (12:1)

The nations forget God (Psalm 2), but God refuses to go away. The God of Israel, their covenant-keeping God, is the One "which stretcheth forth the heavens, and layeth the foundation of the earth, and formeth the spirit of man within him." In this one grand statement the prophet swept away philosophies such as communism and humanism that will give rise to the godless attitude of the nations in the endtimes.

b. What the Nations Find (12:2-3)

The final target of God-hate on this planet will be the Jew and Jerusalem. As the nations of the last days work on getting rid of the last lingering reminders of the Judeo-Christian ethic, they will concentrate their efforts on Jerusalem. The Jews will refuse to surrender the city and will defend it with fanatical zeal. The nations will be so obsessed with Jerusalem that they will be like drunkards who tarry too long at the cup. Thus Jerusalem will become "a cup of trembling [intoxication] unto all the people round about" (12:2).

Doubtless the neighboring Arab states will be in the forefront of the attack. Determined to exterminate the Jewish people and seize Jerusalem, the Arabs will work hand-in-glove with the antichrist. Many other nations will be drawn in as the siege intensifies.

But the Lord told Zechariah, "In that day will I make Jerusalem a burdensome stone for all people: all that burden themselves with it shall be cut in pieces, though all the people of the earth be gathered together against it" (12:3). How true that has been and will be. Britain, in the heyday of her empire, became involved with Jerusalem and found it a very sharp stone indeed. In the end she lost her empire over her ever-increasing desire to find some kind of compromise between Jew and Arab. The United States has meddled with the issue and for her pains has been the target of many terrorist attacks. When Russia meddles with Jerusalem, she will be destroyed. The antichrist will attempt to use his global influence and vast power to seize the city and destroy the Jews, but like all the others, he will find that it is not that simple to solve the problem of Jerusalem. There is a hidden factor in the equation: God and His irrevocable covenant with the Jewish people.

c. What the Nations Face (12:4-9)

Humanly speaking, there will be no reason for the world dictator, with vast military resources at his command, not to be able to conquer the troublesome city. But the besiegers will be up against God Himself. No matter what strategies they employ or what armies they summon, they will be incapacitated by God's direct intervention. "In that day, saith the Lord, I will smite every horse with astonishment [panic], and his rider with madness" (12:4).

The Jewish authorities in Jerusalem will recognize that God is on their side. As in the days of the Maccabees, the defenders of the city will know their God and do exploits (Daniel 11:32). By the ministry of the two witnesses and the 144,000 (Revelation 11; 7), the eyes of many Jews will have been opened to a new awareness of God. They may not have accepted Christ yet, but the moment when they are to become believers will not be far away.

Zechariah prophesied, "In that day shall the Lord defend the inhabitants of Jerusalem" (12:8). The world's hostile powers' ceaseless efforts to take the city will all come to nothing. Evidently the Jews will be weak, but they will be infused with supernatural strength and courage: "He that is feeble among them at that day shall be as David." The fanatical determination of the nations to wrest Jerusalem will be their undoing, for God said, "It shall come to pass in that day, that I will seek to destroy all the nations that come against Jerusalem" (12:9).

2. A Time of Woe (12:10-14)

The result of Israel's end-time suffering will be the wholesale national conversion of the Jewish people to Christ.

a. Israel Convicted by the Spirit (12:10)

The remnant of Israel, awakened at last by their terrible sufferings, will be ripe for a mighty work of the Holy Spirit. The Lord told Zechariah:

> I will pour upon the house of David, and upon the inhabitants of Jerusalem, the spirit of grace and of supplications: and they shall look upon me whom they have pierced, and they shall mourn for him, as one mourneth for his only son, and shall be in bitterness for him, as one that is in bitterness for his firstborn (12:10).

The Jews will come under strong conviction as their eyes are opened at last to Christ, to the One "whom they have pierced." Calvary in all its horror will loom up before them. Suddenly they will realize that right there at the place of the skull outside the city of Jerusalem they crucified the true Firstborn. Their grief and shock will know no bounds.

b. Israel Confessing to the Savior (12:11-14)

Having been convicted by the Holy Spirit, the Jews will confess the Savior. There will have been a considerable spiritual awakening among the Jews even before the final return and unveiling of Christ (Joel 2:28-32; Revelation 7), and many apostate Jews will have perished in the terrible persecutions wrought by the antichrist. It is the remnant of unbelieving Israel who will be instantly converted to Christ at His appearing. It will dawn on them how great their national folly has been in rejecting Jesus as Messiah and Savior.

The whole Jewish population will mourn as they gaze, like Saul of Tarsus, on the One they pierced. In Zechariah 12:12-14 the Holy Spirit emphasized the reality of this national repentance; family by family, house by house, one by one, all will mourn. The mourning will not be mass hysteria, but conviction born of the Holy Ghost.

Backtracking, we note the statement in Zechariah 12:11: "In that day shall there be a great mourning in Jerusalem, as the mourning of Hadadrimmon in the valley of Megiddon." Hadadrimmon was just west of Esdraelon, near Megiddo, where godly King Josiah had been slain and where there had been inconsolable mourning (2 Chronicles 35:22-25). The mention of Megiddo may be a prophetic reminder that the antichrist will have numerous rebellions on his hands toward the end of his brief reign (Daniel 11). When the kings of the East cross the Euphrates and pour into the ancient battlefield of Megiddo, the antichrist will be forced to leave a nucleus of his army to complete the storming of Jerusalem while he concentrates on halting this new threat to his empire.

E. The Compassion of the King (13:1-9)

1. Causes Removed (13:1-5)

a. The Removal of Personal Defilement (13:1)

"In that day there shall be a fountain opened to the house of David and to the inhabitants of Jerusalem for sin and for uncleanness." That glorious "fountain filled with blood / Drawn from Immanuel's veins"[6] was opened at Calvary. Countless millions of Adam's ruined race, including some of Israel's sons, have washed away their sins "in the soul-cleansing blood of the Lamb."[7] But because of stubborn unbelief, that fountain has remained virtually closed to the Jewish people. The blood of Christ is sufficient to cleanse the sin of all the human race, but it is efficient to cleanse only when it is applied to the guilty soul by saving faith. "In that day" the Jews will see that fountain and avail themselves of its cleansing power. That fountain will have been there all along, but the Jews will have been too blind to see it (Romans 9-11).

b. The Removal of Prophetic Deception (13:2-5)

(1) No More False Worship (13:2a)

"It shall come to pass in that day, saith the Lord of hosts, that I will cut off the names of the idols out of the land." Zechariah did not name the idols, but we know that one of them will be the blasphemous image of the antichrist, which the false prophet (a Jew) will place in the rebuilt temple in Jerusalem (Revelation 13).

Perhaps the antichrist will consider it sound policy to set up other idols in Jerusalem, his religious capital—Shintu idols from Japan and images of Buddha and the multitudinous gods of the Hindus, for example. As long as worship of his image is paramount, he may not care if other idols are worshiped too. Perhaps the antichrist will take sardonic satisfaction in establishing a pantheon of all the world's false gods to exacerbate Jewish monotheistic sensibilities.

When the Lord comes, He will cleanse His beloved Jerusalem of all its images and put an end to all idolatry.

(2) No More False Witness (13:2b-5)

Idolatry and false prophets alike are energized by Satan and his demonic hosts. At the beginning of the millennial age, Satan will be incarcerated in the abyss so that he will no longer be able to deceive the nations. The universal judgment of the nations by Christ in the valley of Jehoshaphat (Matthew 25:32-46) will ensure that only regenerated individuals—Jews and Gentiles—will inhabit the millennial kingdom.

The prophetic focus of Zechariah 13:2b-5 is not clear. It seems unlikely that false prophets will arise in the early centuries of the millennium. Perhaps the focus shifts to a time prior to the return of Christ when converted Jews discover that some of their sons have become false prophets; these godly Jews will be so horrified at the discovery that they will personally execute the false prophets, as commanded by the Mosaic law (Deuteronomy 13:6-11; 18:20). Those who escape the execution may show fitting signs of repentance (Zechariah 13:4-5).

Or perhaps the focus is on the later years of the millennium. The early years will be a time of tremendous growth and activity. The regenerated sons of the kingdom will go about the great work of turning the whole world into a garden of Eden. Their hearts will be full of gratitude to the King in Jerusalem. Peace and prosperity will be universal and the laws of the kingdom will be patterned after the sermon on the mount. The pioneers of the golden age will be filled with the Holy Spirit, who will enable them to live holy lives.

The ages will roll by. People will live long—as before the flood. Disease will be conquered and death will be rare. Countless millions of children, grandchildren, and great-grandchildren will be born; all these will know nothing of war, woe, pestilence, famine, and injustice. They will make annual pilgrimages to Jerusalem to see the wonders of the capital, to catch a glimpse of the King, and to see the heavenly Jerusalem above (in stationary orbit over the earthly Jerusalem) shining like a diamond in the sky.[8]

In spite of these ideal conditions and in spite of the ease with which a person born in the millennium can be born again, an ever-increasing number of people will remain unregenerate. Just as children growing up in Christian homes today can become "gospel hardened," so children born in the millennial age will be in peril of growing up "glory hardened." Those who remain unregenerate will dislike the laws of the kingdom because those laws will make any expression of the sinful Adamic nature highly dangerous. Here will be fuel for new unholy fire.

We know from Revelation 20:7-10 that at the end of the millennium Satan will be released from his prison to fan these flames into a universal conflagration. It may be that the prophecy in Zechariah 13:2b-5 refers to the first tentative sparks of a final outbreak of rebellion. Although the world will be filled with beauty and bliss during the golden age, the unregenerate will be discontented. A strange new voice will be heard, the voice of a false prophet. He will promise emancipation from the oppressive tyranny of Jerusalem and hint that a coming liberator is being hindered from bringing his benefits to the race.

The false prophesies will only be whispers at first, but the Lord will be instantly aware of them. Warnings will be issued, but judgment will be stayed for a while to give grace an opportunity to work. However, the infection will spread. The false prophet will win converts, who will emulate their teacher and go even farther astray; indeed they will assume the garb of the Old Testament prophets. The Adamic nature will still be the Adamic nature. Enmity against God is its root; sin and death are its fruit.

The original offender's parents, outraged by their son's wickedness, will take action:

> And it shall come to pass, that when any shall yet prophesy, then his father and his mother that begat him shall say unto him, Thou shalt not live; for thou speakest lies in the name of the Lord: and his father and his mother that begat him shall thrust him through when he prophesieth (13:3).

This execution will have an instant salutary effect. Those infected by the chief offender will come to their senses:

> And it shall come to pass in that day, that the prophets shall be ashamed every one of his vision, when he hath prophesied; neither shall they wear a rough garment to deceive: But he shall say, I am no prophet, I am an husbandman; for man taught me to keep cattle from my youth (13:4-5).

The repentant false prophets will hastily abandon their pretensions and scramble back to their legitimate occupations. Thus for a while the final end-time deception will be stayed. Not until the release of Satan will the infection come to a head.

2. Calvary Remembered (13:6-7)

a. The Scars of the Shepherd (13:6)

The sharp and sudden change in Zechariah's prophetic focus has caused some scholars to reject the Messianic interpretation of

13:6. However, cogent reasons can be advanced for maintaining its Messianic significance.[9]

Verse 6 refers to the sudden revelation of Christ to the Jewish people at the time of His second advent: "One shall say unto him, What are these wounds in thine hands? Then he shall answer, Those with which I was wounded in the house of my friends." The Jews will have looked upon Him whom they pierced (see 12:10).

His hands were pierced by the Romans when they crucified Him, but Christ was not crucified in Rome or Athens. The dreadful deed was done near Jerusalem, the house of His friends. It was the Jewish leaders who plotted Christ's death and forced the hand of Pilate (John 18:35). They hated Him with a hatred set on fire by Hell and they persuaded the common people to clamor for His death. But there were many Jews in Jerusalem who loved Jesus, even though in cowardly fashion they forsook Him. The fact that a month and a half later no fewer than three thousand Jews repented of the deed and were baptized shows that Jerusalem was still the house of His friends (Acts 2:37-41).

Isaiah foresaw those wounds (Isaiah 53:5). David described them graphically in Psalm 22:16. It was these wounds that Christ showed to the disciples in the upper room to still their fears and stir their faith (John 20:19-20). And it was these wounds He showed to doubting Thomas (John 20:24-29). For the remnant of Israel alive at the second coming, these same wounds will again be the authenticating evidence of the finished work of redemption and the reality of His resurrection. They will be the final convincing proof of Christ's identity and redeeming grace.

b. The Scattering of the Sheep (13:7)

Once more shifting his prophetic focus, Zechariah referred to the time of the cross: "Awake, O sword, against my shepherd, and against the man that is my fellow, saith the Lord of hosts: smite the shepherd, and the sheep shall be scattered: and I will turn mine hand upon the little ones." This verse is one of the most remarkable Messianic texts in the Old Testament.

Zechariah was not prophesying about an ordinary sword and an ordinary shepherd. The shepherd was pointedly described as "the man that is my fellow" by none other than "the Lord of hosts." If there were no other similar verses in the Bible, 13:7 would suffice to prove the deity of Christ. No angel in the sky, no anointed cherub, no archangel, or shining seraph could be called God's "fellow"—His equal. The word translated "fellow" occurs elsewhere in Scripture

only in Leviticus (6:2; 19:11,15,17, for instance). Often translated
"neighbor," the word conveys the thought of one united to another
by the possession of common nature, rights, and privileges.

We first read about the sword in Genesis 3:24. As soon as sin raised
its head on earth, God drove Adam and Eve out of Eden. At the gate
of the garden He stationed "cherubims, and a flaming sword which
turned every way, to keep the way of the tree of life." The entrance
was guarded to prevent the guilty pair from stealing back into the
garden to try to circumvent the death sentence God had pronounced on them. Had they been successful in such an enterprise,
they would have lived forever in their sins, become as immortal as
the angels, and been placed beyond the hope of redemption.

The author of Psalm 45 had a brief glimpse of the sword and
issued a call to the coming royal Bridegroom: "Gird thy sword upon
thy thigh, O most mighty, with thy glory and thy majesty. And in thy
majesty ride prosperously" (45:3-4).

And Zechariah foresaw the sword bared at Calvary. He saw the
glittering blade sheathed in the soul of the Savior and the burning
flame extinguished in His blood. God's wrath has thus been
eternally disarmed for all who trust the Savior.

Now the Savior Himself wears the sword as the psalmist foretold.
In Revelation 19:11-16 we see Him armed with the sword and
descending from the sky. His vesture is dipped in blood and He is
crowned with many crowns. Riding a great white horse and followed by the armies of Heaven, the executor of God's wrath is
prepared to "smite the nations."

The crime of Calvary loomed up before Zechariah as he viewed
the sword and the Shepherd. Man's side of the cross was sad and
sordid. But there was another side. The time had come for God to
deal to His own eternal satisfaction with the problem of sin. "Smite
the shepherd," He said. As the hymn writer put it:

> When blood from a victim must flow,
> This Shepherd, by pity, was led
> To stand between us and the foe,
> And willingly died in our stead.[10]

So the Shepherd was to be smitten and the sheep were to be
scattered. The Lord quoted this prophecy Himself, foretelling the
way the disciples would flee in all directions following His arrest
(Matthew 26:31; Mark 14:27). But the scattering of the disciples was
by no means the complete fulfillment of Zechariah's words. The
Hebrew word translated "sheep" in 13:7 is "a feminine singular

collective...used frequently metaphorically of Israel" and the word translated "scattered" is "third feminine plural."[11] The implication is that the unity of the nation would be destroyed and the individual members scattered far and wide. Thus Zechariah foresaw the vengeful uprooting of the Jewish people by the Romans. After the fall of Jerusalem in A.D. 70, large numbers of Jews were deported, and after the failure of the Bar Kokhba rebellion, Roman revenge was thoroughly prosecuted.

The conclusion of this remarkable prophecy states, "I will turn mine hand upon the little ones." The phrase "the little ones" suggests another flock—one that is feeble and faithful. The expression "I will turn mine hand [or bring back the hand over]" can be used in both a good and a bad sense, and the former is the case here. Zechariah and the other Old Testament prophets had no direct vision of either the church or the church age, but we—with the New Testament in our hands and with the benefit of hindsight—can see in Zechariah's words at the end of 13:7 far more than he could (1 Peter 1:9-12). His words were fulfilled when the good sheep of the Hebrew fold were gathered into the flock that the Lord began to assemble on the day of Pentecost (John 10:15-16).

3. Crisis Rementioned (13:8-9)

With another change in focus, the prophecy returns to the subject of Israel in the endtimes, when many Jews will be slain: "It shall come to pass, that in all the land, saith the Lord, two parts therein shall be cut off and die; but the third shall be left therein" (13:8). The carnage wreaked by the enemies of the Jewish people will be horrendous. The world's antisemites will be busy slaughtering Jews until the second coming of Christ intervenes.

Although many will be slain, some will be saved. This remnant will see the returning Christ:

> I will bring the third part through the fire, and will refine them as silver is refined, and will try them as gold is tried: they shall call on my name, and I will hear them: I will say, It is my people: and they shall say, The Lord is my God (13:9).

F. The Coronation of the King (14:1-21)

1. Jerusalem Ravished (14:1-3)

Zechariah saw Jerusalem in the throes of its final agonies before the coming of Christ puts an end to the siege.

a. The Siege of the City (14:1-2a)

"Behold, the day of the Lord cometh, and thy spoil shall be divided in the midst of thee. For I will gather all nations against Jerusalem to battle."

Antisemitism, hatred of Jews, is endemic in Gentile society. From time to time this hatred becomes epidemic and when it does, there is a holocaust. Antisemitism will be curbed by the antichrist—as long as it is in his interest to court the Jews. The Russian invasion of Israel (Ezekiel 38–39) will be the first hint that the Jews are not out of the woods, even though they have a signed treaty with the western powers (that is, the antichrist and the revived Roman empire). Then the antichrist will tear off his benevolent mask and begin the "time of Jacob's trouble," the "great tribulation" of which so many prophecies speak (Matthew 24:15-22). The Jews will put up a stubborn resistance and as the cauldron of the endtimes begins to boil, all nations will be drawn by divine decree toward the Middle East, Israel, and Jerusalem.

b. The Sorrows of the City (14:2b)

"The city shall be taken, and the houses rifled, and the women ravished; and half of the city shall go forth into captivity."

Jerusalem has been besieged so many, many times. The first recorded siege occurred when David took the city from the Jebusites some seven hundred years before the founding of Rome (2 Samuel 5:6-9). Jerusalem was plundered by the Egyptian pharaoh Shishak in the days of Rehoboam (1 Kings 14:25-26) and threatened by the Assyrian king Sennacherib. Nebuchadnezzar of Babylon burned the temple and reduced Jerusalem to rubble. Antiochus the Great took the rebuilt city, and it suffered horribly under the persecutions of Antiochus Epiphanes.

The Roman general Pompey besieged Jerusalem in 63 B.C. He attacked on a sabbath and since the Jews refused to fight on the sabbath, he was soon in possession of the city. Some twelve thousand people were slain. In 37 B.C. Herod, with the support of the Roman army, fought for five months to gain control over Jerusalem. The Roman siege in A.D. 70 was one of the most terrible wars of history. Thousands of Jews were crucified, the temple was burned to the ground, and the city virtually vanished from history for fifty years. In response to the Bar Kokhba rebellion, the Romans obliterated Jerusalem in A.D. 135. They changed the name of the city to Aelia Capitolina, built a temple to Jupiter on the temple site, and banned Jews from going anywhere near the place.

After four silent centuries, the church began to colonize Jerusalem. About A.D. 614 Chosroes the Persian took the city, massacred thousands of Christians, and destroyed the Church of the Holy Sepulcher. Caliph Omar entered the city in 637 and Jerusalem passed into the hands of the Turks. In 1098 the caliph of Egypt sent Afdal, his vizier, to subdue two rival Muslim factions in Jerusalem, and again the city was plundered. In 1099 the soldiers of the first Crusade besieged Jerusalem and in 1187 Saladin recaptured it for the Muslims. In 1244 the Tartars plundered the tragic city and slaughtered its monks and priests.

General Allenby led British forces against the city in 1917 and took it without firing a shot. The Jews and Arabs fought over Jerusalem in 1948 when Israel became a state. In 1967 the Jews captured Jerusalem from the Arabs, united the city, and proclaimed it the capital of the state of Israel.

Such has been the troubled history of Jerusalem. But the worst siege still lies ahead. All the horrors of the past will be re-enacted. By the time two-thirds of the population have perished, the Jews will have lost all hope. It will seem as though the Arabs have finally achieved their goal: the seizure of Jerusalem and the extermination of the Jews. The Hebrew people have never been as desperate as they will be when Zechariah 14:2b is fulfilled.

c. The Salvation of the City (14:3)

But when all seems lost, the miracle will happen: "Then shall the Lord go forth, and fight against those nations." The Lord will return to halt the siege, thrash the nations, seize the antichrist, and disarm the devil himself.

2. Jerusalem Rebuilt (14:4-8)

By the time Christ returns, the world at large will be in a shambles. Devastating wars will have been fought and earthquakes and other natural disasters will have wrought havoc. The entire planet will be in chaos, but nowhere will the ruin be more evident than in Israel and Jerusalem. Therefore some far-reaching physical changes will take place when the Lord comes.

a. A New Valley in the Vicinity (14:4-5)

Zechariah saw the Lord's feet standing on the mount of Olives, the place from which He ascended into Heaven after His resurrection

(Acts 1:11-12). The moment His feet touch the ground when He returns to earth, the mount of Olives will be rent asunder and a valley will appear. The valley will run east and west. Half of the mountain will be to the north of the valley, and half to the south.

At the present time the mount of Olives is at the center of a mile-long line of hills that dominate Jerusalem. The mount of Olives stands 187 feet above mount Zion, 245 feet above mount Moriah, and 443 feet above Gethsemane. Located to the east of Jerusalem, toward the sunrise, the mount of Olives is separated from the city by the narrow Kidron valley. On the other side of the mountain is the wilderness that runs down to the Dead Sea. The road to Bethany and the Jordan river run around the north side of the mountain.

The valley created by the coming convulsion will be a miraculous escape route for the desperate Jewish survivors in Jerusalem. The reference to "Azal" in Zechariah 14:5 has raised some speculation, but Azal is probably a place near one of the eastern gates. Since "the valley of the mountains shall reach unto Azal," the Jews will be able to flee through the gate and down the newly-formed valley.

In another glimpse of the returning Messiah, Zechariah saw Him accompanied by "all the saints." These probably include the angelic hosts and certainly include the glorified saints of the church age, who are now united with Christ in glory (1 Thessalonians 3:13; Jude 14; Colossians 3:4; Revelation 19:7-9). Zechariah, of course, had no knowledge of the church age, but the Holy Spirit, who guided his pen, did.

b. A New Day in the Darkness (14:6-7)

The language with which the prophet described this day is full of mystery and controversy. "In that day," said Zechariah, "the light shall not be clear, nor dark: But it shall be one day which shall be known to the Lord, not day, nor night: but it shall come to pass, that at evening time it shall be light." Here we read of a twilight zone, a day that is not a day, a night that is not a night, a strange kind of darkness that is not darkness, a kind of light that is not light.

Perhaps there will be convulsions in the heavens "in that day." The Lord will be clearly seen, but we know from Revelation 1:7 that He will come "with clouds"; perhaps the clouds will plunge the world into gloom and shadow. The phenomena that accompany this very real and ominous day will doubtless aid the escape of the Jews from the holocaust in Jerusalem and at the same time hinder their terror-stricken foes.

It is not certain whether the length of this new day is the normal twenty-four hours. Zechariah made no attempt to elucidate the mystery that surrounds it. It will be "known to the Lord," he said.

c. A New River in the Region (14:8)

In his vision the prophet saw something never before seen in Jerusalem: a real river. (It is rare indeed for a major city to be built away from a river.) The psalmist foretold this remarkable new development and so did Ezekiel (Psalm 46:4-5; Ezekiel 47:1-12). No doubt the earthquake that will rend the mount of Olives will cause topographical changes and cause a new spring to issue from the site of the temple. The water will flow out from Jerusalem and divide into two branches, one streaming eastward toward the Dead Sea and the other streaming westward to the Mediterranean. This river, unlike so many others in Palestine, will not be subject to drying up in the summer. The waters of the new river will be copious regardless of the season.

3. Jerusalem Rescued (14:9-15)

a. The Lord's Enthronement Reviewed (14:9-11)

"The Lord shall be king over all the earth" (14:9). That is what the antichrist will want to be. He will sell his soul to Satan to secure the scepter of the world. There is no deception he will not practice, no crime he will not commit to reach the pinnacle of power. And all he will receive will be a shaky global eminence that will last barely three and a half years. Then his house of cards, built at such a cost of human misery and woe, will cave in. Earthly power is what Satan offered Jesus in his bold but fruitless attempt to turn Christ into antichrist (Luke 4:5-8). Well, at long last "the government shall be upon his shoulder" (Isaiah 9:6) and the world will own one King and one name.

The promised land will be renovated and repopulated. Jerusalem will be "lifted up" (Zechariah 14:10)—that is, it will be elevated above the hills that have always encircled it; the surrounding countryside will be changed. The changed area will extend "from Geba to Rimmon." Geba, a frontier garrison on the northern boundary of Benjamin, was once held by the Philistines and later fortified by King Asa (1 Samuel 14:4-5; 1 Kings 15:22); the town commanded an important pass through which Jerusalem could be approached. Rimmon was one of the southern towns of Judah

(Joshua 15:21-32). Thus Geba and Rimmon indicate the northern and southern boundaries of the kingdom of Judah. All the land in between will be made "as a plain," said Zechariah.[12]

Not only will the millennial city of Jerusalem be set on a lofty eminence befitting the world capital. Not only will the city be built around the headwaters of a great new river. But all the hills that once surrounded Jerusalem will be depressed into a vast plain. (The landscaping in Isaiah 2:2 is much the same.) Doubtless all this will be accomplished by the same giant earthquake that will split Olivet in two.

In addition to these geographical changes, Zechariah foresaw an enlargement of the city of Jerusalem. (It was a small provincial town in his day.) In naming gates, a tower, and wine presses as landmarks for the new city, the prophet created a picture of order, expansion, and stability and emphasized the fact that his description is to be taken literally.

People will flock to the new city, which will be the safest place on earth. Possibly Zechariah mentioned that Jerusalem will be "safely inhabited" (14:11) because of its stormy history.

b. The Lord's Enemies Removed (14:12-15)

Zechariah seems to flit back and forth from the gruesome to the glorious. Here, as though drawn by a magnet to the gruesome, he gazed on the horrors of the siege that will precede the Lord's enthronement. The prophet described *the scourge* "wherewith the Lord will smite all the people that have fought against Jerusalem" (14:12). This well-deserved and hideous plague will be a living death, like the disease that consumed wicked King Herod because of his countless crimes against the Jews.

Zechariah went on to describe *the slaughter*. In the crisis of the struggle for Jerusalem, panic will strike the troops attacking the city. A kind of insanity, caused perhaps by the portents of the Lord's return, will seize the conglomerate army; the soldiers will fight among themselves, expediting the escape of the Jewish survivors.

The entire enemy encampment will be affected by the plague (14:15). With the Gentile army paralyzed by pestilence and civil war, the defenders of Jerusalem will suddenly see victory within their grasp. They will fall on the enemy and Jews outside the city will rally to the attack (14:14). The last terrible siege of Jerusalem will be over and the victors will gather *the spoil*.

Having had his fill of the gruesome, Zechariah turned his attention to one final description of the glorious.

4. Jerusalem Restored (14:16-21)

a. God and the Heathen Nations (14:16-19)

Now the Gentile remnant appeared in Zechariah's vision. They are classified as "sheep" in the parable recorded in Matthew 25:31-46. At the judgment of the nations in the valley of Jehoshaphat, any Gentile who has extended a helping hand to a Jew will be afforded a place in the kingdom.

Here and there a daring Gentile will shield and shelter a Jew in spite of the interdicts of the antichrist's empire, just as during the Gestapo's reign of terror in Europe a number of Gentiles were courageous enough to hide Jews. Many a brave citizen paid the ultimate price, but some survived.

Viewing the Gentile remnant at the beginning of the millennium, Zechariah wrote:

> It shall come to pass, that every one that is left of all the nations which came against Jerusalem shall even go up from year to year to worship the King, the Lord of hosts, and to keep the feast of tabernacles (14:16).

Toward the end of the millennium disaffection will begin to take root among dissidents, and old hostilities will breed and fester. Although the millennium will be glorious, although the curse will have been removed from the earth, and although wickedness will have been punished and restrained, the golden age is not the eternal state. Unregenerate men will still be unregenerate men. During the first centuries there will be no desire to rebel. The memories of tribulation and judgment will be fresh in the minds of men, and they will enjoy the novelty of peace and prosperity. For a few more centuries, no one will dare to rebel. But during the later centuries some will rebel and they will be punished: "Whoso will not come up of all the families of the earth unto Jerusalem to worship the King, the Lord of hosts, even upon them shall be no rain" (14:17).

The Lord will rule the nations "with a rod of iron" during the millennium (Psalm 2:9). "The family of Egypt" will be among those who will take a lead in the final end-time rebellion (14:18). The mention of Egypt shows that the countries of the world will retain their national distinctives during the millennium, although they will acknowledge the central authority of Jerusalem and they will have Jewish governors and administrators.

We are not told why Egypt was selected for special mention. Perhaps the reason is that Egypt was the first great nation to persecute the Jews and plan their extermination and the first nation to feel the weight of God's displeasure in the plagues. Maybe Egypt will take the lead again. Or perhaps the nationalistic spirit will be revived first in Egypt. In any case, Egypt seems to be the country the Lord will use as an example when He shows the other nations what happens when a land shows signs of disloyalty. Zechariah was referring not to overt rebellion, but to something more cautious and subtle: a deliberate absence from the feast of tabernacles in Jerusalem.

The withholding of rain from Egypt will serve as a warning to other nations. Of course under present-day conditions Egypt never has an appreciable rainfall, but during the millennium the whole Sahara will be a garden. The warning will be clear: "This shall be the punishment of Egypt, and the punishment of all nations that come not up to keep the feast of tabernacles" (14:19).

b. God and the Hebrew Nation (14:20-21)

Zechariah saw in his vision the holiness of the Hebrew nation. There will be holiness in the house of the Lord: "In that day shall there be upon the bells of the horses, HOLINESS UNTO THE LORD; and the pots in the Lord's house shall be like the bowls before the altar" (14:20). In Zechariah's day this inscription was engraved on a plate of gold and worn as part of the miter on the head of Israel's high priest (Exodus 28:36-38), but in the millennial age there will be no difference between the sacred and the secular. Even the bells on the horses' bridles will carry the message, "HOLINESS UNTO THE LORD." In the temple common bowls used for mundane purposes will be as sanctified as the consecrated "bowls before the altar" used for holding the blood of sacrifices. There will be no degrees of holiness. Everything will be holy.

Holiness will pervade not only the house of the Lord, but all the houses of the land:

> Yea, every pot in Jerusalem and in Judah shall be holiness unto the Lord of hosts: and all they that sacrifice shall come and take of them, and seethe therein: and in that day there shall be no more the Canaanite in the house of the Lord of hosts (14:21).

Ordinary everyday things in private homes will be as sacred as the trappings of divine service. There will be no more distinction between profane and holy or between holy and most holy. The pots and pans in the kitchen sink will be as sanctified to God as the vessels of the temple.

"The Canaanite"—the unclean person, the profane person, the person who made merchandise out of holy things in the old days—will be gone forever. Jerusalem will be what God always intended it to be: "the holy city," the central magnet of all that is sacred and pure throughout the whole wide world.

Chapter 12

MALACHI

THE GATHERING GLOOM

I. THE LORD'S COMPLAINTS (1:1–2:17)
  A. The Nation's Spiritual Sins (1:1–2:9)
    1. Denying God's Love (1:1-5)
      a. The Burden Described (1:1-2a)
        (1) How It Was Laid on the Prophet (1:1)
        (2) How It Was Leveled at the People (1:2a)
      b. The Brothers Depicted (1:2b-4)
        (1) The One Loved (1:2b)
        (2) The One Loathed (1:3-4)
          (a) Esau Detested (1:3)
          (b) Edom Desolated (1:4)
      c. The Blindness Dispelled (1:5)
    2. Despising God's Name (1:6)
      a. The People (1:6a)
      b. The Priests (1:6b)
    3. Defiling God's Altar (1:7-14)
      a. The Contemptuous Attitude of the Hebrews (1:7-10)
        (1) Revealed in What They Said (1:7)
        (2) Revealed by What They Sacrificed (1:8-10)
          (a) The Charge (1:8a)
          (b) The Challenge (1:8b-10)
            i. The Governor of the Land (1:8b)
            ii. The Grace of the Lord (1:9-10)
            a. Needed (1:9)
            b. Neglected (1:10)
      b. The Contrasting Attitude of the Heathen (1:11-14)
        (1) God's Name Famed among the Gentiles
          (1:11-14a)

313

(a) The Exaltation of Jesus by the Pagans (1:11)
(b) The Execration of Judah by the Prophet
(1:12-14a)
  i. Their Disdainful Words (1:12-13a)
  ii. Their Deliberate Wickedness (1:13b)
  iii. Their Deceitful Ways (1:14a)
(2) God's Name Feared by the Gentiles (1:14b)
4. Disregarding God's Law (2:1-9)
  a. God's Commandment to the Priests (2:1-4)
  (1) What He Said Specifically (2:1)
  (2) What He Said Solemnly (2:2-3)
    (a) The Thrust of the Message (2:2a)
    (b) The Threat of the Message (2:2b-3)
      i. A Shattering Curse (2:2b)
      ii. A Shameful Corruption (2:3)
  (3) What He Said Surely (2:4)
  b. God's Covenant with the Priests (2:5-7)
  (1) A Lesson from the Past (2:5-6)
    (a) Levi's Ordination (2:5a)
    (b) Levi's Obedience (2:5b-6)
      i. His Godly Inclination (2:5b-6a)
      ii. His Godly Influence (2:6b)
  (2) A Lesson for the Present (2:7)
  c. God's Contempt for the Priests (2:8-9)
  (1) Their Abandonment of God (2:8)
  (2) Their Abasement by God (2:9)
B. The Nation's Special Sins (2:10-17)
  1. Their Detestable Ways (2:10-13)
  a. A Denial of Brotherhood (2:10)
  b. A Distortion of Belief (2:11-13)
  (1) Their Marriages (2:11)
  (2) Their Mockery (2:12)
  (3) Their Misery (2:13)
  2. Their Deserted Wives (2:14-16)
  a. What the Lord Witnessed (2:14)
  b. What the Lord Wanted (2:15)
  c. What the Lord Withstands (2:16)
  3. Their Distorted Words (2:17)

a. Their Words Wearying to God (2:17a)
b. God's Words Wrested by Them (2:17b)
II. THE LORD'S COMING (3:1–4:6)
  A. To Deal Judgmentally with Sinners (3:1-15)
    1. Their Ungodly Actions (3:1-6)
      a. The Lord's Coming in Grace (3:1a-b)
        (1) The Message for the Times (3:1a)
        (2) The Messiah in the Temple (3:1b)
      b. The Lord's Coming in Government (3:1c-6)
        (1) His Immediate Reception (3:1c)
        (2) His Imperial Resolve (3:2-5)
          (a) To Refine (3:2-3)
          (b) To Revive (3:4)
          (c) To Remove (3:5)
        (3) His Immutable Righteousness (3:6)
    2. Their Ungodly Attitude (3:7-12)
      a. In Provoking God (3:7-9)
        (1) Defiantly (3:7)
        (2) Deliberately (3:8)
        (3) Disastrously (3:9)
      b. By Proving God (3:10-12)
        (1) The Challenge (3:10a)
        (2) The Change (3:10b-12)
          (a) Within (3:10b-11)
          (b) Without (3:12)
    3. Their Ungodly Arguments (3:13-15)
      a. How Brazenly They Argued (3:13)
      b. How Bitterly They Argued (3:14)
      c. How Blasphemously They Argued (3:15)
  B. To Deal Justly with Saints (3:16–4:6)
    1. Righteous Ones Remembered (3:16)
    2. Righteous Ones Rewarded (3:17)
    3. Righteous Ones Recognized (3:18)
    4. Righteous Ones Rescued (4:1-3)
      a. The Coming Day (4:1)
      b. The Coming Dawn (4:2)
      c. The Coming Doom (4:3)
    5. Righteous Ones Revived (4:4-6)

a. The Requirements of Moses (4:4)
b. The Return of Elijah (4:5-6)
   (1) The Time of That Return (4:5)
   (2) The Tone of That Return (4:6)

———————❦———————

Malachi, the last prophet of the Old Testament, like John the Baptist, the first prophet of the New Testament, was simply "the voice of one crying in the wilderness." We do not know where or when Malachi was born. We do not know how old he was when he prophesied. We know nothing about his parents, his pedigree, or his occupation. Malachi was just a voice in the gathering gloom.

His name means "my messenger" or "missionary." The Latin translation is *Angelicus;* hence Malachi has been called "the unknown prophet with the angel name."

The voice of Zechariah had faded away along with his glorious vision of the coming golden age, during which "HOLINESS UNTO THE LORD" will be the watchword in Jerusalem. In the hundred years after Zechariah's ministry, something had gone terribly wrong in the promised land. A new urgent and fearless voice was needed and out of the silence it came, awakening the echoes of the hills. Malachi's strident, angry, threatening voice rang out loud and clear and then a somber silence of four hundred years descended. When Malachi finished his prophecy, the Old Testament canon came to a close, so we can be sure that what God said through Malachi was vital to His imperiled people.

Malachi did not give a date for his prophecy, but we are not wholly devoid of clues. Other dates help us track the onward march of time and the progression of Hebrew history:

536 B.C. - Cyrus released his Hebrew captives. Some fifty thousand joyful Jews, full of high hopes and expectations, blazed the trail back to the promised land.

535 B.C. - The foundations of the second temple were laid and optimism still rode high. Then problems arose and reconstruction stopped.

520 B.C. - The prophets Haggai and Zechariah urged the Jews to get on with the rebuilding of the temple.

516 B.C. - The temple was finished at last. The job had taken twenty years, but it was done.

458 B.C. - Ezra the scribe arrived in Jerusalem with a small contingent of new recruits.

445 B.C. - Nehemiah, a high official in the Persian court, arrived in Jerusalem. He was armed with a mandate to rebuild the walls of the city. This decree of Artaxerxes was of prime importance, for it marked the beginning of Daniel's mysterious "seventy weeks," which were to climax first in the crucifixion of Christ and then in His coming again.

433 B.C. - Nehemiah returned to Babylon to report his accomplishments to the king.

420 B.C. - About this time Nehemiah returned to Jerusalem to attack the religious and moral sins he had perceived to be prevalent among the Jewish people.

So we have these signposts. But when did Malachi prophesy? Some scholars think he prophesied during Nehemiah's absence from Judah or during Nehemiah's ministry in the city. But there are problems with this viewpoint. By the time Malachi started to preach, the temple services had degenerated into mere ritual and the sacrifices had been profaned by priests and people alike. This calculated callousness toward the things of God could not have developed overnight, so Malachi must have prophesied a considerable time after the rebuilding of the temple and the restoration of the religious system.

Nehemiah's reforms were so vigorous and thorough that the total collapse Malachi addressed could hardly have taken place in the short time the reformer was away in Babylon. Nehemiah seems to have had no trouble sweeping aside the abuses that did take root during his absence. He was a tough-minded, iron-willed individual, not at all averse to taking an offender by the scruff of the neck and tossing him bodily out of the temple. A man with such a temperament did not need a prophet to lend him support.

In Ezra's day reforms were needed, but not nearly so badly as in Malachi's day. Royal revenues still subsidized the temple services, so there would hardly have been a call for Malachi's denunciations of stinginess.

When we read in Scripture of the days of Zerubbabel and Joshua or Ezra and Nehemiah, we find references to Haggai and Zechariah but no mention of Malachi.

So the probability is that Malachi prophesied sometime after the days of Nehemiah. Sufficient time must be allowed for settled corruption to take root and flourish.

But when *did* Malachi prophesy? Sir Robert Anderson had the best idea. He based his reasoning on Daniel's remarkable prophecy of the seventy weeks (Daniel 9). Daniel was told that seventy weeks of years would sum up the future of his people. The seventy weeks were to commence with the decree to rebuild Jerusalem; the date can be pinpointed as 445 B.C., in the reign of the Persian emperor Artaxerxes. The seventy weeks were to be divided into three periods: a period of seven weeks plus a period of sixty-two weeks plus a period of one week. The first two periods take us down to the cutting off of the Messiah. The third period is still future, for the entire church age has been inserted between the second and third periods.

We may ask why the first sixty-nine weeks are divided into two periods: the first period being seven weeks (forty-nine years), and the second period being sixty-two weeks (four hundred thirty-four years)? As we have noted, the seventy weeks were to begin in 445 B.C. The first seven weeks, then, take us down to 396 B.C. And what was the significance of 396 B.C.? Anderson, a careful Bible student, concluded that Malachi prophesied in that year, and in that year the Old Testament canon was closed.[1]

His suggestion is appealing. It would allow sufficient time for the conditions Malachi described to develop. By 396 B.C. the previous actors in the drama of the repatriation of the Jewish people— Zerubbabel, Joshua, Haggai, Zechariah, Ezra, Nehemiah—were all gone. Decline had set in. Among some of the people there was a spirit of smugness and complacency that eventually produced the Pharasaic party. Among other Jews there was a spirit of skepticism and worldliness that eventually produced the Sadducean party. Sacrilege and profanity marked the religious attitude of the people. Witchcraft, adultery, perjury, fraud, and oppression were the more obvious of their moral and social offenses. The sin of robbing God was widespread. The transgressions of Nehemiah's day had reappeared, taken deep root, and flourished.

God's patience was far spent. It was time for revival or ruin. There was a desperate need for a fresh visitation from God, and God sent Malachi. With the boldness of a spiritual hero, the lone prophet confronted priest and people alike. Their reaction was righteous indignation and self-defense. Seven times this Old Testament

Martin Luther challenged Israel and seven times they answered God back: "Wherein hast thou loved us?" (1:2); "Wherein have we despised thy name?" (1:6); "Wherein have we polluted thee?" (1:7); "Wherein have we wearied [thee]?" (2:17); "Wherein shall we return?" (3:7); "Wherein have we robbed thee?" (3:8); "What have we spoken so much against thee?" (3:13)

God sent Malachi. But the Jews refused him, so the snug little land of Judah would soon be shaken by troubles, persecutions, wars, rumors of war, and military and ideological onslaughts unlike any it had known before.

When Malachi prophesied, the Persian empire was creaking on its cumbersome way to its end. In fewer than forty years the vigorous Philip of Macedon would ascend the Greek throne and by 338 B.C. bring all the Greek states under his control. Then Alexander the Great would succeed Philip and Persia's end would be in sight. The fateful Seleucid dynasty would be founded in Syria in 312 B.C. In this gathering gloom Malachi was given a burden that caused him to speak out for God.

I. THE LORD'S COMPLAINTS (1:1–2:17)

A. The Nation's Spiritual Sins (1:1–2:9)

1. Denying God's Love (1:1-5)

Malachi had a burden, and a heavy burden it was. It had been placed on him by God. The prophet called it "the burden of the word of the Lord to Israel by Malachi" (1:1). Malachi looked at society through the revealing lens of the word of God and, like Bunyan's pilgrim, became aware of a great load on his back. In Malachi's day society was materialistic, secularistic, smug, wrapped in the graveclothes of a dead religion, divorce-prone, callous about the plight of the poor, and conceited in its airy dismissal of God. The prophet was burdened about the alarming sins of his people. They were desperately wicked and didn't know it. He would have to speak out. He knew he might face immediate opposition, especially from the religious establishment; nevertheless he proclaimed the "word of the Lord."

The people thought they had reason to doubt God's love and faithfulness. Malachi 1:2 reveals their attitude: "I have loved you, saith the Lord. Yet ye say, Wherein hast thou loved us?" They had come back from Babylon and with blood, sweat, and tears rebuilt the temple, Jerusalem, and numerous other cities. They had turned their backs on centuries of idolatry and reinstituted the worship of God along Levitical lines. But had God rewarded them? No. Had He restored the kingdom? No. Had He fulfilled the glowing promises of many a prophet? No. Had He sent the Messiah, whose coming had been prophesied by Isaiah and Zechariah? No.

Things had not turned out as expected. Israel was not a great and prosperous land courted by all the nations. In a vast empire she was a tiny province of no account. The Jews were living in one of the stagnant backwaters of the world. How could it be said that God loved them?

In response to their question, Malachi gave them a history lesson: "Was not Esau Jacob's brother? saith the Lord: yet I loved Jacob, And I hated Esau" (1:2-3a). God's love for His people went back a long way. Even before the twins were born, God told their mother, "The elder shall serve the younger" (Genesis 25:23). In His omniscience God designated Jacob as His channel of blessing for mankind. And looking back on history, we see that Jacob (although he had faults and failings) did indeed choose to follow God, whereas Esau (although he had generous impulses) did not. God's decision was not arbitrary; it was based on His divine foreknowledge, impeccable righteousness, infinite love, and immutable purposes.

In the outworking of their national destinies, Esau—the God-hater, birthright-despiser—spawned a nation (Edom) characterized by the most implacable hatred of all things holy. The Edomite religion was both fierce and foul, and the Edomite character was evil. The evil came to a head in the Herods, that serpent brood which did all that it could to destroy both Christ and His church. Jacob, on the other hand, spawned a nation that blessed the world with the Bible and Christ. And his nation will one day bring in the millennium.

Did God love the Jews? Let Paul, that "Hebrew of the Hebrews" (Philippians 3:5), answer by describing his kinsmen: "Israelites; to whom pertaineth the adoption, and the glory, and the covenants, and the giving of the law, and the service of God, and the promises; Whose are the fathers, and of whom as concerning the flesh Christ came, who is over all, God blessed for ever. Amen" (Romans 9:4-5). Yet Malachi's contemporaries asked, "Wherein hast thou loved us?" What a wicked question from a people singularly blessed by God!

Malachi came a bit closer to home in 1:3b. God had delivered both Edom and Judah into the hands of the Babylonians. The Jews He had brought back and blessed. As for Edom, God had "laid his mountains and his heritage waste for the dragons of the wilderness." Still Edom demonstrated pride and self-will: "Edom saith, We are impoverished, but we will return and build the desolate places" (1:4). The result was God's curse: "They shall build, but I will throw down." Malachi referred to the Edomites as "the people against whom the Lord hath indignation for ever."

But God promised blessing for Israel: "Your eyes shall see, and ye shall say, The Lord will be magnified from the border of Israel" (1:5). Malachi was prophesying that Edom would never regain its former glory, but the world would witness God's love and protection for Israel. Israel was God's chosen instrument by means of which He intended to be magnified in the sight of all mankind.

2. Despising God's Name (1:6)

The Lord of hosts is the characteristic name of God in the book of Malachi, where it occurs twenty-four times. In 1:6 the Lord of hosts revealed another of His names: *Father.* "A son honoureth his father, and a servant his master: if then I be a father, where is mine honour? and if I be a master, where is my fear? saith the Lord of hosts unto you, O priests, that despise my name."

The greatest name for God in the Bible is *Father.* It occurs only rarely in the Old Testament, but it was characteristic of our Lord to call God *Father.* In John's Gospel alone the name occurs more than one hundred times. In the Lord's first recorded utterance on earth he used the name *Father* (Luke 2:49). Jesus used the name in Gethsemane and at Golgotha. It was still on His lips when He emerged from the tomb (John 20:17). In His last recorded utterance on earth, He used that matchless name (Acts 1:7). God, by referring to Himself as "father" in Malachi 1:6, seems to have been preparing the ground for the full-orbed revelation of Himself as Father in the New Testament.

God had loved Israel as a father loves his son (Exodus 4:22). Even on the purely human level a son owes reverence to his father just as a servant owes fear to his master. Since God had proved Himself to be the Father of His people, was He not entitled to His honor? Or taking the lower ground, as their Lord and Master was He not at least entitled to their fear? When God asked Israel these questions, the people simply shrugged them off. "Wherein have we despised thy name?" they said.

The prophet challenged the priests particularly. They of all people, called and consecrated as they were to handle holy things, should have reverenced God's name and by their words and example sanctified His name in the sight of the people. It is bad enough when an ordinary believer brings dishonor to the name of God; it is far worse when one of His chosen and anointed ministers disgraces that name. "Thou hast given great occasion to the enemies of the Lord to blaspheme," said Nathan in summing up God's indictment of David (2 Samuel 12:14). The priests' simplest, most basic, most bounden duty was to honor God, so God took a serious view of their behavior that dishonored Him.

3. Defiling God's Altar (1:7-14)

a. The Contemptuous Attitude of the Hebrews (1:7-10)

The sneering, rebellious attitude of the priests was *revealed in what they said.* The word of the Lord came to them through Malachi: "Ye offer polluted bread upon mine altar; and ye say, Wherein have we polluted thee? In that ye say, The table of the Lord is contemptible" (1:7). They were as insolent as Cain, who jibed at God, "Am I my brother's keeper?" (Genesis 4:9).

The priests earned their living by handling holy things, yet they did not care if contemptible things were offered to the Lord. They were concerned with getting their chores done, collecting their commissions, and handling personal business matters. Their hearts were not in the Lord's work. In fact they despised it. Even if they did not actually say, "The table of the Lord is contemptible," their ungodly attitude was obvious. The way they discharged their daily duties—as if their ministry were just a secular job—spoke for them.

The unbelieving priests of Malachi's day are like the liberals in our churches and seminaries today. These unbelievers hold positions of sacred trust and feed off holy things. Yet they have a contemptuous attitude toward the inerrancy of Scripture, the deity of Christ, the virgin birth, the atoning death, the bodily resurrection, the second coming of Christ, and every other cardinal doctrine in the Word of God. When these liberals are challenged, they use double talk and profess to believe the same way we do. "Wherein have we polluted thee?" they say.

The Lord continued his indictment: "And if ye offer the blind for sacrifice, is it not evil? and if ye offer the lame and sick, is it not evil?" (1:8) The attitude of the priests was *revealed by what they sacrificed.*

The word translated "evil" in 1:8 is very strong. Its root word indicates the nature of wickedness, the breaking up of all that is good or desirable. The Greek equivalent, *ponēros* ("evil") or *kakos* ("bad"), is used especially to indicate moral depravity, corruption, and lewdness.[2] These definitions show what God thought of people who culled the undesirable stock from their flocks and herds and reserved these inferior animals for their offerings. The implication is that such people would be capable of any form of moral wickedness. God challenged them to offer lame, blind, or sick animals to their governor in payment of their taxes and see what happened. What an insult their sacrifices were!

Their offense was so great that they were desperately in need of a special dispensation of the grace of God. Malachi said, "I pray you, beseech God that he will be gracious unto us" (1:9). It would be better to close the doors of the temple and allow the fire on the altar to die out than to offer cheap and blemished sacrifices to a holy God. It would be better to offer nothing, to be totally irreligious, than to offer with a contemptuous spirit. It would be better to shut down a seminary or close a church than to operate such an institution in a spirit of unbelief. It would be better to embrace atheism and secular humanism honestly than to perform Christian service hypocritically.

b. The Contrasting Attitude of the Heathen (1:11-14)

Looking ahead, Malachi could see the day when God's name will be renowned among the Gentiles. God said to him, "From the rising of the sun even unto the going down of the same my name shall be great among the Gentiles" (1:11). There has already been an initial fulfillment of this prophecy. Today there is hardly a country in the world where the name of the Lord is not known and where no one worships the living God in the name of His beloved Son. But the Old Testament prophet Malachi knew nothing of Pentecost, the church age, and the worldwide spread of the gospel of Christ. Malachi had the millennium in mind, and his prophecy in 1:11 will have its final fulfillment in that golden age.

Looking at the Jews, Malachi saw a glaring contrast, for they had profaned God's name. The prophet underlined their disdainful words: "But ye have profaned it [the Lord's name], in that ye say, The table of the Lord is polluted....Ye said also, Behold, what a weariness is it!" (1:12-13a)

Nothing could have been more wearisome than the daily round of religious duties required by Jewish tradition. There was so much vain repetition. But behind the sacrifices required by the Mosaic law, behind the prescribed rituals, behind the feast days and the fast days, was a glorious reality: Christ and His cross. The spiritually minded in Israel saw that reality. "Abraham rejoiced to see my day," Jesus said. "He saw it, and was glad" (John 8:56). To those who were not spiritually minded, even divinely-ordained rites and rules seemed legalistic, formalistic, and a "weariness." What the Jews needed was an outpouring of the regenerating, revitalizing grace for which Malachi had told them to pray. Apart from that grace, they would be better off if they abandoned all pretense instead of continuing their deadening routines.

The prophet went on to emphasize their deliberate wickedness. "Ye have snuffed at it [God's altar]," Malachi said to the Jews (1:13b). Today we would say, "You have turned up your nose at it." How terrible must be the state of soul of the person who snubs the things of God, especially the things that speak particularly of Calvary and God's one and only plan of salvation for lost mankind.

There may be some excuse for finding much that passes for Christian worship and service tiresome—boring sermons, dull prayers, uninspiring music, monotonous programs, mechanical routines in drab surroundings. But there is no excuse for being bored with Christ. He is the most glorious, dynamic, exciting person in the universe; there is nothing dull or drab about Him. He is the Creator, the One whom angels worship, the Author and Finisher of the faith. There can be no greater sin than to snub Him.

Malachi added, "Ye brought that which was torn, and the lame, and the sick." He was again exposing those who deliberately misrepresented the Lord and the great sacrifice of the cross. What they offered on the altar reflected their estimate of Christ.

The prophet also emphasized their deceitful ways. "Cursed be the deceiver," he said to the Jews (1:14a). A "deceiver" is one who promises God the best, then offers an inferior sacrifice. Deception in any area of life is despicable, but deception in the things of God is suicidal. What folly thus to insult such a One as the Lord of hosts! The angels who surround the throne of God must view with utmost astonishment the incredible foolishness of human beings who think they can hoodwink God.

"I am a great King, saith the Lord of hosts, and my name is dreadful among the heathen" (1:14b). If God's name was feared among the Gentiles, how much more should it have been feared among those to whom He had revealed so much!

4. Disregarding God's Law (2:1-9)

a. God's Commandment to the Priests (2:1-4)

"Now, O ye priests, this commandment is for you" (2:1). The commandment (implied in 2:2) was to reform their wicked ways. It was couched in terms of a threat: "If ye will not hear, and if ye will not lay it to heart, to give glory unto my name, saith the Lord of hosts, I will even send a curse upon you." The curse was graphically stated in 2:3. God threatened to take the vile filth removed from the animals set apart for the feasts and to spread that filth on the faces of the priests. No greater contamination and disgrace could be imagined. By law this animal filth was to be taken outside the camp and burned. In effect God was telling the priests that, apart from thoroughgoing repentance, they would be put in the place of separation from God and made fuel for the flames of a lost eternity.

In 2:4 God referred the priests to His original covenant with the tribe of Levi, the tribe chosen by Him to be set apart for His service. We read about that covenant in the Pentateuch: When apostate Israel sinned so grievously in making the golden calf, Moses threw down the gauntlet. "Who is on the Lord's side?" he demanded (Exodus 32:26). The only ones to respond were "all the sons of Levi." Rewarding them for this decision, God consecrated the whole tribe of Levi to the ministry (Deuteronomy 10:8-9).

b. God's Covenant with the Priests (2:5-7)

God gave Levi a wonderful covenant "of life and peace" because he "feared" the Lord (Malachi 2:5). The fear of God was conspicuously missing in the wretched priests of Malachi's day. The Levites of Moses' day had a belief that behaved. With their fighting faith and the courage of their convictions, they were prepared to make short work of both apathy and apostasy. The priests of Malachi's day were lineal heirs of the Levites, but their ministry had degenerated into a well-paying job with fringe benefits and social security. Professionalism in the things of God nearly always degenerates into dead orthodoxy or faith-denying liberalism.

Levi was inspired by the fear of the living God and as a result God gave him a threefold ministry: he was an example to all by his words, his walk, and his witness. He was an example by his *words* in that "the law of truth was in his mouth" (2:6). He upheld the inerrancy, inspiration, and infallibility of the Word of God. Levi was an example by his *walk* in that "he walked with [God] in peace and equity." His conduct was such that he enjoyed the constant smile of God's approval and the conscious sweetness of His presence. Levi was an example by his *witness* in that he "did turn many away from iniquity." He did away with apostasy, put the fear of God into the rank and file, defended the faith, and encouraged those who wanted to live for God.

The high calling of the priest was to uphold the fundamentals and fervor of the faith. "The priest's lips should keep knowledge," said Malachi. "They should seek the law at his mouth: for he is the messenger of the Lord of hosts" (2:7). The priestly vocation involved the Scriptures as well as the sacrifices. Occupation with the Scriptures was the first duty of the priest—far more important than his ceremonial duties (Leviticus 10:8-11; Deuteronomy 17:9-11). The priest was to uphold the truth of God.

c. God's Contempt for the Priests (2:8-9)

Malachi made the obvious application. He contrasted the two-faced liberal priests of his day with the original call, conviction, and conduct of Levi. "But ye," the prophet wrote, "are departed out of the way; ye have caused many to stumble at the law; ye have corrupted the covenant of Levi, saith the Lord of hosts" (2:8). Like the skeptical theologians who today destroy the faith of eager young seminary students, and like the Bible-denying ministers who from their pulpits destroy the souls of millions, the godless religious professionals of Malachi's day evoked the displeasure of God.

We know from history where the kind of Bible teaching taking root in Malachi's day led. A cumbersome system of rabbinical interpretation and tradition evolved. To the written and inspired Word of God, the rabbis added what they called the oral law, which in essence consisted of their manmade traditions. Their additions to Scripture included the *Halacha*, a record of rabbinical decisions on questions of ritual; the *Mishna*, a code resulting from those decisions; the *Gemara*, a commentary on the Mishna; the *Midrashic* commentaries on the Old Testament; and the *Haggada*, ritual readings for the first evening of Passover. And so the *Talmud* developed and the *Cabbala*. The *Cabbala* consisted of mystical interpretations and far-fetched speculations similar to the allegorizing of Origen.

By the time of Christ, much of the oral law was well-developed. It was a vast and still-growing encyclopedic accumulation of sense and nonsense, truth and trash, legitimate commentary and worthless tradition. Attacking the oral law cost Christ His life. After the fall of Jerusalem and the discontinuance of the sacrifices, the oral law took new wings. In spite of efforts by saner Jewish scholars to restrain it, it flourished like a vigorous weed in fertile soil.[3] The oral law stifled any hope that the Jews as a nation might turn to Christ, for it locked them into a pattern of Christ-rejecting unbelief.

In Malachi's day, then, besides the problem of priests who

regarded their work in connection with the sacrifices as a tedious but well-paying job, there was the problem of priests who, along with the scribes and rabbis, regarded their work in connection with the Scriptures as an opportunity for playing an elaborate game of Bible trivia. Their interpretive theories were as far removed from genuine Old Testament Judaism as modern liberal theology is from New Testament Christianity.

B. The Nation's Special Sins (2:10-17)

1. Their Detestable Ways (2:10-13)

God was the Father of the Hebrew people not only as their Creator, but also as their Covenantor. Because of their common membership in the wide family of the Father, they should have had special concern for each other's welfare. But the Hebrews of Malachi's day were acting as though God was not the Father of His people, as though there were no sacred ties of brotherhood to bind Jew to Jew. So the prophet asked, "Have we not all one father? hath not one God created us? why do we deal treacherously every man against his brother, by profaning the covenant of our fathers?" (2:10)

The disregard for brotherly love had led to some severe social sins. Malachi looked first at their sinful *marriages:* "Judah hath dealt treacherously, and an abomination is committed in Israel and in Jerusalem; for Judah hath profaned the holiness of the Lord which he loved, and hath married the daughter of a strange god" (2:11). The expression "daughter of a strange god" indicates that these marriages were not with Jewish proselytes, but with women who were practicing temple-worshipers of pagan gods.

Israel was supposed to be a holy nation (Exodus 19:6; Jeremiah 2:3) and was not supposed to worship graven images. To prevent any compromise with idolatry, the law of Moses expressly prohibited marriages with the heathen. The Jews of Malachi's day should have known from the history of their nation that breaking this law was abysmal folly. Solomon's terrible example was proof enough of what always happened. In the days of Ezra and Nehemiah stern measures had been taken to put an end to a renewed tendency to marry into pagan families (Ezra 9:1-2; 10:1-4; Nehemiah 13:25-27), but now the practice was again widespread. Those who entered into such marriages were in direct violation of the first commandment.

In spite of this practical denial of the true faith, the Jews were making a hypocritical attempt to keep up the appearance of orthodoxy. So Malachi looked next at their sin of *mockery.* They continued to bring offerings "unto the Lord of hosts," but the Lord threatened to "cut off" anyone who thought he could deceive God in this brazen way (2:12). No matter who the hypocrite was—master or scholar—God would not tolerate such mockery.

The heathen marriages were causing *misery*. Malachi said to the Jews, "This have ye done again, covering the altar of the Lord with tears, with weeping, and with crying" (2:13). Evidently Jewish wives were being callously divorced so that their husbands could make marital alliances with the families of influential heathen neighbors. It seems that the guilty parties thought that an offering or two on the altar would square accounts with God. But the altar was drenched with the tears of the abandoned wives, and God indignantly refused to accept the offerings of their husbands.

2. Their Deserted Wives (2:14-16)

The guilty men raised their hands in horror, crying "Wherefore?" In effect they were asking, "Why won't God accept our offerings? What have we done wrong?" Their question revealed how eroded was their moral sense and how corroded were their consciences. They had divorced belief from behavior as certainly as they had divorced their wives from themselves. They could not understand that God does not want the offerings of the wicked.

The answer to their question came quickly: "Because the Lord hath been witness between thee and the wife of thy youth, against whom thou hast dealt treacherously: yet is she thy companion, and the wife of thy covenant" (2:14). Malachi was saying that as far as God is concerned, marriage is sacred. No one but Christ spoke more highly of marriage. The marriage covenant is binding. The wife of a man's youth is to be his companion throughout life and the friend of his old age. "The Lord, the God of Israel, saith that he hateth putting away [divorce]" (2:16).

We read the reason for God's insistence on the sanctity of marriage in 2:15: "Did not he make one? Yet had he the residue of the spirit. And wherefore one? That he might seek a godly seed." Malachi was saying that in the marriage relationship God makes two into one. In his explanation he took the Jews back to the garden of Eden. God created just one wife for Adam, although He had the creative power—"the residue of the spirit"—to make him a dozen or a hundred wives. Polygamy was not in God's plan any more than divorce was. His plan was one man, one wife—two people made one and growing together in mutual love as long as they live.

The reason for the divine plan was that God was seeking "a godly seed." He had the children of the marriage in view. In a sin-cursed world, monogamous marriage in itself does not guarantee "a godly seed"—that is, children who love the Lord—but it is a far more conducive environment than a marriage spoiled by polygamy or divorce. What a message for today's divorce-prone society!

Malachi warned the Jews of his day, "Therefore take heed to your spirit, and let none deal treacherously against the wife of his youth." The implication is that divorce has its roots in a bad spirit. How true that is.

God permitted divorce under the law because of the hardness of the human heart, but only in the case of some bodily "uncleanness" or disease (Deuteronomy 24:1). Such a case would involve a woman who was acquainted with the law and nevertheless concealed an "uncleanness," and a man who was unaware of her "uncleanness" before their marriage. Divorce was not permitted because of an illness contracted after marriage—not even leprosy.

The Lord hated the capricious divorces that had become common in Malachi's day and said that the guilty parties covered violence with their garments (2:16). In other words, they put themselves on public display as iniquitous men capable of any kind of violence.

3. Their Distorted Words (2:17)

The Jews attacked the providence of God by bringing up the worn-out argument of the prosperity of the wicked and the suffering of the righteous. Malachi's response indicated that God was sick of hearing the same old slanders served up by immoral people to justify their evil lifestyles. The prophet wrote:

> Ye have wearied the Lord with your words. Yet ye say, Wherein have we wearied him? When ye say, Every one that doeth evil is good in the sight of the Lord, and he delighteth in them; or, Where is the God of judgment?

II. THE LORD'S COMING (3:1–4:6)

A. To Deal Judgmentally with Sinners (3:1-15)

1. Their Ungodly Actions (3:1-6)

Suddenly Malachi's attention was drawn away from the drab sins of his day to a glorious vision of a coming day. The same vision had thrilled many other Old Testament prophets and now it enraptured Malachi.

Against the background of his people's ungodly actions, Malachi saw the Lord's coming in grace and government.

a. The Lord's Coming in Grace (3:1a-b)

"Where is the God of judgment?" the sneering skeptics asked Malachi (2:17). "He's coming," Malachi replied in effect, "and God will send a herald before Him." In 3:1a we read the actual words of the Lord: "Behold, I will send my messenger, and he shall prepare the way before me."

Malachi foresaw the coming of John the Baptist, who founded his ministry on the glorious vision of the prophets (Matthew 3:3; 11:10; Mark 1:2). John was a worthy ambassador, preaching in the power of the Holy Spirit to the conscience of the nation. He brought a compelling conviction of sin to the hearts of the people—from Herod on his throne to the harlot on the street.

Malachi also foresaw the Lord coming suddenly into His temple. By the time Jesus was born, the temple had been greatly enlarged and embellished by Herod, but it was still full of the same old sins. The court of the Gentiles had been turned by the ruling classes of the priests into a market. There animals for sacrifices were bought and sold at a tidy profit for the authorities, and crafty money-changers busied themselves with their clinking coins.

Four centuries of divine silence had come and gone, and after generations of violence the people had finally settled down to a comfortable religious routine in which traditions carried more weight than truth. Smug Pharisees rubbed shoulders with aristocratic liberal Sadducees; Herodians preached rebellion against Rome; Essenes fasted in the deserts. People gave lip service to feast days and fast days. Rich Jews from the diaspora made annual pilgrimages to Jerusalem so they could scrub their souls and see the sights.

The strident voice of John the Baptist stirred the hearts of many, but the religious elite wrote him off as a fanatic. Here and there a godly Simeon or Anna watched and waited for the coming of the Christ, and John caused some excitement by pointing out a village carpenter as the Messiah. But the Man made no move. Weeks passed and He was forgotten.

Then one day He strode into the temple. With His symbolic whip He drove out the merchants and their cattle, upset the tables of the money-changers, and castigated them for turning His Father's house into a den of thieves (John 2:13-21).

b. The Lord's Coming in Government (3:1c-6)

Malachi's prophecy took a sudden leap over the centuries, for his vision of the Lord's coming in grace gave way to a vision of His coming in government. The prophet saw Him in a different guise; He now appeared as "the messenger [angel] of the covenant" (3:1c). The angel of the covenant is the Lord as He often appeared before His incarnation (Exodus 23:20-23; 33:12-16), and this angel will come again for judgment. "Where is the God of judgment?" demanded the worldly and carnal Jews (Malachi 2:17). "Here He is," the prophet said in effect and showed them not a kinsman-redeemer (though that He now is and ever will be), but an angel that could strike terror in any heart.

The covenant angel will come to *refine:* "He shall sit as a refiner and purifier of silver: and he shall purify the sons of Levi" (3:3). We can picture a refiner sitting in front of the fire; his crucible is full of molten metal and he is skimming off the dross. Like the refiner who purifies his gold, the Lord at His second coming will purify all Israel, beginning with the Levites (Ezekiel 48:11). He will use the flames of the great tribulation to burn away the dross.

The Lord is coming to *revive:* "Then shall the offering of Judah and Jerusalem be pleasant unto the Lord, as in the days of old" (3:4). The insulting offerings of Malachi's day were anything but pleasing to the Lord.

The Old Testament offerings will be revived in the millennium. In Old Testament times they were anticipatory; they pointed forward to Calvary. In the millennium they will be commemorative; they will be a vivid reminder of Calvary. "This do in remembrance" will be the idea behind the offerings.

The Lord is coming to *remove:* "I will come near to you to judgment" (3:5). "Where is the God of judgment?" sneered the scoffers. "Here He is," Malachi said in effect as he declared the word of the Lord:

> I will be a swift witness against the sorcerers, and against the adulterers, and against false swearers, and against those that oppress the hireling in his wages, the widow, and the fatherless, and that turn aside the stranger from his right, and fear not me, saith the Lord of hosts (3:5).

The sins the prophet had observed among his people will be prevalent among the Jews of the judgment day too. They will have to reckon with the Lord, for such offenses outrage His holiness.

The only reason the brazen skeptics of Malachi's day were not destroyed for their insolence was the integrity of God. "I change not," He said. "Therefore ye sons of Jacob are not consumed" (3:6). God was simply being true to His righteous character, true to His grace, and true to His covenant promises. If God had not made those promises to the patriarchs, He would long ago have given the skeptics of 2:17 what they asked for: judgment.

2. Their Ungodly Attitude (3:7-12)

a. In Provoking God (3:7-9)

From the beginning the Jews had forsaken God's "ordinances" (3:7). The word translated "ordinances" here can be rendered "statutes" and it refers to special ritual observances. The Jews of Malachi's day had a rebellious attitude toward the sacrificial system, but this attitude was nothing new. The Hebrews had a lot of experience in provoking God to anger. Now He called them to repentance: "Return unto me, and I will return unto you."

But sin had blunted the consciences of the people and dulled their moral perception. (Sin always does that.) So they said, "Wherein shall we return?" They were provoking God defiantly. The Lord responded with one of the great and startling questions in the Bible: "Will a man rob God?" (3:8)

The people were in fact robbing God by withholding their tithes and offerings. They were provoking God deliberately. True, times were hard, but that was no excuse for reducing or totally ignoring the obligation under the law to give God what He demanded (Deuteronomy 14:22-29; 26:12-15).

Feinberg pointed out that there were various kinds of tithes and offerings required by the Mosaic law.[4] The offerings were the first fruits of the harvest—at least one-sixtieth of the corn, wine, and oil (Deuteronomy 18:4). There were at least four tithes: (1) A tenth of what remained after the first fruits were given to the priests went to support the Levites, who held no tribal territory (Leviticus 27:30-33). (2) The Levites in turn had to pay a tenth of their income to the priests (Numbers 18:26-28). (3) A tithe was taken for the needs of the Levites who worked in connection with the tabernacle (Deuteronomy 12:18). (4) Every third year a special tithe was taken for the poor (Deuteronomy 14:28-29).

In Israel tithing was a form of taxation to raise funds to support the religious establishment and finance social services. In the New Testament tithing as such is not mentioned as a church requirement. Grace, not law, governs Christian giving (2 Corinthians 9). However, the principle of proportionate giving applies to the church (1 Corinthians 16:1-2). It is difficult to understand how a Christian under grace can give less than a Jew was required to give under the law. We must be careful that we do not rob God.

God said to the Jews of Malachi's day, "Ye are cursed with a curse: for ye have robbed me, even this whole nation" (Malachi 3:9). They were really robbing themselves, for when they withheld from God that which was His due under the law, He withheld His blessing from them. Poor harvests, faulty investments, and wretched returns were the disastrous results of provoking God.

b. By Proving God (3:10-12)

To change the ungodly attitude of the people, God said in effect, "Put Me to the test. Put your hand in your pocket and start honoring Me with a portion of your income and see what will happen!" Malachi 3:10 records His challenge:

> Bring ye all the tithes into the storehouse, that there may be meat in mine house, and prove me now herewith, saith the Lord of hosts, if I will not open you the windows of heaven, and pour you out a blessing, that there shall not be room enough to receive it.

The Lord made an unconditional pledge to the Jews of Malachi's day. If they scrupulously honored God with their substance, He would reverse their fallen financial fortunes and make them a testimony to the whole world.

God is no man's debtor. The more we give to Him, the more He gives to us. That principle holds as true for us in an age of grace as it did for Israel in an age of law. Any believer with a good heart and a pure motive can put this principle of giving and receiving to the test for himself.

My wife had a widowed aunt who honored God with her generosity. During the depression—"the hungry thirties"—she was the only member of a large family of brothers and sisters (all of whom had families of their own) who had a regular job. She was a charwoman on a ferry boat. The job was hard and unglamorous and paid very little, but it was steady. Week after week this quiet Christian widow toiled away at her thankless task. When payday came, she figured out how much she needed to keep body and soul alive and provide for her son; then she gave her tithe to her church and used the rest to buy bags of groceries for her brothers and sisters. Moreover she opened her home to my wife when my wife's mother was permanently hospitalized. The generous woman took my wife in, cared for her, fed her, and clothed her.

There was no such thing as Social Security for widows in those days and my wife's aunt received no monthly payments from a life insurance company. She fought a daily battle with poverty. But did God let her down? No indeed! When she was old and infirm and could no longer work, God opened His storehouse for her. She had next to no income, but she was taken care of by others. She had a comfortable room, she was surrounded by friends who loved her, and she had more money to spend than she had ever had before. She had given and given and given—with never a thought about giving to get. Then in His good time God gave and gave and gave until she died—and when He called her home, He gave her a mansion of her own.

3. Their Ungodly Arguments (3:13-15)

How accountable we are for our words! How easily we forget that God hears them. He said to the Jews of Malachi's day, "Your words have been stout [bold] against me.... Yet ye say, What have we spoken so much against thee? Ye have said, It is vain to serve God" (3:13-14).

The people said it was useless to serve God; it was useless to walk "mournfully" before God. They resurrected the same old agnostic argument that the wicked prosper, that those who provoke God by deliberate impiety escape punishment. The spiritual condition of the Jews was revealed by what they said. They were ripe for a new round of judgment.

Although there was not a cloud on the horizon, judgment was on the way. In the days of the Seleucids the Jews received a due reward for their deeds.

B. To Deal Justly with the Saints (3:16–4:6)

The rest of the book of Malachi deals primarily with the righteous. God always has His remnant.

1. Righteous Ones Remembered (3:16)

When the wicked flourished, the righteous closed ranks and spoke encouragingly to one another. The Lord listened to the sneering words of the wicked, but He also listened with delight to the godly conversation of His own. Moreover He kept a record of the things they said. We read in Malachi 3:16:

> They that feared the Lord spake often one to another: and the Lord hearkened, and heard it, and a book of remembrance was written before him for them that feared the Lord, and that thought upon his name.

Other Bible passages confirm that God keeps books (see Psalm 56:8; Revelation 20:11-15; 21:27).

2. Righteous Ones Rewarded (3:17)

God thinks of those who love and serve Him as His "jewels," or His special treasures. "They shall be mine, saith the Lord of hosts, in that day when I make up my jewels; and I will spare them, as a man spareth his own son that serveth him."

God has millions of galaxies in space, and in these galaxies are treasures beyond our ability to imagine. He has angels, archangels, cherubim, seraphim, thrones, dominions, and countless hosts of shining ones who hang on His words and rush to do His bidding. Yet those of Adam's race on planet Earth who love Him and talk to each other about Him are His "jewels." How amazing! He promised that He will take special care of His "jewels" and spare them when He visits the world with judgment.

3. Righteous Ones Recognized (3:18)

When the day of judgment comes, the enormous and eternal difference between the wicked and the righteous will be plain for all to see. "Then shall ye return, and discern between the righteous and the wicked, between him that serveth God and him that serveth him not." Malachi 3:18 is God's answer to the sneers of the wicked in 2:17.

Now we only see the back of the tapestry. "Then" we will see the front as well and marvel at the wisdom, grace, and goodness of God.

Not till each loom is silent,
And the shuttles cease to fly,
Shall God reveal the pattern
And explain the reason why

The dark threads were as needful
In the weaver's skillful hand
As the threads of gold and silver
For the pattern which He planned.[5]

4. Righteous Ones Rescued (4:1-3)

The righteous will be rescued in *the coming day* of judgment. This "day of the Lord," foretold by Joel and other prophets, was also described by Malachi: "Behold, the day cometh, that shall burn as an oven; and all the proud, yea, and all that do wickedly, shall be stubble" (4:1). The "day of the Lord" was first injected into the prophetic picture by the first of the Old Testament writing prophets and it is fitting that Malachi, the last of the Old Testament prophets, should remind his sinful people about that day. It is a real day, a terrible day, a day of God's wrath against the wicked.

Malachi saw that coming day in his vision, but he also saw *the coming dawn*. After warning of judgment, God said, "But unto you that fear my name shall the Sun of righteousness arise with healing in his wings; and ye shall go forth, and grow up as calves of the stall" (4:2). The terrible night of the great tribulation will end and a new day will dawn for God's people. Jesus will come and once He has performed the radical surgery of Armageddon and the valley of Jehoshaphat, there will be a time of healing. Then the world will become a safe place, as indicated by the pastoral illustration of calves being loosed from their stalls.

In this world of sin, the wicked often triumph over the righteous, but in *the coming doom* there will be a complete reversal. Malachi foresaw the righteous coming into their own. The Lord said to them: "Ye shall tread down the wicked; for they shall be ashes under the soles of your feet in the day that I shall do this" (4:3).

5. Righteous Ones Revived (4:4-6)

In his closing paragraph Malachi mentioned Moses and Elijah, the two men who appeared on the mount of transfiguration. Both towered above their contemporaries and colleagues. Both passed into eternity under unusual circumstances. Moses died and was buried by God in a secret grave. Elijah, who did not die, was caught away into Heaven in a special, personal rapture.

In Scripture Moses represents the Law and Elijah represents the Prophets. The people of Malachi's day needed to be called back to the Law and prepared for the future, for God was about to close the Old Testament canon. He would say no more to His people for four hundred years—and some of those years would bring terrible suffering.

God said, "Remember ye the law of Moses my servant, which I commanded unto him in Horeb for all Israel, with the statutes and judgments" (4:4). It was the Law, the Torah—not the sprouting Talmud—that God thus endorsed. God's inspired written Word would prove to be the anchor for the soul of the nation when the tempests came and the angry billows rolled. Then God promised:

> Behold, I will send you Elijah the prophet before the coming of the great and dreadful day of the Lord: And he shall turn the heart of the fathers to the children, and the heart of the children to their fathers, lest I come and smite the earth with a curse (4:5-6).

When Jesus came the first time, God did indeed send a forerunner: John the Baptist, who came in the spirit of Elijah to call the nation back to God. The nation responded by murdering John and crucifying Christ. But Jesus is coming again and before He returns, the real Elijah will come, armed with miraculous power to smite the earth with plague and judgment (Revelation 11).

Thus the Old Testament ends. The first book in the Bible ends with a coffin. Isaiah ends on a note of judgment and so do Ecclesiastes and Lamentations. Finally Malachi ends with the word "curse." The rabbis sought to avoid the full force of that dread word by repeating verse 5 after verse 6. But God did not want the word muted. He wanted it to wail out its woe down through the silent centuries. He wanted it to haunt the minds of men, to echo down the years.

God wanted the Jew to find the word "curse" at the end of his Bible. What better preparation could there be for a new beginning in Christ? What better preparation could there be for the coming of Jesus, who would bring blessing? A curse or Christ—that choice was God's final message to the Old Testament Jew.

NOTES

Introduction

1. John C. Whitcomb, Jr., *Old Testament Kings and Prophets*, 4th ed. rev. (Winona Lake, IN: Grace Theological Seminary, 1966).

Chapter 1 - Hosea

1. Shakespeare, *Henry IV, Part Two*, 3.1.

Chapter 2 - Joel

1. Adalbert Merx's opinion, as summarized by George Adam Smith in "The Book of the Twelve Prophets" in *An Exposition of the Bible* (Hartford: Scranton, 1914) 4:656.
2. E. B. Pusey, *The Minor Prophets: A Commentary, Explanatory and Practical*, 2 vols. (reprint, Grand Rapids: Baker, 1953) I:147.
3. In nature, locusts never destroy what was left by their former stages. For example the swarmer does not eat the gnawer's remnant. In other words, when the locust becomes winged, it flies away to ravage other countries instead of staying in the same country and eating the hopper's leftovers.
4. In the King James version the expression is poorly translated in 2 Thessalonians 2:2 as "the day of Christ" and in Revelation 1:10 as "the Lord's day." In both instances the correct translation is "the day of the Lord." See marginal notes in *The Companion Bible* (Grand Rapids: Zondervan, 1964).
5. For a more complete discussion see John Phillips, *Exploring the Future* (Neptune, NJ: Loizeaux, 1992).
6. Egypt's current recognition of the state of Israel evidently will not last.

Chapter 3 - Amos

1. See "Battle Hymn of the Republic" by Julia Ward Howe.
2. See Phillips, *Exploring the World of the Jew* (Neptune, NJ: Loizeaux, 1993).

Chapter 4 - Obadiah

1. Elmslie quoted by George L. Robinson in *The Twelve Minor Prophets* (reprint, Grand Rapids: Baker, 1952) 64-65.
2. Walter Lord, *A Night to Remember* (New York: Henry Holt, 1955) 50.

Chapter 6 - Micah

1. From "Battle Hymn of the Republic" by Julia Ward Howe.
2. George Adam Smith, "The Book of the Twelve Prophets" in *An Exposition of the Bible* 4:539.
3. From the hymn "We'll Sing of the Shepherd That Died" by Thomas Kelly.
4. For a full discussion of this invasion, see Phillips, *Exploring the Future*, chapter 16.
5. See Phillips, *Exploring the World of the Jew*, 132.
6. From the hymn "O Worship the King" by Robert Grant.
7. Shakespeare, *The Merchant of Venice*, 4.1, Portia to Shylock.
8. Smith, "The Book of the Twelve Prophets" in *An Exposition of the Bible* 4:546.
9. Ibid. 4:548.
10. From the hymn "Great God of Wonders" by Samuel Davies.

Chapter 7 - Nahum

1. Smith, "The Book of the Twelve Prophets" in *An Exposition of the Bible* 4:583. The old lion symbolizes Assyria, as in Nahum 2:11.
2. Scythed chariots had cutting blades attached to the hub of each wheel.

Chapter 8 - Habakkuk

1. Also see John Phillips and Jerry Vines, *Exploring the Book of Daniel* (Neptune, NJ: Loizeaux, 1990).
2. Ibid., appendix 7 and pages 69-70.
3. See Phillips, *Exploring the Gospels: John* (Neptune, NJ: Loizeaux, 1989) 52-57.

Chapter 9 - Zephaniah

1. *The Companion Bible*, 1272.
2. See Phillips, *Exploring Revelation* (Neptune, NJ: Loizeaux, 1991) 117-118.
3. See Phillips, *Exploring the Future*, 321,350-353.
4. The phrase is taken from the title of Eugene Sue's book *The Wandering Jew*.

Chapter 10 - Haggai

1. Some scholars say that *Assir* was a person's name, but other scholars say that *Assir* means "prisoner" and refers to Jehoiachin.

Chapter 11 - Zechariah

1. For further comments see the author's *Exploring Revelation* and *Exploring the Future*.
2. From D. W. Whittle's hymn "The Crowning Day."
3. Author unknown.
4. For a more detailed study of the Maccabean wars, see John Phillips and Jerry Vines, *Exploring the Book of Daniel*.
5. See Phillips, *Exploring the World of the Jew*.
6. From the hymn "There Is a Fountain" by William Cowper.
7. From the hymn "Are You Washed in the Blood?" by Elisha A. Hoffmann.
8. See Phillips, *Exploring Revelation*, 251-258.
9. See Merrill F. Unger, *Zechariah: Prophet of Messiah's Glory* (Grand Rapids: Zondervan, 1963) 227-230.
10. From the hymn "We'll Sing of the Shepherd That Died" by Thomas Kelly.
11. See Unger, *Zechariah: Prophet of Messiah's Glory*.
12. Literally, "like the Arabah." See Marcus Dods, *The Post-Exilian Prophets* (reprint, Edinburgh: T. & T. Clark, 1956) 123.

Chapter 12 - Malachi

1. Robert Anderson, *The Coming Prince* (reprint, Grand Rapids: Kregel, 1957) 72.
2. See *The Companion Bible*, appendix 44:viii.
3. See Phillips, *Exploring the World of the Jew*.
4. See Charles L. Feinberg, *The Major Messages of the Minor Prophets— Malachi: Formal Worship* (New York: American Board of Missions to the Jews) 125-126.
5. Author unknown.